Tom Chetwynd was born in London i...
Downside School and studied Theology at London University.
His mother, Bridget Chetwynd, was a novelist, and he himself
started writing at the age of seventeen, with an impulse to record
a vivid waking dream that appeared in his first novel, *Rushing
Nowhere*. After an intensive period of exploring his own
unconscious – which resulted in novels, scripts and stories
written in symbolic language – he turned his attention to dreams
and produced his *Dictionary for Dreamers* which has enabled
many people to discover the value and significance of their own
dreams. Since the success of this dictionary, he has concentrated
on the wider significance of symbolism as a whole, not only as
it affects the individual through his own personal waking
dreams, but also as it appeals to his unconscious through
myths, fairy-tales, religion, literature, art and cinema. The last
years have seen a major breakthrough in the understanding
of the value and meaning of symbolism – that there is only
one symbolic language which is used by dreams, creative
imagination and myths in expressing the unconscious, the
imagination and the soul. His subsequent *Dictionary of
Symbols* and *Dictionary of Sacred Myth* have been compiled
largely from the fruits of this recent research. Besides these
three dictionaries, which form a trilogy of the Language of the
Unconscious, he has also written *The Age of Myth*.

Dictionary of Symbols

TOM CHETWYND

Thorsons
An Imprint of HarperCollins*Publishers*

Thorsons
An Imprint of HarperCollins*Publishers*
77–85 Fulham Palace Road,
Hammersmith, London W6 8JB

First published by Paladin Books 1982
Published by Aquarian Press 1993
Published by Thorsons 1998
10 9 8 7

© Tom Chetwynd 1982

Tom Chetwynd asserts the moral right to
be identified as the author of this work

A catalogue record for this book
is available from the British Library

ISBN 1 85538 296 2

Printed and bound in Great Britain by
Caledonian International Book Manufacturing Ltd, Glasgow

For
HÉLÈNE

How could that twig bear such a fruit?
They'll wonder –
Not knowing you're the tree, the root.

Acknowledgments

This dictionary is compiled from the works of psychologists and others who have devoted a large portion of their lives and energies to unravelling the relationship between symbolism and the working of the human psyche, which plays such a central part in determining human life and destiny. It is particularly indebted to the writings of C. G. Jung, Emma Jung, Georg Groddeck, Marie Louise van Franz, James Hillman, D. Streatfield, Liz Greene and others, listed in the Index of Authors. Also to J. E. Cirlot who compiled his own invaluable dictionary of symbols nearly a quarter of a century ago, which has contributed so much to elucidating the nature of symbols.

I would personally like to thank Giselle Scanterbury for her help in recommending certain authors to me, Richard Kennedy for his suggestions and assistance in preparing and polishing the final manuscript. Ruth Newton for her initial work on the drawings and diagrams, and Mark Straker for finalizing these. I am also especially grateful to Eva Hunte for her care with the editorial work of transforming a monstrous manuscript into a princely page: the elegant result gives little hint of the difficulties overcome on the way. Finally I would like to thank gassho Kyudo Nakagawa Roshi for his part in the affair, and Sochu Suzuki Roshi for his.

Introduction

How to Use the Dictionary

1 A Symbolic Way

This dictionary is especially compiled and designed for those people who want to explore and develop the resources of their own psyche by means of symbols. Symbols have always been treasured as a means of releasing sources of energy from the unconscious. By gradually integrating conscious with unconscious content in the psyche, they affect the quality of your personal life, bringing value and meaning to it.

The dictionary aims at being a kit, an instruction manual, to help the individual – aid rather than hinder the natural processes of growth and transformation in the psyche. This is no more difficult than gardening or cookery except that, whereas there exist many excellent, well-tried comprehensive guides to these areas, anyone setting out to cultivate his own psyche has not been so well served.

In this aspect, the dictionary is most especially indebted to Jung and his followers, who have (particularly in the last decade) managed to explain convincingly why symbols are of such vital, everyday concern.

2 Symbolic Language

People often get interested in symbolism first through the accumulated symbolism of the past: fairy-tales and myths, nonsense verse and religious symbols, novels and plays with powerful symbolic themes like *Faust* or *Peer Gynt* – though there is often just as much symbolism in modern cinema and science fiction. Events that never took place, and aren't at all likely or even possible, may have a compelling fascination.

For example, if 'Sleeping Beauty' were presented as an historical account of the way Louis XIV met his bride, it would be merely ludicrous. Yet the story remains haunting, and it is the object of the dictionary to explain why (*'SLEEPING BEAUTY'*).

There is such a wealth of symbolism that no dictionary could be exhaustive. But this is not necessary because there are certain underlying principles and themes which keep recurring in symbolism. The dictionary shows the way symbolism actually works through many clear key examples so as to enable the reader, who becomes familiar with these inner workings, to be able to interpret other symbolic material for himself.

3 Dreams

Dreams are one small section of symbolism. They use the same symbolic language, and many of the images that appear in dreams can be looked up both in this dictionary and in my earlier *Dictionary for Dreamers*. The way the same symbol (perhaps first experienced by primitive man in a dream or vision) has been expanded into myth and symbolism generally, very often throws considerable light on your dream (by 'amplifying' the dream images).

4 A Way In

But even more important, a powerful symbol from a dream can lead the individual into the wider and richer field of symbolism in everyday, waking life, where the imagination is always at work whether we are conscious of it or not. In the same way, a particular myth or tale which exerts a special fascination may be a way of opening up the symbolic dimension of an individual's life. The dictionary provides an opportunity to see the relevance, and even the intellectual rigour, of symbolism, which otherwise might get dismissed.

5 Deprived of Symbols

Many people do not remember their dreams and feel the lack of symbolism in their lives, as if it's something they are excluded from, a mystery, a blank. But just as everybody dreams most of the night, and we don't notice it, so everybody's waking life is full of symbolism but operating at an unconscious level, and therefore irrationally, even dangerously. Recognizing symbols, knowing that they refer directly to patterns and processes at work in your own psyche, is the important function of 'withdrawing projections'. So quite ordinary objects and people we encounter daily may have a special inner significance and value for us – just as they may appear in dreams in this capacity. For example, husband and wife may have a different inner (or symbolic) significance for each other as representing the masculine or feminine sides of their own psyche; this can complicate marriage below the surface until it is recognized, and then it may become a powerful tool in integrating the psyche (*MASCULINE/FEMININE; ANIMUS/ AMINA; WEDDING; EROS*). Part of the battle of the sexes is a result of the inner rift between feeling and thinking. Symbols (of their nature) gradually heal just such rifts in the psyche.

6 Overwhelmed by Symbols

Until recently it was fairly rare for an individual to be so overwhelmed by his rich symbolic life that he was unable to cope with ordinary, everyday concerns (sometimes called 'implosion'). But it is certainly becoming more common, especially among the young who are nearer to their unconscious (which dominates childhood thinking) and it can be triggered off by drugs. Symbolism integrates the particular, restricted life of the conscious Ego with the grand, unconscious dream, and it works both ways. It re-introduces us to the grander reality of our lives, which are in contact with remote stars, remote periods of history, etc., but which we suppress for utility reasons. But symbols have evolved with man, and primitive man especially was all too inclined to be overwhelmed by the horror and splendour of life as a whole, seemingly chaotic. Symbols are man's ancient way of ordering this chaotic array of direct experience, assimilating it to his particular life and destiny. They exclude the irrelevant and focus the individual's attention on the particular application of the grander vision of vast space, endless time. In the same way the dictionary works both from symbols to everyday life, as well as from everyday life to symbols: e.g. from macrocosm to microcosm and back.

Conscious Ego and unconscious Self complement each other perfectly, like two halves of a jaggedly broken disc which fit perfectly once they are brought together. Such discs were the origin of the word 'symbol'.

7 Comparative Symbolism

By showing that symbols refer to the inner world of the psyche, psychology has also brought to light the relationship between the different systems of symbolism. Whereas the forms are very different, the meaning and value for the individual may be the same. And those sections of the dictionary devoted to Related Symbols, could help to provide a basis for understanding the fundamental similarity and accord, where in the past misunderstanding has led to bitter clashes, and subsequent personal disillusionment. Whereas once related to each other, the different systems bring objective validity to the processes at work within the psyche.

8 As a Reference Work

As a reference work on psychology, myth and folklore, this dictionary is designed to complement others already in existence: J. E. Cirlot, Jean Chevalier (ed.), A. de Vries, J. C. Cooper. It is the result of the most recent research into symbolism which only became available in the seventies, research that has shed so much new light, that it is indispensable for any complete or convincing picture of the way symbols work. This dictionary also concentrates on important aspects of symbolism that have been less emphasized or neglected in other guides; for example, symbols cannot be understood purely intellectually for they must arouse feelings; nor can they be understood outside their context (e.g. a dragon in the sky is not the same as a dragon in a cave, the Four Elements with which they are associated govern the meaning). Symbolism is deeply concerned with wholes, perceived by intuition, that is, whole patterns and whole sequences, and the interaction of the parts in context. So it doesn't help the individual grappling with the symbolism to divide up the twenty-two trumps of the *TAROT* or the signs of the *ZODIAC* into alphabetical order.

The Pattern of your Psyche and the Sequence of your Life in Symbols

Symbols are concerned with what is of greatest importance to man, his own life and his own mind, the central focal point of that life. They depict the pattern of the psyche, the sequence of the cycle of life, and the interaction between the two. As well as playing his own unique part in the order of things, the individual shares in a communal fate, the communal destiny of Man. Individual destiny and human destiny, are interwoven, inseparable.

Symbols express the binding force of the universe. Eros as the great snake, coiled around the cosmos and holding it together. They also articulate the relationship between the different parts; without this clear expression of interaction, which arises spontaneously from the feeling function of the psyche, everything tends to fragment. Society breaks up into warring factions: masculine against feminine, black against white, one class against another, etc. Even the psyche itself breaks into complexes, different nuclei of energy contending with each other, – which often leads to great internal stress. And this, of course, is reflected in the symbols themselves, which have become fragmented into isolated units and thus mere curiosities on the fringe of life. This is the way in which symbols become divorced from their function, which is to work from the core of life to grasp Wholes and relate the Parts.

Psychology has once more bound symbols back to their source in the human psyche and in the life of man. Each system of symbols arising from the human psyche is an expression of the very structure of that psyche, and thus the best way of getting to know one's own mind, its latent energies, its conflicting forces, male and female, etc. 'If psychology were taught through the literature and books people already know (rather than special textbooks) it would be grasped far more readily by the ordinary individual' (Groddeck). Because symbols express the human psyche, of which they are a product, and always refer back to the human predicament as it is, they can all be related to each other. This is the great service which psychology has achieved in this century: to grasp the relationship between the different myths, fairy-tales and other symbolic material of all nations. What had always been considered a confusing morass of conflicting data suddenly fell into place as a unified whole. Certainly there were slight variations in expression, but this only helped to clarify the central theme, namely Man's life, the life of each particular individual, you and me.

In the past symbols were used to express the preoccupations of the time, with each particular society relying on a specific series of symbols and knowing no other. But suddenly, with the enormous influx of information brought about by the increase in literacy and improved communications of the last couple of centuries, the possibility of living with a single set of symbols seemed to be gone for good. Men's convictions and insights into the nature of living experience disintegrated in the face of a mass of confusing detail. However, the great danger in the past had been to take – or mis-take – the symbols too literally, thus failing to grasp the underlying reality to which they referred, the dynamic structure of the cosmos and the psyche, and the interaction of the two. In other words, living experience: life, here and now.

Life in its purest form is experienced as a unity: every twinkling star is part of the child's experience, it is only the intellect which separates the individual from the star by two thousand years. This tends to alienate man from his environment, from his world. But symbolism re-establishes the contact on a grander scale than ever before. Through symbolism man is in direct contact with a light which shone two thousand years ago, and many millions of miles away: such is the extent of his life, of his everyday experience.

Because dictionaries are the product of the intellect, they tend to dissect and fragment experience by their very nature. And for symbolism this would destroy its integral unity, its most important feature. However, by expanding the entries a little and referring the reader to related subject matter, it has been possible to adapt the dictionary's format to its subject matter. In this way something of the full range of symbolism can be expressed for the first time without sacrificing its essential cohesion, and in a form which is readily accessible to the ordinary reader who is interested in discovering the findings of psychology in relation to his own psyche, and the way in which these have been expressed throughout the centuries in symbolic terms. At the same time the layout will inevitably introduce him to other vivid examples of related symbols from other cultures, which may refresh or shed light on the ones with which he is overfamiliar: for when symbols grow old and stale, they too disintegrate and wither away to make room for the new.

The Arrangement of the Dictionary

As with the interpretation of dreams, the understanding of symbolism depends upon the recognition of essentials; otherwise one inevitably gets lost in a plethora of conflicting detail. Thus the entries in this dictionary describe the major characteristics that constantly recur in all symbolic material. With the recognition and identification of these character- istics, the essence of symbolism falls into place, and the particular variations and details can be easily grasped in relation to the specific society or individual with which one is concerned. This is true both of the dreams of the individual and the fruits of his imagination, as well as of the myths and symbols of a particular group or society.

The dictionary has various types of entry which reflect the many different levels on which symbolism works:

i. *Complete systems of symbolism*
There are complete systems of symbolism outlined broadly and briefly, to preserve their integrity. For those who lived and utilized these systems, each was complete and sufficient in itself. For example, see *ALCHEMY, GREEK MYTHOLOGY, I CHING, ZODIAC*.

ii. *Key symbols*
Through major, or typical symbols (see Two *BROTHERS*, Four *ELEMENTS*, Four *SEASONS, PATTERNS*), which are often common to the different main systems of symbolism, the unconscious, by way of the imagination, reveals its

archetypal structure – the patterns of energy which affect the sequence of life as it unravels through the years.

iii. *The qualities and functions of the psyche*

However, many different symbols can refer to the same essential – though invisible – reality of the psyche. Psychologists have often tried to demonstrate the way in which these realities manifest themselves in a variety of forms. They have taken examples from many different societies and eras in order to present a unified picture of the relationships between *CONSCIOUS/UNCONSCIOUS, EGO/SHADOW,* and the inward relationship with *ANIMUS/ANIMA* – all psychological realities which have tangible effects on our lives, but which need to be clothed in symbolic language in order to be visualized. These entries (working from the psyche to the symbol) give a varied cross-section of the symbols which have been used – with such amazing consistency – throughout the ages to depict the qualities of man's mind.

iv. *Negative/Positive Symbolism*

Wherever possible Positive and Negative symbols of the same archetypal force have been placed side by side. This is because the main work of symbolism is to heal the rift between conscious and unconscious mind – which may be connected with the two separate hemispheres of the physical brain. The aim is to integrate unconscious content into everyday experience: to drag dark irrational feelings and intuitions into the light of rational consciousness and thereby extend the boundaries of the rational mind. These forces often appear as negative symbols first, but can be transformed by recognizing them and coming to terms with them – possibly through active imagination – into equivalent positive symbols. Much relevant information is given about how to cope with the life situations in which the negative or positive symbols occur, so as to enable the individual to restore inner wholeness and so fully realize the potential of his or her life.

v. *Symbolic Sequence*

Many complete *SEQUENCES* have been included to

demonstrate the development of events in symbolism, depicting the way in which the energy of man unfolds into the action of life and affects it, as, for example, in *SLEEPING BEAUTY* and *FAUST*. Occasionally the reader is referred to other entries which precede or develop from a particular symbol in sequence; thus the entry *ORIGINS*, *SPLITS* into *OPPOSITES*, which demand to be related in the *UNION* of Opposites.

vi. *Index*

Where the reader wants to find out more about particular, individual symbols, then the majority of these can be found in the Index. However, in the main body of the text they will be found in context, probably with other, related symbols, which will all help highlight their significance.

vii. *Cross-references*

These have been set as follows: See also *EXILE*; or the *TREE*; Man is the *MEDIATOR*.

By familiarizing himself with the core of symbolism, whether by dipping into the dictionary, referring to entries of personal significance, or by working on his own symbolic life in dreams or active imagination, the individual should soon be able to make the symbolic connections for himself. Enough actual examples, in their proper context, gradually elucidate what every child or primitive society has always known: that symbolic language works, and has a vitality and significance that extends beyond conventional forms of communication.

Anyone who has used his imagination will already realize that the language of symbolism expresses profound truths about his life. However, the precise significance may only be recognized years later, and then perhaps only with outside help. This dictionary is designed especially for those seeking such help, and may throw light on their own symbolic work.

Being ABANDONED (Exposed)
Inner Life threatened with the danger of Inner Death

There are two aspects to this recurring image.

i. *An Ego figure, such as the Child Hero, is left alone to confront dark, sinister and destructive forces – as Hercules was abandoned to fight with the serpents in his cot.*

In the stories, the dark, primeval forces attack from without in the form of serpents or wild beasts, but in reality they are signifiers which refer to the dark forces inside the Hero. This image represents the beginning of the work of distinguishing the Ego from the Shadow.

ii. *Or, a figure of the Self: the Infant is exposed – usually abandoned and left for dead, either on water, in a wilderness or forest, or on a bleak hilltop – but is rescued from outside, either by a Hero, for whom the Infant is the object of his quest, or else by chance, such as by peasants or local villagers.*

This symbol refers to a much later stage in the creative work of life, when the ordinary, conscious personality is strong-willed, mature, developed – and suddenly this is not enough. A new side of the individual, the Self, is born in the unconscious and, like a new-born child, must take its chances there, exposed to the inner flow of Life (the waters) and the barren wilderness of the unconscious. The helplessness of the Infant emphasizes the passive qualities which are essential for this stage of the imaginative work. It is crucial to trust the processes of nature (the unconscious), and be as open and receptive to the products of the imagination as the Infant to its fate.

Related Imagery:-

On the cosmic level this symbol is depicted in terms of global catastrophes, with Mankind under threat of annihilation, like the Infant, but rescued in the final hour, against all odds – such as in the case of the Hero of the Flood (Noah, Utnapishtim). See also *EXILE.*

Sequence:-

The beginning of any work (see *ORIGINS*) is accompanied by one of these symbols of abandonment. In the early part of life the helpless child going off to its first school, the Youth leaving home for the first time or else inwardly struggling

1

with the dark side of his character, in all these cases, the Child Hero is appropriate.

Whereas later on, a passive openness to a much wider range of experience is indicated. This often involves reclaiming part of your personality which was originally exiled by your own dominant, conscious Ego.

Some examples of the recurring theme of Abandonment:-

In Myth: OSIRIS, *abandoned in the swamps;* HERCULES *in his cot; and* DIONYSUS, *left to be raised as a girl and a ram.*

In Legend: Sargon and Moses, who were both placed in baskets on the water.

In Fairy-tale: Hansel and Gretel abandoned in the forest; 'The Three Golden Hairs of the Devil' (Grimm).

In fiction: Charles Dickens: Oliver Twist.

ABOVE/Below
as in SKY/Earth
The Oneness of the Whole, the unity of opposites

Symbolism is based on the principle that the Cosmos is a unified whole, in which everything is related, however disparate. Though the patterns of nature may be intricate (and therefore appear confusing), they are in fact consistent rather than chaotic (see CHAOS). Thus, *what happens above* is most especially related to *what happens below*. The Sky is related to the Earth as husband to wife. (Whether the male tree, or pillar, plunges into the soft, round celestial sphere, or the male lightning impregnates the womb of Mother Earth, these are the two halves of the totality of Life, VEGETATION as well as ANIMAL LIFE.)

The Inner world of Mind must be clearly distinguished from the Outer world of substance (Matter) – and then related to it. The respective contributions of Life and Matter have to be distinguished and related in Man's experience of reality.

Related Symbolism:-

See also IMAGINATION, INNER/Outer, Cosmic MAN and MEDIATOR.

Examples:-

PATTERNS, the Vertical Line. Also the Six-pointed star of Ishtar.

The Cosmic AXIS. Or the *TREE.*

In Egyptian myth when the Sky Goddess, Nut, consummates her union with the Earth God, Geb, this depicts the vibrant relationship of Above and Below, of mind and matter.

The same is true when the Sky God Uranus, fertilizes the Earth Goddess, Gaia, in Greek myth.

BODY. Mind/Body.

See also *MIRROR.* The *COSMOS.* The *ELEMENTS.*

Postive/Negative Symbolism:-

The Winged Serpent, Or the Lightning, contrasted with the serpent, Or dove/serpent: Whatever exists below in the dark realm of unconscious (*UNDERWORLD*) is essentially the same in structure, when brought up into the light of consciousness (i.e. salvaged). So everything in the underworld has its counterpart in the upper world. And man is the Mediator between the two.

Personal Symbolism:-

It is chiefly a matter of temperament, whether you prefer to visualize the realm of Life descending into Matter from above, or basic material existence evolving by stages towards higher states of consciousness. The two visions complement each other. Ideally, the movement is conceived in both directions: from Above down, and from Below up, with appropriate symbols to express this.

ABYSS
Source of wisdom

An abyss of fresh water was supposed to lie beneath the earth and at the rim of the world, and was the source of all rivers, springs, etc. It was associated with the God of Wisdom (e.g. Ea in Mesopotamia).

A source of life and vitality that lies below the surface of reality. It is especially a source of Wisdom accessible to Intuition. It can be discovered by a process much like water-divining. What appears divided and different on the surface (i.e. many rivers, streams, lakes, etc) is all from one source, which is profound, deep, like the profoundest depths of the mind – with its refreshing qualities, once tapped.

The image is closely linked with dissolving into the softer

more malleable state of unformed potential – an attitude where everything is fluid and ready to change; in contrast with rigid, fixed attitudes where nothing can change. Attitudes need to be put back into the melting-pot and re-formed, at least four times during a life (*PERIODS OF LIFE*) if the symbolic work is to be accomplished successfully, before the final dissolution at death when the sharp steel of the spirit vanishes from sight, cp *King Arthur's sword* (i.e. spirit) *Excalibur*.

Related Symbolism:-
DISINTEGRATION/Integration.

Symbolic ACTIONS
Doing something impresses and changes the psyche, more than just thinking or dreaming.

An important part of symbolic action is acting in a particular way, solely in order to contact and develop that side of your personality. The introvert may loathe parties but force himself to go in order to work on his ability to relate, his extravert Feeling. Jung, an intuitive, attached enormous importance in his own life to working with his hands on stone, not because of the objects he produced but because of the effect upon himself. Each aspect (*INNER* and outer) of the *Four FUNCTIONS* can best be activated by doing something rather than thinking or dreaming about it. This is particularly important in relation to the *INFERIOR Function* where the results may be ridiculed by the intellect, which misses the symbolic point.

Related Symbolism:-
ALCHEMY is an example of a profoundly symbolic activity. See also *RITUAL, COMPULSIONS*.

ADJECTIVES
The adjective, which qualifies and gives the feeling tone, often determines the symbolism rather than the noun.

Because symbols refer to the inner reality, a round and rosy sun may be the equivalent of a round and rosy apple, both referring to round, rosy aspects of your inner life. This is so, even when adjectives aren't specifically mentioned. Applying this simple principle can dispel much of the apparent confusion surrounding symbolism.

Adjectives are like the attributes of a god or goddess, images of the significance, the value and feelings associated with the noun (or god), and this is the particular concern of symbols. Or the adjective may refer more directly to the meaning of the symbol than the noun.

The powerful bull is related symbolically to the powers of nature, sun and storm and refers to the power of man.

Anything soft, smooth, round or undulating may be an attribute of such a goddess, and refers to the gentleness of the feminine in nature and people.

For example, the attributes of Venus may be an apple, shell, dove, myrtle or rose.

Note:-

Children whose dominant *FUNCTION* is Feeling, often litter their early prose with adjectives.

Four AGES OF MAN
The symbol of regeneration

The Golden, Silver, Bronze and Iron Ages are often assumed to be a series of gloomy degenerations. But this is an interpretation of a symbol by a classical and dominantly intellectual civilization which has lost touch with the cyclic essence of symbolism. In fact, the Ages correspond to the four stages of the process of regeneration in Alchemy – the black of the earth (the unconscious), the white or silver of air (Anima, a feminine light in the unconscious), the red of copper especially (the energetic – fire – use of the unconscious content in physical life), and the gold of transformation.

It is worth noting that the order of the symbolism may have been unconsciously altered – there are many instances of this which can be traced – to accord with the current degeneration of symbolic life itself. In the same way, swords – or spades – in the *TAROT* have become the suit of ill omen, in accord with the dark and negative use of intuition.

An even gloomier vision of the Four Ages of Man was

projected on to the future, in a reversed mirror image (see *MIRROR*) from the unconscious, and was overtly related to the lifespan of Man. Future men would be born into the full maturity of a Golden Age; then, through a process of degeneration, would pass via Silver to a Bronze Age of strife and war, and finally emerge, as wrinkled, grey-haired babies in the second or last Iron Age. Such premonitions are often valuable projections of the psyche, illuminating the unconscious potential which will influence the future.

ALCHEMY
Dissolution and coagulation – the separation of the various ingredients of Life, and then the recognition of the relationship that exists between them.

The alchemical symbol is not the representation of a finite process, but signifies the repetition of processes in common, everyday Life to discover life's true value and meaning (the gold). It is concerned with working towards a transformation of Life, and such labour can be divided into two stages, two aspects, related to the major *SPLIT* in the sequence of Life and the pattern of the psyche: Dissolution and Coagulation. The symbolic representation of these two aspects of the work, the division between the active and passive elements of the cosmos, is usually articulated as the difference between Male and Female – between king and queen, sun and moon, day and night, life and death, form and matter, the volatile and the heavy.

These symbols refer to different aspects of the division of Mind and Body, of Inner and Outer (see *INNER*), which can only be finally realized in death. However, much can be grasped from a pseudo-death – a period of withdrawal, incubation, fasting or isolation: indeed, any process which divorces the subject from normal experience, and gives him the opportunity to discern the nature of the living organism in a vacuum, and then relate it to the material universe. The result of this separation and the subsequent union – this process of dissolving and coagulating, disintegrating and integrating – is to relate conscious with unconscious, the personal life of the individual with cosmic, universal Life (see *Cosmic MAN*).

The Stone became more valuable the more often the process was repeated.

The Goal of Alchemy: Although it has been argued that some alchemists did discover the secret of turning lead into gold by nuclear fission, their work and objectives – to find the elixir of Life, to transform base metals into gold, to force the transforming essence (or principle) of life, the Homunculus, to rise like a genie from the retort – actually remind us of symbolic *GOALS*, which lie in the beyond, and are not evoked so that they might be attained but rather because they give direction to the work. They are goals related to the End Time.

The Philosopher's Stone was the secret of Life itself, related, on a cosmic level, to the first germ of life on Earth (see *COSMOS*). If the Alchemist could impregnate the Stone with his own life, then he had discovered the secret of the Creator.

The work above was divided into a pattern of four, and further developed into seven stages. The four aspects of the work – and of the psyche – correspond to the four *ELEMENTS*, as well as to particular colours and minerals (see Chart on page 8).

The pattern of the psyche is static. It is divided into conscious and unconscious, and then further subdivided into Sensation, Thinking, Feeling and Intuition. The process of the work moves in a circular sequence.

i. It starts by sinking into the Black – the unconscious – where parts of ourselves have been exiled or abandoned. The Alchemists started with the premise that something was amiss; that Matter and Life were somehow dislocated. Consequently, the ordinary light of everyday consciousness must be extinguished.

ii. Then the white moonlight appears, the feminine light of the unconscious. Its components had to be separated and analysed.

iii. These elements – both individually, and in terms of the whole of which they are part – must now be assimilated by the conscious mind, much as dreams can be understood.

iv. But the process is not complete unless the golden sunlit

7

waters which blend the conscious and unconscious elements – of feeling and intuition especially – actually water and feed the earth and bring forth fruit. In other words, they must be used in everyday Life.

Then the process must start again.

Where there are seven stages, the first four remain as above, though described in varied symbolism that stressed the

Chart of the Fourfold sequence of the Alchemical Work. The basic principle was taking apart and putting together (as in other mending processes).

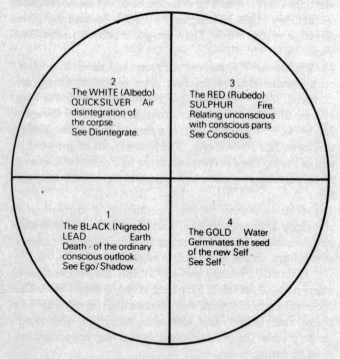

2
The WHITE (Albedo)
QUICKSILVER   Air
disintegration of
the corpse.
See Disintegrate.

3
The RED (Rubedo)
SULPHUR   Fire.
Relating unconscious
with conscious parts
See Conscious.

1
The BLACK (Nigredo)
LEAD   Earth
Death · of the ordinary
conscious outlook.
See Ego/Shadow.

4
The GOLD   Water
Germinates the seed
of the new Self.
See Self.

Note:

There were also three preliminary stages depicted by colours, and suggesting a way of descent into the black:

1. Yellow, leaving the sun of ordinary ego consciousness behind.
2. Blue, for the sky empty of sun or ego.
3. Green for dissolution in the sea. Sinking within.

All the stages were associated with planets, metals, etc.

unique, essential features of the work, which took a lifetime to complete. The fifth stage is something new, thriving on the opposites, Fire and Water, Earth and Air. The sixth stage can be conceived of as an attempt to elevate the work from the personal to the collective plane, from the particular to the archetypal, from the realm of men to the summit of the Gods which could only be achieved through the rituals of sacrifice – through denial and suffering – in other words, through sublimation.

In the final stage the collective conscious life must fuse with the collective unconscious, to form a new, enduring experience of the Self at one with the Cosmos, united in a single Reality, which remains ever the same through a constant metamorphosis and renewal.

Chemistry, Psychology and Alchemy: Alchemy was the bridge across which the rich symbolism of the ancient world – Arab, Greek, Gnostic – was transported into our own era by people who lived in a world described by its language. Thus symbolism fell from the rarefied heights into the melting-pot, and began to be tested in a continuous, dynamic interaction with the findings of chemistry.

True symbolism is not fantasy, though both are the products of the *IMAGINATION*. Symbols attempt to express such fundamental principles that are synchronistically true for the outer world of Matter *and* the inner world of the psyche, both of which stem from the same source and consequently behave according to the same principles. Over the centuries Alchemy provided ample proofs to substantiate this duality, since its practitioners continually applied archetypal symbols to a microscopic universe, and time and again the symbol demonstrated its validity in both spheres, the psyche and Matter.

Examples:-

Fluids could be distilled – and the product was a concentrated and purified essence. In the same way, the Emotions, isolated and concentrated, revealed their most valuable fruit.

Amorphous blocks of Matter could be broken up and analysed, dross and scum discarded, or purified by fire. The chemical effects of fire and salt, paralleled – and, indeed, exemplified –

the way that bitter experience could sometimes purify the character and eradicate corrupting elements.

Gross substances could be refined; the heavy could be made volatile – for example, water could be turned into steam – the evasive and mercurial could be tethered, the dry could be moistened. Everything is subject to decay, yet even this is merely another facet of transformation, since the essence of Life is indestructible:

All these processes are equally valid, in symbolic terms, when applied to what we now call *COMPLEXES* or the contending forces in the human character. Central to the work of the Alchemists was Mercurius, quicksilver, and the hermaphrodite, which could relate the various complexes and principles. As Hermes – the equivalent of Mercurius in traditional myth – the messenger of the gods could move between heaven, earth and the underworld, spreading knowledge and uniting opposing elements. It should be noted that a great deal of traditional mythology regained its relevance in the hands of the Alchemists, once it was integrated into their processes, and the visions erupting from their unconscious.

Related Symbols:-

Much of the symbolism in this dictionary would have been familiar to the Alchemists, who provided many terms such as 'dissolution', 'condensation', 'fixation', 'projection' since appropriated by psychologists.

Books:-

Jung, C. G. *Mysterium Conjunctionis* [Jung's masterpiece], in *Collected Works*, Vol 14 (1963).

Grinnell, R. *Alchemy in a Modern Woman* (1973).

ALCOHOL, such as soma, beer, wine
Releases the unconscious for better – or worse

A lowering of conscious activity, a dimming of the conscious mind which allows the inspiration of unconscious intuitions to break through. So it has always played an important part in ritual. It is a symbol of the spirit and of love (Sufis). It has been used to rouse any content from the unconscious, especially the ferocious animal instinct for battle, and the mating instinct after Bacchic frenzy and orgy. (See *DIONYSUS*.)

Negative Symbolism:-

The destructive side of the unconscious: uncontrolled, unassimilated.

Personal Symbolism:-

Intoxication is a way to find out something about your *SHADOW*, which is the first step in relating to the unconscious. For example: people who are too extravert, and pay no attention to the inner realm, could eventually feel compelled to drink alone with their own visions and hallucinations from that source, while shy, introverted people drink in company (see *COMPULSIONS*). There may also be some symbolic link between drinking and immaturity, the bottle and the baby's bottle (see *CHILD*, Negative).

Distilled Alcohol (i.e. Fire Water): When set alight is an image of the *UNION* of fire and water, of emotion and intuition, of above and below (fire rises/water descends).

Red and white wine: The sun and the moon – the sun ripens the grape which the moon causes to swell (symbolically the cause of growth because it waxes). Or the blood of life, and bones of death.

ALLEGORY, metaphors, similes
Consciously contrived comparisons are not true symbols

Whereas symbols express the relationship between man and the cosmos, by using images from the outside world as the only possible means to depict aspects of his own inner nature, the conscious intellect, limited to its own resources, misunderstands and misappropriates this device. By dressing up one clear set of outside facts in terms of another, without relating them to man's own life, as experienced from the inside, which is the central reference point of symbols, their reality is betrayed (see *INNER*/outer). Allegory is an attempt to manipulate symbolic modes of expression. Symbols erupt spontaneously from the unconscious, while allegories are man-made substitutes. Symbolism is the language of nature speaking to man, the whole man of emotion and intuition, as well as of sensation and intellect. However, there is no clear boundary line between the two, because unconscious material creeps in spontaneously as soon as people exercise their imaginations. (For example, George Orwell's *Animal Farm* is partly a political essay dressed up in farmyard language, but also partly a fairy-tale of the human predicament.) And true symbols may be contaminated by conscious interference.

It is chiefly important to avoid the intellectual pitfall of interpreting one true symbol in terms of another related symbol, thereby reducing symbolism to allegory, as well as missing the point.

The ALPHABET. Words
The basic units of the universe

Underlying the complexity of the universe are the simple units from which it is built: just as a simple row of letters can be arranged in different combinations to describe everything that exists, and every product of the imagination.

Alpha to Omega: The first and last letters of the Greek alphabet, therefore the beginning and end of all that exists. Juxtaposed, they represent the great cycle of time where the beginning meets the end, like *the SERPENT Ouroboros*, a symbol of the All, i.e. of God. (See *ORIGINS, GOAL.*)

M, (Mmmmmmmm, as in Aum (Hinduism) and Mu (Zen)): As the basic humming sound of man it is almost one with the sound of the breath exhaling, and is symbolic of the essence of the universe, without the shape or form or consciousness.

Words: As intermediaries between the life of the mind and material substance, relating idea to object. From the time of the Pyramid Age, the word has symbolized the creative force of consciousness. Matter, substance, only exists through consciousness (see *COSMOS*).

Example:-

In the *KABBALAH* the ways of wisdom were identifed with the letters of the alphabet, and linked the *NUMBERS* of the Sephiroth.

Related Symbolism:- See *ELEMENTS* or *ARCHETYPES* for similar basic units of matter and mind.

12

Book:
Bayley, D. *The Lost Language of Symbolism* (1912).

ANCESTORS
Symbols of the forces that moulded your psyche

As the final product of generations of evolution, we embody our ancestors: each upward step from sponge to modern man has left its mark on the psyche, which also registers genetic decline.

Often the cemetery was placed at the centre of the town or city – much like the roots and trunk of a tree – and, as time passed, the city grew and extended from this centre like branches:

The personal and collective unconscious. The present generation is the final product, the living fruit, of all preceding generations: a walking testament to the premise that the essence of Life can only be transformed, never destroyed.

Personal Symbolism:-

The evocation of one's ancestors has recently been rediscovered as a method of gaining access to the inner complexes and conflicts of the Self. Their blood runs in your veins. The brilliant members of your family – as well as the black sheep, the heroes, the cowards, the drunks and the suicides – can all be used as especially appropriate images to represent the entire range of your inner personality. This is partially a spontaneous process, but there is, of course, always a danger of only identifying with those of our forebears who confirm the conscious image that we have of ourselves. But unless we are prepared to face the entire picture, this is a sterile and misleading exercise that fails to take into account the many conflicting elements of the Self, which could ultimately elucidate current difficulties.

Related Symbolism:-

Reincarnation.

ANGELS/Demons
The benevolent and malicious forces at work either on or in the unconscious psyche

ANGELS

Historically both angels and demons were usually the deposed gods of a former religion, or conquered people, which could not be eradicated totally from popular favour or fear. And they have provided occasion to preserve tenaciously some features of the pagan pantheons, which reflect patterns of the psyche governing the processes of everyday life. There are vestiges of their relationship with the Aenneads of nine gods, with one central high god and eight others arranged around, corresponding to the points of the compass, the elements, the seasons of the year, and the relationship between these basic factors.

The different types of invisible powers, from Seraphim to angel, refer to the scale values, the *LADDER* between the highest and the lowest aspects of man's field of vision.

The correspondence between Angels and demons arises from the fact that the underworld is a reflection of the upper world in dark, distorted form – i.e. it is the same but experienced negatively by intuition functioning unconsciously, and so in an inferior manner.

Symbolism attempts to convey that it is the interaction between your state of mind and outside facts that determines your living experience. Winged-delight in contrast with seething-torment is a perennial concern of man, regardless of the images.

ANIMA See ANIMUS/ANIMA

ANIMALS general
The animal instincts, often unconscious and dangerously primitive, but also a source of vitality.

The physical body and the animal instincts in man. Most especially the instinct of aggression, the mating instinct, and the herd instinct, which includes the individual's reaction to figures in authority. Animals frequently depict the dark unconscious aspects of the psyche such as the Shadow, the Animus and Anima, and the Inferior Function which have usually got stuck in primitive archaic forms.

There are no civilized instincts and the psyche experiences considerable embarrassment and conflict trying to reconcile the civilized veneer with basic animal needs, which can be much stronger and fiercer than the Ego alone. For example, animals recognize the herd leader or parent by such signs as bellowing, mane, antlers, and people are liable to be carried away by similar insignia, uniforms, or the voice, without recognizing what is happening. The inner image, by which animals recognize a mate, is more specialized and less subject to error and deceit, but in man is still a frequent cause of disaster, when he *PROJECTS* an image on to a person. If the conscious mind cannot go along with the instinct, its only power is to hold out against it until some more suitable object presents itself. *BULL-FIGHTING* is a good example of symbolic action to cope with and master animal aggression. *Wearing skins, leather clothes, furs* may be an attempt to activate the Dionysian (See *APOLLO*/Dionysus) side of our nature, or an irrational demand for attention from the animal side of our nature. Hairy people and people dressed in skins may take the less civilized *SHADOW* role. (See The *BROTHERS*.)

A woman who helps cope with animals: Inner feminine attitudes are sometimes better at coping with aggressive instincts then heroic determination (See *ANIMA*). Sexuality and aggression are, in any case, related symbolically as two aspects of passion.

Gods who turn into animals, or vice versa, animals which reveal godlike qualities: The sacred and valuable side of the animal instincts.

Fighting the animal: is grappling with the Shadow (See *EGO/Shadow*).

Figures trapped in animal form: indicate failure in humanizing the animal instincts and emotions.

Animals shying, panicking: refers to the fear that is felt in the guts, the animal region of the body (See *PAN*).

Sometimes the animals point out their great age: They existed long before man and are nearer to the origins and source of life. This side of them cannot be ignored. People who turn a blind eye to the animal world are the most likely to be possessed by bestial compulsions. (Freud speaks of the lust for killing being inherent, and art as a kind of sop or compensation for what we sacrifice in becoming civilized, on

15

a par with wishful thinking and daydreaming. But Jung suggests that symbols arising spontaneously from the unconscious can transform this brutality and give new direction to the energy.

Trying to get people who have been bewitched as animals, back into human form: Integrating and humanizing the animal instincts. It may take years to tame the wild irrational feelings (see '*BEAUTY and the BEAST*').

The herd: The social group in contrast with the *INDIVIDUAL*.

Carrying an animal: coping with an animal passion through a difficult phase or period of transition.

When animals kill all who venture near: they destroy human qualities for the sake of animal ones.

Or the animal may guard an imprisoned female figure: and so be preventing the *ANIMA* from playing a part in life.

Animals guarding the treasure: the brutish passions which may prevent the individual from realizing the true potential of life, the *SELF*.

The Animal Man
Symbol of the inner conflict between Nature and Culture.

This symbolic figure includes those primitive people who look after animals, animals with human characteristics, and is closely related to composite creatures, part animal and part man:

The conflict and/or reconciliation between the natural side of man and the civilized. Animal instincts, especially sex, in conflict with law, moral codes, social behaviour.

This conflict is never completely resolved and has many facets. The combination of man and animal is the focal and central point of all animal symbolism. There are figures close to the animal realm in a riotous, brutish unrestrained way (like the *Centaurs* and *Cyclops*); and, at the opposite extreme, godlike figures who restore the harmony of nature, and turn the world back into paradise (like Nizami's Majnun). And in between there is every shade and grade of being. The wild natural man has always had a strong appeal, even in the very ancient Babylonian myth of Gilgamesh where he appears with his attractive, wild companion

Enkidu. But this becomes more pronounced as the valuable animal instincts get more threatened in an increasingly complex civilization.

Examples:-

Voltaire, *L'Ingénu* (1767). A French Canadian brought up by Red Indians but thrust unexpectedly into the mannered French society of the epoch – a striking early example of the Noble Savage theme and the need to return to nature.

Mowgli, in the *Jungle Books* (Rudyard Kipling, 1894).

The Noble Savage in *Brave New World* (Huxley, A. 1932). The civilizing influence becomes an unpleasant act of vivisection in *The Island of Dr Moreau* (Wells, H. G. 1896).

The film *Derzu Uzala* (Kurosawa, Akira, 1975).

Composite animals especially if part human, like Centaurs and Mermaids.

Indicates that important facets of the psyche have remained unconscious, and therefore confused. But these figures may be mediators between man and nature.

i. Because these creatures don't exist in the outside world, they refer directly to the inner world, and in particular to contact with the unconscious where the content has not yet been differentiated. The fusion of animals – or animals and men – indicates that the different parts have not been clearly distinguished. For example, the upper half, the conscious ego, may have been humanized, but the feelings (fish and horses) are still primitive, irrational and in need of conscious attention. But these figures remain joined to, therefore related to, their instincts and so have something vitally important to offer the Hero (with whom the reader is supposed to identify, as if it were his own life that's at stake). Note:- The very fact that such freaks are not likely to appear in the outside world is used to help pin-point their meaning, which is inner. The fact that the human and animal parts are inseparably linked, is also meaningful. Thus the image is a compressed bundle of meaning: the meaning is its only point.

Or:

ii. When particularly godlike beings are concerned, such a being may depict the successful differentiation and reunion

17

of the different aspects of the psyche. For instance, Jung interprets the Mithraic god *Aion* in this way, as the particular union or combination of psychic factors which enable the individual to unlock the secret of life. This secret, which is the recurring theme of symbolism, is perfectly intelligible to the conscious Ego, but not appealing. Only the essential *SELF* can exult in the flux of life. (See also *CHANGE/Changeless, UNION OF OPPOSITES*.)

Or:-

iii The ingredients of the composite animal may refer to basic ingredients of symbolism such as the wings from above united with the snake from below. (See *ABOVE/Below*). Or animals representing earth, air, fire and water may be combined (see *ELEMENTS*). Or animals from the zodiac, combined to give powerful images of the processes and transformations of time. (See *SPHINX, ZODIAC, TIME.*)

Contrasting animals
Contrasting ideas

A lot of symbolism is in pictorial rather than story form and dates back, as such, before writing, when many important features of symbolism are already clearly discernible, especially man placed between contrasting forces of the animal kingdom. Or the tree of life may be the *MEDIATOR*, holding the balance between opposing symbols, representing variously *INNER* and outer, *ABOVE* and below, etc.

For example, Lion/Eagle or Lion/Unicorn: physical existence in contrast with spiritual essence.

Talking animals
Nature trying to communicate with man and influence him.

Symbols attempt to regulate and control the system of the mind (psyche) in accord with the dynamism (energy) of the world of instinct.

Talking animals try to mediate between these two worlds in myth and fairy-tale.

Sometimes the animal's advice is just what is needed and entirely positive: – when it is time to rely on the instincts.

But at other times disobeying the animal, though it leads immediately to trouble: that is, inner tension, may nevertheless be more richly rewarding at the end of the fairy-tale or of life.

Womb Animals
   In context these may be related to processes of rebirth
The pig is the womb animal of the Earth, sacrificed to the Earth Mother.
The Dolphin is the womb animal of the sea.

Particular Animals See main part of Dictionary or Index.
Book:-
White, T. H. *The Book of Beasts* (1954), for interesting aspects of medieval animal symbolism.

ANIMUS/ANIMA
Symbolic figures (see *PERSONIFICATION*) **of the masculine forces in a woman, and the feminine qualities in a man.**

These lie in the *SHADOW* realm of the unconscious, and, as with everything unconscious, it is easier to get to know them through the imagination than through the intellect.
For Emma Jung they are the main waking path or bridge to the unconscious, and therefore the route to the *SELF*. For a man, the Anima is the feminine guide across that bridge, to the other side of himself. As the feminine *MUSE* was the inspiration of the poet, so the Anima is the guide and inspiration for the ordinary man in the creative work of living: making something of each day (a work of art), in contrast with merely existing and getting through time. For a woman the Animus performs the same function.
So if you are a woman, everything in symbolism that is classed as male: refers primarily to masculine forces at work in your life. These may be experienced cosmically as the masculine side of nature, or as the men in your ordinary extravert life, or experienced inwardly as the personified Animus figure.
If you are a man: The same is true of everything feminine in the world, and your relationship with it. The archetypal figure experienced inwardly is a symbol of the relationship between man and all that is feminine at whatever level. The feminine principle in nature, the core of the archetype,

cannot be experienced directly, but only as it manifests itself in women etc. Men get cut off from this experience, if they lose contact with the part inside themselves which responds and corresponds to the feminine.

NEGATIVE side of both:- Like the *SHADOW*, the figure of the opposite sex has many dark menacing qualities, which may be the first to manifest, indicating the time has come to tackle the problem.

The Symbols:-

The harmonious relationship of the sexes is a major concern of symbolism, from the sacred *WEDDING* of *ZEUS* and Hera, the *UNION* (conjunction) of *ALCHEMY* to the Happy Ending (see *GOAL*) of fairy-stories. It is an integral part of the larger problem of the union of *CONSCIOUS* and Unconscious.

Book:-

Jung, E. *Animus and Anima* (1957).

The ANIMUS – the Masculine figure in the woman's psyche
The Father, Brother, Husband and Son to the feminine conscious Ego

All the complex, mythical, incestuous relationships – as in the royal families of Ancient Egypt – are symbolically related to the changing role of the Animus in a woman's life. Councils or courts, of gods or men, are a common representation of this symbol, since the Animus may manifest itself in the form of a group voice or an accepted belief. Quite often, corporate opinion allows us to adhere without thought; this is clearly a danger, and all such beliefs should be examined in the light of inner experience.

Symbols deal with the typical situation of the Traditional Woman, who is well-adjusted emotionally, but occasionally refuses to analyse her world because she fears that such an examination might impede her feminine power. But by contrast, the Animus – the thinking function – has, in many modern women, received so much lavish attention – as a consequence of the role of women being questioned and redefined by society – that it now dominates the psyche, and might well impede a true expression of Self. That is to say, it is possible, and even common, for certain women to have a typically masculine conscious Ego with Anima problems; once this has been recognized, it is, of course, easier for a woman to develop the feminine side of her nature than for a man.

Symbols, relevant to the *ANIMUS*:-

The head is the focal point of the Animus in contrast with the heart. And all the symbols of the masculine thinking world are, for a woman, symbols of the Animus side of her nature. But the dark, negative side of the symbol will be experienced more vividly, will be more meaningful in the typical situation.

The dark sun, the Black Sun (Sol Niger) or sun in eclipse, as well as a darker form of the sun hero, such as *Black Knights* or *Princes*: But the symbols will keep changing and transforming in accordance with developing stages in the relationship with the Animus (see *FUNDEVOGEL*).

In body symbolism the developing Animus may manifest in a voracious appetite, the appetite of a growing boy, that is, the growing boy within the woman in this case.

The Animus is also associated with breathing, and problems with breathing (e.g. asthma) may be one indication of a new phase in coming to terms with the Animus. *Primitive male figures like giants*, especially if associated with the underworld, represent for the conscious feminine Ego, the Animus, malformed or partly animal, indicating an early stage of its development, and the need for transformation. *Satyrs, devils, Pan figures: HEPHAESTOS and also Loki, an underworld fire spirit*, also represent this male figure within the Mother Earth side of a woman's nature. *Woṭan or Hermes*, or any figure associated with guiding souls to the underworld (i.e. guiding the inner spirit, initiating it into the realm of the unconscious), would represent a highly developed and clearly distinguished Animus, godlike and therefore capable of transforming the inner life. *Dionysus was served by women who danced frenziedly, ecstatically, in order to become possessed by the god:* In psychological language, in order to rouse the inner masculine Animus from the depths of the unconscious.

Negative Symbolism:-

The Animus is an elemental, unruly force, not at all easy to control. And guidance into the unconscious can itself take the negative form of being lured into the pit, as *Orpheus* or the *Pied Piper* lured men and beasts. In confrontation with the Animus, a great deal of psychic energy is taken up, and may be used in inner turmoil if not directed purposefully. (See *BLUEBEARD* for Negative Animus.) However, if understood, the Animus offers the chance to become free from the limitations of the personal conscious Ego.

Personal Symbolism:-

Many women have no difficulty letting the imagination run on, especially about dark strangers, and, though this must not be blocked, it is only the beginning of grappling with the Animus. It is particularly important to get to know what he thinks, how he thinks, where he gets his opinions from, whether they are second-hand or truly individual. And distinguish between the different sets of opinions fed into him: which ones came from the father, the husband, the newspaper, or other groups of people (church etc.)? What does he really think about them? Is he just one of the herd? What does he think of himself? What does he think of you (the woman)? What does he want or demand of you? What right has he, what are his plans anyway, and, in particular, what can he do for you in return?

The business of getting to know him may seem a bit awkward and artificial, though not much more so than getting acquainted with a difficult person in the outside world, but later, with particular difficulties and crises, the inner dialogue can be valuable and rewarding. Fiction, drama, etc., consist of this creative interplay, but it is just as necessary to be imaginative about the creative work of the living (of which fiction is a by-product).

Note:-

The attraction which women often feel for weak – or even crippled – men, could derive from seeing in the outside world a reflection of their own inferior masculine side: the Animus. Though this is also related to Mother Love. See *INFERIOR FUNCTION*, of which the Child is also a symbol, and actual children sometimes suffer from contamination with the Mother's inner psychological Animus problem.

Book:-
Grinnell, R. *Alchemy in Modern Woman* (1973).

The ANIMA, or Female Shadow Figure in a man's psyche
The Anima is Mother, Sister, Wife and Daughter to the masculine conscious Ego, in the inner world of the psyche

The youth, or infantile man, has a maternal Anima which transforms into the younger figure when he matures.

This figure is a *PERSONIFICATION* of the heart rather than the head: the feelings, and especially the feeling of being alive which gets lost sometimes. It is the source of receptiveness and sensitivity.

Just as a woman needs patience to carry and nurture her young, so the Anima is a source of the patience required to nurture the seeds of future development.

Just as women spin fantasies about their offspring, so the Anima spins fantasies. Which means that a man can't make any contact with his own unconscious, which expresses itself in imaginative symbols, without some recognition of his own feminine qualities. This is part of the feminine openness and emptiness (emptied of conscious purpose especially) which enables the unconscious to manifest itself without interference.

Symbols relevant to the *ANIMA*:-

Nymphs, water maidens, Valkyries, etc.: connected with the wellspring of life, its origins and power of regenerating and revitalizing the man, a source of new fresh possibilities.

The symbols are often threefold in nature, e.g. three graces, three gorgons: because the Anima can manifest in various ways, it has different faces, different aspects, some positive, some negative, thus embodying the feminine as a group.

This threefold nature of the symbol is often related to the three phases of the moon:

   i. The full moon: The natural fecund mother, who provides physically.

   ii. The dark moon: The unnatural dark mother who sometimes offers the possibility of transformation – but only through suffering and deprivation (see The *MOTHERS*).

23

iii. The New Moon: The youthful newborn Anima, who replaces the Mother Anima and so releases the Youth from her archaic power which threatened to bind him in perpetual immaturity.

The colour white, because of its association with the moon, is often connected with symbols of the Anima. This includes white birds, white animals, etc. For example, the White Serpent, or the lady who turned into a white worm at night (Bram Stoker) refers to the Anima in a primitive state.

White Goddesses (e.g. Artemis): the Anima at a more refined stage of development.

The princess enchanted by a spell, trapped in a castle, or otherwise in the clutches of the witch: the youthful positive Anima is still trapped in its archaic maternal form.

The difficulties involved in rescuing her: refer to the steps which need to be taken (within the psyche) in order to transform her.

Rider Haggard's *She* is often quoted as a typical Anima figure.

Positive/Negative Symbolism:-

The Anima contains extremes and symbolic material often indicates this.

The priestess or fairy who initiates the Hero may also be the witch who threatens to destroy or degrade him. In the Ancient Near East, the goddess Anat was also a whore who transformed men into animals: Which expresses the dangerous double-sided nature of the Anima. It has a monstrous side which can swallow the individual who is trying to integrate it. It may fill your cup – that is, your life – with a potion of love, inspiration, or transformation – or poison.

Cybele, whose priests emasculated themselves; or Circe who turned men into pigs on her island; or Calypso: All refer to the hazards of a primitive neglected EROS, with the Anima still stuck at the mother/witch, or negative mother, level. People who stay there too long become soft and emasculated: the conscious masculine Ego is caught and bound, whether by a spell or other means – indicating unconscious compulsions – and eroded.

Sometimes glass or ice cuts off the Anima which may be depicted in a torpor of unconsciousness: The mind is seeing the

Anima and the problem, but this is not enough. The feelings must be activated too.

The well-integrated Anima
Enables the man to relate with flexibility and vitality

When the nature of the Anima is understood clearly and brought under conscious control, a man can express his feelings appropriately without sentimentality. And many even show coldness when necessary. (See BETRAYAL.)

After the SHADOW side of the personality has been fully accepted and integrated in youth, around the mid-point of life, just when masculine attitudes are fully developed, but can start to get crusty, then is the moment ripe to come to terms with the feminine Anima (see HERCULES's fate).

If you succeed in assimilating her qualities into your all-male Ego it will show in vitality, subtlety, relatedness and imagination. You will feel more in tune with nature, more flexible, flowing like water along paths of least resistance, turning answers to the wind, and able to talk with conscious ambiguity rather than unconscious confusion, vacillation, ambivalence. In order to guide others, the qualities of nature are needed, a certain cunning and coldness, and ability to betray.

The Anima in Personal Symbolism:-

Emma Jung points out that the analytical viewpoint – that is the critical masculine outlook – has grave limitations, if left unchecked and unrelated to the Anima, as the personification of the man's feeling function. This is especially true in relationships where perfectly correct (but utterly inappropriate) thinking creeps in to sever and destroy those relationships which are not usually served by discernment or objectivity, but by sympathetic feeling. A sense of value, of what is important and what matters, is needed, especially to combat the urge for reasonable arguments in matters of love, which are futile, because irrelevant to the situation.

In order to experience the imagery of your own unconscious all intellectual activity must be deferred, and used to analyse and criticize later, rather than be allowed to block the flow of the imagination. It may be helpful to pretend you are a woman daydreaming, like the male novelist who found he could only write in the first person as a woman (i.e. through his feminine Shadow or alter ego). Sexual fantasy may have revealed some features of the Anima, who can then be held by the imagination, till she leads on down fresh paths to other transformations and visions.

Woman-chasing, when no actual woman proves satisfactory: may indicate searching in the wrong direction for the Anima (see *PROJECTIONS*).

Book:-
Hillman, J. 'The Feeling Function' in *Lectures on Jung's Typology* (1971).

ANXIETY. Angst. Fear
The Negative side of desire. The desire to face the Unconscious is in conflict with the Ego's fear of its consequences

The aspect of anxiety relevant to symbolism is the fear of the conscious Ego breaking up in the face of the Unconscious, the angst that · repressed content will break in, expressed symbolically, for example, as *corpses rising from their graves to harass the living*, and all the other typically chaotic ingredients of myth and folklore intruding upon life, like the threat of madness.

In other words, the chief source of anxiety is the conflict between conscious and unconscious, and it is precisely the work of symbolism to reconcile these two opposing forces in the individual's life. The first step is to recognize the unconscious by its effects (i.e. the fear it produces). The imagination then clothes and bandages the invisible forces (in this case the dreads), visualizes them in symbolic form in order, first of all, to be able to distinguish between them. It then relates them to the conscious Ego, which is thereby transformed into the individual Self.

The process is never at an end, but once it is begun with determination, the anxiety becomes the legitimate ally in the work of making the potential Self into a reality. It acts as a goad when a spurt of energy is needed for the next move. Fear is described psychologically as a negative wish: a true wish but experienced negatively. Once the nature of the wish is realized then the fear is transformed (see *WISH*). Although symbols give shape to our fears, this is for the practical reason of coping with the fear.

Fear of women (heroes who do not know fear, learn it from women): the reverse negative side of reverence, excitement, longing. In the same way longing for success inevitably involves dread of failure. But once this is understood, it is possible to transform the fear. See also *PAN*, for animal panic.

APOLLO/Dionysus
The struggle between intellect and passion. Or between Ego and Shadow

The heroic side of a man's nature, his bright, conscious *EGO* in contrast with a soft, effeminate side, the dark god of wine, love and sexuality. Wine lowers the barriers of consciousness, and so allows the unconscious to break through.

But these two gods are two aspects or manifestations of the same force. At a more primitive level they are one, both associated with the serpent oracle (at Delphi and Thrace respectively) and both gods of destiny.

Conscious determination, left to itself, has a very short, if meteoric run. It is the alternation of work and rest that gives a destiny that enduring indestructible foundation.

Apollo was only later associated with the sun in Greek myth, supplanting Helios the older sun god (William Smith). Other attributes, such as his bow, suggest that he was originally a storm god. For example he sends flashes of lightning for the Argonauts: This would make him a symbol of intuition as well as intellect. Like the serpent, lightning was associated with oracles and the powers of divination. Apollo epitomizes the qualities of mind in contrast with body.

Dionysus was brought up as a girl and later as a ram: which points to the feminine, emotional side of his nature, his receptivity, as well as the instinctual animal side.

Both are gods: indicating the sacred quality of the different *FUNCTIONS* of the mind, which are to be revered. There is a price to pay if one or other is despised or neglected. Dionysus's fantasies and moods are projected into the outside world which teems with his unconscious confusions,

27

while the Apollonian side of man stands aloof, bewildered by what is going on: sexual lusts, animal drives that involve suffering, being torn apart (like Dionysus).

The most respectable matrons joined in the orgies connected with the cult of Dionysus, god of wine, who wore an ivy wreath, like an evergreen vine and was later connected with all vegetation: As a ceremonial part of life, this letting go on particular occasions seems to have preserved the stability of society rather than broken it up. And this is something to be reckoned with in coping with the individual personality.

Dionysus travelled as far as India civilizing mankind. He is especially representative of the oldest and most primitive life form, vegetation: that is, the deepest layer of unconscious life.

The mask on the cup from which his initiates drank depicted the terrifying exterior of nature.

Apollo's twin sister Artemis is the equivalent force of Apollo in women. *Aphrodite was loosely related to Dionysus (they had an affair).*

Related Symbolism:-

The *BROTHERS*, the *SUN/Moon*.

Death in Venice (Thomas Mann) is an instance in recent literature of insufficient respect being paid to the Dionysian side of life, until it erupted, destroying the conscious, intellectual aims of the central character.

In society hippie movements, especially the 'flower children', would be a symbolic reaction against the too deliberate, systematized orientation.

The very real dangers inherent in allegiance only to Dionysus or *PAN*, on the other hand, are rather obvious: drunkenness, debauchery, drugs, apathy, etc.

Personal Symbolism:-

Too much conscious drive can be self-defeating because life eventually comes to feel so stale, flat and not worth living that you can't be bothered any more. On the other hand, uncontrollable passion disrupts and disturbs life – whether pursued as a conscious aim in life, or erupting from below. What seem to the intellect to be mutually destructive and opposing forces, in the (fairly long) process of living become mutually beneficial, alternating in a balanced way, and both contributing to the whole pattern of life. They are not just both valid in themselves, but they are actually helpful to each other.

In achieving the balance, there is a difference between the first part of life and the second. In the first part Dionysus looks after himself, and the striving can be concentrated on the heroic qualities of Apollo. In the second part it is the other way round, and people who are beginning to get into ruts of work need to relearn how to play, if their lives are to remain in any way fresh and flexible.

Not thinking, but acting in full conscious awareness, is what resolves the problem, reconciles the opposite poles.

Apollo also has his own dark underbelly of wolf, rat and plague, just as Dionysus has his bright, civilizing aspect. Just as there are no strict demarcation lines in the psyche or in nature where everything is in a state of flux and transformation, so with myth.

APPLES, including Golden Apples
Conscious knowledge which may cut us off from natural life

Like the round and rosy *SUN*, this is another symbol of the conscious mind which has become alienated from the blissful ignorance of the animal realm and the animal instincts (see *SPLIT*). Animal innocence came to an abrupt end as mankind ate of the Tree of Knowledge, just as the romp of childhood comes to an end for each child on reaching the age of reason.

Paris awards the Golden Apple to 'the Fairest of them all', namely Aphrodite, the dove and reunion: But it doesn't heal the rift, or prevent the strife continuing. Quite the opposite; this decision in favour of the Goddess of Love cannot carry us back to a state of union with nature, rather it is the initial cause of the Trojan War, escalating the conflict with the other goddesses involved (*Hera* and *Athene*).

The apple itself was provided by the Goddess of Strife, Eris, who wasn't invited to the wedding feast: Variations of the theme recur throughout myth, legend and fairy-tale which are primarily concerned with the conflict between conscious and unconscious.

Symbolically the goddess of Strife is the divisive characteristic of Ego-consciousness, that is, Egoism, always competing to be the fairest, to possess the fairest woman, or to win the war.

When one half of the apple is poisoned as in 'Snow White': one side of the apple is equated with sleep and death, both unconscious.

Positive Symbolism:-

The golden apple is also ultimately the HERO's passport to paradise, beyond the Western horizon: Although the apple caused immediate distress, the animal condition governed by instinct is not to be preferred to a fully integrated godlike consciousness, which endures through dying and rising, like the sun. If this is to be achieved, the myth implies that the Goddess of Strife meanwhile must be admitted to the feast of life, and given due attention – she likes to be noticed – as a necessary preliminary to reconciling the opposite ingredients of the psyche; in this case the Mother Archetype, *Hera,* the Anima, *Athene,* and the Love Goddess, *Aphrodite.*

Related Symbolism:-

See *APOLLO,* whose symbolism is related whether he was 'the apple God' or not.

KABBALAH: The blazing spheres on the Tree of Life also refer to the ultimate fruit of life, the golden apples of redeemed consciousness. But on The Tree of Life the parts are related in harmony; upper and lower, masculine and feminine.

Personal Symbolism:-

The basic *SPLIT,* then, is between knowledge and life. Knowledge involves dissecting, but it can be absorbed and integrated into the act of living, though not the other way round.

Jung compares symbols themselves to apples on the tree of life (the tree of the unconscious). There is a plentiful crop for everyone, so you can pick – or starve.

The ARCHETYPES. Typical features of life
The forces simultaneously at work in nature and in man
   First principles, which govern the forces and patterns of life.

The original single whole, the All, is grasped as the One. This

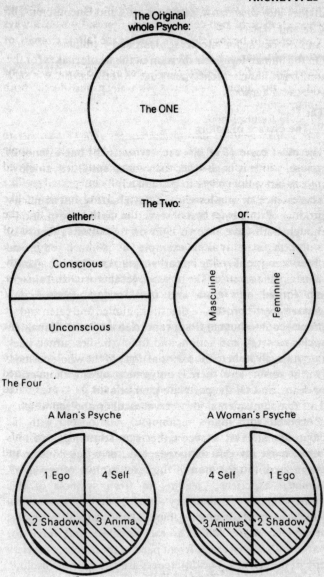

The Original
whole Psyche:

The ONE

The Two:

either:

Conscious

Unconscious

or:

Masculine

Feminine

The Four

A Man's Psyche

1 Ego   4 Self

2 Shadow   3 Anima

A Woman's Psyche

4 Self   1 Ego

3 Animus   2 Shadow

Note:-
The Ego is quite cut off from the *SELF*, and must first be integrated
with Shadow and Animus/a before the *HERMAPHRODITE* Self can
encompass the whole psyche in a fully conscious way.

divides into *OPPOSITES*, of *CONSCIOUS* and Unconscious, of Life and Matter.

And divides again into *MASCULINE* and Feminine.

On the human level, this division of the whole makes for the four basic human archetypes: *EGO, SHADOW, ANIMUS/A, SELF* (see the diagrams).

The One
The essence of nature

The most basic of all the archetypes is the one essence of nature, which is none other than the essential self, single in *ORIGIN* but split in order to germinate.

This essence, or quintessence, is not a fantasy, but as much a product of long empirical observation, as of introspection – though both have thrown light on it. Darwin's theory of evolution is a typical example of detailed empirical observation confirming an earlier intuition, that life is single in origin and essence. The observable facts of earth, rain and sun turned into grain and fruit, metamorphosed into animals by the process of digestion, hunted and eaten and so processed into human flesh, vaporized into unseen qualities such as energy and action, and finally bodies turned back into dust, all point to the essential unity of the whole cosmos. On the cosmic level there is only one cosmos without crack or seam, and all the parts are inter-related.

This one fundamental idea pervades all symbolism which is concerned with man's meaningful relationship with his environment. This is seen either as a relationship of love between clearly differentiated parts, or a relationship of union, akin to the union of the sexes in their offspring.

Personal experience, leading to fresh symbols of this underlying unity, is necessary – not in order to grasp the idea which is simple enough – but in order to galvanize this archetypal unity, which is the principle and force for harmony between the different parts of the psyche, of society and of the cosmos. The differences are relative not absolute.

Symbols relating to the one:-

NUMBERS: ONE/Many, also *ZERO*.

The Quintessence (see ELEMENTS) and the Philosopher's Stone (see ALCHEMY and STONE).

The Two
Nature is split

Nature splits into *MASCULINE* and feminine in order to reproduce. In symbolism this archetypal split is expressed on every level from god and goddess, down through to the mineral realm where every object can be given symbolic gender because of associations with male or female characteristics.

Nature is split or divided many other ways, into conscious and unconscious, inner and outer, active and passive, above and below, dark and light, etc. Although each division is distinct, and can't be precisely equated with any other division – for male, active and light are not exactly or even vaguely equivalent, any more than are female, passive and dark – nevertheless a symbol like *YANG/Yin* may sum up the idea of nature-divided-into-two. If misunderstood, this ignores all the subtle variations and shades of meaning. But symbolism aims at being so fundamental that it can be applied to the particular situation and found relevant; it is in relation to the everyday situation that the finer distinctions come out. At the same time, the particular situation and problem is illuminated by the archetypal perspective.

Related Symbolism:-

INNER/Outer, CONSCIOUS/Unconscious OPPOSITES.

The Fourfold Structure

Symbolism is inevitable. It doesn't deal with what may or may not have happened in a remote age, like geology, for example, but deals with immediate experience. Although man may be confronted by chaos on the one hand or at one time, he is also confronted by order. Typical patterns and sequences emerge in different contexts and are inter-related. The basic feature of the patterns is that simple units are linked up to form more and more complicated combinations.

Some Symbols of the Fourfold Archetypal Patterns and Sequences:-

The Four SEASONS of the Year, which are related to *the Four PERIODS of Life; The Four ELEMENTS; The Four DIRECTIONS; The Four Suits in the TAROT.*

ARCHETYPES

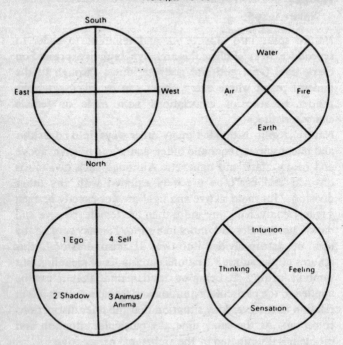

Note:-

These basic fourfold structures have borne fruit in elucidating symbolism, whether applied to personal dreams, individual fairy-tales, or particular myths.

Other Combinations
   Simple basic ingredients build up into the complexity of nature and the human character

The complex combinations which relate man to the cosmos are endless but any system of symbolism is bound to confine itself to eight or twelve subdivisions of basic experience. The *I CHING*, one of the most expansive systems of symbolism, concentrates on sixty-four, that is 8×8.

Symbols:-

The more complex Archetypal Patterns and Paths of life. Especially the *I CHING*.

34

A working pattern of the *ARCHETYPES* within the psyche.

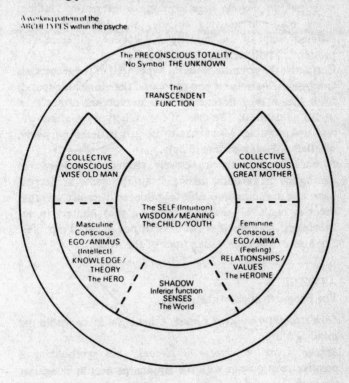

Also *The CHAKRAS: KABBALAH*, the spheres on the Tree of Life; *The Planets or Heavenly Spheres of the ZODIAC PATTERNS; The TAROT: GODS AND GODDESSES.*

The Archetypes are clothed in many different symbols, all pointing to their essence in different ways.

Personal Symbolism of the Archetypes:-

The individual cannot escape the basic framework: four periods of life and four ways of grasping reality. Beyond that, however, he is free to select the ingredients and mix the combinations of his choice. As the fairy-tales indicate, the art is in the choosing.

One writer argues convincingly that even the image of the Ego growing and expanding into the True Essential Self is just another stereotype, limiting the true, personal freedom which reaches beyond ideas of growth and fulfilling your potential, to include degenerating, disintegrating, failing, going mad, committing suicide, etc. There are many different ways of soul-making and as many different end-products. Myth reflects this diversity.

Certainly, the potentially useful hypothesis of the archetypes can become harmful if you get bound (let alone hidebound) by it (i.e. if they degenerate into stereotypes rather than useful guidelines). The core of the archetypes is unknown, and unknowable. Much has to be just suffered passively, whether willingly or unwillingly.

Symbols and myth are closely related to patterns of instinctual behaviour, arising from the same archetypal base, and are sometimes able to influence them in a way that theories can't. So the only criterion that matters is not theoretical, but whether it works or not in life. Your life. See also *COMPLEXES, FUNCTIONS* of the Mind.

ATHENE
The Personification of the Anima

Born straight from Zeus's head: Athene is a force within the mind of Man.

Athene is the protectress of Heroes, thus symbolizing a positive relationship with the Anima, protecting it against the dark forces of the feminine. *It was she who taught men the use of bridle and yoke*, a representation of an inner female principle, the mastering of which enables men to bridle their passions – thus avoiding false projections and compulsions – and yoke the male and female sides of their inner being in harmony.

She is the principle by which a man can combine Power and Wisdom, since Athene herself is the unification of the power of her father (*Zeus*) and the wisdom of her mother (*Metis*). *The olive is sacred to her* since her embodiment of harmony and balance is the means to peace, tranquillity and order. *The owl was the animal closest to her, and she introduced the art of weaving*, which suggests Athene's relationship with introverted intuition, the wisdom to see the pattern and meaning of life.

Negative Symbolism:-
All this balance and splendour can become inflexible and sterile. This aspect of Athene's nature is reflected in her shield which bore Medusa's head, and in later fairy-tales where the birds symbolically associated with her had the power to turn man to stone.

ATLANTIS
The lost continent sunk beneath the waves
The unconscious

The various theories about Atlantis and its historical reality in no way affect its symbolic appeal, since its fascination is related to our yearning for pleasures which have gone before – the secret worlds of childhood, or all-embracing excitement of first love – rather than the truth about a lost civilization which may, or may not, have existed. The enthusiasm which one feels for a particular period of history is a consequence of a natural identification with mankind as a whole as a collective consciousness, perpetually seeking to retrieve chunks of the past, by way of historical research, archaeology, etc., which had been lost in the collective unconscious.

Related Symbols:-
The Hyperboreans, who lived idyllically beyond the North Wind (see Ashe, G. *The Ancient Wisdom*, (1979)).
Any *Golden AGE or Lost PARADISE.*

The World AXIS
This important ridgepole rose symbolically from the navel of the world – the central mound or omphalos – to the pole star.
Time

This Axis is a representation of the enduring principle which supports reality, as the spine supports the body, or a tent pole holds up a tent. Thus it can be seen as the central core of life; the invisible principle which connects – or unites – mind with matter, without which there would be no living experience. It is the vertical spine of Cosmic Man – the central reality of life, yet unseen and intangible. It is the force which triumphs over inertia, degeneration and decay.

AXIS

Related Symbolism:-

The *DJED* Column in Egypt: all that was stable and enduring beyond the passion and death of Osiris.

This idea of continuity through time is related to Phallic symbolism, the continuity of man through procreation, and also to the symbolism of the Last Sheaf of corn put aside for the following year's harvest. It is also echoed in the more ancient *standing stones* (see *CENTRE*).

Other symbols: Wooden Pillars (Asherahs) on High Places, The Date Palm, The Pole and the *SERPENT, NUMBERS, ONE/many BODY/Spine* and the *TREE OF LIFE*, the Vertical Line in *PATTERNS*.

Note:-

Steles (boundary stones) were optimistically meant to mark boundaries which would endure for ever.

BABOON

The dawn – symbol of birth and *CREATION*

Only in Ancient Egypt was the baboon sacred; it was tied to altars, and mummified after death. This is because it was associated with the dawn, in much the same way as we associate the cock with daybreak (fairly arbitrarily, since many birds participate in the dawn chorus and there are many other activities which commence with the rising of the sun). Daybreak symbolizes the experience of birth – and rebirth – after the extinction of our normal perceptions of Time and Space in sleep.

Personal Symbolism:-

It is unlikely that your alarm clock will hold the same significance as the chattering of monkeys on the dawn of a new day. However, there are occasions at first light in the city when a neighbour's alarm, rattling out across the empty streets through closed curtains, can, in certain moods, convey something of the cosmic clock (*TIME*): the difference between sleeping and waking, extinction and experience, death and life. In this way a common appliance could become as potent a personal symbol as the baboon was for the Egyptians.

BANQUET
The satiation of desire

Sharing meals with gods, banqueting at the end-time is a representation of the inner spirit being satisfied through wisdom, bliss, etc.

In fairy-tales the Jinn spread banquets in a symbolic way related to another dominant theme of the fairy-tale, the *WISH*, in this case fulfilled, but in other stories it is often thwarted.

Related Symbols:-
The Horn of Plenty, cornucopia and other bags, pots or jars which contain inexhaustible supplies.

Negative Symbols:-
The legitimate wish for satisfaction can be mishandled by a variety of follies as, indeed, many of the fairy-tales tell us. Then life can provide us with an equally endless supply of things we *don't* want. In other words, the greater the desire, the greater the fear, since these are the positive and negative sides of the same impulse.

See also *PANDORA, ANXIETY* and *WISH*.

BEADS
Strung in circles
The cycle of time: the number of beads may refer, albeit roughly, to the number of weeks or other temporal divisions of the year.

Related Symbols:-
Goddesses with strings of skulls around their necks or waists refer to the negative, devouring side of time.

'BEAUTY and the BEAST'
Transforming the *ANIMUS*. Or coming to terms with brutal Nature.

This fable is the symbolic manifestation of a woman confronted with her fierce, cruel, and as yet malformed *ANIMUS*, which needs to be integrated and transformed. It is a story which highlights the necessity of coming to terms with

39

the masculine forces in nature, in their different forms and transformations.

On the sexual level the Beast is a fusion, in the girl's mind, of Father and lover. However, the incest taboo makes all relations on the physical, natural level repugnant. The emotions at play are still vague, primitive and ill-defined; thus they are trapped at the animal level.

On the cosmic level Beauty is the feminine soul – of a woman or a man – which has to reconcile itself to the cruel side of nature, which also provides for all our needs. In this sense the story is related to all the transformations of gods into animals: these all clarify the relationship between the spiritual essence of life, and brute, physical existence. Only by love – oblivious of the conscious Ego, but at one with nature – does the face of nature transform and reveal its radiant aspect.

In social terms the contrast and conflict between the socially beneficial modes of living and the wild, adventurous side of life are also symbolized in this tale. *The Kind Father/The cruel Beast:* The positive and negative sides of the same *ANIMUS*. In relation to an actual Father, the love relationship contrasted with the fear of incest (see *WISH/fear*).

Related Symbols:-
APOLLO/Dionysus.

Book:-
Jung, C. G. *Man and his Symbols* (1964).

BEE – Honey
The inspiration or wisdom which discerns the essence of life

Honey, which the bee extracts from many different blooms, can be seen as a representation of the essence of life which lies beneath the surface of existence (see *ESSENCE/Existence*). The essential oneness which underlies appearances is further emphasized by the way in which bees work together as a single unit. Hence they are an image of corporate identity. Each man is part of a great whole: mankind, of which the *KING* or *COSMIC MAN* is the symbol. If he identifies with this larger whole, then he is immune from personal extinction. Thus bees are the sacred attributes of many goddesses, and honey is a divine food which nourishes wisdom, a symbolic manifestation of the sweetness of the Earth and the sap of life.

Related Symbols:-

'The OWL and the Pussycat', who took honey and money, when they set out on the sea of the unconscious.

BEETLE
A symbol of Creation

In Egypt the word for the 'scarab beetle' is very similar to another meaning 'The Becoming One'. Thus, partly because of the play on words – which is often enough when a visual image is required for something which is difficult to imagine – and also because the beetle rolls its eggs along in a ball of its own dung, the creature became the symbol of dawn and creation. Perhaps its blue colour related it in the minds of the Egyptians to the sky.

Negative Symbolism:-

Its industry and brittle shell are representative of the façade which many adopt for work, which eventually becomes the most dominant attribute, taking over the personality completely, as in Kafka's *Metamorphosis* (1912).

BETRAYAL
The dark side of trust, which it shatters

i. Inner self-betrayal. The first painful shock of encountering the Shadow or the Animus/Anima.

ii. Leaving the protection of a secure childhood and taking on the responsibilities of adult life.

iii. Encountering the dark side of Nature, as if thrown out of paradise into the world as it is.

Positive/Negative Symbolism:-

Betrayal is the dark side of trust which it shatters. And also the dark side of forgiveness to which it may lead. Without coming to grips with the dark side of nature there is no possibility of development. But unless it can be related to the wider symbolic context of meaning and value, betrayal is simply brutal. If the individual is swallowed up by the dark side of the psyche, he inevitably acts from it (i.e. viciously). Betrayal is based on trust, but breaking this trust may be a part of love leading to independence and maturity.

Sequence:-

ABANDONMENT is followed by betrayal.

OSIRIS abandoned, then betrayed by Seth.

Whereas the *ABANDONED* child is looked after by nature (for example, nurtured by wolves), later the *YOUTH* is also betrayed by nature. No reconciliation with Nature is possible without being able to take these blows. Nature gives birth, provides and feeds, but also sends disease and death. The mature individual needs to be in tune with nature's ways, which involves integrating the *ANIMA*.

Betrayal is a down to earth fact, more common in life, than specifically symbolic; nevertheless the actual betrayal whether of Isaac, Job, Julius Caesar, the utterly forsaken Christ, the Jews by the Nazis: all point symbolically to the dark side of the mind, and of life.

Man betrayed by woman, whether Adam by Eve, or the husband by his wife in the French domestic triangle movie: the recurring betrayal by the Anima, which first as mother image turns dark and sinister, and later as the feminine Shadow, has a way of bedevilling life, even when outside circumstances are secure.

The eternal YOUTH unable to mature or grow up is most especially subjected to recurring images of betrayal: because betrayal is an inevitable experience at some point in life; if it is not assimilated, reckoned with, it continues to hold sway. It arouses strong emotions of resentment (which is a device to stop it sinking back into the unconscious), but some people get stuck at this stage, of festering conscious resentment. Unacknowledged hopes of living in blissful paradise forever backfire as cynicism. And the incident of betrayal (whatever it was) points inwards to a deeper self-betrayal, of which the other was only a symbol, a split between life and ideals. The refusal to shoulder the responsibility of living out the ideals, bringing life and ideals together (see *ABOVE*/Below), prevents the transformation of life. The immature conscious Ego is betrayed by its own Shadow and Anima. Because the Ego fails (or refuses) to understand their purpose in making themselves felt, he cannot mature.

Book:-

Hillman, J. *Loose Ends* (1975).

BIBLICAL SYMBOLISM
Layers of tradition, preserved and treasured on account of their symbolic significance for the inner man

The Bible has yielded up its symbolic fruit in many different forms to almost as many sects. To the Jewish tradition (as, for example, in the Zohar), to the Christian Fathers (the extravert, official face of Christianity), to the Gnostics and the Alchemists – a neglected Shadow – introverted – side of Christianity.

Because the books are presented as straightforward, historical documents, their symbolic value and meaning tends to be obscured. Also, for many of its readers, it has been wrenched from its dramatic context: the Cycle of the Year, which is symbolic of a man's life. Thus, even if they were not consciously recognized as such, many of the books' episodes and events would naturally relate to sequences and patterns in each person's own life. In this way the individual's life and destiny would be related to the life of the race – the life-story of Mankind.

Much of the material in the Bible comes from an epoch and region which had contributed all the basic foundations of symbolism. The books present much the same symbolic picture of man's condition as that reflected in the outpourings of the Ancient Near East (Mesopotamia, Egypt and particularly Homer's Greece), but in a highly condensed, more consciously discriminating way. Because it was a living drama it had to appeal each new year and to every generation; this may account for its continued fascination for different races in different eras, long after the shaping of the material had been completed. In other words, the long formative process tended to favour the survival of the archetypal and symbolic elements – of enduring value and meaning to anyone, anywhere – at the expense of what was long-winded, or of only passing interest.

The Seven Days of Creation

Taken in Reverse order. See *MIRROR*.

In personal symbolism, this can be related to the seven steps required to reach ever deeper layers of the unconscious.

These stages can be experienced internally, as the subject progresses towards that foundation of archetypal experience – preconscious totality (i.e. a 'positive regress'). In Ancient Mesopotamia this corresponded to the seventh or eighth level of the ziggurat, where there was no image of any god.

i. In order to get back to his *ORIGINS* man must first attain inner peace, which resides in the silence of contemplation . . .

ii . . . then he can discover and relate to the bestial side of his own nature (the Shadow figure) represented as the creatures who were created on the same day as man . . .

iii . . . as he plunges into the deeper waters of the unconscious, he discovers that at this stage he is at one with the slimy, crawling embryos in the sea . . .

iv . . . and moving back another day – and in common with most other systems of symbolism, particularly alchemy, man must then relate sun and moon, night and day, conscious and unconscious . . .

v . . . to be preceded by what is sometimes referred to as the vegetable soul: an enduring form of life and being which is barely conscious; hardly able to distinguish between night and day . . .

vi . . . then matter itself is dissolved in the waters of the unconscious . . .

vii . . . yet there is still light which, as the Zohar points out, is quite independent of the sun and the moon, for it is the inner light of life. (The Upanishads refer to a similar illumination, which continues to shine after all others have been extinguished.) At each end of this process is a period of rest in brooding silence (whether for God or for man): the entire cycle is contained within the passive state.

It should be noted that, in the context of symbolism, the whole process of Creation is related to the stages of contemplation. In Mesopotamia and the related cultures of the Indus Valley, Egypt and Canaan, some form of yoga seems to have been practised from the Third Millennium B.C. (see Butterworth, E. A. S.).

The Fall

The Garden of Eden, with its four rivers, and guarded by a monster with the flaming sword, to protect 'the way of the tree of Life'.

   This is the archetypal description of the treasure of life, which is difficult to get close to and grasp.

There is a specific allusion to the fourfold nature of the psyche, which is represented by the four rivers. But the garden is also identical to the ancient's image of the world; with its four rivers – the Tigris, Euphrates and possibly the Nile and the Indus – and its limits encircled by monsters. This is an indication that if our world is to be returned to paradise, then man must first re-enter his own, inner realm. This can only be achieved through a return to archetypal origins.

Freud saw the garden from which man was expelled as the mother's womb, which is the physical and sexual embodiment of this same archetype.

The Brothers

Cain/Abel, Jacob/Esau et al.

   The rift between the conscious and the unconscious (see also
   BROTHERS).

Jacob tricks his brother, the more primitive Shadow figure, out of his spiritual resources (his birthright), and with the co-operation of his mother dresses himself in animal skins in order to delude the father, who prefers the older, more primitive, animal son (the bestial side of man), and thus represents the opposition to transformation.

See also *SPLIT* and *TRICKSTER* as a key figure in the process of transformation.

The Recurring Themes:-

The story of Creation serves as an introduction to, and a summary of the sevenfold symbolism, represented by many different forms: the seven-branched candlestick, the seven-day week, the great seven- and eight-day festivals, and in some traditions (Koran, Dead Sea Scroll) a year divided into seven parts by feasts, each section of which was seven weeks long (totalling forty-nine weeks; the extra three were made up by week-long festivals). These can be interpreted as the symbolic proliferation of the way of the tree of life, with its various stages which amalgamate life's numerous experiences; integrating them inwardly, as well as consolidating them outwardly.

The image of the plagues of Egypt is like an inversion of the Creation, since each blight deprives Man of an element vital to his formation. It highlights disintegration as the negative side of creation, and provides us with a foretaste of the End of Time.

The Flood and the crossing of the Red Sea reflect the inner psychic process dissolving the old order in times of crisis, to facilitate the transition to a new phase of life. Old attitudes must be sunk before the new can emerge. On the cosmic level, it is like dissolving the universe and waiting to see in what shape it will reappear – if it reappears!

The wilderness filled with serpents is a symbol of the unconscious lying beyond the edges of the civilized world, to which the group longs to return – negative regression.

The Divine Plan
The Pattern of events for individuals and for the whole people

In the Bible God occasionally intervenes in momentous events in History – such as Exodus – and often communicates through His prophets. But the pattern of the chronicle also suggests a symbolic blending of Spirit and Matter, an alternating of dark and light – as in the case of Joseph, who rose from prison to the position of chief vizier; or from the Wilderness to the Promised Land for the children of Israel; or else in the alternation of War and Peace in Judges and Ruth. The effect is symbolically satisfying, for it suggests the significance of every event, its part in the overall pattern and vision, its value and meaning. This is in contrast to the common perception, which emphasizes the SPLIT between spirit and matter, mind and body, which is expressed in the contrast between symbolic events (myth) and physical events (history or life story), creating the illusion of separate, disjointed worlds. Whereas the Biblical narrative achieves the ultimate goal of symbolic work – the union of opposites on the vertical axis (see *ABOVE/Below*, *SPIRIT/Matter*, and *PATTERNS*).

The Heroes – Joseph, Moses, Samson, Job et al: are symbolic representations of major stages of transition and development of the collective consciousness. They have been compared to the other heroes of the ancient world, who are, perhaps, more obviously rooted in mythology, rather than history (see *HERO*). Like the Kings of later years, they are the focal point of the corporate identity and destiny, but also provide the archetypal background for the pattern and sequence of individual destiny.

The Women – Sarah, Ruth, Deborah et al: display the entire range of feminine qualities – from the ever youthful and seductive, to the enduring warrior women of darkness, who inspire fear.

The Twelve Tribe arrangement (Amphictyony): this image has its parallels at Sumer and Delphi, where the groups were responsible for providing tribute for the central shrine on a monthly basis. The origins of this custom are probably related to the *ZODIAC*, of which Abraham was supposed to be the father (Eusebius). The earthly rota can then be seen as a symbol of the revolving constellations and, through the mediation of man, the earth reflects the perfect order of the celestial sphere.

The Song of Solomon: Although as a love poem this work should not be underrated, as a celebration of physical love it should be seen as a part of a long tradition, in which such passions are the outward, material appearance of the Archetype of *UNION*: that is, the union of conscious with unconscious, feminine content (for example, the black Shulamite lady as the image of Shadow and Anima). If we compare Sufi poems from the same region, but composed later, we discover a wealth of overtly erotic material, accompanied by profound spiritual insights – a combination which is, for the most part, totally unacceptable in the West.

The Prophets and Wisdom literature: reflect the maturity of

47

the race, as well as the manhood and old age of the individual.

The vision of the End of Time: The last pieces of writing to be included in the Bible – executed in a visionary, 'apocalyptic' style – were concerned with the end of the world. The prophets had already pondered on the theme – the Day of the Lord – in much the same way as an individual will become concerned with reflections upon death after he has passed the mid-point of life. Isaiah speaks of the days when the cosmos will be rolled up like a scroll, and in the Upanishads (probably written at about the same time) there is a similar reference to the world being rolled up like a piece of leather. In modern symbolism a comparable image is that of a roll of film being packed away when the show is over.

Thus the overall pattern of the Bible conforms to the pattern of life itself, and is a reflection of the human predicament. This relationship is developed throughout the text, within each of the individual themes, life stories, contrasts, etc., which have mostly been preserved because of their lasting, symbolic appeal. This is another way of saying that each image refers beyond itself to the order of the universe, the patterns of society, and to the sequence and patterns of the individual's life and mind. Because this archetypal material is a product of mind, it must inevitably refer back to the mind. Order can be discerned in the cosmos, but it also needs to be created by man. The symbolic quality of the narrative is entirely contingent on its value and meaning for the individual *now*, rather than upon the validity of its historical content. This is why drama and fiction are usually symbolically richer than factual reports.

The Image or Conception of God as idol: Whether this plan – this order – is discerned in nature and events, or created in the mind and projected on to nature and events, it has its common origin in the archetype of the UNKNOWN. This archetype lies before the beginning and after the end; beyond the horizons or edges of the universe and encompassing the whole as we know it. To be drawn towards this context – which is the context of our own existence – is not the same as having an image of what it is.

It is Unknown and unknowable, yet the core of existence

fixed at the centre-point of an individual's life.

Symbols point outwards through time and space, beyond the confines of any symbol – however concrete or abstract. Although they may be able to guide intuition and feeling beyond the limitations of Ego-consciousness to the broadest possible vision of reality for man, symbols are always, in the final analysis, inadequate. There is no image for the nature of reality. The ultimate symbol is no symbol. In this respect Biblical symbolism is in accord with all other traditions, echoing, for example, the 'Not this, nor that' of Hinduism. Books:-

Jung, C. G. *Psychology and Religion* in *Collected Works*, Vol. II (1958).

Rahner, H. *Greek Myths and Christian Mystery* (1963), for fascinating but minutely detailed comparisons between Homer and equivalent symbolic themes in the Bible, such as the willow, the mandrake root.

Hooke, S. H. *Middle Eastern Mythology* (1963), for Biblical material in its context of neighbouring mythologies.

Goldziher, I. *Myth among the Hebrews* (1877).

Kluger, R. S. *Psyche and the Bible* (1974).

BIRDS
The Quest of the Mind for the heights

The image of the bird is a reflection of the thoughts, fantasies and symbols which dwell in the upper regions; it is a representation of those symbolic flights of fancy which carry man into the realms of the unconscious. It can also signify the mind, trapped in a primitive, subhuman condition. Birds act like messengers between man and the cosmos in which he dwells.

Even now, with the advent of the age of flight and the technology which has taken man to the moon, individuals tend to lose sight of the extraordinary qualities of the human mind in everyday life. Not only can it explore the ends of the earth and the limits of the sky, but it can reconstruct a lost Age of Dinosaurs which existed long before the first man.

The qualities of the birds – bright, golden or dark, nocturnal: determine which aspect of the mind's content is being

49

symbolized; whether the bright, conscious, positive side (eagle or falcon gods), or the dark, unconscious side which is often identified with the Anima or feminine soul.

In the context of ornithological symbolism, the Giant Bird is the Mind from which all others emerge, on which each depends and to which all are related. It is the generative essence.

If the bird should darken the sun, such as the monstrous crow which overshadows Tweedledum and Tweedledee, this is a symbol of the dark, unconscious Shadow which blots out the conscious Ego.

Birds with human heads, such as the Ba-soul in Egypt or the Harpies in Greece, and also the parrot, which has a human voice: All these are more specifically indications of particular human characteristics – whether positive and instructive, or negative and destructive. Only recently has the mind been conceived as a part of the body – in the past it was envisaged as extending far beyond corporeal confines, and assumed to survive quite independently.

There is an Ancient Egyptian text in which a man discusses the prospect of suicide with his own Ba-soul: it seems to him like a return home after a long and difficult journey. He longs for it in the same way as he lusts after a drink at his favourite tavern.

The Sufi poet Attar describes a flight of birds consumed by the sun, which can be interpreted as an image of the souls of men, stripped of all temporary appearances and limitations and at one with the essence.

Related Symbols:-

The volatile *ELEMENT* – air, gases and steam.

ICARUS, the bird man.

A feather of the bird is sufficient to symbolize the entire creature.

The movement of the bird is twofold

  i. It rises from the earth to the sky above, like the shift from body to mind; transcending bare, physical existence.

  ii. It swoops down to earth – as, for example, when the Phoenix eats its own wings: ideas and ideals have to be brought down to earth before they can be incorporated in life. Even the most inspired thoughts are vacuous until.they have some influence on the pattern of events. Only when symbols can be integrated into everyday life do they become of real, enduring value. Otherwise precious glimpses of the realms of the unconscious slip away elusively, and may even leave the individual more disappointed than before. It is getting the content back across the threshold from the unconscious which presents the difficulty here.

Particular birds:-

Dove, *the attribute of the Love Goddess as well as the Holy Spirit.* This is the Archetype of Relationships and Values which arise from feeling. The union of distinct, individual entities (*UNION*).

The Goose
The condition of Ecstasy (see Joseph Campbell: *The Flight of the Wild Gander*). Was the prehistoric symbol of the trance of the spiritual leader or Shaman. But apart from this historical detail, the symbol does not seem to differ from the usual significance of the bird the world over.

Goosey, goosey gander, who wanders upstairs and takes a man by the left leg and throws him downstairs, because he wouldn't say his prayers: a rhyme which combines the symbolic themes of above and below. Birds as messengers reveal the plan of the cosmos and enable man to live in conformity with it, or else be hurled down by the negative and sinister left side of life.

In Egypt, the goose laid the Cosmic Egg, as in later folklore it was to lay the golden egg: the symbol of the Earth Mother, the womb of the cosmos. (Note:- By an appropriate piece of synchronicity, the first set of nursery rhymes ever printed used to be sung by a Mrs Goose of Boston to her grandchildren. But it is only because it is so symbolically apposite that 'Mother Goose' has been attached to nursery rhymes ever since – a granny of another name would surely have been forgotten long ago?)

The Peacock's Tail
Symbolizes the innumerable eyes of the individual *COMPLEXES* and of the collective unconscious.

Like the stars in the sky, or the fishes' eyes under the sea, these see in a different way from the sunlight of conscious vision. These independent eyes (centres of consciousness) provide a vision which extends far beyond that of Ego-consciousness. It includes a blaze of vivid insight, comparable to the brightly coloured tail.

As a Negative Symbol, it signals the danger of the Ego becoming swollen with self-importance when it mistakes the brilliant colours of nature for its own brilliance.

The Peacock was the Bird of Hera (Juno): Unconscious Nature.

The Pelican

Self-*SACRIFICE*, since according to legend this bird fed its young from its own breast.

The Phoenix – *which rises from the ashes of the fire*:
   New life.

This is the symbol of the phenomenon which manifests itself when life is at its most bleak, when everything has disintegrated into ashes; then, something unexpected emerges to fill the vacuum. This is the opportunity for fresh life and inspiration to surge up from within. Such an image is as appropriate for civilizations as it is for individuals.

Along with Osiris, the phoenix was identified as the dawn sun, rising brilliantly through the greyness of the first light: which is an allusion to the continuity of life, through cycles of change and transformation (see also *ORIGINS/Rebirth*).

On the cosmic level, the call of the Phoenix proclaims the message of life; it declares all that has transpired, as well as everything which is to come.

'BLUEBEARD'

He who kills his wives and keeps the corpses in a secret room.
The Bluebeard myth can be seen as the manifestation of a woman's negative *ANIMUS*, which destroys her own femininity.

(Like a character in a cartoon, we all have nine lives in the inner realm, thus we can be destroyed time and again.) It indicates too much male conscious thinking, with insufficient feminine feeling.

The Room: is the secret chamber in the mind of the victim herself, to which only a relationship with a man – or relating to her Animus – can provide the key.

But she is forbidden to enter that room: as with every gaze into the realms of the unconscious, there are many risks involved. In this instance, the vision of the dead (i.e. unconscious) side of her own femininity.

She is rescued by her brother: or by her positive *ANIMUS*, which can only occur *after* she has confronted the horror of the negative side of the same force.

She inherits the castle's fortune: or the treasure of her own personality.

On the cosmic level this story has been related to the solar myth of the sun slaying the feminine dawn as it rises to its zenith. However, the meaning for the individual is the same: a surfeit of conscious, masculine Ego can threaten the twilight realm of feminine feeling.

The name 'Bluebeard': the colour blue emphasizes the inner masculine qualities of the intellect of an intrinsically male attribute (beard), but sited within the woman.

THE BODY – Flesh
The Intermediary between the life of man and the cosmos

The body provides a complete, self-sufficient system of symbolism. All of its organs are related, both to the outside world and also to the *COMPLEXES* in the psyche. The body is not simply a mass of matter, but a dynamic force of inter-related functions – just as the mind is a dynamic inter-relationship of complexes. The body acts out a physiological mythology (Robert Grinnell).

We do not experience our bodies *directly* very often and when we do, it is either as pain or as an external object. We do not experience the living organism. The body functions unconsciously and, more than any other symbol, it is intimately connected with the unconscious mind. Which goes some way towards explaining why the actual use and movement of the body, when systematically executed, can affect the unconscious mind when words and thought are of no use.

THE BODY

Negative Symbol:-If the body reacts negatively – and it is only on these occasions that we become aware of it – even though the source of the complaint may not be obvious, it is often possible to interpret the action which the unconscious is demanding through a reading of the body's symbolism. The unconscious will always make its requirements known and protect its own interests, at the expense of the body.

The Symbolic Body/The Flesh

The Symbolic – or imaginary – body is a total expression of the psyche and is inseparably linked to it

The general similarity of all bodies – two eyes, one nose, etc. – is a reflection of the overall conformity of human nature. More especially, it is the Symbolic Body of the Cosmic Man which expresses this unity, as well as exemplifying the tendency for each of the separate parts to relate to the single whole, the Universal Man of which the individual is a particular instance. The Imaginary Body expresses the power and extent of the mind – the universal, collective Conscious and Unconscious. Whereas the Body of Flesh and Blood expresses the Ego and Shadow (of both sexes) and reveals the limits, frailty and dependence of human existence; a revelation which deflates the tendency towards self-importance. The frail, almost pathetic body of man acts as a reminder that the experiences, accomplishments and forces at his disposal all exist outside of himself – although they may be lived from within – and cannot be equated with brain, intestines, etc., even though they are interrelated and interacting with these.

In any case, by one means or another, it is important, particularly during the second half of life, to befriend the body and enlist its co-operation whatever the nature of the symbolic work. One should value and respect its impulses, even if you do not necessarily go along with them. The masculine mind needs to be tender with the feminine body/flesh and not treat it as an object. When this sentiment is put into practice, the body is grateful and exudes a graciousness which compensates for the ugliness of the ageing process (Hillman, J.).

Mind/Body
The body mediates between mind and Cosmos.

As an expression of mind (conscious and unconscious) the body becomes an intermediary between inner and outer, between Spirit and Matter, and the source and the centre of the UNION of the opposites.

Like so much that is fundamental to symbolism, this is another obvious concept, or thought, easily dismissed by the intellect as trite or facile. The difficulty comes not in thinking it, but in living it; actually getting the body to play its intermediary role properly and stop interfering, coming between the interaction of the human mind and material cosmos. Thoughts are not enough to get the body practised and disciplined in its role of intermediary. Whereas the language of symbolism has always galvanized its co-operation, for · better or worse; only afterwards can the conscious Ego be allowed to interfere with its powers of veto, modifying or qualifying the effects.

Much of symbolism is concerned with this most basic relationship of mind and body. For example, most *ANIMAL* symbolism is mainly concerned with it, and at another extreme Prospero's relationship with Caliban in Shakespeare's *The Tempest.* But the primary symbols are the parts of the body, experienced as powerful images full of meaning and value in themselves.

The body as a whole
Is related to the symbolism of the Zodiac as a whole, indicating that it can be elaborated into a complete symbol-system adequate in itself.

It has its top and bottom half, its right and left sides – the *SPLIT* of symbolism between conscious and unconscious, masculine and feminine, social and wild. With arms and legs splayed like spokes, it gives the circular wheel of life with its four main divisions corresponding to the horizontal plain and the four points of the compass, whereas head (or heart) and genitals, joined by the spine, correspond to the vertical axis.

THE BODY

Note:-

If you have a feel for symbolism you will not be worried by the slight disregard of the physical facts, of arms and legs splayed and spinning round the spine. Lying on the vertical axis the head and guts are both central, and of central importance. The guts (tanden, solar plexus, and lower abdomen) are a centre of energy, while the head is a complete circle in itself, the inner keep of the fortress (for the body is also the stronghold of armour, protecting its treasure, the life of the individual).

A man doing perfect cartwheels, is an image of the circular pattern of man's life combined (related and united) with its movement through time, a lifetime.

The body at different stages of transformation. YOUTH juxtaposed with Old Age, or the Child with Man or Woman occur frequently in symbolism (see *MYSTERIES* at Eleusis, or Samothrace) to depict the crises of change in the process of living through the different *PERIODS* of life. Also symbolized by the different ages of the gods and goddesses.

The body deformed, an inferior or undeveloped aspect of the psyche (see *DWARF*).

The five limbs of the body (four plus one, the head); and the five senses; and four fingers plus thumb: Link body symbolism with symbols of 4/5 (*NUMBERS*, 4/5), the four elements plus essence, in relation to the four functions of the psyche plus the centre, including the will.

This can be extended in order to relate the body to the prevailing sevenfold symbolism, by counting the seven openings (orifices) in the body by which we contact the cosmos – two eyes, two ears, nose, mouth and anus. This is not an arbitrary extension of playing with numbers. The relationship is already there between the order of nature and the order of the psyche, and symbolism seeks a succinct and convincing way of expressing it – as does maths for different ends. The intricacy of the body provides a wealth of such images which, when they arise spontaneously from the unconscious, or are presented in the right context, have the awe-inspiring (or negative horrifying) impact of all true symbols.

The body cut up, an image of distinguishing and analysing the complexes of the psyche (see *SACRIFICE*).

The body is also a symbol related to the circular vessel of transformation. After being separated and sifted out, the ingredients of the psyche are bound together in a new (chemical-like) structure. The binding together is accomplished by feeling rather than thinking. On the cosmic plane it is like the original Greek Eros, a god encircling the world holding all its ingredients together. In this the whole body is a symbol of the (feminine) feeling. It is the carrier of individuality and life.

Particular parts of the body:-

Blood (monster, animal or human)
  The inner life, the inner truth of man.

The special qualities of whatever creature the blood comes from, can be absorbed, integrated in this form. For example:-

Extracting blood. Distinguishing between inner truth .and external appearances.

The Hero drinking the blood of the witch, hag may be absorbing vital feminine qualities in order to complete his own nature (*HERMAPHRODITE*).

Blood is also an intermediate state between the solid body and the aetherial nature of man and so is an agent of union between the two.

Breathing
  The vital masculine spirit, and the *Animus* in women.

Eye
  The conscious ego
The intermediary between the lights of the cosmos (sun, moon, etc.) and the more primary inner light of life (which still continues bright in a lucid dream, even though no other light contributes). These three – sun, eye and mind – are three aspects or manifestations of the archetype of light, especially the light of the mind, which is why the eye and the sun are interchangeable as symbols. Like the Word, the eye is a source of creation because nothing fully exists until known, and thereby bathed in the light of life.

So the eye brings form and order out of chaos.

One-eyed, like the Cyclops, limited, one-tracked.

The sacrifice of an eye (like Wotan in order to get the runes), Blindness. The sacrifice of something physical (including an animal) is often done for the sake of inner gain. The psyche is like a balance to the physical realm: what one loses, the other may gain. For example, 'Seers' (visionaries) were often traditionally *blind* as if they'd swapped outer visions for inner (for example Tiresias in Ancient Greece).

The third Eye (associated occasionally with Zeus as well as Shiva and Buddhist figures). The inner eye; insight, Vision; the light of the mind.

Being greedy to see, either eagerly sightseeing, or paying exorbitant prices for the 'vision' of the artist, may represent a hunger for inner visions of the mind's eye.

Many eyes in the dark, such as fishes' eyes under the sea. The nuclei of unconscious complexes. Dim and luminous fragments of the personality, glowing independently (compare *STARS*).

For Hair
See *HAIR* in main part of dictionary.

For Hand
See *HAND* in main part of dictionary.

Head
   The thinking *FUNCTION*.

Head/Stomach, or body. The spiritual and physical as in related symbolism of *ABOVE/Below, APOLLO/Dionysus*, etc.
Two heads refers to the inner *SPLIT*, two different ways of looking. The contrast in world views may appear symbolically as *two different worlds*.
Three heads may refer to different phases of the *MOON* and of life.
Many heads, many different appearances of one reality.

Heart, *sometimes surrounded by flames:*
   The life principle, the vital force that distinguishes the body from the corpse (cold).

Heart/Tongue. Life in contrast with Order; commands proceed from the tongue.

Liver, *which is large and dark and full of blood:*
The active life with all its passions, such as greed, jealousy, wrath. The seat of fate or destiny which is much affected by these passions.
Note:-
This is why the liver of animals was especially important in various forms of *ORACLE.*

Spine.
The Will. The inner principle of the Union of Opposites, especially the union of thoughts with deep feeling. See also *SERPENT. Kundalini,* and *CHAKRAS.*
Symbolism related to the body:-
Especially *The HEALER/Sickness.* For physical *Symptoms as Symbols.*
Also *COMPLEXES; COMPULSIONS; SEXUAL SYMBOLISM.*

BOW and ARROW
Intuition

An attribute of the Goddess of the Hunt (Artemis) whose hounds sniff out their unseen prey. The bow is related (by shape) to the crescent moon: Feminine intuition. *When associated with the storm or storm gods:* The arrow is like the *LIGHTNING* leaping direct to its mark, and the bow is like the rainbow, flourished after the storm.
Note:-
The strong composite bow in the ancient world was built up in layers of horn, wood and sinew, possibly in an attempt to emulate the rainbow.
Book:-
Herrigel, E. *Zen and the art of Archery,* throws light on the relationship between archery and the inner intuitive man who can hit the mark without any of the usual conscious means – in the dark without looking.

Cupid's bow
The darts of love, emotion

But there seems to be some link between sublimated sexuality and spirituality (which is normally associated with celibacy) as if one were the reversed inward side of the other.

BRIDGE
Links this side with the other side, conscious with unconscious

But there is an interesting half-bridge in the Grail legend, which swivels at the centre. The Knight gallops at it with trust, and just as he would have plunged to his doom, it swivels, so that he can complete the crossing by going back over the same half: the way looks impossible to the conscious Ego, but this device sets the scene in looking-glass land (see *MIRROR*) where everything is reversed. It seems to point directly to the phenomenon which psychology calls 'positive regression' (i.e. going back over the same ground in order to go on, back through the layers of the unconscious in order to mature). It could also represent the first and second halves of life which correspond to each other, as opposites. The centre of Life is a crucial turning point (see *PERIODS* of Life).

The BROTHERS. Sometimes Twins – or just two unequal males:
Civilized controlled activity in contrast with primitive behaviour

The conscious male Ego, and his Unconscious Shadow. The *SPLIT* or conflict within man is represented symbolically as two. In the case of twins it is more obvious that they represent two halves of a single unit.

The same basic principle applies to the psyche as to nature: you must first take it apart in order to put it together again. The pre-conscious unity, totality, is split, and there is considerable difficulty in fitting the parts together again. The difference between the totality at the beginning and the union at the end is consciousness. The whole process starts with a split of consciousness, which is slowly expanding its field of vision and awareness. Consciousness is part of creation, giving form, name and order to what is otherwise only potential, chaotic, unknown. This is the major theme of symbolism, which puts into images the continuous relationship and interaction between the different parts within the whole. There isn't any more at the end: all is all-there-is-in-the-matter. But instead of just existing, it is known to exist. And taking it to pieces is the ordinary way of getting to know anything.

When it comes to the brothers, the primitive – more animal, more physical – side of man is distinguished from the later, more civilized – more conscious, thoughtful – though frailer side.

The relationship between these two brothers goes through four different phases:

   i. At first the conscious Ego is a treasure, a frail new-born thing, like an offspring of the Shadow, a small younger brother, in fact, which the older Shadow figure protects and admires.

In one of the oldest stories in the world, Gilgamesh, who is King of the City (and first archaeologist), is for the most part helped by the wilder and more primitive Enkidu, lord of the forests. Note:-

W. F. Albright saw in these encounters between civilized and wild men which feature prominently in early myth and literature an actual historical meeting of Cro-Magnon man with Neanderthal man, which is perhaps the most striking of all images for the continuing struggle between Civilized Man and his Primitive Ancestor, whose blood still runs in his veins. See Albright, W. F. *From Stone Age to Christianity* (1957).

   ii. Then there is a stage of near equality, when the struggle rages most fiercely, with the victory going to one side and then the other. The savage may persecute (savagely) his more refined brother, loathing his new ideas, while the more highly evolved Ego outwits and derides the more primitive but also the more natural side of life.

   iii. At the third stage the Conscious Ego gets the upper hand, and begins to eliminate its rival systematically. Conscious attitudes are over-valued and equated with good. And the Shadow – the wild, Nature in its raw state – is all lumped together and identified with evil.

iv. But this is no longer tenable. In the final stage – which is the point we've reached now – the Ego feels alienated and depressed because he is beginning to miss his brother. There is a call from the wild – from the Noble Savage – which echoes through nearly all imaginative literature since Voltaire's 'Ingénu'. (See *ANIMALS*, The Animal Man.)

In the wider context of the split or division of nature, taking the whole apart and reassembling it solely in order that it should become known, the different phases in relating to the Shadow become part of a recognizable sequence.

Particular Brothers, or pairs who typify the split between Ego and Shadow. Sometimes there are more than two brothers indicating further differentiation of the male psyche into its different *FUNCTIONS*:

OSIRIS/SETH.

Gemini, the twins in the Zodiac.

Castor/Pollux, also called the Dioscuri, who were exceptionally close and undivided, but who had two other dark, obscure, less defined (i.e. Shadow) cousins with whom they squabbled, Idas and Lynceus.

Baldur/Loki, in Nordic myth.

Aleyin/Mot, in Canaanite myth.

Zeus, who ruled the upper world in contrast with his brothers Hades and Poseidon, who ruled under earth and sea.

There is something symbolically a little odd about *Cain*, the grower of crops (i.e. the settled, civilized, more highly evolved social state) being the killer and wanderer, while *Abel*, who looks after animals, represents the refined side of humanity. Unless Mesopotamian myth has been adapted by a nomadic people?

Jacob represents the refined, inner conscious man, in contrast with *Esau*, the first-born (though only by moments), therefore the older, more primitive life-form – for this reason the Father may represent the Shadow too. This story is rich in detail, all totally relevant to Jung's archetypal Ego/Shadow conflict, culminating in the reconciliation of the two brothers at the end (see also *LIGHT/DARK*).

APOLLO/HERMES, half-brothers, especially in incidents like the stealing of cattle, and various exchanges between the two.

Fairy-tales frequently start off with two or four brothers setting about their tasks in various ways, throwing light on the merits and faults of conscious and unconscious approaches. But as fairy-tales (by their nature) give voice to the hidden subterranean view, the opposite of the dominant conscious attitude, it is usually the *INFERIOR* shadow figure, in tune with the animals, etc. who fares best.

St. Michael/Lucifer, his brother archangel who became the cloven-footed *Devil*, complete with animal tail.

In more recent fiction, there are the brothers in *The Master of Ballantrae* (Stevenson, R. L., 1889).

See also *EGO*/Shadow, *CONSCIOUS*/Unconscious.

Personal Symbolism:-

Actual brothers sometimes follow the archetypal pattern, of going different ways and playing each other's Shadow role. Then, relating to the actual brother (or somebody else with the same characteristics that are the opposite of your own) may help to heal the inner rift.

BUILDINGS, City
The mind, conscious and unconscious, transforming matter

Every product of the human mind is bound to bear some relationship to it, and this relationship between outer and *INNER* is precisely the concern of symbolism. So buildings, just as much as fairy castles, can be symbolic of the mind which produced them, whether individual or corporate. They display conscious plan, but also unconscious factors at work – whether neglected or repressed.

Castles. Citadel
The Self

Like other buildings, with conscious and unconscious parts – sometimes symbolized as two castles, the centres of two different kingdoms which need to be united. The image of the castle emphasized that it is as difficult to get to know the inner Self as it is to storm a castle. In a more modern setting, away from fairy-tale, Franz Kafka's *The Castle* would be a good example of the Self which he cannot reach because civilization has swamped nature with endless formalities and paperwork. This is in contrast with the natural barrier of thorns in 'Sleeping Beauty'.

A female figure (the Damsel), incarcerated or enchanted, usually plays a key role: The role of the *ANIMA* – or indeed the whole castle may refer to the feminine matrix, protecting the unborn *SELF.*

Cities, towns, villages
Refers to Human Society and individual life

Towns used to be laid out as part of a ritual with everything done and chosen for its symbolic value. For example, the cemetery might be placed at the centre of the city, as representing the trunk of the tree of life (see *ANCESTORS*). Then there might be eight gates into the city, with one of them sealed, representing the path of life round the circumference of the city, with its four major and four minor periods of transition or turning points. The eighth might be sealed up representing death.

City: The community or society that lives in it. The Mesocosm, mid-way between the Individual Man (Microcosm) and the Cosmos.

In a modern city the lack of overall vision and the unrelatedness of the individual parts to the whole: suggests the neglect of inner factors such as Intuition, which is concerned with Wholes, rather than fragments, and Feeling which is concerned with relating the individual parts to each other.

House

Personal Symbolism:-

Equally in the individual house, many aspects have a symbolic significance and arouse feelings quite out of proportion to the facts. For example, an exaggerated dread of cleaning out the downstairs loo may be connected with clearing up some other very different problem, perhaps connected with sexuality. The symbolic significance of the actual house is the same as the dream house (see my *Dictionary for Dreamers*).

Temples, churches
The pattern of the psyche

These, most especially, are built according to designs which are highly satisfying because they represent the overall pattern of the psyche in mandala form (see *PATTERNS*). Particular features represent particular aspects of man's life struggle.

For example, gargoyles on the outside of the church, like the monsters guarding the treasure: The negative side of the unconscious, which manifests first, before it can be transformed.

Twin towers: represent the *SPLIT* in the psyche.

The dome, an earthly material representation of the sky: unites all into a single whole, like a universal umbrella for all the different factions of life.

Cloisters, facing the four directions, like the four SEASONS: The four periods of man's life; walking round a cloister, with its tree or fount in the middle, would be related to the journey of life.

The BULL
Power

For the ancient world the bull was a symbol of the High *GOD*, associated with the creative power of Spring (Taurus in the Zodiac), the power of sun, moon, and storm which roars like a bull. But also manifest in earthly forms, such as the bull which is still one of the most powerful of the domesticated animals. Symbolically there is no root contradiction in the essence of power (i.e. power itself) taking different forms in the different spheres and elements of life.

See also *CATTLE*.

Bull Fighting
Symbolic action to control lust and frenzy, or negative power

When passion, with its positive and negative aspects in sex and violence, was fiercer, then bullfighting – as symbolic action – was widespread throughout the Mediterranean world. Jung felt it had survived only in Spain for the symbolic reason that there only is society still predominantly matriarchal as in the ancient world, and the feminine values of Eros (passion) are highly esteemed, and reach full maturity early – like the bulls. And men still lack the qualities of Logos (quick thinking), symbolized by the bullfighter, with whom the Spanish crowd naturally identify. Whereas Jung suggests that the rest of Europe would identify with the bull, and in any case need to stir the reluctant bull within them: they must get out of their easy chairs and woo.

BUTTERFLY
The psyche

Two well-developed, beautifully patterned wings, and two less so: The four FUNCTIONS of the psyche of which two are normally more developed, while two remain inferior.
Caterpillar/Butterfly. See TRANSFORMATION.

CADMUS
The hazards and rewards for the man who tries to relate to his inner feminine side, the ANIMA

Cadmus is sent in search of his sister, Europa, who has been carried off by Zeus: Jung sees this as the separation of man from his spiritual Anima – the inner damsel, or Lady Soul – who is the object of the quest in so many later tales.
Next he must find and follow the cow, which is later sacrificed to Athene: The cow is a symbol of the whole feminine realm. When a man stops projecting his Anima on to actual women – symbolized by the flesh of the cow, which is sacrificed to the spiritual Athene – then the spiritual Anima becomes an ally.
These newly discovered inner, feminine resources are later able to secure him his bride, according to one account. On a more mundane level he must sacrifice his incestuous love for his sister in order to set free his emotions, and redirect them.
A dragon devours his companions: The negative side of the feminine manifests, probably the archaic MOTHER within, who would keep him immature and puerile if she could, symbolized by swallowing him back into her womb.

He slays the dragon and extracts its teeth, which turn into mighty warriors when sown in the ground. He throws a stone in their midst, and they begin to slay each other: He retrieves something of vital, inner importance from the Mother, connected with his own masculine powers. This results in a period of intense inner struggle, between conscious and unconscious. The stone may be related symbolically to the *APPLE*, which also causes strife.

Five warriors remain and help the hero build a city. And Cadmus is given a wife, Harmonia: The individual is in accord with Nature, signified by the *NUMBER* Five. Masculine and feminine are in harmony. All looks well.

However, Cadmus continues to be persecuted by Hera, who turns him and his wife into serpents: Hera, most especially, is the high goddess of feminine maturity and of nature. It would seem that his relationship with the feminine remains stuck at the primitive unconscious level of serpents.

But the serpents are happily entwined ever after on the Islands of the Blessed: which suggests there may be compensations for being reconciled with the Anima, even when the process is not recognized in a fully conscious way.

CADUCAEUS
The balance of opposing forces throughout the universe.
Also the movement in the dance of life, separating and joining.

The Caducaeus is two intertwined serpents on a pole and is an attribute of various gods and goddesses in the Ancient Near East, especially Hermes: This is a development of the single *SERPENT* and pole, meaning the unchanging world axis in contrast with the everchanging phenomenal world. But the main feature of the phenomenal world is duality – light and dark, conscious and unconscious, masculine and feminine, intertwined (represented by the two serpents). At head and tail they are united, at the beginning and the end they are one, but in between they are taken apart and put together, differentiated and reunited, coagulated and dissolved in the process of living (see *DISINTEGRATE/Integrate*).

They are the serpents of Force and Form, and by their intertwining they create the different spheres or Worlds,

formed by the loops in their bodies (i.e. the different levels of existence, or of conscious life in man).

Related Symbols:-

The figure 8, symbolizing the joining of the two worlds of mind and matter, is a simpler version of one aspect of the caducaeus, while the symbol of infinity (∞) is also an abstraction of the double serpent symbolism, just as the zero is symbolically related to the Ouroboros (the circular serpent with its tail in its mouth).

CANAANITE MYTH

A highly sophisticated symbolism widely influential throughout the Ancient World, but only fragments remain.

The fragments and scraps that have been recovered particularly from Ras Shamra (ancient Ugarit at the mouth of the river Orontes), addressed to an audience familiar with the mythology, leave many lacunae, which the new library recently dug up at Ibla - or some other not yet discovered source - may help to fill. Unless the bulk of the work, possibly written in the oldest alphabetical writing, the

Sinaitic script, was applied to paper or leather, which has since rotted away in the damper climates north of Egypt.

The position of Canaanite myth, both in time and space, is nevertheless crucial to understanding the relationships of the different mythologies in the Ancient Near East. It was situated at the crossroads between Egypt and Greece, between Mesopotamia and Crete, and in time, the very advanced Canaanite civilization spanned an important epoch in the development and diffusion of symbolic language, when the power of the West Semites extended to the Indus Valley in India, as well as Crete and Mycenean Greece, and there is evidence to suggest that their fleets sailed much further afield.

Books:-

Nevertheless, in spite of scanty documentation, Gaster, T. in *Thespis* (1950) has convincingly traced the origins of Greek Drama back through Canaanite ritual to Egyptian origins. The crisis and resolution which are the essential feature of drama are also fundamental to symbolic language arising from the unconscious.

He suggests the tentative identification of *Baal* with ZEUS, *Yam* with *Poseidon, Mot* with *Hades*.

There are other familiar symbolic themes such as MOTHER and Son, Ishtar and Tammuz, the dying and rising god whose death provokes great lamentations, known earlier in Mesopotamia and later in Greece. And the Warrior goddess, Anat, wading through the blood of her victims, who may have been an earlier, more raw and unconscious version of the refined Athene. Mot is cut into pieces as in the original sacrifice of primal man. (See *SACRIFICE*.)

Also Gray, J. *The Canaanites* (1964).

Gordon, C. *Before the Bible* (1962).

CATTLE

Especially when a certain number of them is specifically mentioned:

The horns of the New Moon, therefore weeks or months of the year, TIME itself.

When the colour of the cattle is white, red and black: the white, new moon; the full, red harvest moon, and the black, old, extinct moon (see *MOON*).

A unicorn of these colours: The same, but with the moon visualized as a single horn.

Fifty cattle: Either the four years of the Olympiad (i.e. 48 months – symbolism is always a little vague and arbitrary about facts) or the fifty-two weeks of the year.

A recurring theme in myth is the stealing of the cattle, e.g. Hermes steals Apollo's cattle and hides them in a cave; Ulysses' men pilfer Hyperion's cattle, etc.: Refers overtly to the disappearance of the moon from the sky but, because of the associations with the years, it refers to the thief of the years – a lifetime stolen from us. But the reappearance of the moon suggests recapturing the years (through memory, as in Proust's *Remembrance of Things Past*, recovery of time lost, or through some other experience of the enduring quality of the time and of the past).

There is nearly as much cattle rustling in ancient myth as in the modern Western film. In the Western it often goes on at night, and its appeal to modern audiences may be because of strong unconscious associations with this mythical theme.

The cattle belong to the light, the Sun god or the father of the sun (Hyperion): The dark swallows the moon, night steals the day, death consumes life.

A CELTIC QUEST

The quest is for the *ANIMA*, the feminine principle, and the *SELF*, a wiser, older man, in this case King Arthur.

John Layard has examined the archetypal themes in a Welsh legend, which brings to light especially the sequence of events in grappling with the Anima, and reconciling the Ego with the Self.

He is particularly explicit about the Two *MOTHERS*. There is the natural mother, who nurtures the physical side of the hero's life, but turns primitively dangerous and intractable – turns into a wild pig and a vicious hag, in fact – when he starts on his spiritual task. This is in contrast with the black stepmother or godmother, of many a tale, whose negative stimulus turns out for the best in the long run.

The relationship between the Hero (the *EGO*) and King Arthur (the Self or *HELPFUL FIGURE*) is also explicit, as they contend against powerful inner forces, represented by the Hag, deep in her cave, sending out her negative Animus in the form of Wild Boar. They eventually win the prize, the female Anima, from the hag-ridden Giant.

John Layard also shows how the sexual (Freudian) interpretation of such tales complements the inner, archetypal one. In both aspects the ancient tale is relevant to everyday life now. A youth still has to transfer his sexual affections, awakened in infancy, from the actual mother (or mother substitute) to the mate, as well as distinguishing between the masculine and feminine spirit within himself and relating them to each other.

Book:-

Layard, J. *A Celtic Quest* (1974).

The CENTRE

Whatever is of enduring importance. The core or hub of life, on which the centre of time and space depend for their existence.

Combines ideas such as the centre of the universe, the centre of life, the centre of the community, and the centre of the psyche in the overall idea of whatever is most central, most important. Sometimes will-power.

The central point: the meaning.

It is the nature of the symbolic mind to be able to relate to the idea of the centre, whatever it is, and adapt fluidly when new centres are discovered.

Taking symbols literally is to let the rigid, intellectual approach creep in. For example, when Copernicus demonstrated that the sun was the centre of this galaxy and not the earth, the reaction was an outburst of intellectual Ego-centricity. Copernicus himself based his hypothesis on Platonic symbolism: the sun was more important than the earth, therefore it must be more central (Karl Popper), which Copernicus then set out to demonstrate. In ancient Egypt, for example, the Sun God (Ra) had always been more important and more central than the lethargic Earth God (Geb). Anybody with a feel for symbolism will realize that

71

what shattered the medieval world was nothing to do with the relative positions of sun and earth, but whether man himself was merely peripheral, rattling round the edges of creation, a view that has gained increasing ground ever since. Which is logical enough, looked at one way, but the symbolic view looks at it another way: life is central, and it is only the interaction between life and inanimate matter (whether gaseous, liquid or solid) that creates light, distance, weight, texture and all the rest of the sum total of reality as it is experienced.

In this context the earth becomes a symbol of the *EGO*, which is peripheral.

And the sun a symbol of the *SELF*, which is central, thereby bringing together individual and cosmic symbolism, inner and outer. Of all life forms we know for sure, man's is the most highly evolved and therefore symbolically the most central. Nevertheless, the symbol of the Centre can point indefinitely beyond the life of man to whatever life form is more central, more essential, even if it hasn't come into existence yet.

The Symbols:-

From the beginnings of symbolism the Centre has been a dominant theme (Butterworth, E. A. S.).

The early statuettes of pregnant figures are symbolically related to the later highly developed symbolism of the *Omphalos*, or creative mound, the womb of creation, at the centre of the world. With the emergence of patriarchal society, this mound is surmounted by a standing stone or pillar signifying the phallus as the enduring central pillar that props up reality by ensuring the continuity of life, without which the cosmic tent would collapse. Later Nippur, Jerusalem and Delphi were each considered such centres of the world, as was Mt. Fuji.

The Cosmic AXIS, the ridge-pole of space, and the central pivot of time on the cosmic clock are subsequent derivations, and elaborations, which lose their force if severed from their roots in sexual symbolism.

In *BODY* symbolism this, in turn, is related to the spinal column, with its centres of consciousness (chakras, like wheels threaded through the centre), the highest of which may (or may not) be able to plunge beyond the relative experience of time and space, mediated through the senses and the limited brain, as if sticking out through the Pole Star above the whole cosmic tent.

In the psyche the idea of reaching the centre involves getting a free pass to any other *COMPLEX* or nucleus of energy within the psyche, and so being able to call on the different available forces at the appropriate moment. In contrast there are those stuck at the edge in the Ego, unable to find the centre, and so left at the mercy of unconscious compulsions and motivations.

All the different symbols of the centre:
> **combine to suggest a mythical point where the centre of the Cosmos and the centre of Man's life is one and the same.**

This emphasizes that the centre is not inside man, but is at the centre of the relationship and interaction between man and the cosmos.

See *Cosmic MAN*.

The CENTRE/Circumference or edge: The fixed in contrast with the volatile; the still centre in contrast with activity and turbulence. Like *the hub of the wheel*, the centre is the unmoved principle of all movement. (See *SERPENT/Pole*.)

Related Symbolism:-
PATTERNS; KABBALAH, The Tree of Life; *MAZE; ONION.*

CHAKRAS
Centres of consciousness.

The chakras were depicted as lotus flowers or wheels situated around the spine in an ascending order: And represent levels of consciousness, from ordinary, everyday awareness, which is related to the base, animal instincts of fear, greed and lust in the lower part of the body, up to cosmic consciousness.

There were six chakras, each associated with an organ of the body, a god, an animal, a symbolic colour and number – and a seventh with no image: This is consistent with all the different symbolism dealing with the different stages of the development of consciousness, which can be aligned roughly with stages on the way to realizing the potential *SELF*. All

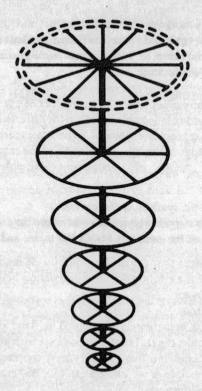

such attempts to become an increasingly aware whole individual seem to be in accord with the long-term aim of evolution.

Related Symbolism:-

The *ARCHETYPES*, which personify similar levels of awareness, from the unconscious animal instincts, through personal consciousness, towards collective consciousness and finally union with the pre-conscious totality for which there is no figure, no image.

Book:-

Evans Wentz, W. Y. *Tibetan Yoga and Secret Doctrines* (1935). Gives specific experiences connected with the different centres of consciousness.

CHANGE/Changeless. Flux/Stability
Everything keeps turning into something else – but so slowly we don't notice it. This is the trick of the universe in order to renew itself, and stay the same.

This is a recurring theme in symbolism, not only in the form of magical *TRANSFORMATIONS*, but also in all the different symbols which contrast the ephemeral with the *ENDURING* (see also *ESSENCE*).

The Symbols:-
The waxing and waning moon, in contrast with the constantly circular SUN: all such symbols contrast appearances with reality.

PROTEUS, the Greek mythical figure who could change his shape, like later magicians and witches: Although the symbolism may seem bizarre, this is only to provide striking images for something that we easily take for granted because it is such an ordinary feature of everyday life – which is in a state of flux. Everything changes into everything else, but so slowly we don't always notice it. Symbolism speeds up the process, like speeding up the film to see what happens in the process of growth, or it may personify *TIME*, as the magician who can change one thing into another.

Evolution is a good example of how life takes different forms, transforms from shape to shape, over a long period of time. But inanimate matter is not excluded from the process either: water, earth and heat, all swell the potato or grape, which are turned into chips and wine in due course, which are then consumed, and changed again into flesh and blood, to be worked off in energy. Finally the corpse dissolves back into the mud, in an endless cyclic process.

In the same way, the world as a whole – and symbols often refer to such wholes – is constantly changing, yet as a whole remains more or less the same. It changes continuously in order to renew itself, in order to stay the same.

The main principle of this change is the parts separating and regrouping. It is the same archetypal process in nature as in the psyche: distinguishing the different parts in order to reassemble them in different combinations.

CHANGE
Related Symbolism:-

TIME, the Father of the Gods: it is time which effects the changes, whether of water into wine or Child turned into Old Man, or Old Woman. (See *PERIODS* of Life; The *ELEMENTS*.)

CHAOS
The unconscious in its most primitive disorganized state and therefore in need of attention.

The image also depicts the dread of facing the dark, inner world of unconscious forces.

The Symbols:-

Ra battles with the Monster Apep, nightly.
Marduk splits Tiamat into rain-filled clouds and sea.
Jahweh subdues Leviathan.

Chaos like the great, primeval monster of the deep, surrounds both man and the cosmos at once. All heroes have to contend and do battle with it. But it is formed of the very stuff of the world, which has to be laid out and ordered into a coherent universe. The H-bomb is probably the nearest, modern, equivalent symbol of what the monster of chaos meant to the ancient world. But Chaos threatens the social order, as well as the individual (with madness). Only man, by his conscious and creative grasp of reality, can prevent his experience of life breaking up into a morass of meaningless data, an incoherent stream of pointless and unrelated events.

Positive Symbolism:-

Like nearly all symbols, this one has both a positive and negative side. Positively, it is the symbolic experience of *DISINTEGRATING* into chaos and *DEATH*, dissolving the conscious Ego in the unconscious, in the hope that it will re-form anew, bringing with it unconscious content from the depths, where Chaos reigns.

The CHILD
The part your childhood continues to play in adult life.

The promise and potential within the individual, all the possibilities for change, development and *TRANSFORMATION* within the psyche, are summed up in the image of the Child. However, this source of creativity and wonder is still at a

76

childish – and foolish – phase of development. The child, who is dependent and vulnerable, may harbour dark, ugly secrets, such as primitive cravings or archaic, destructive impulses, all of which need to be slowly transformed in the light of consciousness.

The Symbols:-

The Child Gods.

Each particular god, when represented as 'Child', may refer to particular functions in the psyche still in their primordial state – depending on the qualities of the particular God in question.

The child Zeus: New-born intuition.

The child Apollo: Newly differentiated thinking powers. For a woman this might provide an intermediary symbol for making contact with the Animus.

The child Dionysus: The realm of feeling in sweet new-born shape, meant to appeal.

The child Hermes, messenger between the gods: Of the four, this Divine Child most clearly represents the newly emerging Self, the principle that will relate and unite the complexes and archetypes within.

The glowing child – and radiant children – that feature frequently in myth, legend, fairy-story, and fiction, such as the child in Eliot, G. *Silas Marner* (1861) or Kipling, R. *Jungle Books* (1894–5).

Childlike/Childish.

Potential new growth emerging into the light of consciousness, in contrast with a retarded infantile *COMPLEX.*

At best the child within is full of creative imagination and spontaneity, and is the *PERSONIFICATION* of the playful side of life. When the figure is recognized for what it is, and met halfway, it can be related to other aspects of the psyche, most especially through the Animus (or Anima), which act as its guardians within the psyche: tutor (or governess) to its worst excesses.

In contrast, the infantile 'inferiority complex' is neglected and ignored (because feared) but all the more demanding for that. Passive, and at the mercy of fantasy, its naïve overoptimistic wishes are never fulfilled. Symbol of the auto-erotic. Altogether a bit of a monster and often spoilt and resentful.

But the Child within the psyche can only be contacted whole, with its dark negative sides, as well as its positive sides. Whenever there is conflict between the Adult and the Child, the golden rule (as always, with different parts of one's own personality) is to take both sides. The individual must not let the child alter him, but nor must he (or she) just chastise and correct it in trying to make it grow up.

The Child is a symbol of an enduring feature within the psyche, a force that is there to the end of life whether recognized or not, and is therefore not to be confused with actual childhood which gets left behind.

Projected in marriage: The child-within often tries to nestle into the partner's affection and get his or her way, and there may be quite a struggle between the two 'children' clamouring to be pampered.

Projected on to children: Adults are sometimes over-romantic and silly about children, and use them in other ways as the only source of refreshing their own jaded outlook. These are the types of parent who are unwilling to let the children grow up. Alternatively they may have child after child as if it were the only way of recapturing the valuable qualities of the child, which are really qualitites within themselves in dire need of attention.

Postive/Negative Symbolism:-

Dwarfs, elves, or any little people may represent the enduring qualities of the child in subsequent *PERIODS* of Life – often infantile and negative.

Peter Pan is a detailed representation of the ambivalence of the Child archetype, partly a source of wonder and partly an infantile horror – stuck with his daydreams in never, never land.

The Water Babies (Charles Kingsley) are similar.

The Divine Child/the Infantile Shadow: The most blatant characteristic of the child is that it is exorbitantly demanding, which leads to extremes. It is authentic but inadequate.

As a positive ally, all the fresh new wonder of childhood can be carried forward through each new phase of life, but without the pathetic limitations and helplessness of childhood.

Most outstanding personalities, in history as well as myth, but especially the Sages, often act direct from this simple Child Self, but appropriately. People who fulfil their destiny have rarely excluded the child from their life.

For many the child gets lost or crushed chiefly by the over critical approach, considered suitable for the Adult. This infantile Shadow, firmly lodged in the depths of the psyche, represents the arrested and inferior side of the personality, an 'enfant terrible' who has the power and knack of suddenly messing things up at the last minute. The exclusively Adult personality lives in increasing dread of his sudden emergence. However, relating to this child and discovering its valuable qualities can amount to a symbolic rebirth, which may salvage a life from ruin.

Note:-

But if 'Childhood' is to have the right symbolic effect throughout life, it isn't only a question of relating to it properly later, but it requires living it properly in the first place. One of Freud's lasting achievements was in relating so much adult ineptitude to childhood experience, which was still active and destructive.

Related Symbolism:-

Being *ABANDONED* and *BETRAYED*, are both important events in the life of the inner Child.

APOLLO/Dionysus, where Dionysus is also a personification of the playful side of life.

Book:-

Hillman, J. *Loose Ends* (1975).

CHRISTIAN SYMBOLISM

Christianity echoes the major symbolic themes of the Ancient Near East, but applied on a conscious personal level to the man, Jesus, and through him to each individual.

Forged in an atmosphere where symbolic themes and ideas prevailed, and emerging from the widest possible context of symbolism – that of *BIBLICAL SYMBOLISM*, as well as *GREEK* and *EGYPTIAN* symbolism – its concern is precisely with the same archetypal questions about the nature of life, the relationship between man and the cosmos, and the destiny of man.

God/man:
   The relationship of spirit and matter.

The eternal and enduring essence, in contrast with the ephemeral and continually transforming appearances, is the main concern of symbolism, to which all other concerns are subordinated. And these two are not just loosely related but are identical. Life cannot be divided from life, existence from existence, or reality-as-it-is from reality-as-it-appears. One 'I am' is of the same nature as another.

Related Symbols:-
PATTERNS, The Vertical Line; The Cosmic *AXIS*; The pole around which the *SERPENT* writhes.

Adam/the Second Adam.
   Man and Cosmic *MAN*. Or *EGO* and *SELF*.

The old Adam was the man of Flesh, the New Adam was the Man of Light. The work – for the Alchemists and others – was to transform one into the other: man into Cosmic Man. By *SACRIFICING* the conscious Ego, Christ – the second Adam, crucified on the central mound of the world, where the old Adam was buried – restored the unity of the psyche and the Cosmos, and gave access once more to the Tree of Life at the *CENTRE* of Creation.

Creation/Man.
   Matter is dark and formless without the light of life.
   Consciousness, at first cut off with only a small bite of reality, penetrates layer by layer towards the core.

The different levels of consciousness are depicted in the *BIBLICAL SYMBOLISM* of Creation in seven days, and applied to the individual life of man explicitly in John's Gospel which opens, 'In the beginning . . .', and relates seven aspects of the cosmos with seven aspects of man's personal life. His seven miracles are selected to recapitulate creation, and to show man as the second creator of the universe. As the discourses make plain, the miracles are signs: symbolically signs of seven stages on the inner path of reuniting living spirit with dead matter.

Christ is identified with each aspect of creation in turn.

He is the light: That is the light of life – at one with the transcendent hub of all the action and energy of the universe.

He walks on the water: He reverses the separation of land from sea: symbolically the separation of cosmic consciousness from collective or cosmic unconsciousness. These two must finally be dissolved in order to reach the preconscious totality, the source of eternal spiritual waters – that is, the light of life.

He turns water into wine and multiplies loaves: His symbolic action speeds up the natural processes of transformation, and the miraculous increase and abundance of nature. But these in turn point to the inner transformation achieved through contact with the unconscious vegetable soul. So long as we are at one with the great vine or family tree of human life, we endure forever, as root or fruit alternating (see *VEGETATION*).

The blind man is cured: This is related symbolically to the creation of sun and moon and the symbolism surrounding them, which relates to aspects of personal consciousness, and unconscious (see *SUN/Moon*).

Jesus cures the cripples by the pool: Related to the waters that brought forth moving creatures, primitive life forms, which may be closer to nature than man, and so act as mediator. This is the realm of man's inner *SHADOW*.

And he raises Lazarus from the dead: He recreates man, the final triumph of creation, little less than God. But only if the man is inwardly renewed through living contact and experience of stages of his own evolution, still existing in the psyche as layers of consciousness, through which he can contact his *ORIGIN*.

On the other side of total dissolution in the waters of the womb, as Jesus advises Nicodemus, lies the light of man's essential nature, which is distinct from the dark void of matter – without life – yet penetrates and pervades all matter.

Negative Symbolism:-

The dark negative side of this same symbolic theme is expressed in John's Apocalypse, which could symbolically be divided into seven equivalent days of destruction at the End of Time. From which the same insight into the nature of life and energy emerges, separate and distinct from matter, distinguished so as to be reunited – separated so as to be put together again in a new combination – with mind over matter, and transforming it, rather than being submerged in

Eve/the Second Eve.

The power of the feminine, but with its dark side inadequately represented.

Eve, as the dark side of the Feminine and of Nature, who brought sin and death into the world, is rather a vague figure for such an important symbolic role in contrast with the amazing array of Gorgons, Sirens, Harpies, Furies, and Amazons of Greek myth, representing every shade of the feminine force in nature when it manifests itself negatively. Knowing that the forces (which a symbol represents) may manifest negatively if approached wrongly, and being aware of the very real havoc and misery this may cause, induces deep respect for the archetypal powers that are symbolized. So people who understand the effects of symbolism (Jung, von Franz, for example) on world events have attributed many of the shortcomings of Western civilization to the absence of a clear and terrifying symbol for the dark side of the feminine. It leads quickly to a lack of respect for the positive side of the Feminine: namely, Nature, relationships and values; the Eros side of life which, when not actually derided, is usually given second place to careers and finances in the West. (See *COW*.)

The Mother of God: In the context of symbolism has to fulfil the functions of all the Goddesses of Antiquity, both as Virgin Queen of Heaven, crowned with stars, with the moon for footstool, and as Mother Earth, clothed in red and black – more common in icons of the Eastern Church.

As the second Eve, she represents the material world which gave birth to the physical race of mankind, protectress of all men including sinners as the Earth Mother. But as the Queen

of Heaven, she mediates and reconciles the opposites:
Human/Divine, Earth/Spirit, Evil/Good. She saves the
human realm by pulling God down into it (von Franz). She
personifies, or embodies, physical humanity with all its dark
sides, as well as its light; and as such is the fourth immanent
side (or Person) of God, who cannot be extracted from his
creation – for he is in every particle of it – nor identified with
it.

Note:-

The idea of the Quaternity of the Godhead, symbolically
indicated by the three arms of the Cross, pointing upwards
to the Trinity, and the fourth beam thrust into the ground
(matter), is not just a recent product of Archetypal
Psychology, but appears in traditional theology. For
example St. Maximus saw humanity as the revelation (final
unveiling) of God's spirit, just as the Spirit was the revelation
of Christ, and Christ of the Father, and each was assigned to
one of the Four Ages in History.

Book:-

Lossky, V. *The Mystical Theology of the Eastern Church*
(1957).

The Trinity and Incarnation:
  Relate the one source of life with many individual lives.

God Immanent in the world, and God Transcendent beyond
the world unite in the Incarnation: man is the *MEDIATOR*.
There is unity at the root of variety. The Godhead,
symbolically the one essence, is related to – or indivisible
from – the multiplicity of creation.

Related Symbolism:-

NUMBERS, One/Many.

Personal Symbolism:-

As with so much symbolism, this refers to direct experience,
and the agonizing conflict between *INNER* and outer, until
this conflict is suddenly resolved through the mediation of a
third symbolic factor, which restores total unity. The Spirit
is usually the personal inner experience of the Mediator,
crossing the abyss between man and cosmos, because all is
brushed with the same wind, infused with the same godlike
life.

The Trinity in Personal Symbolism: Turning inwards away from the everyday world to discover the Spirit of life, and thereby ascending to God, the symbol of symbols, or essence of *ORIGINS*, and Cosmic *MAN*. Then emptying of yourself, and returning to earth incarnate for everyday life. Then repeating the process.

Related Symbolism:-

See also *DEATH*, The Books of the Dead, for the three planes of Bardo. These can be related to the phases of the work in *ALCHEMY*.

See also *INNER/Outer*.

The Kingdom of God, or the rule of Christ.

> **The rule of the *SELF*, so that the Kingdom of the psyche is no longer divided, conscious against unconscious.**

Symbolism points always to inner factors of the psyche and is especially concerned with which particular complex or archetype is in command, where the power lies. The renewal of the King may be one of the oldest rituals out of which symbolism itself evolved. He represented the corporate identity of the people, in close relationship with the powers of the cosmos. In contrast with the Personal Ego, whose power in society is limited, just as its power within the psyche is limited. Only the King – the Self – contacted from within can bring together conscious and unconscious, and thereby bring the whole psyche of complexes and archetypes under the control of the will. This power, which Christ called the Rule of God (the centre of his message) and which his followers called the Rule of Christ, is totally other than the ordinary conscious Ego. In fact, the ordinary conscious Ego has to be eliminated – crucified – before this power manifests at all.

This is the culmination of the symbolic work, the union of opposites, of conscious and unconscious, in an 'individual' – which means one who is not divided against himself. The Ego is experienced as only one peripheral factor, or complex, in the organization of the whole psyche. Its *DEATH* was symbolic only, pointing (as always with symbols) to something more real, the person's actual death in the near future.

Negative Symbolism:-
Hell ruled by the Devil:
Apart from being an all male preserve with no Queen, hell is a fairly standard *UNDERWORLD*, the dark negative Shadow aspect of the rule of God (with seven levels down).

The Events in Jesus's Life:
   Are presented as a summary (or recapitulation) of the events of History.

So he is presented not only as the second Adam, but also the second Moses, with a similar slaughter of babies accompanying his birth, forty days in the desert reflecting forty years in the wilderness, presenting the New Law to substantiate and fulfil the Old Law. Like Moses whose face shone so that he had to wear a veil, Jesus is also transfigured beside Moses. Like Joshua he crossed the Jordan where he is initiated by John. And as the new David he makes his way to Jerusalem for a royal procession.
In the context of symbolism this refers to the way every life depends on the unbroken chain of former lives, of which it is the end-product. Each life is the individual personification of Life itself.

The Crucifixion:
   The inner experience of *DEATH*.

Death of the Ego, which is the necessary prerequisite for rebirth – into the Self. The route to the unconscious.
Human nature is torn between paradise above and hell below, between good to the right and evil to the left (the two thieves), the intolerable paradoxes of life, the intolerable conflict of opposites which tear man asunder between the highest and the lowest, the first and last, symbolized by the four arms of the cross. These are the four poles, the four extremes of life.
The God of love is also the god of wrath, the god of the Archangel but also of the Devil, the Alpha, of beginnings, birth, providence, but also the sinister side of the Omega, the end in death and corruption, abandoning his son, and with him all mankind to their fate. This conflict ends in the descent into the underworld, the recovery of the whole

collective unconscious from its beginnings, which leads on to the prefiguring of the End of Time.

Related Symbolism:-

Compare *DEATH* for other instances of this image which is central to symbolism.

Personal Symbolism:-

The cross is the image of the *via negativa* or apophatic way of the ascetics who emptied themselves of their Ego by dying to the world.

Resurrection, Ascension, Assumption.

Resurrection: The penultimate transformation within the world of matter.

Ascension and Assumption: The ultimate metamorphosis into pure invisible action, energy.

These are symbolic events prefiguring the End of Time, the ultimate destiny of mankind. What exactly was the nature of the event, as a freak occurence out of gear with the ordinary life of man, will not become clear until the same thing happens again, and again.

There is a recognizable tendency (in spite of many set-backs) for the matter or substance of the world to become increasingly refined or spiritualized through a slow process of *TRANSFORMATION* and *CHANGE*, i.e. dinosaurs turn into Dante. It is a process by which matter is shaped, modelled and increasingly brought under the rational control of the conscious will and mind. Symbolically it is Man himself who must rise from the dead, i.e. the slumber of unconsciousness. As a prefiguration of the final end of this process, resurrection and ascension are symbols of the unity of spirit and physical nature that are meaningful and of value for anyone. If they genuinely prefigure what will take place, they are more valid as symbols for mankind, than as a singular event.

Note:-

Joseph Campbell rightly points out that if these symbols are taken literally, then it must be decided at what speed the bodies were travelling in their ascent; if at the rather uncomfortable speed of light, then they would not have quite reached the Milky Way yet. It's easy to see the ludicrous side of this. The difficulty for anyone nowadays is to grasp what is so meaningful, so all-important about such symbols that Jung could consider the pronouncement of the dogma of the Assumption as one of the most significant events in the twentieth century.

The End Days.
The ultimate destiny of man, which gives direction to his endeavours meanwhile.

You need to know where the North Pole is, in order to achieve the right orientation, direction, and so in symbolic language it is often stated that the goal and the way are the same. They are not just related but identical, because the vital forces symbolized by the archetypes are always concentrated in the present moment, now, which is in no way segregated from the past or the future (it is always flowing out of one into the other).

It isn't some surprise End of Time sitting waiting to spring out, that is of symbolic concern, but the part which the End of Time plays now, creatively or destructively (see *GOAL*).

The three worlds, Heaven, Earth, and Man: reflect the three types of mysticism: God Mysticism, Nature Mysticism, and Soul Mysticism. (See Happold, F. C. *Mysticism* (1963).)

Transformation:
The immanent and enduring essence of reality – God – appears in a continuous state of transformation.

Mankind as a whole acts as mediator between the spiritual world and the physical, sharing in both. God transforms matter by penetrating it with his life. By his share in that life, the individual is one with the life that pervades the whole universe. Thus Christ identifies with mankind, with God, but also with bread and wine. Bread and wine, eaten, turn into flesh and blood (by the normal process of digestion) and these turn into spiritual energy, and vice versa. This points to the core of symbolism which seeks to heal the rift between God and man; between conscious and unconscious; between life and matter.

Books:-

Rahner, H. *Greek Myths and Christian Mystery* (1963).

Jung, C. G. *Psychology and Religion* in *Collected Works*, Vol. II (1958).

Rieu, E. V. (trans.), *The Four Gospels* (1952).

The *CHURCH FATHERS*, especially Clement, Origen and lastly Jerome (influenced by Isaiah, Plato and Philo), saw the most significant meaning of scripture as symbolic and referring directly to the human soul. For Origen the words were a vast ocean or forest (both symbols of the unconscious) of mysteries, presenting patterns and types of human existence, in a way that anticipates Jung's *ARCHETYPES*.

CINDERELLA

Concerns the *INFERIOR* function in women, often Introvert Intuition, which is the neglected side of their personality, needed to complement extravert practical qualities.

The Ugly sisters are given everything physically by their natural MOTHER, while Cinderella is totally deprived: this contrasts paying attention to outer physical needs, with self-denial in search of inner riches.

The Fairy Godmother produces gifts which are valid up to a point: The gifts of the imagination, though they provide a glimpse of another realm, are not lasting. They vanish away and leave you as you were before. Above all they cannot see the individual through the midnight hour which is the hour of death, when only rags and ashes are left.

However there is a spirit which can effect a true transformation of life, via the shoe: The shoe may symbolize the female genitals, or organs of procreation – a very physical symbol of the way life endures eternally, only by changing and renewing itself.

Note:-

Because in an older version of the story Cinderella is called Leda and gives birth to twins, Harold Bayley traces the origin of the story to the myth of Zeus ravishing Leda in the form of a swan, which suggests the story may also be concerned with the union of spirit and matter, with the masculine spirit taking the initiative.

CINEMA
Deprived of true symbolism, man satisfies his craving with celluloid.

The cinema is particularly well suited to give a flickering nocturnal form to the life of the imagination. The nature of the experience is not far from dreaming. So it is hardly any wonder that films are packed with symbolic themes that provide an unconscious balance to conscious waking life.

The fact that the symbols are predominantly negative – *UNDERWORLDS* of crime and horror – no doubt reflects the widespread neglect of the unconscious, which erupts in its dark shadow aspect in the cinema, as an initial way of becoming recognized, without doing any more harm than similar incidents in dreams. But, as Jung pointed out tirelessly, these same neglected unconscious phenomena not only threaten to take possession of the individual – with obsessions, compulsions, phobias, etc. – but they are also at the root of sudden eruptions in society, such as Nazism in Germany.

Related Symbolism:-

For themes that recur in cinema, see *CATTLE, CRIME, DEATH,* the Undead, *HORROR, SCIENCE FICTION, SPY STORIES, VAMPIRES.*

CLOTHES
The body.
Either:-

    i. Anything which divides *INNER* from outer.

Artificial man-made fibres – i.e. systems, taboos, conditioning, etc. – which cut the individual off from direct experience, or from the central reality (see *CENTRE*). This is a typically introvert attitude.

Or:-

    ii. Flesh and blood itself (see *BODY*), layers of substance which build up into the concrete experience of reality. When shed layer by layer in Arallu (the Mesopotamian land of the dead), it is like shedding the senses themselves, and only a vague insipid dusty life remains. This is a typically extravert attitude.

89

CLOTHES

Particular ways of dressing: as a symbol of individuality in contrast with social conformity, this often arouses exaggerated reactions which point to powerful repressed feelings on this issue. Most people tend to repress their resentment at the extent to which society has ignored or crushed their personal aspirations from schooldays onwards. This hidden resentment may erupt when they see others who flaunt their freedom from social strictures. (See *INDIVIDUAL/*Group.)

Because of their close connection with the body, obsessions, phobias and compulsions, really about the body, are transferred to clothes.

Shoes
Female genitals.

So, for example, because other protruding limbs of the body, like feet or fingers, may be symbolic of the phallus, *gloves* and *shoes* may be symbolic of the female genitals, as in *CINDERELLA.*

The old woman who lived in a shoe: As she lived for nothing else but her female sexual organs she inevitably kept on having children, till there were too many.

Covering the lowest part of the body, shoes further refer symbolically to what the individual may consider a debased aspect of human nature, which may need attention, may need to be integrated; particularly for a person floating in intellectual realms, shoes may take on symbolic significance (i.e. a significance out of all proportion to their actual use).

CLOUDS
Forces of nature, which bring life after drought.

Intermediaries between heaven and earth.

They also form an intermediate phase between substantial reality and ethereal reality: that is, between space and action; between matter and time.

The clouds may form a complete psychological landscape, with ethereal mountains, towers, etc: Mental images of reality, insubstantial forms.

Being taken up into a cloud: Being transformed into pure

energy. A cloud is like steam, a stage in the process of melting and etherealizing solid substances.

The clouds around Mt. Olympus, which protected the gods from the eyes of men: As intermediaries the clouds are also barriers that obscure the invisible spiritual realities of pure force. These clouds can only be penetrated by a flash of intuition, symbolically the equivalent of LIGHTNING *from the clouds.*

Book:-

The Cloud of Unknowing, by an anonymous fourteenth-century English mystic, describes the way into the psychological inner clouds of the mind (which dull the activity of the conscious Ego) and how to journey through them into a universal reality of the SELF or COSMIC MAN.

COLOUR

Whatever you spontaneously associate with a particular colour will usually be an indication of its symbolic significance.

As soon as any form of symbolism gets cut off from its roots and becomes too abstract, it is liable to become grotesquely distorted very quickly, by conscious interference.

The revived interest in symbolism centres round the fact that it continues to have a direct impact on the individual via the unconscious. So if you ask anybody which colours he would associate with feeling, thinking, intuition and sensation, his answers shouldn't completely differ from the accepted symbolism, because feeling is associated with fire and the blood; thinking with the sky and air; intuition with flashes of light; and sensation with the earth (either brown or covered in green).

In much the same way all the lighter range of colours will refer to aspects of the conscious mind, while deep colours will refer to the unconscious or introvert side of whatever subtle force is being depicted or suggested by the colour.

Contrasting colours may be used for contrasting aspects of the psyche and life, the so-called 'cold' bluish colours in contrast with reddish colours can denote contrasts not just of feelings, but between passive or active approaches to life. The reason for this becomes clear when the colours are associated with aspects of nature: the still sky or pool in contrast with leaping flames and racing blood.

The great range and variety of colours which can be arranged in order of intensity
Are especially suited to expressing the range and intensity of feelings, of values. The quality of life.

But a series of colours can be related symbolically to any other series and so symbolize sequences of events, layers of the psyche or other processes, though this is more a conscious use of colour than a symbolic expression arising spontaneously from the unconscious (see *ALLEGORY*).

White/Black.
Conscious/Unconscious.

For example the black Knight, the black Crow, like the descent into hell or St John's dark night of the soul, may symbolize a period of *DISINTEGRATION* and germination in the unconscious, before experiencing new insight, the white light of ecstasy.

In this context white and black *TRANSFORM* into each other – as in nature – black clouds bring white rain and bright flames leave charred ashes.

White: Related to the moon which waxes pregnant, and therefore moon goddesses, the feminine realm, and man's *ANIMA* within the psyche.

Particular Colours:
These show the type of associations which affect colour symbolism.

Blue, related to the sky (e.g. The Blue Rose), the inner spiritual essence.

Green, the colour of vegetation, but also of corpses (e.g. Osiris was depicted as green). Nature in all her aspects: the cycle of birth and death.

Grey, like ashes. The fire of love is out, therefore Egoism and indifference.

Ochre robes, worn by condemned criminals, outcasts, and so adopted by Buddhist monks.

Pink, the colour of flesh, sensuality.

Purple, a mixture of red and blue, but also like grapes crushed to make wine, the difficult transmutation of inner spiritual values into outer concrete events, with the suffering involved. But this synthesis of mind and matter is also the source of power.

Red, like blood and dawn, outer worldly activity and existence.

Benz, E., Portmann, A. (*et al.*), *Colour Symbolism* (1972).

COMPLEXES

Including Inferiority Complex, Mother Complex, Father Complex.

Archaic and primitive forms of the *ARCHETYPES*, and because still unconscious they manifest negatively in relation to the personal *EGO*.

Most people realize that the Ego – or ordinary everyday 'I' – is not in complete charge of the situation or of their lives. There are other moods which sweep over them in waves, other forces which drive them, and some of their reactions have been 'conditioned'. Complicated bundles of feeling lurk in the unconscious, and from that well-camouflaged vantage point may jump out to molest the Ego and often thwart its conscious plans and activities. And this is usually the way we first recognize a Complex: when strong feelings disturb the psyche, disrupt normal behaviour or shatter our ordinary idea of ourselves.

The Ego's best defence is to become conscious of these forces and learn to control them, which can only be done by taking up a position midway between the Complex and the Ego, between feelings of inferiority and superiority, between feminine and masculine attitudes within.

In order to do this, the Complexes first have to be recognized as powerful Inner figures, personifications of inner forces, and not confused with actual people in the outside world. Note:-

The complexes, like the *ARCHETYPES*, can be loosely related to the Animal Instincts which partly accounts for their brute force. As follows:

The Ego Complex, when the Ego is grossly over-assertive: is related to the instinct for self-preservation.

The Inferiority Complex, which arises from the Archetypal Shadow: derives from animal aggression towards rivals. The desire to succeed and dominate involves the fear of failure and inadequacy.

The Mother/Father Complex, as the first negative manifestation of Anima and ANIMUS: has its roots in the Mating Instinct of animals.

The Symbols:-

The actual Family: Parents especially are initially abused as powerful symbols of disruptive Inner Forces and this leads to a great deal of friction between adolescents and their families.

Other PEOPLE: The whole process of getting inside other people, knowing what they are thinking, knowing what they are really like, exercises the imagination quite as much as the powers of observation. To a large extent we 'create' the characters of the people around us out of our own inner material. And if we keep a sharp eye on the process – and discriminate between what we actually observe and what we invent – we can begin to assemble sketches of our own personal Complexes: our own Inferiority Complex will be assembled from people we despise, etc. This can be done in the street or on the bus, but the work becomes more exacting in relation to people close to us (see *PROJECTIONS, PERSONIFICATION*).

Personal ANCESTORS: who can be imagined in a long procession behind the individual, like the Ka souls carried behind the King of Egypt.

The BODY, with all its organs and limbs, especially if any of them are manifesting negatively: Just as the body needs to be directed by the conscious will – and not twitch involuntarily – so the different Complexes, which are like the limbs of the psyche, need to be brought under conscious control.

The UNDERWORLD, with its legions of demons, spirits, ghosts and dead: may represent repressed Complexes, and their powers of destruction.

All the symbols for the ARCHETYPES may appear in more primitive archaic forms representing the Complexes.

Negative Symbolism:-

No Complexes: The worst possible way in which the Complexes can manifest in everyday life is by their absence. If they are successfully repressed and all contact with them cut off, this would result in life becoming vacuous, lonely and empty. Because the Complexes are centres of Feeling, they are the inner source of relating to other people and making contact with the outside world. Once recognized, they can be transformed into the helpful Archetypal Figures, who enable the individual to fulfil his potential.

ARCHETYPES/Complexes: Chart of the Complexes as they correspond to the Archetypes.

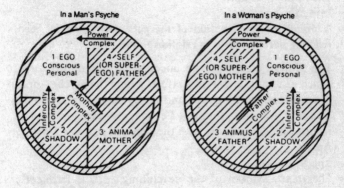

The Inferiority Complex.

A manifestation of the personal Shadow, that part of our make-up which we despise.

The qualities of the Shadow, when experienced from the limited viewpoint of the Ego, may come across as waves of disappointment, dim vague feelings of resentment. The Shadow, as the personification of all that we despise about ourselves, can make its presence felt in an oppressive and disturbing way.

The main division across the centre of the psyche is between *CONSCIOUS* and Unconscious, between *EGO* and Shadow. The Shadow can be visualized as one (hermaphrodite) figure, or as legion. But the symbolic process of growth and development involves recognizing that the *SPLIT* is always between *OPPOSITES*. The Inferiority Complex needs to be balanced by equal and opposite feelings of Superiority, and vice versa – depending on which particular attitude is in possession of the field at the time. The (temporary) conscious attitude has to be modified in relation to the Shadow reaction, before it's possible to integrate the two. This very process helps to locate the True *SELF* at the centre of the psyche. Like dissecting lines, it is a matter of taking up a position midway between the two extremes, and so holding the balance, which can never be achieved by the Ego alone. From this central position the Self acquires a detached and objective view of the Ego and its limitations.

The Mother Complex
In a Man's psyche:
A primitive manifestation of the personal Anima for men, reacting unconsciously in relation to the Ego.

The Mother complex is an unconscious and unruly force, which can have devastating effects within the psyche – until it is consciously recognized and slowly transformed into the Youthful Anima, a fount of Feeling, and the source of all relationships, especially with the opposite sex. See *ANIMUS/* Anima.

The Symbols:
The *HERO*, symbol of the developing *EGO*, is frequently depicted struggling with his Mother Complex. (See *OEDIPUS. FAUST. A CELTIC QUEST and especially the Two MOTHERS*.)

In a Woman's psyche:
A primitive and archaic form of the Inner *SELF*.
A woman may be tied to her Mother Complex, as if by an inner umbilical cord, which makes her the puppet of her upbringing, her early conditioning and other unconscious forces, which are centred round her Super-Ego and her True Self. Once the cord is cut, the Inner Figure – clearly and consciously distinguished – may become the Inner Guide, the *HELPFUL FIGURE*, the personification of that particular woman's potential maturity. (See *SELF*.)
Negative Symbolism:-
For a girl, when the Mother Goddess is missing, Hecate turns

up: With negative feelings towards motherhood and a loathing for children.

The Father Complex:
In a Woman's psyche:
If left to his own devices this Negative *ANIMUS* figure may cause considerable havoc which will affect not only a young woman's relationships with men but also her thoughts and judgements.
The Symbols:-
See *BEAUTY and the BEAST* and *RUMPELSTILTSKIN.*

Three blind mice, who all ran after the farmer's wife, who cut off their tails with a carving knife: the nursery rhyme depicts the activity of blind *COMPULSIONS* deriving from the unconscious Father Complex, which drive a woman from behind till she turns and analyses them with conscious discrimination. The symbol of the knife (like the *SWORD*) discerns but also castrates, that is robs these masculine impulses of their negative and destructive power. 'Did you ever see such a thing in your life?' highlights the fact that the complexes, and compulsions arising from them, are not often consciously discerned. The wisdom concealed in these nonsense rhymes is one way to account for their enduring fascination.

In a Man's psyche:
The Father Complex is associated with the actual father and other figures of authority, but so long as it is confused with them this will affect a young man's ability to achieve independence and mature gracefully.
It is the area of the Power Complex – which needs to be refined – but if it is lacking altogether a man remains ineffectual and childish.
Symbols:-
See *YOUTH/Old Man; SATURN.*

Other Particular Complexes.
   All other Complexes can be regarded as particular facets of the three more familiar complexes above.

As with the Inferiority Complex above, one way of coming to terms with them is to pair them into *OPPOSITES.*

COMPLEXES

For example the Naïve Child can be set against the Crusty Old Cynic, the Starry Eyed Adolescent against the Jaded Wife, the Hardboiled Professional against the Spoilt Brat, the Despotic Tyrant against the Self-Pitying Martyr, and vice versa – and so on: We all usually have plenty of both sides in us somewhere, and it's just a question of locating or presuming the other side, lurking in the unconscious. This process involves letting go of particular Egotistic standpoints – which fall into perspective – and gradually establishes the Archetypal *SELF* at the centre of the psyche in full conscious control of what goes on there.

Personal Symbolism:-

It is rare for personal Complexes to reflect the outside world directly. Usually, in the Inner Realm, the mass of humanity gets mixed together in the Unconscious, and then redivided according to symbolic criteria, *LIGHT* and dark, *MASCULINE* and Feminine, important and unimportant. And it is out of these categories that the curiously mixed dream-figures emerge – in dreams the Queen comes into the same category as your mother, Feminine and Important, and so can be interchanged with her. But these Composite Figures – or Complexes – also play an active part in everyday life, whether you are introvert enough to notice it or not. The device of *PERSONIFYING* them affords the chance to see them in action in order to relate to them – or come to terms with them if they are being destructive.

See also Personal *MYTH*.

COMPULSIONS

Symbolic action arising from excess of bottled up feeling, without clear rational control and often against conscious aims.

Including phobias, obsessions, moods, behaving or talking automatically, especially if the spontaneous gesture or remark belongs more appropriately to somebody of the opposite sex: All such involuntary compulsions arise directly from the unconscious and are a symbolic indication of its content. The centres of energy in the unconscious manifest more naturally and directly in the form of action than thought.

(See *COMPLEXES*.) Or may affect the body directly (see *HEALER*/Illness).

The Symbols:-

Such compulsions can be personified as tyrants manipulating the individual like a puppet from the shadows of the unconscious. They need to be recognized for what they are, powerful figures, often animals – or half-animal – who ravage the land, who force the hero to do their will in myths, fairy-stories, etc. The hero in turn has to wait his opportunity to escape.

Polyphemus, the one-eyed cyclops, from whom Ulysses escapes, by wit and trickery, the one-tracked demon of compulsion. Without giving in, or consenting intellectually, the will is often nevertheless trapped and powerless in the situation.

The hero or heroine of the tale is sometimes set an arduous task like sorting grains of sand and seed, which can only be done with the help of birds or INSECTS. Conscious discrimination is needed to sort out the inner world. Precision cures obsession, because one matches the other with intensity: intense thinking to match intense feeling.

Related Symbolism:-

SEXUAL SYMBOLISM, Compulsion*; ALCOHOL.*

Personal Symbolism:-

Obsessions about incidents which took place long ago in the past, but suddenly recur with a deep exaggerated sense of regret, may in fact be symbolic of the present situation. As with dreams some former failure may keep coming to mind, not because it matters in itself any more, but because it is essential not to fail again in the current challenge. Or if you once spoilt your chances by antagonizing people at the wrong moment – by being too overbearing, or too supercilious or whatever – being haunted by the incident may be a fairly obvious warning not to make the same mistake again.

Alternatively, somebody who had quite dismissed (i.e. repressed) the idea of having a child found herself wandering round a baby shop, without being able to remember how she got in there at all. Or another woman who had dismissed the idea of marriage in order to pursue her art suddenly felt an irresistible urge to steal a beautiful madonna and child for which she needed the assistance of a man she knew. Only later did she realize that her unconscious wanted her to marry the man in question and have a child by him. Whenever the emotional reaction is excessive, intense, out of proportion with the incident, it's worth looking to see if it has some symbolic significance.

CONFLICT

OPPOSITES, **or opposing forces, in the outside world are symbols of conflict in the inner realm.**

All derive ultimately from the basic *SPLIT*, or rift, between Conscious and unconscious. The preconscious totality – the single universe, interdependent with life – is split a different way for each individual. The individual affects the community he lives in and is affected by it, so that a dominant conscious attitude emerges, different for each society and each epoch. Alongside the neglected unconscious, shadow parts lie in wait in opposition or emerge into open conflict. Eventually the pendulum swings (by a law or principle sometimes called enantiodromia) and what was the dominant conscious attitude gets lost in the unconscious, while new attitudes crystallize and take conscious shape out of the unconscious. And the trouble starts up again but from another angle – just where nobody was expecting it.

Emma Jung and others see it as the special task of our time to bridge this rift and find the balance between the opposing forces.

Related Symbolism:-

OPPOSITES: UNION of Opposites; The *MEDIATOR*. Also *SPLIT: CONSCIOUS/Unconscious; EGO/Shadow.*

CONSCIOUS/Unconscious

The contrast between rational and irrational behaviour, or voluntary and involuntary action: as well as where we focus conscious attention and what we dismiss or fail to notice.

Symbolic language, whether in myth or fairy-story, often calls attention to the unconscious content of the psyche, whether as a warning of its dark destructive potential, or as an incentive to discover its treasures, and so enrich the conscious life.

It isn't easy to define the threshold between conscious and unconscious content of the psyche. Perhaps, as some psychologists suggest, it is better to leave the borderline a little vague. Nevertheless, a vague idea of what we're talking about is absolutely necessary and fundamental to the understanding of symbolism at all.

Since the conscious content manifests in dreams which can be noted down, it cannot be equated with the totally *UNKNOWN*, all that lies totally beyond the range of ever being assimilated by the individual, or conscious Ego. What is distinctive about the unconscious is that it is not under the direct control of the ordinary waking will; it operates without conscious attention, like dreams. When you turn your conscious attention to the matter afterwards, you realize that unconscious forces have been at work, forces that are part of yourself but *SPLIT* off. So there is a distinction between conscious actions, regulated by the ordinary 'I' of everyday life, such as picking up a drink; and unconscious actions, like breathing, digesting, and creating a baby in the womb, whether beautifully formed or malformed, whether boy or girl, which is all outside the range of conscious control. So most physical functions, as well as vestiges of the animal instincts, fall at present into the sphere of the unconscious, and indicate something of its power. Then again there are many experiences in life from early infancy which have left a deep impression on the mind, though we can't recall them consciously any more. Beyond that there is the hereditary factor of which we are the endproduct: the psyche, as it is, cannot be dissociated, severed, cut off from the processes which went into its making; the experience of mankind in the past has affected the evolution of the mind as it is now, and is directly responsible for much of the way it functions, at this particular stage of its development. This interaction between past experience and present mental structures Jung has called the Collective Unconscious. Symbolically it can be visualized as the relationship between the tree and its fruit.

CONSCIOUS

The real distinction between Conscious and unconscious, is, as suggested above, the difference between voluntary and involuntary, the difference between rational and irrational. And symbolism seeks to unify and relate these opposites by bringing to light all that is irrational, and involuntary, so that it can be transformed in the right relationship with the rational side of man; who is then freed, liberated from unconscious forces which would otherwise control his life. Note:-

Reason has been falsely identified with the Thinking *FUNCTION*, but only people whose Feelings are lost in unconsciousness feel erratically, negatively, beyond the reach of will or reason. But feelings can be just as much rational or irrational as thoughts (James Hillman). Equally intuitions have been considered supra-rational when they lead to great insights, discoveries, hypotheses, or merely idiotic superstitions; and even the physical senses can surely be directed consciously and rationally.

It is the prize of consciousness – symbolically stolen from the gods – which makes man a rational animal. Every interest in the unconscious is not a retrograde desire for unconsciousness, but is present in order to extend the sphere of consciousness, to penetrate on beyond the present boundaries. Symbolically it is to make contact with the barbarian hordes beyond the boundary, before they find the weak spot in the wall, sweep in and ravage the capital.

The symbols:-

CREATION Myths: The dividing of order from *CHAOS* reflects an equivalent division of conscious from unconscious content.

MIRROR: reversed reflections symbolize equal and opposite factors in the unconscious.

The *BROTHERS; LIGHT/Dark*.

Related symbolism:-

*DISINTEGRATE/*Integrate.

Also *SPLIT; EGO/Shadow; UNION* of Opposites.

CORD. Ropes, Thread:

Any link of an inner nature, but most especially the

psychological umbilical cord, the fixation or involvement in the mother.

Hence, suicide by hanging may be related to involvement in the Mother Complex, resulting in difficulties in the realm of the feminine. (see *CRIME*, Hanging).
Thread. The thread that binds reality together.
Related Symbolism:-
MAZE, *Ariadne's thread.*
Also EROS. The FATES.

The COSMOS
The World or Worlds.
The Individual's 'Big Body' on which he depends for survival – and from which he can't be separated. The full extent of your experiences, your life interacts with matter.

Man is not shut up inside himself, but his experiences extend to the limits of the cosmos. For this reason his life-force is seen symbolically as co-extensive with the universe rather than confined to his body.
The cosmos itself is dead.
As mere inanimate substance, the cosmos doesn't have any of the qualities of existence – such as space, light, heat, heaviness, or distance. These are all qualities of experience, and dead matter can't experience anything. It does not realize.
So the world reaches its culmination in being known – or imagined; as, for example, when we imagine a world without life where the sun continues to shine on a rocky shore. Man himself is the second creator of the world, as Jung put it. Furthermore it is a matter of common everyday experience that through our senses – especially our eyes – and through our minds, we extend into the cosmos and even beyond.
Symbols try to find adequate expression for this experience, this relationship and interaction of life and matter.
The symbol:-
Cosmic MAN.

Two Worlds, Macrocosm and Microcosm:
  Two different experiences of the one world.

Firstly, the conscious mind acquires direct knowledge of the outside world through the experience of the senses. In this vast world we appear to ourselves as tiny figures who can't be represented by a dot on the globe.

Secondly, we can shut our eyes and find an inner world, still intact, complete with kangaroos and distant stars. Or alternatively project a vivid world around us in dreams. From this world view it is we who contain the cosmos: either it all fits inside us, or we expand into the macrocosm till we can hardly pick out our own tiny bodies from afar.

Two such disparate experiences of reality require to be reconciled.

Related Symbolism:-

See *INNER/Outer*.

Three Worlds:

Three levels of consciousness, such as cosmic consciousness, ordinary everyday consciousness, and the unconscious.

The symbols:-

In traditional symbolism these were the Celestial Sphere, the Human Sphere, and the Demonic Sphere.

Similarly, the *SELF*, the *EGO* and the *SHADOW*, each experience the world differently.

Related Symbolism:-

The sky represented pure life, while the earth symbolized dead, unconscious matter, and the lightning interaction of the two brought offspring in a third realm between the other two: the realm of vegetation, animals and man, all *MEDIATORS* between *ABOVE* and below.

GODS. HEROES and Demons, or BIRDS. ANIMALS, and SERPENTS: Much symbolism is on three levels, always referring to three levels of consciousness.

Roots, trunk, and branches of a tree: Sometimes the tree is turned upside down so that the enduring can come from the heavenly sphere.

The three strides of Vishnu.

The three gunas, height, appearances, darkness.

The Ankh Cross, see PATTERNS.

Each sphere contains the other: hence those sages who identify with the Macrocosm, become of great value in the human realm even though they lead secluded lives. Whereas, when society is disintegrating it is not easy for the isolated psyche to be integrated.

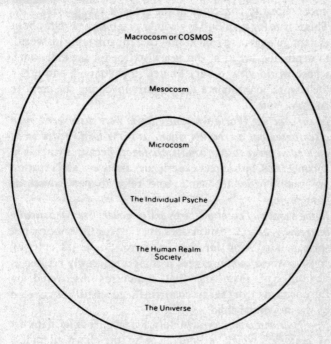

COW
The feminine in nature, the fecundity of heaven and earth.

A lack of respect for the feminine side of nature (including human nature) has been projected on to the cow as well, in present Western society, which has no vestige for us of that otherworldly radiance that suffuses the Ancient Egyptian representations of the cow.

Seven cows of Hathor are seven reaches of the sky: The feminine path or way. Seven steps between birth and death in the life of a woman.

See *CATTLE*, also *BULL*.

CREATION MYTHS

Express the inner process of becoming more and more conscious of the world.

Bit by bit man brings new content across the threshold from unconscious to conscious in the creative act of living.

This is true for mankind as a whole, grasping new data about distant galaxies and split atoms, thereby enlarging his world, in depth and breadth. But it is also true for the individual, whose world view is very limited in childhood, and it is a life's work to complete the picture, involving the creative *IMAGINATION*.

In the Ancient World when new lands were discovered, man often acted out a creation ritual, as if the land needed to be created in order to confirm its existence: Because symbolism is concerned with direct experience, discovery and creation are symbolically the same, and refer to new conscious content.

In the same way creation, birth and discovery are symbolically interchangeable: Creation does not exist for the unborn, but springs into being for the new-born. So far as entering consciousness is concerned, a rhinoceros newly created is no different from the first rhinoceros discovered by European man, or the rhinoceros in the zoo, newly discovered by the individual child.

New Year and Dawn: are symbolically smaller units in the act of creation, which is equivalent to the dawn of man's consciousness. New Year was especially the time for ritual re-enactment òf creation, whereby man imposes mental order upon the fleeting variety of direct experience. It is memory which brings stability to experience, and lays out the beginnings and the ends (see *TIME*).

Negative/Positive Symbolism:-

The work of bringing unconscious content into the light of consciousness also transforms man's dark negative feelings of being lost in an alien cosmos. Man orientates himself by means of mental concepts such as order, direction, boundaries, which transform his experience of the cosmos from being terrifying, confusing, or just strange: and relate him to his environment.

Note:-

But this systematizing can be overdone, and it may be that modern man needs to rediscover the impact of direct experience. His conscious control is so tight that the real experience of life eludes him: he is no longer disturbed by sleep where space and time dissolve and slip away into nothing, to be partially replaced by the chaotic disorder of the unconscious otherworld of dreams. He is all too sure of his limited Ego world, and so can hardly grasp his precarious position semi-stuck to a big ball of fiery mud, spinning through endless space and time. But in reality his position is no different from that of primitive man, only his focus of attention has changed.

Related Symbolism:-

See *ORIGINS, and SPLIT:* for stages in creation myths which reflect stages in the creative act of living.

HEPHAESTOS: the God of artistic creation in Greece.

DWARFS and GIANTS: for unconscious impulses seeking a creative outlet or expression.

BIBLICAL SYMBOLISM, Creation: for the relationship between seven stages of creation and seven levels of consciousness.

Destruction/Creation:
   DEATH **and rebirth.**

Creativity:
   You risk damaging your personality if you neglect your creative faculty.

In Personal Symbolism:-

Creation myths refer to the individual's own creative capacity. When people neglect their own inner creativity, neglect the task of recreating the universe over again for themselves – not just the dead material universe, of course, but the other people in it, the world of relationships, values and meanings too – it has been found to affect other aspects of their lives. For example, sex and creativity are not just symbolically linked (as procreation and creation) but appear to be interdependent, intertwined in the same deep archetypal root. So that failure to use inner potential has led to impotence which, in turn, was only cured when the individual found an outlet for other creative impulses.

CREATION MYTHS

When the creative work of living is neglected, there is also a compensatory overvaluation – and envy – of creative art, which is then put in an isolated compartment, cut off from everyday living, as if it wasn't a direct product of life. By providing a special box for the talented or creative, the individual hopes to evade the personal responsibility of the creative task of living, of which art is an inseparable part. Often it is impossible to stimulate the creative faculty without doing actual creative work, such as painting, writing or whatever (see symbolic *ACTION*, and the *INFERIOR FUNCTION*). In any case this material form of creativity provides some of the symbols for the more subtle creative work of life; pregnancy provides others. So, for example, an artist may feel pregnant with ideas, but prefer to bask in that feeling rather than give birth to what may turn out a disappointing offspring. This is especially true of the Eternal *YOUTH* type, whether an actual artist or not. Women sometimes resort to having another actual baby, in order to evade the inner task.

Dissolving into the unconscious, or remaining near the unconscious source of life, is an essential beginning, and can be compared with the period of germination in nature. Creative ideas and impulses must be given time to grow roots underground, without being tampered with, that is, without conscious interference.

Contact with the Muse: is symbolically equivalent of contact with the *ANIMA* for the ordinary individual, or in the case of a woman the *ANIMUS*. This is an essential step in the creative task.

Book:-
Franz, M. L. von *Patterns of Creativity Mirrored in Creation Myths* (1972).

CRIME/Punishment
The dark forces of the unconscious, which the Collective Conscious Ego, in the form of Society, fears and punishes.

The criminal: The *SHADOW*.
The 'underworld' of crime: The collective Shadow element in society, the dark neglected side of dominant collective

attitudes, sometimes brutal and animal, but also more refined aspects of the inner cravings that are denied open expression.

The quota of crime fiction: As always, symbolism makes no distinction between fact and fiction, since it is primarily concerned with the inner world, in this case the inner *SHADOW*. The dark sinister criminal is the embodiment of the unconscious, and in a thriller this figure is a murderer, threatening to kill the conscious Ego, in order to satisfy its own more primitive cravings.

But of course the symbolic solution of putting him safely behind bars has no lasting effect, so the next thriller has to be collected from the shelf. Till the criminal within is finally tracked down.

Punishment of crime:

   Is often a symbolic solution, compensation, mis-taken physically and literally.

Flaying is symbolic of changing skin and therefore of transformation.

The cross represented the ideal man perfectly developed (see PATTERNS). Therefore crucifixion: forcing a man to conform to the ideal.

Drawing and quartering a man, or tearing him apart in other ways, such as on the rack, by beasts, between trees. The punishment for dissenters. The primordial man was so *SACRIFICED*, but society, when centred and co-ordinated, manages to reunite the parts, in the sense of forming a corporate identity. The criminal disrupts this, so what he does to society is done to him.

Prison, dungeons, chains. Just as the unconscious binds the will, and compels the individual to act from his dark shadow side (see *CONSCIOUS/Unconscious*), so the criminal is physically bound, deprived of freedom.

Stoning (especially of the prophets) for offences against the inertia of tradition. It is as if the stones themselves rose up against such an infringement of the status quo.

Hanging: Refastening the criminal to his Mother Society by another umbilical cord (see *CORD*).

The corpses of suicides were mangled, and dragged through the streets. As a physical display of what had taken place inwardly, in the form of lack of respect for life.

Burning at the stake: Tying to the central world-AXIS and transforming by fire.

Note:-

These actual historical punishments manifest an unconscious symbolism at work which, once understood as referring to the inner needs of the individual in relation to society, indicates the age-old need for the psychological approach to the criminal, now widely favoured. Otherwise the symbol gets mis-taken literally.

The Symbols in Myth and Fairy-tale:-

The basic crime, depicted as stealing fruit or fire from the Gods. Is becoming conscious, acquiring a rational mind. Animals cannot commit crimes, but in becoming conscious man loses his basic instinctive animal existence.

The inherent punishment is exile, prison, or chains. His knowledge cuts him off from the instinctive free relationship with nature, splits his world in two so that his conscious self becomes aware of his inner predicament, experienced as confinement or exile in the material world, from birth to death, the life sentence (*'Tied to a dying animal'*, or *chained to the rock like Prometheus*).

Related Symbolism:-

The themes of trial and judgement whether after death or now (as in Franz Kafka's *The Trial*) are symbolically related to this awareness of the human predicament.

Zeus punishes his wife Hera, by dangling her from the clouds with anvils tied to her feet. As the block on which the blacksmith strikes with his hammer, the anvil is a symbol of the passive feminine role which Zeus is impressing upon his wife – after her rebelliousness, with her masculine Animus, Hephaestos. See ANIMUS.

The Damsel in the High Tower. The female Anima trapped within the male. Or: a woman caught up in masculine problems.

The Hero in the Dungeon. The Animus in the depths of the feminine realm. Or: a man caught in Mother or Anima entanglements.

Being in and out of prison many times. In fairy-tales may be a sign of initiation, a familiarity with the underworld, at the depths of experience. A deep knowledge of the dark side of life and how to relate to it; above all how to get out of it. That is, someone who has tackled his own Shadow, and so has the ability and experience to help anyone else in a similar predicament.

Note:-

As with prison, the difficulty is not so much getting into the unconscious, as getting out of it again; and getting something out of the experience.

This may partly account for the great popular appeal of figures like Jack Shepherd who escaped again and again from prison.

Book:-

Streatfeild, D. *Persephone* (1959), for a fascinating psychological investigation of the symbolism of James Hadley Chase's thriller, *No Orchids for Miss Blandish* (1942).

CROWN or Halo
The splendour of the fully conscious mind.

From rays of the sun, light itself, originally an attribute of the gods only, then of their representatives on earth, who mediated symbolically the conscious light of man.

The complete circle of consciousness, the full awareness of reality.

When combined with the diadem of the moon, integration of conscious and unconscious light.

Related Symbolism:-

See *KING*, for the corporate identity of man which allows each little light of consciousness, working in unison, to become one great light. Kings or Saints became focal points for unity. Compare Trade Unions today.

CRYSTAL
Invisible matter. So a union of spirit and matter.

Gazing into a crystal ball: reflects an empty conscious mind, receptive to the emerging content from the unconscious.

CRYSTAL
Related Symbolism:-
See *GLASS*.

DANCE
Reflects the patterns and threads of energy which bring order into chaos, on the cosmic level, as well as on the personal level.

Circular dances, for example, round the Maypole: The cycle of time and movement around the world Axis (see *CENTRE*).

The symbolism of DEATH. Books of the Dead.
Unconsciousness.

Also the spiritual realm.
At death the flesh of the material body is abandoned by all the force which possessed it; and left to *DISINTEGRATE*. In a symbolic death, all contact with the outside world is cut off, as are all incoming thoughts, in an attempt to simulate the experience of death, and so acquire spiritual insight.
The land of the dead: The realm of the unconscious.
And the common dread of the dead awakening, of corpses stirring: is equivalent to the inner dread of the repressed content of the unconscious rising up.

The Books of the Dead:
*For example, the Egyptian **Book of the Dead**, or the Tibetan **Bardo Thodol**.*
Refer to the psychic journey inwards and down into the unconscious.

It is from the experience of the unconscious – rather than the actual experience of the after-death-state – that their material is derived.
Death makes clear the distinction between the physical substance of man – the corpse – and the living energy; in religious language the difference between the visible body and the invisible soul or spirit.
In the Tibetan system, there are three planes of existence beyond death: That is, three levels of unconsciousness. As so often with symbolic material, the events are described in

reverse of the natural order of experiences, that is in terms of a soul descending and entering matter (see *MIRROR*). But Jung prefers to treat them in their natural ascending order of inner experience:

i. The instinctual, animal and sexual, plane of existence, which seeks rebirth. (*Sippa Bardo.*)

ii. Form without matter.

The plane of images, symbols and archetypes – all the residue of actual existence. The experience of unleashed fantasy in a riot of forms, which need to be integrated. When these are arranged into an ordered plan they form the Mandala.

Mere actual life is distilled into a subtler mind form, not unlike the Platonic realm of Ideas. (*Chonyid Bardo.*)

iii. *The pellucid blue light:* Pure existence, pure essence, or pure energy. Although this realm is beyond knowledge and beyond the symbol, it is not experienced as dark, empty or vapid. On the contrary it is the most positive and exhilarating experience of the *UNKNOWN*, as Pure Reality without form or attributes or qualities which are relative and dependent upon the way the sense organs and imagination are fabricated. (*Chikhai Bardo.*)

This sequence of a deliberately selected set of symbols is the ground plan and guideline to similar, but more confused, sequences of spontaneously produced personal symbols: A recurring pattern of symbolism is psychic *DISINTEGRATION* – equivalent to physical disintegration at death – which is a necessary step towards maturity.

The first step is the blotting out of ordinary limited everyday attitudes, so as to become aware of a wider range of reality. The inner reality of the unconscious, expressed in a riot of imagined forms, cannot be directly related to everyday life. Hence the misery and madness of people thrown back and forth between these two, which are in violent conflict, if this is allowed to become a permanent state of vacillation, rather than an intermediary stage: once clearly recognized for what it is, the tension may be accepted and valued, precisely because it demands to be resolved by a process of transformation in the psyche. See, for example, *SPLIT, OPPOSITES, INNER/*outer, or *CONSCIOUS/*unconscious.

Both then need to be wiped out, in order to experience the Unknown Reality, without the distortions of the individual senses or inner misconceptions, and this experience transforms the everyday life style, as well as the life style of the pure imagination, validating both as partial views of reality that complement one another.

In psychological language the *Bardo Thodol* describes the three major stages in the process of individuation – achieving individuality by integrating all parts of the psyche, and thereby attaining an Undivided *SELF*. The work may take a lifetime, or be left unfinished at the end.

Macabre figures of death:
Such as skeletons with a scythe madly dancing, drumming or blowing the trumpets of doom. Or just worm-eaten meat.
   Announce the death of the Ego, which is just the first step towards any higher awareness.

This step, like the figure, is repellent to the conscious mind. Though the figures are often fascinating to children, whose Egos are less developed, less highly differentiated.

The After-Death-State.
   The most powerful and central of all the symbols of *TRANSFORMATION and re-centring*.

Positive Symbolism:-
After death there is nothing left, the whole cosmos is extinguished as in sleep. The death of the individual corresponds symbolically to the end of the world.

But beyond that, everything is left the same except one lump of flesh, one lump of matter, which is changing. This may involve reassessing where the centre of one's being is, not intellectually so much as emotionally: what is of most value, one lump of flesh – physical symbol of one Ego – or the whole cosmos – symbol of the Self.

Another symbol of this is the great circle of existence and transformation in the Bhagavad Gita, *where mankind marches in the mouth of Vishnu to be munched up, and reappears the other side to continue on the round, i.e. the self-consuming Ouroboros, but applied direct to human life. The* physical body, the psyche and the cosmos all live by perishing (*TRANSFORMATION*).

One of the difficulties of the Ego in facing the experience of death is that the highly specialized individual personality appears intensely preferable to the spectre of expanded consciousness, with inevitable associations of the communal porridge-mix. (See *PEER GYNT*.) But a more realistic *IDENTIFICATION* with the processes of nature would also take into account the way the process tends towards more and more specialized forms. The more highly evolved creatures are also the most refined and the most individual. After millions of years of evolution, and out of millions of different combinations, if we were satisfied with the particular bunch of characteristics handed out at birth, perhaps that is cause to trust whatever process is involved. Symbolism as usual tries to depict the patterns, the forces at work, the life process, without the specifications of non-symbolic language, so that man can live in relation to whatever forces are at work, even though he doesn't know exactly what they are. Unfortunately, symbols such as re-incarnation are then taken literally and people claim to know all about what is fundamentally unknown. The great advantage of psychology has been to refer symbols back to the psyche of which they are an adequate expression.

To accept the life process, which landed us in this predicatment, isn't easy, but the alternative is non-existent.

The impulse to suicide:
May be a symbolic urge for transformation.

But involving over-confidence in the positive side of the death-symbol, and a lack of due regard for its macabre opposite side.

Equally it is symbolically indicative of an impatience to transform, quickly, often a last-minute, and rather desperate attempt to make up for lost time in people who have become arrested, especially emotionally arrested, in that they have failed to transform at particular crises and turning points earlier in life.

Ideally, if recognized as the symbol of an inward psychological impulse, it can be a most vivid personal transformation experience for the psyche. Many Zen stories, for example, emphasize the way personal desperation (usually egocentric) precedes a new awakening.

Or:-

Suicide may also be a drastic attempt to keep unconscious content repressed by killing it off once and for all.

Symbolic Death.

An important psychological inner experience, which requires to be recognized before facing the second half of life. See *PERIODS* of Life.

In the Sequence of Life:-

The mid-point of life (between thirty-five and forty-five) when the Ego is well developed, is a great turning point and time to confront the second part of life culminating in actual death. And so, it is the time for this psychological inner experience. The failure to take this symbolic mid-point (the zenith, before the decline) seriously can render the whole second part of life vapid, a pale vestige of the first half, repeated in rather nauseous form.

Symbolic Death/Actual Death: We cannot experience, or anyway savour, the moment of actual death. As with our own *BODIES* we can only experience death through the imagination.

The value of the experience appears to be that it leads to individual wholeness. This may be because we have to face death with our whole being: feeling as well as thought (Voltaire); body as well as spirit.

The Symbols, and Related Symbolism:-

The Gods and spirits of the dead, such as: *OSIRIS* (Egypt), *Rephaim* (Canaan), *Orpheus* (Greece). See also *EMBALMING*.

The *UNDERWORLD as land of the dead.* The difficulties of getting into it and back out of it reflect difficulties in retrieving content from the unconscious.

In Zen, the Great Death is the symbolic experience of extinguishing the conscious Ego, by cutting off all sensation and thought; derived from and comparable with other *YOGA* practices.

The Shamans practised symbolic death in fasting, trance, and feigned executions.

The Greek MYSTERIES appear to have included crossing to the other world.

Odin, wounded and abandoned, was left nine days and nine nights dangling from the Cosmic Tree, till he was freed by magic. He derived new vigour from the experience.

The Sufis also extinguished themselves – symbolically – in order to discover the land of immortality. *Most heroes in myth have to face death, or the land of the dead, at some point.*

In fairy-tales, sleep as in *'SLEEPING BEAUTY'* and various other fairy lands and realms are related to the land of the dead, and refer to similar experiences within the psyche.

Necromancy, seances: The dead are raised to reveal the truth which lies buried in the unconscious.

By contrast, carrying a corpse (disposing of the body): Thrusting unsavoury material down into the unconscious. Sometimes trying to take an awkward step towards the unconscious.

Vampires, the undead: Splintered parts of the personality which have not been integrated and which are disturbing life, draining conscious energy. See *VAMPIRES*.

Book:-

Jung, C. G. *Psychology and Religion* in *Collected Works*, Vol. II (1958), for his commentary on the Tibetan Book of the Dead.

DEMETER and Persephone
The cycle of human life.

Holding up a piece of corn: Unites the idea of motherhood with the way the Earth provides. Both corn and mother combine into the image of Earth-Mother as provider, identifying the life of man with the corn, which dies and grows with the cycle of the seasons.

It was threshed, ground, made into man-shaped cakes (like gingerbread men) and eaten. The whole is broken down into bits, but the bits are formed into a new whole: there is continuity through the change.

With her daughter Persephone, who descends into the underworld and returns. Re-echoes the theme of continuity, in man as in nature; the transition – or *TRANSFORMATION* –

DEMETER

between Youth and Age, and maturity giving birth to youth.
Note:-
Here the symbolic ritual may have been trying to capture
what nature says silently to man.
Related Symbolism:-
MYSTERY Cults; also the *MOTHER*.
Book:-
Kerenyi, C. *Eleusis: Archetypal image of Mother and
Daughter* (1967).

DEPRESSION

**Has the psychological effect of lowering (depressing) the level
of consciousness, and thereby allowing unconscious content to
break through.**

If extreme, this comes near to a symbolic death experience –
like the black (nigredo) phase of Alchemy which at best can
be the prelude to new insights of such emotional intensity
that they appear as revelations from the outside.

Being DEVOURED, Swallowed

The conscious Ego devoured by the unconscious in the psyche.

The corpse swallowed up by the earth in the physical realm.
A life devoured by time. This aspect is stressed if there is any
oblique reference to the Moon, which marks the months and
is swallowed by the darkness for three days. The three
aspects of the symbol are linked and interwoven in the
dominant idea of *DEATH* and *TRANSFORMATION* in nature.
The old continuously perishes in order to make room for the
new, in the realm of time (i.e. yesterday disappears in order
to make room for today). The old perishes in order to give
substance to the new in the realm of matter. And the psyche,
in a continuous state of flux, lives by perishing.
Symbols:-
*SATURN devouring his children. He is time itself (Cronos of the
Greeks), the cosmic clock.*
*A great deal of devouring goes on in myth and fairy-tale by all
kinds of monsters, ogres, creatures living under the sea, etc.,*

118

but usually suggesting some particular aspect of the above symbolism, which is not unrelated to the process of sexuality: of being swallowed and reborn via semen or womb.

DIFFERENTIATION
In psychology, applying the analytical thinking function to symbolic material, which can be useful — but only after the *IMAGINATION* has been allowed a free hand.

Then it is a valuable sorting process, which is particularly necessary when confronting the tangled complexities of the unconscious: to sort *INNER* from outer, *CONSCIOUS* from Unconscious, etc. But it is secondary.

The danger of the thinking *FUNCTION* is that it has become so closely allied to the conscious Ego (even in many women), and if it gets in first, with its hyper-critical and utility attitudes, there won't be anything to differentiate.

The Symbols:-

INSECTS. SWORD, from stone, wood. The GORGON, Medusa. Which is one clear example of the importance attached to careful differentiation in the Ancient World, where the unconscious appears to have been more powerfully felt.

Separating gold from sand, grain from chaff, ore from dross, etc.: reflect similar processes within the psyche: differentiating what is valuable from what is worthless.

The Four DIRECTIONS
The psyche divided into four, whether as Four *FUNCTIONS*, or Four *ARCHETYPES*.

In symbolism the four directions are usually arranged:

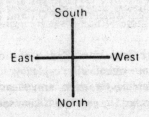

DIRECTIONS

And these four quarters not only correspond to the fixed pattern or structure of the psyche, but also to the dynamic sequence of life. They provide the digits on the Cosmic Clock, and measure the day, the *SEASONS* of the Year, and the *PERIODS* of man's life.

Also *NUMBERS, Four.*

Note:-

Both the *I Ching* and the *Zodiac* place South at the top of the page (in contrast with the ordinary map). This is more satisfying symbolically because it corresponds with the sun at its zenith.

Diagram of Directions of Symbolism

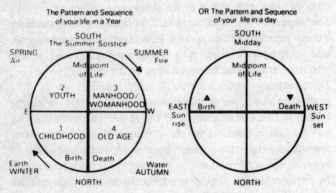

The Pattern and Sequence of your life in a Year.

OR The Pattern and Sequence of your life in a day.

Related Symbolism:-

The Four Cardinal signs of the ZODIAC, originally in the Age of Taurus, were Bull, Lion, Eagle and Man: they reappear in many guises as symbols.

They are probably loosely related to the four sons of Horus who guarded the four horizons, with the Hawk-headed and Man-headed pair more or less identical, and the Dog-headed and Ape-headed equivalent to the Ox and Lion.

DISINTEGRATE/Integrate

Psychologically, or symbolically, exploding into the Cosmos, and then reassembling the parts around a new nucleus or *CENTRE* in the psyche. The gain is self-knowledge.

In the language of *ALCHEMY*, it is to Dissolve and Coagulate. So long as people *PROJECT* all their experience on to the outside world, then all the conflicts are experienced as a clash between themselves and the outside reality. But when everything in the outside world is found to have a counterpart within, the clash and conflict is experienced inwardly. Then this feels like a breaking up, a flying apart, a disintegration of the personality.

In the continuous interaction between *INNER* and outer, as between two sides of the looking glass (*MIRROR*), the inner viewpoint imposes its patterns and prejudices on the outside world. The outside world is solid and intractable, and if the inner realm is mixed with it, it too congeals, grows stale and flat. But to withdraw the whole cosmos inwards, to see everything in it as shadows and reflections of your own complexes, the personal and collective unconscious, is to bring all the hard bitter antagonism between the noble and vile in mankind, between the masculine and the feminine, right within your own feeble physical frame.

It can be described symbolically as swallowing the world whole: not in a nice sewn-up image – like the *CADUCAEUS* – but in all its gory detail. This is linked with the process of *IDENTIFICATION*: identifying with every man, woman and beast in the universe.

In an extreme case – and extreme cases often illustrate the point best – where the conscious Ego is not sufficiently developed, this break-in of reality (called implosion) causes an irrevocable disintegration of the personality – schizophrenia, madness, false identification with Napoleon, and so on.

But in the ordinary strong individual, it is a very fruitful experience, the experience which fertilizes the little limited Ego (Egg) which then begins its long period of growth outwards into the self: the cosmic, universal, undivided *SELF*. When all the forces of the cosmos – whether you see them in miniature, as microcosm, or not – clash in the inner realm, it is very different from when they clash in the outside world, because the inner world is a melting-pot where everything can be turned into fluid potential, whereas in the outside world the same forces have crystallized into hard rock. It's like the difference between throwing yourself off a high roof and hitting the paving stones, and throwing yourself off the same roof, but hitting water.

So what looks like – and, more important, feels as if it's going to be – total break-up of the personality, splintering of the complexes, a hideous shattering of life, suddenly turns into a softer dissolving in which the parts of the personality can be taken apart more gently and put together again in a new shape.

This is comparable, physically, to the dissolving of a man back into a sperm-drop, from which he emerged; born of a blood-clot, or a sperm-drop as the Koran states. For a woman it is shrinking into one ovum in order to give birth. The symbolic offspring creates a new cohesion in the inner realm of the psyche.

In the melting process all kinds of fantastic distortions come to light. This is the time when fantasy runs riot, and any kind of merman or monster can put in an appearance.

But it enables hard, stale, flat, conscious attitudes to be freshly blended with underlying natural needs. What seemed like impregnable fortresses of obvious truth and common sense suddenly totter and crash. They come to be seen as mere obsolete prejudices, of limited or relative value only, once measured against the spontaneous vitality of the unconscious.

The Symbols:-

The Alchemists, who were responsible for preserving the best traditions of the symbolism of the Ancient World, even into the scientific era, stressed this process of dissolution and coagulation as the fundamental principle of nature and of all their work. A healthy symbolic tradition can be recognized easily from the fact that new symbolism emerges alongside the old, in contrast to a tenacious clinging to forms that don't actually work any more. Thus this application of the ancient archetype (presumably discovered primarily through the experience of the psyche?) to chemical processes was to add a whole new dimension and level to this principle at work throughout nature. See *ALCHEMY*.

The SACRIFICE of Cosmic *MAN*, which is at the very roots of symbolism and which Theodore Gaster sees at the roots of

Greek tragedy – and therefore all tragedy – expresses this same archetypal experience.

SETH cutting up his brother OSIRIS into fourteen parts, that are no doubt related to the fourteen slices taken off the moon and then added to it before it is whole again, must have been of poignant concern to man because of the similar process taking place within his own psyche. The different pieces are shattered and fall away; before the whole can be repaired again. Compare *EMBALMING*.

In the realm of vegetation this is further related to the threshing of the corn in little pieces, each one of which can grow into a whole again. As with Osiris but also Mot in Canaanite myth.

Also see *DEATH*, the Books of the Dead.

Related symbolism:-

UNION of *OPPOSITES*, for more about integration.

Personal Symbolism:-

No doubt the mythical and archetypal descriptions of the process are on a grander scale than the personal experience which may involve small insight at the expense of a lot of suffering. However, if this insight is not dismissed as negligible but valued, the means of increasing it are now known and opened up. A process once discovered can be repeated. And it is at the end of a lifetime that the personal experience may match the archetypal description.

Note:-

Symbolic descriptions invariably contract time and may describe a whole life of struggle in terms of one short episode, whether in myth or fairy-tale.

Contrary to what many people think, there is little risk in confronting the irrational unconscious side of your nature. The danger lies rather in keeping your head stuck in the sand. It may be a bit disturbing, but it can be very exhilarating and fascinating too. The real threat is usually from the other direction: the processes of inner growth and transformation get stunted; leaving crippled psyches cramped in little steel cages – in the limited frames of reference of their conscious Egos. It is by no means so easy to contact the unconscious. Marie Louise von Franz describes a long period stuck alone in a shack on a hillside, without anything happening at all, except that she began to become frightened of burglars breaking in. Suddenly it clicked how utterly irrational this was as there was no one for miles around. She had made contact with her unconscious *ANIMUS*. The irrational often indicates the presence of symbolic unconscious material.

DJINN, or Jinnee

The powers of the psyche which at first appear dark and menacing because unconscious: but are transformed when brought under conscious control.

The first impression is always that it would have been better if they'd never been let out of the bottle. But often they bring great rewards in due course.

Like most psychic phenomena they can transform and take many shapes, but especially favour shapes between animal and man: indicating instincts and complexes within the unconscious that are particularly potent for being near to the animal realm (i.e. unconscious forces that are in chaotic form, and can't be assimilated until they have been clearly recognized, distinguished).

Related Symbolism:-
See *ANIMALS*,

DOGS/Wolves, Jackals

The animal instincts as helpful intermediaries between man and nature; or as negative aggression.

Dogs help man hunt the wild animal and round up the domestic animal: So they are symbols of the right inner relationship between man and his animal nature.

Their good nose for scenting unseen prey, or intruders: Intuition, which is aware of other people's inner nature, senses when something is wrong, and is not easily deceived by others.

Negative Symbolism:-
Hunting hounds, or dogs which attack: Male aggression, and often used to represent the masculine aggression of the *ANIMUS* in women.

124

Often associated with the UNDERWORLD and with death: And so represent the forces which hunt and hound the conscious Ego, and tear it to pieces from the depths of the unconscious. Then *DEVOUR* it.

Dogs, wolves or jackals, unseen, but howling eerily at night: The unseen forces of the unconscious which are related symbolically to the spirits of the dead.

The many-headed Cerberus, with snake's tail – and entwined with snakes – guards the THRESHOLD to the UNDERWORLD: Man must brave the animal instincts in hideous negative form and subdue them to his will before he can retrieve other content from the unconscious.

In the same way in the Egyptian underworld Anubis is dog-headed. Artemis, the Huntress, or Hecate with her hounds of death and war; also the witch with her familiar: The dark destructive force of women, when their unconscious male *ANIMUS* is unleashed.

Related Symbolism:-

On the cosmic level, the planets course across the field of fixed stars as if combing the celestial sphere for heavenly quarry, on behalf of the Moon Goddess: The night sky, like the underworld, is symbolic of the unconscious realm where the light of the conscious Ego must be hunted down, so that the individual may plunge deeper into the abyss of nature which is feminine.

DRAGON

The life force. Or Mother *COMPLEX*. The essence of Nature, which manifests in the four *ELEMENTS*. The underlying invisible force that flies and devours like *TIME*.

Negative/Positive Symbolism:-

In negative form the dragon is the ultimate enemy of the HERO: That is, the Conscious Ego, which is attacked from outside and inside. The dragon symbolizes the Earth itself, matter which devours corpses, and swallows the light of conscious life.

The dragon in caves, or the depths of the sea: Is the living embodiment of the *UNDERWORLD*, where it dwells. It is the epitome of the Unconscious in the sense of the extinction of the conscious Ego: the oblivion whether of death or sleep, or unconscious motivations and compulsions.

The abode of the dragon: determines much of the symbolism, whether negative or positive, material or spiritual.

The dragons of the sky or fresh water, sometimes winged or crowned: Creative intuition has transformed the relationship between the Ego and forces of nature. Such dragons were more common in the East where the inner symbolic work of transforming dark unconscious forces into triumphant creative forces was more widely considered the major concern of life.

The dragon is often associated with a particular element, earth, air, fire or water: Which may mean a particular FUNCTION of the mind, such as intuition, emotion, sensation or intellect, is acting negatively and in need of transformation. See the INFERIOR FUNCTION.

St Michael's triumph against the dragon-devil: he succeeds in thrusting these forces into the underworld, thereby repressing rather than transforming them: so the battle continues to rage on the human level.

The final battle has been postponed till the End of Time: The ultimate question is always the same: What is going to happen in the end? Will the dragon devour everything including itself?

Where the dragon guards the treasure: The treasure is the positive conscious aspect of the same life force, as experienced by the Self not the Ego.

Related Symbolism:-

In Alchemy basic matter which has to be transformed into the QUINTESSENCE is the equivalent of the dragon.

See also Mythical MONSTERS.

The monstrous Apep forever attacks the Heroic company of the Sun on their perilous voyage and devours the Moon bit by bit: He is the enemy of light and man's conscious life, which he devours bit by bit till it's all gone.

The SERPENT, Ouroboros, is of the same family.

The Dragon is also a Composite ANIMAL: the confused ingredients of the psyche need to be clearly distinguished and newly related to each other, before the whole can be transformed into the Quintessence.

DRAMA
Especially Greek tragedy evolved from ritual:
Enacts the tension and crisis of man's predicament, which is ultimately resolved only in the Cosmic *SACRIFICE*.

Drama, and in particular Greek tragedy, evolved directly out of the myth and ritual surrounding the death and replacement of the old King, and the cosmic sacrifice of primal man. Like the ritual it expresses the paradox of *DEATH* and *TRANSFORMATION:* a moment without a future is at the same time a major transition.

William Archer diagnoses the central ingredient of all drama as conflict building to crisis and resolution. This is also the structure of dreams and other symbolic material arising from the unconscious.

Through *IDENTIFICATION* with the figures in the drama, the psyche hopes to resolve its conflicts vicariously and thereby avoid much of the personal tension.

The Symbol:-
DIONYSUS, the object of the Cosmic Sacrifice, is also the God of Tragedy, which developed from the ritual verse in his honour.
Book:-
Gaster, T. *Thespis* (1950).

DREAMS
Dreams have provided the key to the personal relevance of other symbolic material.

On the other hand, the rest of symbolic language provides the context and overall structure of the unconscious viewpoint, as it surveys especially man's predicament, the human lot.

The dream, as a symbol: The fleeting ephemeral and illusory quality of the ordinary level of human consciousness, that is Ego consciousness. Like a film, the Ego projects its own experiences which cut man off from reality. Until he can see through the device and withdraw *PROJECTIONS* (see *MAYA*).

Dream/reality, as when Alice is told that she is just part of the Red King's dream. Or in the case of the Japanese poet who dreams of being a butterfly, but on waking can't be sure whether he's not just a butterfly dreaming that he's now a man: Here the dream is used a symbol for re-centring beyond the range of the ordinary conscious Ego.

DWARF
Including goblins, elves and other deformed or stunted figures: **Unconscious impulses that are still only half-formed, primitive. Therefore especially the** *INFERIOR FUNCTION.*

If ignored, slighted, unrecognized, they invariably take revenge: this refers to the effects of repression, which leaves such impulses limited and primitive instead of developing them into something more worth while.

Outright destructive dwarfs and goblins: mischievous, immature, childish impulses. Like children the dwarfs usually can't concentrate for long. Children correspond symbolically to an earlier, more primitive phase of evolution, as do dwarfs.

Helpful dwarfs: little creative impulses, or good ideas that may save a lot of trouble. The valuable playful and childlike side of man (see *CHILD*). This valuable creativity in everyday life just disappears if the fleeting ideas and inner whispers are ignored. Nearer the earth dwarfs are inwardly wise with earth values.

Dwarfs/Giants: The creativity of dwarfs is linked with erotic play (they are little phalluses) but in an inward fantasy way, whereas giants may represent the big, flabby, physical phallus, always hungry for more (see *GIANTS*).

In pointed hats, like witches and magicians in similar hats, and other upward pointing symbols: Impulses, forces aimed at becoming conscious, as the new shoot of a plant is pointed to push up from below the earth, i.e. from the unconscious.

Priapus, son of Dionysus and Aphrodite: the neglected inferior side of the parents' virtues.

The Hunchback of Notre Dame (Victor Hugo) mostly symbolic of inferior feeling function.

See also *RUMPELSTILTSKIN;* and *HOMUNCULUS.*

EARTH

In the psyche, the *FUNCTION* of sensation. Stability.

In the cosmos, substance, matter. All that is solid, well-ordered.

But the earth in symbolism may be held up, supported by a living figure, e.g. Atlas, the elephant or the tortoise: the nature of material existence depends on life, and not the other way round.

The earth is further bound together by a band of life, for example in Egypt the serpent Sito, in Greece the original form of Eros: stresses that the material substance of the world depends for its cohesion and continuity on the forces of life.

For the Ancient World, the earth was under continuous threat of dissolution in the waters or the void that surrounded it: The fear that ordinary common-sense, everyday life will break up in the face of powers of which man is not fully conscious, nor in control, namely the archetypal powers of the unconscious; and on the cosmic level, forces such as black holes or the latent power in the atom (see *CHAOS*).

Earthquakes: Personal *DISINTEGRATION*.

The Earth Goddess: The beneficent side of *NATURE*.

In the Egypt the Earth God, Geb: The listless, awkward, slothful side of material existence.

Related Symbols:-

MUD; NATURE; ELEMENTS; COSMOS; also *VEGETATION*.

EATING/Spitting out

Becoming conscious.

Taking in the outside world, 'digesting' experience, and thereby internalizing it.

Absorbing whatever is eaten. It is the process of life to turn material existence into the inner experience of the psyche, i.e. memories.

But this can work the other way round, as with the symbol of the bird eating its own wings: The flight in the realm of the mind when digested becomes physical and down to earth: there it has its effect.

The Ouroboros serpent – or other symbolic figure – which eats itself: On the cosmic level refers to the closed system of the cosmos, which is continually at work eating itself, both physically, and spiritually, i.e. in re-digesting the experience of itself it becomes increasingly aware of its nature, and transforms that nature in the process.

On the personal level it is the same, because man is a replica or individual reflection of the cosmos, and there is nothing for him to take in except his own life, his own existence, his own nature, but this existence extends beyond his body, and beyond his personal conscious Ego. By taking in, digesting his whole experience of life, he integrates the remote and unconscious parts of his personality.

Eating/being eaten: Conscious swallows up the unconscious and vice versa. Life feeds on death – corpses, meat literally – but also symbolically in the way the conscious present feeds on the unconscious past, which in turn swallows up the present, in an endless cycle of self-renewal (see also Being *DEVOURED*).

Eating live snakes or other abominations: Absorbing features from the underworld and shadow realm which may lead to new insights.

Spitting out: Projecting inner content, *COMPLEXES*, etc. into the outside world.

So spitting out snakes and other slimy creatures (as above): Projecting Shadow content into the outside world.

This is a fairy-tale theme: where the inner mind is given form and substance either as pearls and treasure or as repellent creatures which magically speed up the ordinary process of life by which the inner potential of the person slowly becomes manifest in his or her life style.

Swallowing: May also refer to repression: trying to keep unconscious content from manifesting in the outside world; trying to hold it down in the lower realms of the abdomen. For example, as in the story of *FUNDEVOGEL*.

Creation is sometimes accomplished by spitting forth the world, e.g. Atum created that way as an alternative to masturbation, and the spittle of the gods was mixed with clay to make men in Mesopotamian myth: Creation and rational consciousness are closely linked symbolically (see *CREATION*).

We become conscious by taking in the reality that was

unconsciously spat forth. The two processes reflect each other as with other *CONSCIOUS*/Unconscious material. See *MIRROR*.

Cosmic EGG
The origins of conscious life.
In one account it is laid by four slimy creatures: the fourfold division of the world – as in the four *DIRECTIONS* or the four *ELEMENTS* – in unconscious form:
i. Nothingness – instead of Earth substance.
ii. Nowhere – instead of the air, atmosphere, which symbolically provided a space for man between earth and sky.
iii. Darkness – without the light or warmth of the sun or fire.
iv. The boundless, endless, undefined – in contrast with the waters which symbolically circumscribed the world and gave it shape.
Or the egg may be laid by the goose (see BIRDS, Goose).

The Personal EGO/Shadow
Everyday attitudes in contrast with everything in your psyche that is outside your immediate control.

The Symbols:-
Civilized Man/The Noble Savage.
Conflict with any previous or more primitive phase of evolution, as in the war between Gods and Titans in Greek myth.
Conflict between man and animals, as in BULL, Bullfighting.
The BROTHERS, including OSIRIS/Seth.
Related Symbolism:-
See *ANIMALS, The Animal Man*, *EROS/Thanatos*.

The Ego:
Is one *COMPLEX* within the psyche: that is only one segment or quarter of the whole; but it is the quarter with which we normally identify. See *IDENTIFICATION*.

Especially after the mid-point of life – around forty – people who live exclusively in this segment get a bit limited and boring, rather like home movies. They even bore themselves sometimes.

EGO

The Symbols:-

The HERO, related symbolically to *the SUN*.

Sometimes the Hero is too pig-headed, and won't listen to other voices in the story, or causes trouble by being over active: Indicates a context where the Ego tries to interfere in situations that are outside his domains and beyond his control. Active interference is out of place. Better to be more passive and await developments.

Symbols of the Woman's Ego: *The HEROINE* and *the MOON*.

The woman's heroic role is often in the realm of relationships, bringing people together or reconciling opposing forces: The masculine Ego orders and differentiates the chaos, separates the layers of creation, till the living experience begins to look like a dissected corpse, and the well-ordered cosmos is in danger of turning into a well-structured prison. Then it's time to turn to disorder, which Claudel calls the 'delight of the imagination' – and of the feminine.

The Shadow:

Everything at work in the psyche apart from ordinary waking consciousness.

First experienced as dark and alien or lying on the far side of a barrier, but separated from the Ego as dark is from light: This apparent barrier between conscious and unconscious is an illusion, a trick of the light. And the Shadow is the personal embodiment, or *PERSONIFICATION* of the dark side. Any power or force in the psyche neglected by the conscious Ego remains unconscious and therefore irrational and potentially destructive.

The Symbols:-

The Villain of the story, often in command of the situation because the King (or father) is so weak: which depicts a situation where the unconscious shadow controls a person's fate because his Ego is too ineffectual.

Neglected figures who are exiled, or thrust into the UNDERWORLD but from there manage to cause a lot of trouble: depicts a situation where the absence of certain qualities, which have turned negative as a direct result of being thrust aside, neglected – may be affecting that situation, though nobody can detect how or why.

The Fairy who is not asked to the banquet, or the despised goblin: also come into this category, which is much like the heel of Achilles, one small neglected area through which a whole life can be destroyed.

See also *INFERIOR FUNCTION*.

A Woman's shadow is symbolized by the dark side of the MOON, the rabid dog, the wolf, Hecate: Moon myths are lessons in feminine psychology (Jung).

Just as the Hero has a weak spot – of being too gullible or whatever – a dark side, so the Shadow figure usually has a soft spot. For example he may be supposed to kill the child but leaves an escape route: Indicates one way in which Shadow and Ego each contain something of the other, the seed of transformation into the opposite. Hence the caution against putting too much reliance on one side of the personality only. Related Negative Symbolism:-

The negative aspect of any symbol refers to a particular power or force neglected in the unconscious, and therefore always referring to one aspect of the Shadow.

Ego versus Ego.

   It takes a strong Ego to challenge the Ego: that is, to break down one's limitations and make room for wider experience.

Integrating the Shadow.

   Part of the Shadow, such as its fierce vitality, can be of great value when under conscious control. If you don't keep your eye on the other part, you won't be able to take evasive action.

The Shadow is the modern psychological name for an ancient symbolic figure, the embodiment and epitome of all that is most vicious, brutal and vile in the human character. To get to know this, and to accept responsibility for it, is the difference between being naïve and being experienced. Much of it never can be transformed. It is part of the data of living, which cannot be ignored either; we have to adapt ourselves around it. The malice that is always there, generation after generation, unalterable, ineradicable, was the side consigned to unquenchable hellfire in traditional Christian symbolism. But there is another side of the Shadow – which needs to be distinguished, strand by strand on clear calm nights – which is primitive but full of vigour and other valuable ingredients. It may start foreign, menial, barbaric, or animal – and it's often best treated like an animal – but these qualities connect us with the roots, the instincts of mankind, the whole range of his past experience. This side contains the fierceness of the personality, which can be destructive, but can be very useful in all kinds of situations, when under conscious control, in order to protect what is precious and not have it pushed down by anybody a bit more forceful. It's often essential in order not to be ineffectual; for example in bringing up children, or to avoid becoming henpecked. In the same way a certain amount of cunning is needed in order not to be duped at every devious encounter.

Because the Shadow represents the whole of the Unconscious, it very rightly has a powerful fascination. It is the source of many *COMPULSIONS* and cravings that are of a mixed nature. Fanatical, bigoted delusions may contain within them seeds of lofty ideals, just as the other way round heroic pretensions can hide greed, complacency or the craving for power. Sometimes the Ego needs to be able to preserve and rescue itself from its own Shadow, forewarned and forearmed. And even to find some symbol of sufficient power to counterbalance the fascination of the dangerous demoniac longings. Only accepting full responsibility for the Shadow's cravings, by living constantly in close relationship with it, will you gain any power over it.

Ego/Self:

By extending and growing into the Shadow realm – both its feminine and masculine sides – the Ego expands and grows into the whole potential *SELF*.

The Ego is first experienced as the only and all important centre of consciousness within. But once the rest of the psyche has been recognized, it is as if the limited Ego realm is shattered, and the inner nucleus becomes the True Self.

The Symbols:

The seed, the acorn, or the egg: The Self emerges from the Ego as the bird emerges from the Egg.

The Ego and the Self are as different from each other as egg and bird, or acorn and oak tree; yet they are also the same.

For this reason the whole later development of the Self

depends initially on the strong development of the Ego, which is as vital for each child now, as it was for mankind at the youthful stage of its development. In symbolic terms a rotten egg or mouldy acorn cannot produce a fine bird or a magnificent tree.

The Ego is initially a temporary product, or personification of the Self. Just as the egg and acorn were first the products of bird and oak, as well as turning into them, so the Self gives birth to the Ego, which then grows back into the Self, but renewing and transforming itself on the way.

EGYPTIAN MYTH
Is full of pristine archetypal symbols.

The Ancient Egyptians were fundamentally idealists, anticipating Platonic ideas in their conviction that the mind can penetrate beyond appearances to reality. Living closer to their own unconscious mind than we do, their literature is full of archetypal patterns and figures in stark uncontaminated form. Most especially their cult of the dead reveals their familiarity with the working of the unconscious soul, expressed in symbolic terms, which are the only terms available for the ultimately indescribable inner realities of man and hidden working of nature. See *EMBALMING*, and also *DEATH*.

Myth, ritual and the visual arts all combined to express symbolic meanings. Their temples were images of the Cosmos in the form of the primordial mound, the nucleus of nature in man and the universe. The dawn was identified with New Year's Day, and the beginning of the world; when the eye of Atum (the eye of consciousness) is sent out alone into the vast primeval ocean, searching. The Word is another symbol for the creative idea that brings form and order into matter.

The relationship between life and the cosmos in which man finds himself is reflected in the idea of the form of each entity being supplied by the Ka, or soul.

The kings and the rulers of the provinces were sons or incarnations of the Gods over the same regions, which emphasized the connection between the religious sphere and the human.

However, Egyptian myth has barely been investigated for its relevance to the life of the psyche, partly because the themes of Greek myth, and fairy-tales, etc. are more familiar, but partly by accident simply because nobody has devoted as much of his attention to the archetypal themes as they appear in Egyptian myth, as Jung did for similar themes in Alchemy.

Related Symbolism:-

OSIRIS/Seth; EMBALMING; LOTUS.

Books:-

Rundle Clark, R. T. *Myth and Symbol in Ancient Egypt* (1959).

Wallis Budge, E. A. *From fetish to God in Ancient Egypt*, 1934, shows how many of the main foundations of religious ideas (that persist to this day) were already laid in Ancient Egypt, probably as early as the Pyramid Age. For example Incarnation, Trinity, in that an Ancient Egyptian would not have worshipped a Pantheon of gods, but only his particular family God, the God of his Province, and the High God. The

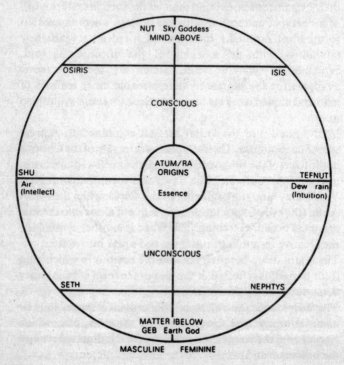

Power of the Word which effects Creation – linking the conscious mind with the form of material existence.

The Nine Gods (Ennead) of Heliopolis, the offspring of Atum, image of the original bisexual germ or seed of life, who gave birth to Shu and Tefnut by his lonely but pleasurable emission. These two were locked in embrace until they were divided and gave birth to sky and air, who in turn gave birth to the next four, Osiris, Isis, Seth and Nephtys. In the diagram they are arranged in a typical symbolic pattern suggested by their order of birth and their nature, so as to show their possible relationship with other pantheons and *PATTERNS* in archetypal symbolism: depicting the stages by which the One Power generates an indefinite variety of objects and beings.

The ELEMENTS

The sum total of the universe including man. The positive forces but also the destructive forces, when out of control.

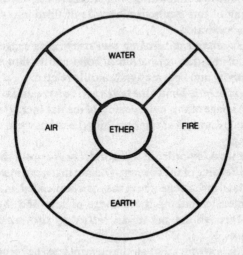

Everything in the material universe, including man, can be divided into solid (Earth), liquid (Water), and Vapour (Air), and these three are transformed one into the other, through the agency of Fire (energy): In man solid food is digested into the bloodstream and turned into the breath of life, energy, as well

as invisible thoughts, memories, images. In this way nature corresponds to human nature. In their context Earth, Air and Water are aspects of spatial reality while Fire symbolizes the process of time.

Liquid is the intermediary state between the solid and vaporous: Similarly within the psyche there is a state between rigid attitudes and empty vacuous imaginings, where the life of man can be blended with the material of the cosmos, affecting it, changing it, perfecting it.

Liquid is further related to potential forms lying in the unconscious.

Vapour, steam, gases, smells, all that rise and dissolve invisibly into the sky – like the DJINN from the bottle: The mind and imagination of man – as well as his memories, like dissolving traces of former actions – together form an ethereal, or psychic, body: the living organism in close relationship with the cosmos. *CLOUDS* of smoke or steam are sometimes used as intermediaries or heralds between this realm of pure action and the solid material world. Also see *ALCOHOL*, which shares something of this symbolism because distilled into vapour, and reconcentrated.

A body sweating and breaking into steam: also suggests the process of the transformation of solid matter into energy: work activity and heat are symbolically related.

The flow of breath: Unites the *INNER* and outer realm, as well as being an image of the invisible flow of mental energy which is of the same duration as our breathing, i.e. stops when we stop breathing.

Fire: the working-order of the world, the energy of the body and the life force of the cosmos. The fact that it can melt solids (e.g. metals) into a state where they can be blended, may have contributed to making it an image of love and therefore union. Through the sun it was related to *TIME* which also transforms.

Ether: The mere fact that all the elements can be turned into each other, indicated that they must be of the same essence at root. Beyond the appearances lay the quintessence (see *ESSENCE/Existence*).

In some combinations the elements are incompatible (e.g. as when water puts out fire) but these same two elements combine to foster the growth of plants as warmth of the sun and rain: This became an image of the way the opposite elements of life could be mutually destructive, or wholly productive of a third principle, if combined in a different way, as part of the process of living. See *UNION* of Opposites.

Related Symbolism:-

In most ancient mythologies the elements were personified as gods, who were then given particular elements for their domains. For example, in Mesopotamia there was the Earth-mother under various names, the sky-god (Anu), the water-god (Ea), and the god of the storm representing fire and life force. In the same way in the ancient *EGYPTIAN* pantheon at Heliopolis, the original life force divided itself up into the elements. And in Greece three major gods, the brothers Zeus, Poseidon and Hades, divided their realms between air, water and earth.

They are also related to the symbolism of the *ZODIAC* and *I CHING*. And every other system of symbolism that attempts to depict the structure of the universe in relation to the nature of man. For example, see *PATTERNS*.

Positive/Negative Symbolism:-

The Earth: Gives birth, provides, but also devours everyone born.

Air: The breath of life, but also the gale of destruction.

Fire: Is near to the highest good as light and heat of the world, and so a symbol of conscious life, but also scorches and withers.

Water: The beneficent rains, the destructive floods.

Together they form the sum total of the universe, with its positive and dark negative sides.

Fire and Air: Often depict emotion and intellect as the more active conscious (therefore rational) of the four *FUNCTIONS* of the mind.

Earth and Water: as sensation and intuition are considered more passive, low-lying and unconscious faculties in man.

Note:-

Though this does vary from individual to individual and collectively for different societies, but this basic distinction may be valid, and help explain why water sometimes depicts the feeling-realm, i.e. when feeling is more passive and unconscious.

ELEMENTS

In traditional medicine rather than psychology, the elements:
Used to be associated with the inner man via the humours (choleric, sanguine, phlegmatic, melancholic). Just as there was a perpetual balance between the elements in the outside world, in spite of continuous flux and change, so in the inner realm.

Personal Symbolism:-

Standing in the sea, with your feet on the bottom, and your head out in the air: can be a symbolic experience of the unity of man with his environment, in the inter-relationship of the solid, liquid and ethereal realms in nature and human nature. Simple actions of this kind can be satisfying at a very physical, unconscious yet symbolic level. (For example, compare *JOURNEYS/Walking*.)

EMBALMING

Distinguishing between Ego consciousness and Life itself. Then reuniting individual life with the undivided life of the Cosmos.
See *DISINTEGRATION/Integration*.

Inscribed within the pyramids can be found the whole process of individuation. But even when the realm of the dead is interpreted as the present realm of the psyche, it isn't easy to grasp the value and importance to the Ancient Egyptians of mummification, which arouses in us only disgust or derision, largely because of our own lack of adjustment towards death and towards the unconscious.

The ritual of transforming the king into an Osiris, and giving him his lion-body, involved distinguishing the Ka-soul from the formless Ba-soul, as well as separating the corpse from the entrails (the viscera) so that they could be re-combined in incorruptible form: Reflects the spiritual disciplines, of cutting off sense-experience, and inner images, to reside in the unconscious realm of being, at one with the stars of the night sky which the Ba-soul went to join. Such spiritual disciplines are an intensification of the ordinary experience of living on four different planes:-

i. The intuition of pure being (the Ba), just life, just existence without quality or limitation.

ii. To this the intellect adds form (the Ka); provides images.

140

iii. This, in turn, is distinct from the gut-reaction to life; the feelings (the viscera).

iv. Finally the physical experience of the world (the body). *The entrails were further subdivided into lungs, intestines, stomach and liver; and protected by the four sons of time, who represented the four directions of space:* Each aspect of life, each plane of being, can be further subdivided in relation to the others. But especially moods, feelings, may arise in response to physical events, to others' moods, to intellectual stimulus (or lack of it), or to intuitions of being.

Note:-

In this way the experience of the single individual grows increasingly manifold and complex, and this is reflected in structures of symbolism such as, for instance, the *I CHING*.

Related Symbolism:-

Turning lead into gold for *ALCHEMY*.

Also *BODY*, with its organs as images of the Complexes in the psyche; *DEATH*, as a symbol.

ENDURING/Ephemeral

Continuous *CHANGE* **and** *TRANSFORMATION* **keeps everything much the same as it was. This is the means by which the Cosmos manifests the principle of Enduring.**

Similarly man not only endures but evolves through casting off old bodies and making new ones.

The major concern of symbolism is with the eternal images, the patterns of reality, and sequences of life, the distilled essence, the enduring core which doesn't change, and the way these essences are related to the flickering phenomena of life. For Coleridge the dimension of myth was The Vast; it is measureless, unbounded time: time as it is spread out in front of the mind without any seam between past or future, which both stretch away endlessly.

When this realm gets lost, or goes dead, because it has sunk back into unconsciousness, then it turns negative and threatens every aspect of ordinary everyday life, which, by contrast, flickers along in strict chronological order. It threatens the cohesion of society, and the meaningful pursuit of individual destinies. Human life, robbed of vision, becomes degraded and miserable.

Once the symbol no longer stirs the unconscious, it either has to be abandoned or transformed. But when looking at traditional symbolism, it is axiomatic that it was meaningful and mattered at the time: it roused the deepest intuitions, and referred to whatever was of the utmost importance to the individual and to society. Whatever was being expressed symbolically, was held in the highest value.

These intuitions and values were expressed in symbolic form, often living symbols from nature, because mere explanations are ineffectual. They fail to make contact with the unconscious depths of the personality, which aren't an esoteric extra dimension at all, but the brute bodily existence, everyday physical reality. This is how symbols can affect us while ideas and dogmas may leave us cold.

The Symbols:-

SERPENT/Pole; Or NUMBERS, One/Many; Or the Cosmic AXIS; The CENTRE, and all such related symbolism; PATTERNS, the Spiral; The Pole STAR, and wheeling constellations.

EROS

The Archetype of Relationship.

   The principle of attraction and involvement.

It is the symbol of the forces that bind together: the force that locks relationships, from sexual compulsions to yearning for the unattainable.

Originally Eros was the cord or serpent that bound the ideal world together, before it broke up into this world (Empedocles):
As such, on the personal level, Eros represents the vessel of transformation.

The binding force of the cosmos is necessary to bring about the process of evolution in nature. So on the personal level, if the vessel is broken, no transformation is possible. Such opposites as masculine and feminine cannot be held together unless the cord which binds them is strong enough: unless the vessel is of sufficient radiant power; unless the archetype of Eros himself is active in the life of the individual – under whatever guise or symbol, in whatever form: for example, friends grappled to your heart with 'hoops of steel'.

Eros/Pothos: Pothos represented the idealized, internalized side of love, often connected with the birth of those wandering heroes who search for the unattainable, the Transcendent (such as Prometheus, Ulysses or Jason) through the mysteries of Samothrace, where he was embodied as eternal *YOUTH*, beside the changeless features of old age (i.e. Puer and Senex).

Eros/Psyche: Tells the story of the longing of the mind of man for a god which it cannot see. Once man glimpses the object of his yearning consciously he is punished for it. (See *HEROINE*.)

Note:-

There are many tales on this theme of catching sight of gods and goddesses, and in each of them, man is trying to get a clear conscious view of the forces of nature which are ultimately hidden. The story of *BEAUTY AND THE BEAST* derives from the same theme; the punishment is death but it is mitigated, and transformed into erotic love at the end.

Eros/Thanatos. Love-gods in contrast with death-gods: Man's life stands between these contraries of love, birth, life and sickness, old age, death and decomposition, and in the depths of the unconscious the two are intertwined. For example, masturbation has been found to evoke fantasies of death. And in the unconscious, values are reversed: Eros becomes over simplistic and cosy – as well as over-populating the world. Doom, deception, misery and quarrels also have their place and a right to exist, especially when they counterbalance facile stereotypes of self-improvement.

Eros/Logos or Eros/Apollo: The contrast between the archetype of relationships, for which women may live and die, and the archetype of ideas for which men may live and die (see *OPPOSITES*).

Note:-

The Eros side of life is always represented by a male god, presumably as the more suitable object of pursuit for women. Whereas the Muse (of ideas) and Wisdom are both feminine for contrary reasons.

Related Symbolism:-

All male love gods: compare *Tammuz, Adonis, Frey.*

Kama, the Hindu God of love, who rides a sparrow armed with bow and arrow.

For incarnations of enlightened spiritual love, as the binding force for the individual, society and the cosmos: Buddha, Jesus, Krishna.

ESSENCE/Existence. The Quintessence
The idea of the essence combines the original seed with the enduring nucleus of life.

The sperm-drop and ovum appropriate material from the world around them – bread and potatoes – to form the man; and then shed them in the form of the corpse.

In the cosmos it is equally the life-principle which gives form to the material chaos, existing more as a thread or force through time, than in any bulky way in space.

DEPRESSION denies existence, possibly in the unconscious hope of grasping the essence of life, which is related to its meaning: the essential point.

The Quintessence, as fifth ELEMENT, from which the others derive, is another expression for the single archetypal life force, which then divides into air and fire, water and earth – in the psyche into intellect and intuition, feeling and senses – and subdivides.

Symbols attempt, in a makeshift way, to describe the patterns of this force. This is the difference between the Tree as a symbol, and a tree simply as a part of existence, for example.

Personal Symbolism:-

The Individual *MYTH* is related to the essence of a particular life, while the life story tells of existence.

EXILE
The dominant Ego rejects an aspect of its own larger Self; throws it out into the unconscious represented by the wilderness beyond the bounds of its own territory.

The Ego is as possessive of its realm as any other tyrant and wants to remain the undisputed ruler. As a result, it always lives in fear of being overthrown.

Newly-born children, whether children of the Gods in myth, or of the king in fairy-tales: Often represent this threat of new unconscious conflict, and so are banished – if they aren't devoured, swallowed back into the unconscious.

For contrast see *ABANDONED*.

Note:-

In the hands of the Kabbalists, and Jewish exiles, whether from Israel or Spain, exile became a meaningful symbol of man's lot and destiny: and reflects especially the cosmic *SPLIT* of Masculine and Feminine. For them this accounted for the harsh masculinity of the wrathful God of their tràdition who had withdrawn and become divided from his feminine side, the Shekhinah.

EXTRAVERT/Introvert
Energy flows in a different direction for each.

For the extravert the flow of energy is primarily towards the world of people and things, but this involvement may equally be negative, against the world, and still a part of extraversion. *The introvert* draws the world in, absorbs it into his own inner realm of images and values.

But whichever way the energy flows there is no breaking the relationship, interaction between cosmos and psyche which are interdependent.

For Jung the psyche has three modes of activity.

    i. *UPWARDS/Downwards*: Up towards the transcendent spirit and downwards, penetrating matter (see *ABOVE/Below*).

    ii. *CONSCIOUS/Unconscious.*

    iii. *EXTRAVERT/Introvert*, on the intermediate horizontal or human level of existence (see *PATTERN*).

The contrast between absorbing, concentrating and spiritualizing the data of the cosmos (which is certainly related to the process of forming symbols and making myth,) ideally needs to be balanced with an equal and opposite flow of energy out into the Cosmos.

Personal Symbolism:-

In *The Perennial Philosophy* (1945) Aldous Huxley described the extravert as dreading the loneliness of solitary confinement, while the introvert has an equal and opposite loathing for the barrack room. In the same way the extravert dreads dying of some insidious inner disease, while the introvert lives in dread of blows from the outside world, culminating in a fatal accident. But each has the other alternative personality ready to take over from the Shadow realm.

The Symbols:-

Fleas, rabbits and other creatures who survive by breeding and pouring out into life: The extravert.

The hedgehog or the elephant with their strong defence mechanisms: The introvert.

The whole symbolism of *Day and Night*, as related to *Summer and Winter*, in the cycle of time and the seasons includes provision for a symbolic balance between *INNER* and Outer factors.

Most symbols arise from and refer to the neglected unconscious inner realm, with its inflowing force from the cosmos, to balance the conscious extravert bias of the dominant collective view. But by contrast, in the East where the inner journey has been taken more seriously and the bias has often been introvert, commonplace symbols of responsibility towards the outward extravert side of life have become highly charged, such as the washing of a bowl, the movement of a frog.

But as always with symbolism it is the balanced *UNION* of opposites, the two-way flow of energy in this case, which is the aim and goal.

Don Quixote/Sancho Panza: Introvert/extravert. Also symbolic of Mind/Body, Spirit/Flesh.

FABLES

For the most part are consciously devised *ALLEGORY* without true symbolic content.

For example with Krylov's fable of the stone: it complains about the shower of rain which gets all the praise, although it just comes and goes while he's endured in that particular field for years and years, the moan of the worthy plodder – a reversal of the hare and tortoise. As products of the imagination the stone and the rain do have echoes of symbolism; in this case, the archaic intractable forces of life in contrast with change and transformation.

But see Robert Louis Stevenson's *Fables* for some modern adult myths.

See also *INFERIOR FUNCTION*, for symbolism of *Lion/Mouse* and *Hare/Tortoise* (Aesop).

FAIRY-TALES
Speak directly from the unconscious and appeal directly to it.

There is a long tradition of passing down the living wisdom of the human race in story form, and fairy-tales especially seem to be related to the wisdom and insights of *ALCHEMY*, which preserved and elaborated more ancient symbolic traditions. They reduce ancient mythical themes to more human proportions, and relate them to everyday concerns.

Fairy-tales reflect typical phases in the struggle of every man to fulfil his potential and achieve individuality. Most of them are fairly superficial and don't get much further than confronting the personal Shadow (see *EGO*/Shadow).

Starting with the device, *'Once upon a time'* – which means once and for all, or outside time – in many different ways they make it very plain that they are really about the enduring essences and forces of nature rather than particular instances in everyday existence. In this they balance the collective conscious attitude, which is always inclined to repress this realm because it threatens the conscious Ego. Fairy-tales speak directly from the unconscious and appeal directly to it: anything in life which can't be grasped by the intellect strives for realization through symbolism, and fairy-tales are one outlet for this symbolism.

Most of the stories would be quite absurd if given an ordinary historical setting. The figures in them are plainly products of the imagination, figures of fantasy rather than figures-of-flesh. Marie Louise von Franz has derived very interesting insights just by counting them and noticing such points as how many of the figures are male and how many female at the beginning of the story, and comparing this with the end. For example, there may be four figures at the beginning, predominantly of one sex, and this imbalance between male and female attitudes is causing sickness or misery of some sort; but the story ends with a double marriage indicating that

147

the balance of the psyche is restored (see *MASCULINE/ FEMININE*).

Fairy godmothers: elemental feminine forces of emotion, relationships, values.

The fourth, youngest, weakest figure, who often redeems the situation: the weak *INFERIOR* Function which gets neglected, left behind in the unconscious but can be the source of renewal for the psyche.

Each tale;
   May depict a whole life.

Fairy-tales usually dwell on themes of urgent social importance, where the need is greatest, and are the popular version of symbolism.

One important clue to understanding them is that the events described are drastically compressed. A struggle with the Shadow, which may be spread over ten years in life, can be told in one short incident – as in a dream. A longing that would take an ambitious lifetime to fulfil is a wish granted instantly – though there may be no chance of another *WISH*, precisely because life has run out.

Particular Examples:-

See *'BEAUTY AND THE BEAST', CINDERELLA, RUMPELSTILTSKIN, SLEEPING BEAUTY.*

See also *DWARF, WITCH.*

Books:-

Franz, M. L. von *An Introduction to the Interpretation of Fairy-tales* (1970); *Shadow and Evil in Fairy-tales* (1974); *Problems of the Feminine in Fairy-tales* (1972); and *Individuation in Fairy-tales* (1977).

The FATES – The Moerae or Parcae
The whole sequence of life. Life, is the realm of the Feminine.

There are three fates, Clotho who spins the thread of life, related to ORIGINS and the new moon; Lachesis, the full moon, who measures the length of it with her rod or staff; and Atropos (atrophy) who cuts it with her shears, who is the moon as an old crone (see *MOON*). Their symbolic significance is perfectly explicit, but sometimes there is just the thread or the spinning wheel in a tale which makes sense only when referred back to the fates themselves.

By some accounts even Zeus could not change their decrees: The particular masculine powers of thought, etc., are not relevant in the feminine realm of life.

Related Symbolism:-

Brahma, Vishnu, and Shiva, as Creator, Preserver, and Destroyer in the Hindu Pantheon.

Spring, Summer, Winter, in a three SEASON year.

Compare also *The FURIES.*

FAUST

The story of an ordinary man living by his unconscious, guided by the symbolic material arising from that side of his nature, without the usual conscious aims or strictures.

Faust's pact with the Devil: He becomes bound to unconscious impulses. On the other side, by abandoning conscious striving he is carefree, childlike, without clear aim (see CHILD). By ordinary conscious standards he becomes an idler, a day-dreamer, a seducer, a magician, a traitor and a murderer. Yet this will leave a trace that endures throughout the ages, decided by the forces of the underworld which are of constant interest to mankind.

God/Mephistopheles: The light and the dark side of the masculine psyche: the Self and the Shadow. The dark side (the Shadow), provides the way to deeper layers of the unconscious.

The Mothers: The feminine realm of Nature, untrodden, unknown; an underground world entered through a cave, the depths of unconscious life.

By entering this other world, Faust is to become master of the two worlds, two kingdoms: these are the two worlds that are so much at the centre of all symbolism, the conscious and the unconscious, the alive and the ghostly, the ephemeral and the eternal, the world of substance and the world of symbol, the appearances and the essence.

The key: The secret of crossing into the unconscious is inextricably linked with sexuality. Not refined emotion but basic animal sexuality which is the physical cause of the endurance of the race, and this physical side has an inner counterpart in basic sexual fantasy.

In the underworld are the beautiful ever youthful Helen; the boy of ecstasy, Euphorion; and Mephistopheles in the mask of a hag: Echoes a recurring theme in symbolism of the juxtaposition of Youth and Age, Masculine and Feminine. Related, all four form the complete cycle of life, taken as a whole, ever the same.

The ultimate and unattainable goal: The curious elusive quality of the realm of Mothers, refers to difficulties of making real and physical what is vague, and mostly lost altogether in the depths of the unconscious – such as early memories of our lives, our life in the womb.

Incest: As a fantasy, the image of reaching the Mother is insufficient. Only the actual and physical union of mother and son, down the ages, makes for eternity, and this is the terrifying symbol, which dogs symbolism – ever since its rebirth centred on the Oedipus complex. Although the union of mother and son is inadequate, unless realized physically and sexually, nevertheless like all symbols it becomes merely ludicrous if mistaken literally (as incest in the afternoon). But the way towards this ultimate physical union of male and female, of youth and age, of mother and son, is itself the goal, and must not be given up until union with the Anima is complete, real and alive.

Faust salvages a tripod with a circle on top, from the realm of the Mothers: The tripod seems more convincing as an ultimate source of power when related to the symbol of the Ankh cross of Ancient Egypt, for example. It implied the bringing together of the three worlds of mind, flesh and unconscious; the raising of the unconscious realm to physical reality. See *PATTERNS*.

Note:-

The impression left by the drama is that the struggle with the unconscious is solitary, but with fleeting glimpses of the throbbing reality of the cosmos and its figures, which makes for inward self-sufficiency.

Related Symbolism:-

See *MOTHER/and son; YOUTH/and age; MASCULINE/Feminine; DEMETER/Persephone.*

Books:-
Groddeck, G. *Exploring the Unconscious* (1949).
Goethe, J. W. von, *Faust* (1808 and 1832).

FISH
The most precious content of life which can only be appreciated through the realm of the emotions *(Sea)* or intuition *(Freshwater)*.

As symbols themselves are products of emotion and intuition, so fish can be symbolic of the world of symbols, in contrast with the purely materialistic earthbound approach to life. Fish are the treasures from the waters, which in general symbolize the psyche in contrast with the body: the unconscious rather than the ordinary conscious.

Sacred meals of bread, wine and fish: integrating the material realm (*bread*), the emotional love (*wine*), and the spiritual (*fish*). This was part of the mystery cults which grew up in opposition to the dominant intellectual consciousness of the Classical Age, and acted as a balance to it.

Negative Symbolism:-
The destructive monsters of the deep such as Leviathan or the Kraken, or sharks with gaping jaws, etc.: The destructive passions, or repressed emotions.

The jellyfish:
   A symbol of the highest significance.

As a round fish, it is linked with the symbolism of the Circle (see *PATTERNS*). Eight tentacles link it with the eightfold wisdom – the eight steps between birth and death that lead from earth to heaven, or the eight centres of consciousness, the *Ogdoad*. Therefore the symbol of that which is of the highest significance, namely the Quintessence in Nature; or the true centre of the individual, the Self.

The fact that the jellyfish could burn (sting) from under water added to its significance as the union of fire and water – it was alleged to be able to cook what it caught before eating it. It was the radiant and radial star of the sea.

Negative Symbolism:-
The unquenchable spark of lechery which could not be put out even under water.

151

FISH

One species is called Medusa – who was given snakes for hair as a punishment for her lechery: the creative centre (sexuality) can also be a source of destructive forces. But these conceal further creative powers – of *Pegasus who sprang from within Medusa* (see *GORGON*).

Book:-

Jung, C. G. *Aion*.

The fisherman,
such as the Fisher King in the Grail legends:
   The wise man, who can bring up the treasures of the deep, from the depths of the mind.

Fishermen and their wives are common in fairy-tales, with this significance: bringing back the treasure presents as much difficulty as reaching it. This is where Melville's Captain Ahab in *Moby Dick* comes to grief; also Hemingway's old man of the sea who brings back the bones only, which won't feed anyone.

Fish's eyes:
   Eyes into the unconscious.

Different self-governing complexes peering out at the dim domains of the psyche.

Related Symbolism:-

Like LIGHTNING, the HARE, and SNAKES – fish also dart about: and therefore symbolize flashes of intuition. The intuition leaps swiftly and takes in a wider field of vision than the one-tracked intellect.

The FROG, also leaps, but is distinctive in that it can move from the depths of water to dry land, and back. Its form, not unlike an embryo child, links it with the new-born Self: inner creativity, and the sexual drive turned inwards, sublimated, and roaming through the fresh-water ponds of the psyche.

FLAGS
Depict symbols of union.

The fascination of flags is largely symbolic. They usually contain ancient symbols for the *UNION* of opposites, such as the cross or the circle, since their object is often to unite. But

the designs also express the distinctness of the different factions that are related by being placed on the same flag, though not merged. As with quartering of coats of arms.
Flagpoles and flags, sometimes appear in symbolic literature: as the epitome of the symbol which, for example, had sunk out of view in *'SLEEPING BEAUTY'*.

The FLOOD
Devastates the ephemeral forms, but doesn't destroy force.

It is a manifestation of force, energy, and leads to regeneration.
A return of the whole of nature to the uterine waters, the womb, and rebirth from it.
Particular Examples:-
Heroes of the various accounts of the flood:
Utnapishtim, in the Mesopotamian story of Gilgamesh; *Noah*, in Hebrew tradition; *Deucalion*, in Greek myth.

FLYING. Wings
Transformation into the spiritual realm.

The powers of the mind, which was always symbolically capable of raising material forces into the realm of pure energy, action, with an increase of power rather than a loss of it.
Note:-
The fact that the symbol is not a fantasy at loggerheads with reality but an expression of the forces of reality could be illustrated here by noticing that the powerful symbol of man's flight has overcome the objective 'impossibility' of it. The *WISH* has overcome the insurmountable barrier. The imagination or vision has overcome intellectual scepticism which ran high in Victorian times. Even H. G. Wells, in *The Sleeper Awakes*, could not envisage anything like Concorde. In symbolism the way that the material world changes, adapts, and transforms as a result of the symbolic work and in accord with it, is a consequence – even a by-product – of the work itself. For this work, the inner resources have to be discovered and related, linked up: the resources of mankind

in general, the collective consciousness, as well as unconscious, the intuitive faculties as well as the physical. *Wings:* are needed to tackle the elusive qualities of the inner psyche. As for example in the fights with the *GORGON Medusa, or the Chimera*. It takes a winged spirit to grasp the inner emotions, motivations etc.

Related symbolism:-

See *ICARUS; BIRDS; ELEMENTS, volatile steam, gases.*

FOOL

The *CHILD* in adult form, that is, the child within the adult.

Spontaneous and genuine like a child. Often the *INFERIOR* function, which is stunted, and *DWARFISH*, but nearer to the unconscious, so hence its value.

The king's fool, who was tolerated and appreciated whatever he did or said, as in 'King Lear' for example: The right relationship between the mature side of the personality, and the inferior unconscious side, which has to be lived inwardly by everyone else. This inner realm was represented by the *KING* and his court.

The fool or idiot has often been taken as a symbol of spiritual wisdom in contrast with worldly sophistication, as, for example, by the Sufis: Which accords with their deeper understanding of the unconscious hidden side of life.

The Harlequin, an Italian version, is often supposed to be invisible: that is unconscious, spiritual.

Harlequin and Columbine: The Shadow and Anima. See *EGO*/Shadow and *ANIMUS*/Anima.

His chequered suit: The interplay of *OPPOSITES*.

Clowns: Often play either the under-developed childlike emotions – found more in men – or the inferior intellect, which is ignorant or pig-headed – more common in women, traditionally.

The Fool in the Tarot pack, the joker of ordinary playing cards: Is basically as above, the irrational and unconscious, with all its potential for transformation. However other symbolism has been packed in.

FOX/Wolf
A primitive form of *TRICKSTER*. **Animal intuition.**

Just as animals refer to the animal instincts in general, so the particular animals refer to particular aspects. The fox represents intuition at a basic animal level, animal cunning. The highest spiritual aspirations (i.e. wisdom, speculation, subtlety) are trapped or cursed in animal form, caught in the unconscious, and remaining primitive. The *ANIMUS*, or masculine side of women, is often a crude form of this mercurial, lightning spirit.

Negative Symbolism:-

The Wolf: The dark side of aspiration is devouring greed for substitutes that never quite satisfy, which results in cold resentment. Apollo and Mercurius as Figures of Intuition, both have this dark negative form. And the Werewolf, like everything else associated with *HORROR* stories and films, is an image of the moonlit realm of Intuition gone badly wrong – that is, misused and warped.

But the wolf can also refer to the dark side of the feminine unconscious in general, that is, of the Ancestral Mother.

For example in 'Little Red Riding Hood' the grandmother/ wolf: The positive/negative aspects of the same symbol. One changes into the other and back again: the grandmother is inside the wolf and vice versa.

FROG
Fertility, creativity, a vital impulse.

The spirit of nature, whether through sexuality giving birth to actual children, or inwardly giving birth to creative work (see also *FISH*).

So the frog often appears in fairy-tales as herald of change to initiate new developments. As a symbol of transition from land to water, the liquid realm of the psyche where transformation is possible, it refers to *TRANSFORMATION*: potential embryo turns into a Prince (Animus).

Frog/Toad: The earthbound basic materialist attitudes, symbolized by the toad, lack the power to transform, in contrast with the frog above.

FROG

Note:-

Toads are ugly enough anyway, but an irrational aversion for them, whether there is actually one in the garden or not, could include this symbolic element, a fear of being stuck in the material realm without developing the creative imagination, to transform your life.

The FUNCTIONS of the mind or psyche

All symbols give visible form to the invisible forces of life: most especially the inner *PATTERNS* and workings of the psyche, which determine both the *SEQUENCE* of life as well as man's experience of the *COSMOS*.

There are Four main Functions in the psyche; each approaches reality from a different point of view and with a different question. Each grasps a different part of reality.

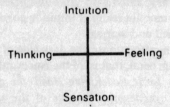

The Symbols:-

The Four DIRECTIONS.

The Four ELEMENTS.

The Purusha, who was three-quarters in heaven (i.e. thinking, feeling and intuition) and a quarter on earth (i.e. sensation). See Cosmic *MAN*.

The Four Pillars of the World, or *the Four Wheels of a Chariot.* (see *NUMBERS, Four.*)

The ARCHETYPES.

The Four SEASONS, which depict *the Four PERIODS* of Man's life, relate the pattern of the psyche to the sequence of Man's life, suggesting that the physical body and senses are developed in Childhood, then a Woman's Feeling and a Man's Thinking, and vice versa in the third period, with Intuition left for the last phase of life. See also *ZODIAC*, for a more complex and therefore realistic scheme.

Related Symbolism:-

Most symbols can be referred to the Cosmos, the human society, and also the inner psyche. So in relation to the psyche, for example, *ABOVE/Below* refers to Intuition/Sensation functions.

The content to be retrieved from the *UNDERWORLD* is very often related to a function of the mind lost in unconsciousness, and so acting erratically and inadequately. *MASCULINE/Feminine*, in terms of the Functions, may refer to Thinking/Feeling. Although the man may be the Feeling type and the woman the Intellect, it is important for the two to complement each other in a relationship rather than share the same deficiency. This is also true for larger groups and companies. See Personal Symbolism on page 160 for more precise descriptions of the different types.

When referring to the psyche, the *CENTRE* and related symbolism would refer to the *TRANSCENDENT FUNCTION*.

Extravert/Introvert Functioning of the Psyche:

Each of the Four Functions above can operate in an *EXTRAVERT* manner, with energy flowing towards the outside world; or an introvert manner with the energy flowing towards the *INNER* realm.

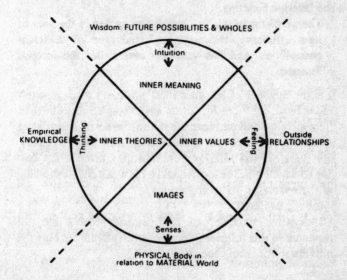

FUNCTIONS
Conscious/Unconscious.

Each function has a further possibility of operating in a positive *CONSCIOUS* rational way, under the control of the will. Or in a negative unconscious way, acting autonomously outside the control of the conscious will.

And the evidence so far suggests that these two major factors, Extravert/Introvert and Conscious/Unconscious, are interwoven in each individual according to a pattern.

The dominant conscious function will have a particularly weak counterpart in the area directly opposite to it in the diagram on page 157. So the thinking person may have feeble atrophied feelings and vice versa, while the intuitive may have a poor relationship with the physical realm of sensation. But also if the dominant conscious function is extravert, its particular weakness will be in the introvert area of the opposite function.

So that the person whose life is dominated by the archetype of Knowledge, in the diagram, may be particularly weak on Values, and vice versa, whereas, for example, the introvert intuitive who sees meanings and takes in whole patterns of life at a glance, may stumble over the particular awkward details of material existence right in front of him.

The Inferior Function.

The problems of life are inclined to gather in the area of least efficiency, the most neglected area of the eight possibilities. And this area has been called the Inferior Function.

It is the bugbear of life, just what you can't manage, can't understand, can't do. It is often easier to pick this out than those strong dominant features of the character. These latter are sometimes taken for granted since they come so easily, and therefore the Inferior Function may provide the best clue to which type the individual is: his weak points showing up the nature of his strong points.

Symbolic Material:-

All negative symbols, all dark sinister forces are not unrelated to this Inferior Function which affects not only the individual but whole societies.

But there is another side to the Inferior Function: just because it is that side of life most deeply buried in the unconscious, it provides the means of discovering the unconscious, of relating conscious and unconscious, and is therefore the means of completing the personality. See *DWARFS, FOOL*, or *RUMPELSTILTSKEN*. It is a source of extraordinary renewal, especially in the second part of life. See *INFERIOR FUNCTION* especially for other relevant symbols.

Mythological/Logical.

The Symbolic World View in contrast with the Intellectual materialist world view.

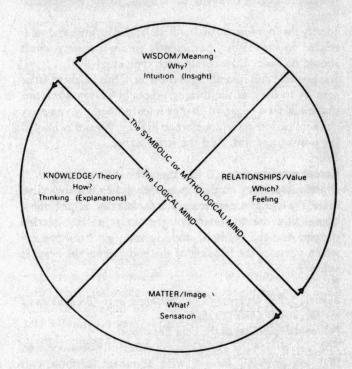

Very often the four functions can be split across the middle with two dominant conscious attitudes, and two inferior unconscious ones, both on the individual and social level.

FUNCTIONS

Until recently Western society has been predominantly extravert, intellectual materialist, i.e. primarily concerned with matter and empirical knowledge, in mounting reaction against an earlier medieval symbolic attitude: the turning point came with the Renaissance.

By contrast the Symbolic World View expresses feelings and intuitions (with an introvert bias). It is concerned with values and relationships, also the underlying meanings, insight into the meaningful patterns running through existence – also foresight, hypothesis, speculation, plans, visions. This side of life, having become the neglected Inferior Function of a whole society, is suddenly missed by quite a few. And so the pendulum begins to swing back again, after five hundred years.

Ideally the four functions should be held in balance and well-related to each other, particularly within a society which should be easier than within each individual.

It is possible that something of the fruit of this balance can be seen by looking at the turning points in history when one dominant view began to change into another, e.g. the early classical period in Greece steeped in the myth and symbol of the previous period. And the Renaissance.

Note:-

Recent research suggests that these two different centres of consciousness may reside in two separate hemispheres of the brain: the logical speech centres in the left side of the brain – dominating the right side of the body in right-handed people. And the symbolic mind in the right hemisphere – which operates the left side of the body where the heart is situated.

Book:-

Jaynes, J. *The Origins of Consciousness, in the Breakdown of the Bicameral Mind* (1976).

Personal Symbolism of the Four Functions:-

For each person the Functions are differently developed, so that you probably have a main dominant function, two subsidiary functions and an inferior function, or else two superior and two inferior functions depending on where the line between conscious and unconscious falls in your particular case.

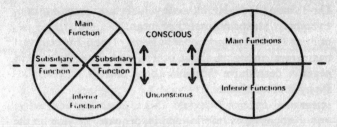

Much of the personal significance of symbolism is lost if you don't work out which is your dominant function, and which is your inferior. Dreams continuously refer to the functions that are atrophying in the unconscious: partial glimpses of facets of your personality which require attention. But myths and fairy-tales complete the picture of how to tackle the problem and what to do about it to avoid becoming a crippled and deformed psyche, partly living only.

The Sensation Type: If extravert, you are master of observing detail. If introvert, you absorb impressions deeply, and notice the inward sensations, memories as they occur, the galaxy of inner image and detail. Both are sensitive to tastes itchiness, pain, noise, and physical bodily sensations.

Inferior Negative Sensation, as experienced mostly by Intuitive types: A lack of regard for the facts, and the flesh of life. Thousands of living people may be ignored or massacred in pursuit of the Vision. Often the brilliant Vision – of the Intuitive's Main Function, working perfectly – gets the blame, quite wrongly. This causes much confusion if not discerned clearly. And this is the same in everyday life: it isn't the attention to possibilities and impalpables that causes the bungling; but the failure to pay attention to such physical symptoms as tiredness or hunger, or alternatively overeating and oversleeping out of casual disregard for all such matters. Inferior sensation mismanages sex and money.

Symbolic action to integrate sensation: Working with stone or clay, or other material substances, as the *ALCHEMISTS* did. Noticing the here and how, of tastes, aiming at making manual work and physical experience yield up their treasures; reviving the thrill and satisfaction almost certainly experienced at times in childhood.

161

The Thinking Type: His ultimate value is order, organization. Everybody must say what they mean.

Inferior Thinking, experienced by Feeling types: The extravert has cynical thoughts about others, and the introvert has negative destructive thoughts about himself. Their philosophy is secondhand.

Integrating Inferior Thinking: This is much less destructive once recognized as Inferior and inadequate. Relying on the main function – the strong reliable feelings – the individual can assess the thoughts at their true value which is little. Only by giving way to the secondhand opinion that thought is more valid then feeling, is the individual taught to rely on his inferior function.

The Feeling Type: Has a proper evaluation of the Cosmos and an appropriate relationship with it. He handles his feelings expertly. The feeling function is expressed by style. He knows the value of beauty and relationships. If introvert, he projects value on to truth and purposes; he is master of the art of slowness, and the organic clustering of time. With his correct values, he distinguishes important factors and sets standards without recourse to words. He needs attention whether love or anger.

Inferior Feeling, mainly experienced by Thinking types: Dark irrational emotions and passions: you fall in love, which is an instinct of the unconscious, but are unable to refine that love in the vessel of transformation (i.e. marriage) which feels like a cage or trap. (See EROS). Often empty 'niceness' and well-intentioned 'goodness' are products of thought not feeling, and may end in fearful rows. No hierarchy of values by which to sort facts or thoughts. Crude loves, crude hates without conscious control or command of the situation: it all seems to happen to him or her, as with every manifestation of the unconscious.

The work of integrating Inferior Feeling: Trust spontaneous feelings but pursue them, and make something of them, never losing sight of a friend or a love. Discover your ultimate value: what you value and devote your time to genuinely, whether self, sex, money, ambition for fame, work, service, politics and religion, or gambling and kicks.

Gestures of wooing, such as bringing flowers, may be thought to be hypocritical because they don't correspond to current feelings but they may be true to the original love and provide a way through the present numbness of inadequate feeling as if by massaging the bloodless limb. Dance and colour affect the feelings. Words repeated may intensify the feeling, without adding to the sense. See also *ALCOHOL*, which releases Anger or Love.

The Intuitive Type: Creative people, people with hunches, whose chief concern is with future possibilities: they sow but don't stay to reap. They have a nose for the invisible and the impalpable. They perceive wholes and can compress much into a flash. Poets and prophets are often intuitive.

Inferior Intuitions, of Sensation types especially: They are liable to be full of dark forebodings. If they don't manage to erect an iron curtain against all potential developments, then these appear negative and menacing because from the unconscious and beyond their control. They may be full of dark suspicions. And the fantastic is crazy. They have a negative response to saints and yogis often, let alone priests and churches.

Integrating the Inferior Intuition: As always by relating to one's own inner function, but knowing that it is inadequate, and not confusing the distorted view with the reality. This is a way of acquiring true objectivity in relation to the functioning of your own psyche; of becoming less naïve about fantasy (or the ghost story) by going into it more deeply. And of valuing other's people's intuition in the form of inventions and hypotheses, because they reach beyond the here and now, the facts, and are capable of transforming the future.

See also *INFERIOR FUNCTION*.

FUNDEVOGEL (a fairy-story collected by the Brothers Grimm)
A story concerning the role of the Animus.
A forester finds a boy-child, left in a tree top by a bird: That is the spiritual male side, underdeveloped in the top part of the tree, the head.

163

FUNDEVOGEL

His rather primitive cook wants to eat the child: she wants to return it to the inner unconscious realm, which suggests it's the woman's Animus. She is unrelated to the man in whose house she lives – she's just the cook.

The forester's daughter warns the boy and they leave together. Unlike the forester and the cook, they swear to be together, related: In the unconscious, undeveloped child side of the story – children are always nearer to the unconscious – there is a good relationship between male and female, by contrast (i.e. new potential for the development of the Animus in the girl).

The cook sends out her servants to bring the boy back. But the girl and he turn into rose and rosebush, clock and tower, and the servants can't find them: the blind destructive forces of the Animus cannot reach the vegetable and mineral layers of the soul, and are not acquainted with the potential transformations in the psyche.

Finally the girl and boy turn into duck and lake, the cook tries to drink the lake but the duck pulls her in and drowns her: The archaic backward looking woman, who wants to prevent transformation, is herself swallowed up in the unconscious, leaving the boy and girl free to develop in union (i.e. leaving the girl free with her Animus, found for her in the forest by her father).

Note:-

This story anticipates the present development of women towards greater independence, freedom, masculinity, in intellectual careers – and via the unconscious may have contributed to preparing the way for that development.

The girl and the cook are the positive/negative aspects of the Feminine. And it is the girl's initiative which plays the chief part in overthrowing the archaic feminine attitude. In particular the transforming power of the intuition.

See also *TRANSFORMATION, TRICKSTER.*

The FURIES. Erinnyes, or Eumenides
The darkest and most unconscious of the Feminine Forces, in Nature and in life.

These may dog a man's life in the form of unconscious

compulsions, as they dogged the life of *OEDIPUS*, and other heroes of Greek tragedy.

Alecto, that is the Unnameable: All that can't be named or given form by the conscious mind. The horror of what might lie below the threshold of consciousness, like unborn embryos and abortions.

Megara, the Resentful One: The forces opposed to destiny and life.

Tisiphone, Vengeful Destruction: Crimes against life cause life itself to turn negative, destructive and disintegrate back into unconsciousness.

They are variously represented with underworldly attributes, such as dogs' heads (perhaps for scenting their invisible prey), bat's wings (for following it swiftly), and serpents for hair (i.e. rays of conscious thought turned dark and primitive).

See *MASCULINE/FEMININE, The Feminine; UNDERWORLD.*

GAMES
Are a direct expression of the patterns and conflicts of the psyche.

Games in general are symbolic of the patterns of life – with chequered patterns referring to chequered careers, of dark episodes alternating with light, ups with downs. In the course of life, the different conflicting forces move, inter-relate, lock and fly apart: usually red versus black, conscious versus unconscious, in the basic life conflict. The symbolic significance of actual games sometimes gives them an irrational appeal, an obsessional quality as with children's 'crazes'.

Ball games: Masculine virility.

Related Symbolism:-

Games are related to the playful inventive and positive side of the *CHILD* archetype. Jung admired the English for being able to make a game out of anything – they were the first apparently to turn the laborious business of climbing a mountain into a sport.

See also *SEQUENCE*, for the symbolism of Chess and Draughts.

Personal Symbolism: particular symbolic games:

i. *If you draw a square, a circle and a triangle:* and then turn them into pictures, these pictures can be interpreted symbolically.

ii. *Equally if you think of a garden:* describe it.

Then think of a house in it: Describe the house. Where are you standing?

Finally you are holding a glass: describe it, and what is in the glass.

And a key: describe it.

You hold the key above the glass, and you drop it: what happens?

iii. Or there is the game, where one person in the room thinks of anybody in the room (or other people mutually known).

Then the other person, or the rest of the people there, in turn ask questions like: If he/she were an animal what animal would he be? If he were water? For example would he be a spring, a well, a bucket of water, the sea itself? If he were a cheese? Anything goes. As soon as possible you have a guess who the person is, and guesses are limited.

Note:-

These games are quite useful in that they demonstrate how near the symbolic realm is, and how it can be fairly consistent, between a variety of people.

i. *The square:* refers to the earth symbolically, i.e. material outward existence. So, for example, the person who fills it with prison bars feels fairly trapped by his material circumstances at present.

The circle: refers to water and the inner life, so if it is turned into a sun, for example, all is fairly sunny within, even heroic (see *SUN*).

The triangle: refers to fire, the passions and sexuality. If the triangle is drawn pointing upwards in the first place, then emotional life is usually more conscious and rational, better differentiated. Pointing downwards, it is more dark, regressive, unconscious – as in the case of an intellectual who paid little attention to his emotions, who turned the triangle into a picture of a pram, so:

ii. *The garden:* will represent the inner psyche with special regard for the natural feelings for life. The flowers and flower beds represent cultivated emotions and particular *COLOURS* will be of symbolic significance.

The house: will represent the home life, the family, and the more consciously worked structures of life. The individual's position will throw light on where he stands in relation to these two, whether in the house or facing the house, i.e. more involved and tied to the home, or away from it.

The glass (like the square above in i)*:* represents the person's actual life and circumstances; the content his inner life.

The key: his sexuality; and dropping it into the glass marks the effect of his sexuality on his life.

Note:-

This inner *LANDSCAPE* may include all kinds of fascinating symbolic features, which can probably only be deciphered with intuition, combined with a familiarity with symbolism. What is significant is that so long as people respond spontaneously, the results do seem to be symbolically relevant, and revealing. The symbolism can be extended to cover the inside of the house and attempts made to assess the introvert/extravert qualities of the person. Or the territory beyond the edges of the garden as unconscious Shadow realms.

GENEALOGIES. Family Relationships

May refer to quite different relationships between symbols, or different parts of the psyche, Thinking and Feeling or Conscious and Unconscious.

The relationships between the figures in myth, fairy-tale, etc. are usually symbolic, referring to qualities and interrelationships within the psyche, or between forces of nature in the Cosmos.

167

GENEALOGIES

The further back down the ancestral line usually leads deeper into the unconscious, which in the course of time, by a process of differentiating and relating, has given birth to increasingly refined conscious offspring, who supersede and overthrow the old order. This reflects the running battle between conscious and unconscious, each of which threatens to swallow up the other. Most mythologies refer back beyond this period to a Golden Age of preconscious totality when, for example, the Gods, representing the Archetypes of the Unconscious, ruled the earth, before the birth and splitting off of the conscious Ego (see *ARCHETYPES*).

Apart from reflecting the relationship between unconscious and conscious, these genealogies may provide a sequence in the differentiation of masculine and feminine. Typically, just as a lot of primitive life forms are bisexual, so there are phases in childhood where the male and female psyche are less clearly differentiated, and in the same way the first gods often contained both sexes.

Descent through the father's line: May indicate a relationship through intellect, i.e. not a blood relationship at all, but causes and effects of relying on the Thinking *FUNCTION*.

Descent through the mother's line: May indicate that feminine qualities of Feeling are at the root of what is being talked about.

Offspring: Often different aspects of the one psyche.

Note:-

In referring to the psyche, myths and fairy-tales, relate especially to the collective social psyche of the time, which influences the individual psyche.

See *GIANTS, Daughter*, for example.

GIANTS
Primitive Neanderthal tendencies which want to stay that way.

Giants inhabited the earth before men, which indicates that they symbolize a pre-existent part of humanity that has got left behind, being archaic, primitive and backward looking. They represent the neglected, earthy material side of the unconscious including extravert sexuality (contrast the *DWARF*).

They *PERSONIFY* the tremendous force of the unconscious, usually in its negative destructive aspect. Views, discoveries and visions that are larger than life, and can tear a man's psyche to pieces may all take the form of giants (i.e. experiences which can't be formulated properly and may be very destructive).

Giants hold human beings prisoner or devour them, they are basic, backward, entrenched sides of life, refusing to change and incapable of it, and so they threaten the ongoing conscious Ego.

Giants are often hagridden: i. Early or primitive human societies seem to have been ruled by the Mother (matriarchal). And still today, the Anima, partly formed by the relationship with the actual Mother, plays a vital part in coming to terms with the forces of the unconscious.

Or: ii. The giant may represent the Animus, i.e. the masculine side of Woman's nature, which can be utterly ruthless, without mercy or reason. Because it is still primitive and unconscious, it is irrational and beyond conscious control.

Or: iii. The erect phallus, always bound to fall to women. Uncontrolled passion.

Battling with the giants, as the Gods did battle with the Titans in Greek myth. Or trying to outwit the giant, possibly in order to steal its treasure: Indicates an intermediary stage in dealings with the unconscious, where the conscious Ego has become wily enough, and well-enough equipped mentally – often special sets of weapons are required – to meet the unconscious on equal terms. The giants are symbolically closely related to *ANIMALS*; also to the more primitive *BROTHER*. Slaying the giant is much the same as slaying the monster.

But later it may become necessary to put the bits together and try to revive it. The giant is not unlike a negative form of the Cosmic *MAN* or the cosmic man gone wrong.

Positive Symbolism:-

The helpful giant: The force of the unconscious is double-edged, and even the giant sometimes appears as a symbol of its positive powers, brute force but well-directed: the strength and the passion needed to get great tasks done. Like the unconscious, the giant may do the task for the individual, but in this case a huge task. The difficulty comes in stirring the energy of the creature enough to overcome its passion for laziness, its colossal lethargy. From the legends it appears to take a genius or a sage to do this.

The giant's daughter: As daughter of the dark unconscious side of the mind, the youthful differentiated side of the Anima. Both the giant and his more resourceful mother may have to be overcome in order to reach her. See *ANIMUS*, The Anima.

GILGAMESH/Enkidu
Hero and Shadow (see *EGO/Shadow*).

When man becomes a social political being he gets cut off from a freer, wilder side of himself, from the spirit of nature (and the Gods,) and needs to relate to it again. This seems to have been recognized early and described in the relationship with the more animal Enkidu, who helps with witchcraft. See also *The BROTHERS*.

GLASS. Crystal
Matter rendered invisible, spiritualized.

Negative Symbolism:-
This has the danger of separating the emotions and the body from what can be seen with the eye (the intellect).

The GOAL
Symbolic goals nearly always refer to some aspect of becoming the New Man, reborn and enlightened.

Jung found that all manifestations of the unconscious were purposeful – in spite of working long hours in a madhouse. Symbolism is always working towards a goal, towards completion. And if anything works towards a specific end, this seems to imply a certain unconscious foreknowledge, a potential, some antecedent force at work. From the mere fact that the unconscious psyche counterbalances one-sided tendencies, and vital deficiencies, we can infer an inherent direction or goal. In the same way, in Nature the unconscious forces tend towards more highly evolved forms, such as the eye, the human being, which suggests a direction and therefore some kind of goal.

The goal of the psyche appears to be increased awareness, higher and higher states of consciousness, in the widest sense – all four *FUNCTIONS* in the psyche used in a more rational and vibrant way. It is an end without end. The end or goal is also the way to it. There is no real distinction between the two. In the realm of feeling the aim or goal is to keep on feeling more deeply, more widely, which is also the way to the goal.

Although the goal is ultimately unattainable, it is not to be dismissed for that reason. The difference between what we are and what we become is determined by the goals we work towards.

And in the end, it's the process of becoming which is the only goal worth the effort anyway: the New Man, reborn, enlightened, decisive.

Meaning, as well as confidence in the future, is symbolized in the goal, but once there is a fresh vigorous start, as James Hillman points out, then that end is fulfilled, in contrast with stricken imagination, spontaneity gone, the creative spark extinguished, which may be the result of removing the goal: or of taking the goal too literally, putting it away in the remote future, and so robbing the impulse of its force now. The Goal gives direction: without it we become disorientated and unable to face reality. We can't think, feel, will or act, without the perception of some goal, according to A. Adler.

The Symbols:-

The Happy Ending: as in '*They got married and lived happily ever after*': The reaction against symbolism in general involved a particularly violent antipathy for the 'Happy Ending' which wasn't true-to-life, when mis-taken literally. But as a symbol of the union of masculine and feminine forces in the cosmos, in life, and in the inner realm, it is an image of two forces that are never far apart, never more than momentarily parted – and this temporary separation may only be a delusion of the Ego.

See *WEDDING*.

GOAL .

In fairy-tales apart from marrying, the Hero often becomes king: Indicating complete rule over the inner realm of unconscious *COMPLEXES* and freedom from the pressures and compulsions that fetter the will, and negative forces that imprison and even destroy parts of the personality. See *KING.*
Frequently the narrative emphasizes that because the direction and goal are wrong, this leads to disaster: This usually refers to the long-term aims and goals of a lifetime. Time is compressed.

Tragedy: Is usually concerned with meaningful death, as making way for change and transformation and is as much a part of the symbolic goal as the happy ending, which requires this counterbalance.

Related Symbolism:-

Treasures, see STONE/Jewels.

The WISH.

ALCHEMY, The goal of Alchemy.

BIBLICAL SYMBOLISM, The vision of the End of Time.

And such images as *Paradise, the HORN of Plenty, WATER of Life, Fruit of some special tree* that grows only in the unconscious and bears *golden apples, silver pears*, which may be symbols related to the golden sun of conscious rational knowledge, or the silver moon of unconscious awareness.
The lance and arrow are sometimes symbolic of perceiving and aiming for goals.

Personal Symbolism:-

Note your conscious aims and purposes, and work out what their exact opposite would be, especially in terms of the opposite inferior *FUNCTION*, and from there try to discover the symbolic pattern, directions, and goals towards which the unconscious might be striving. Notice especially the qualitites of whatever has upset your conscious, rational aims and see if it doesn't throw light on other different unconscious purposes. Without abandoning the rational aims and outlook, it may be possible to extend these to allow for the unconscious needs, and to embrace the other symbolic goals.

GODS/GODDESSES
The masculine and feminine forces in Nature and in Human Nature.

The evidence unearthed seems to suggest there was first just one Mother Goddess in primitive matriarchal society: The womb, in a sense, has remained the ultimate matrix of all symbols, as *ORIGINS*, the whole story of evolution from amoeba to man, recapitulated in nine months. It is a focal point for much psychology. It is related to the symbolism of the *CIRCLE*, and forms a principle of family and social life. When evolved into the *MANDALA*, it establishes the principle and pattern of cohesion between the parts. In the womb the *BROTHERS*, often twins, were one.

This is the symbolic or archetypal pattern of the feminine whether in Nature, woman, or as man's Anima, as valid now as in the earliest accounts of the Goddesses. Such archetypes ignore superficial variations in favour of what is typical.

The male God:
Embodies the active masculine force in Nature. (See *PERSONIFICATION*.)

Possibly with the historical *SPLIT* off of a more active male conscious Ego – which takes place at a certain moment in the story of each child, as it must once in the story of mankind – there appears a male God, with many of the attributes of the male conscious Ego. Plainly these attributes are projected, but this does not mean man invented the masculine forces in Nature. Every symbolism recognizes and makes it emphatically clear that the forces which the symbols (or mental images) describe, exist outside man in Nature, of which man is part, and has a particularly grand share. Modern archetypal symbolism of psychology is just as emphatic about this: the God Image or The Wise Old Man, though only an image, is an image of something real. In a way, the Animal images (theriomorphic) made this clearer: it was the force of the bull or the flight of the gander that was in question.

The opposition of male and female forces in the world, related to the opposition between male conscious Ego and feminine unconscious, has dominated symbolism, which reflects life: phallic and yonic, yang and yin, etc. (see *MASCULINE/FEMININE*).

Triads of Gods:
Male, female and offspring, which appeared as early as c. 8000 BC.
See Kenyon, K. *Digging up Jericho.*
The child god as *MEDIATOR* **unites the opposites (see** *UNION*).

The primary movement of symbolism, life, and the psyche, separates the male and female parts and then unites them in their offspring.

In symbolism this is related to the differentiation of above and below, of mind and matter (or life and matter) which when combined make for the human experience of reality. Man, born of the earth like the animals, but possessed of the fire of consciousness, becomes the *MEDIATOR*.

Note:-

This symbolism is still active and consistent behind the intellectual outgrowth in Christian doctrines of the Trinity: God Transcendent and God Immanent are reconciled through the Incarnation.

Particular Gods:
> **A more precise awareness of distinct aspects of the masculine forces at work simultaneously in the psyche and in Nature.**

As the different male forces became clearly distinguished, together with the way they worked, acting and interacting in nature and in man, the gods could be given more clearly defined characters. This process, though ultimately obscure, can provisionally be explained in terms of the archetypal processes of unconscious projection still at work in the individual now. Experiences of tremendous power that turn life upside down – or the right way up for the first time – are felt as an inbreak of revelation from beyond, which can only be described in figurative terms. For this reason, it is doubtful whether the originators of the myths could have ever mistaken the symbolism in a naïve and literal way. So long as the gods were still related to their proper reference points in the forces of nature and the human psyche, they were valued for the light they threw on both. Whereas once they are taken literally this arouses immediate scepticism – let's climb Olympus and see for ourselves – and the myth is soon defunct. If it is replaced by another, there is no great loss, but, as Jung said, if Pan or God is dead (i.e. sunk in unconsciousness) it's no good pretending he's alive – which only adds stupidity to unconsciousness. He must be brought to life.

Gods as personified forces of nature: Although the gods embodied all the forces of nature, such as *TIME, STORMS, SUN, MOON, ANIMALS, VEGETATION,* or the *ELEMENTS*, which have always been powerful symbols in themselves (and remain so in dreams, etc.) the fact that they are *PERSONIFIED* points especially to the relationship between these cosmic forces and man: in response to nature it is the mind of man which is struck by the radiant and overwhelming power of the cosmos.

Note:-

This explains why Egyptian, Greek and Roman gods could easily be identified with each other and even with Nordic and Vedic gods.

The pantheons of the gods, and the High God: The many centres or nuclei of life within the psyche. Reflects the attempt to arrange the forces of life according to a hierarchy of human values.

They are the personification of the archetypal forces of life, which are active in the three spheres:

   i. the life of the psyche with its complexes.
   ii. the life of society.
   iii. the life of the cosmos as it is related to man.

Particular Goddesses:
   Increasingly differentiated feminine forces.

These reflect especially the ambivalent nature of the feminine forces of life: or in any case man's attitude to them, of love and gratitude, but also of fear and loathing. These appeared projected on to the goddesses themselves, as a benevolent side which provided and protected, but also a fearful and loathsome aspect which destroyed. Innini, for example, who as Heroine retrieved Tammuz from Arallu, loved the shepherd boy's bird of bright colours, but also broke its wing, and spurned and whipped the men she turned into jackals, horses and swine.

Like the Anima they may play mother, sister and wife to the same person. They could be virgins and harlots, existing in a realm beyond duality. Put another way: they are all the conscious intellect can grasp plus a lot more. And even when the Virgin goddesses (like Athene, Artemis) were differentiated from the Love Goddess (Aphrodite) they all still have a dark negative side, sending disease, cutting down the enemies, or inflaming the passions with wild animal lusts.

The Black Goddess:
For example, Isis, Artemis, Parvati, or the Shulamite Spouse in The Song of Songs. Also the Black Madonna:
The dark unconscious feminine powers which manifest first.

The maternal black earth which can remake what it once made: so Isis can remake Osiris. The dark side of man's Anima which, when disrobed, has a great light within it, an inward transforming power.
Whereas Parvati, when sad, is only given a golden skin by the gods: She is only transformed superficially. The black depths of the feminine unconscious remain obscurely dark with the result that when accused of being black by Shiva, she retreats, fleeing from union with the light conscious principle. (Compare GORGON, Medusa.)

Monotheism:
   The essential unity of the psyche in communion with the Cosmos.

Quite apart from the genuine insight into the wholeness of existence, the single essence without seam, psychologically there is a tendency for the monotheistic idea to harden intellectually into the monolithic, the uniform, the one-tracked. This is to over-emphasize the One at the expense of the many. (See NUMBERS; ONE/Many and related symbolism.) And may lead to intolerance of the variety of life. This can be illustrated historically in the incredibly heated feuds, schisms and heresies that have dogged Christianity, concerning such points as whether the Holy Spirit proceeded from the Father *and* Son, or from the Father *through* the Son, in contrast with Hinduism where every shade and variety of belief is seen as forming a valid part of the whole. Christians are barely beginning to see the enormous value of such condemned heresies as Gnosticism, rich in poetry and symbolism, which was more aware of the many emanations, many levels of consciousness between the one essence, and the multiplicity (or variety) of existence in the material world.

God is a symbol of symbols. Jung, C. G. *The Symbolic Life* Collected Works, Vol 18, Part III.
(See *UNKNOWN*).

GOLD
The enduring and untarnishable essence of life.

Whatever is of the highest value.
The whole Self, the conscious rational mind: not just the thinking function, but rather those *FUNCTIONS* which have been brought into the light of consciousness.
Gold/Silver: The conscious mind in contrast with its Shadow. Compare *SUN*/moon. Like the moon, silver turns black, and needs to be repolished; so it is a symbol of the corruptible, changing side of nature, which needs to be transformed.
Silver: is the bride of gold. Those who seek it are often in need of the feminine forces of life.
See also *ALCHEMY; METALS; RUMPELSTILTSKIN*.

GORGONS
Three sisters, two of whom were immortal, with claws of brass, tough scales, tusks like wild boars, and wings:
Among the harshest forms of the feminine impulses, neglected and turned negative in the unconscious.

And therefore most especially man's neglected Anima, often depicted as triple in form, Mother, mate and Virgin daughter – like the three phases of the moon, old, full and new.

They are winged and fabulous, which refers them direct to the inner world of mind, like all monstrous creations that don't exist in the outside world.

Medusa, the Cunning One, desecrated the chaste Athene's temple with her wild inappropriate passion (she was ravished by Poseidon) and was given snakes for hair: Medusa was the human – the only mortal of the three – and therefore nearly conscious, near the threshold of consciousness. She is the dark, female shadow side of Athene, ZEUS's positive Anima, or feminine soul, born direct out of his head. This dark, shadow side of the feminine nature is not often so clearly differentiated as in Greek myth. In contrast with the radiant Athene, hers are the dark serpent rays of the unconscious realm.

Those who look at her direct are turned to stone: The archetype of life is feminine: when this languishes neglected in the unconscious, people are robbed of life. They may get stuck in dead, rigid, masculine intellectual formulae, or trapped in obsessions – usually work – compulsions, fixed patterns of behaviour.

Women who are possessed by the Animus, taken over by the male side of themselves, equally lack the more fluid feminine attitude, and so often manifest the same lifeless obsessions.

In order to slay the dark exterior negative form of the feminine, the Hero (Perseus) has to look at her reflection only, in his shield: This points vividly to the necessity of looking inwards, into the MIRROR of the unconscious, in order to do battle with this negative force, and not make the mistake of attacking projections in the outside world which will only harden the situation irrevocably – turn it to STONE.

Once slain, Medusa yields her treasure, the Golden Sword (Chrysaor) and the Winged Horse (Pegasus) conceived by Poseidon in Athene's temple: This is a recurring symbolic theme, that the dark figures are closely related to, if not identical with the bright radiant forms of the same archetype.

For example in Charles Kingsley's *The Water Babies* the repulsive hag Miss Done-by-as-you-did, is none other than the beautiful Miss Do-as-you-would-be-done-by.

Medusa becomes the emblem on Athene's shield: the dark

shadow side of the feminine is integrated and useful. And hidden within her hideous exterior are probably the feminine qualities of intuition (see *SWORD*) and inner values, inner feeling – the passion that desecrated Athene's temple, but now sublimated and reborn winged, i.e. as inner, creative inspiration and passion. When the physical side of the passion is sacrificed it finds its ethereal form, in Pegasus.

GRACES
Aglaia, the Brilliant One; Euphrosyne, she who brings joy; and Thalia, the Festive One.
Three aspects of the positive side of the Feminine force, possibly distinguishing feminine intellect, emotion and intuition (?). (*See MASCULINE/FEMININE.*)

Graces/Gorgons, or Graces/Phorchyds (who were the three hags with one tooth and one eye between them): The contrast between feminine charms and grace, and the dark, negative forms was probably intended. (See also *GORGONS*.)
The feminine in Nature, in Woman and in the Man's Anima, can only be confronted and accepted whole.

The GRAIL Legend
Reflects the developing consciousness of a Christian man in the First Millennium, and describes the inner journey.

The Grail Castle: is a magical world hard to find: that is, the unconscious.
The hero, Perceval, must perform other tasks before he can cross into that realm: that is, he must develop his conscious Ego, solving other problems in the outside world.
The knight's sword: shows that he is no longer governed by brute passions – he can master the animal in himself – and his powers of conscious discrimination give him a truly human sense of proportion.
The old Fisher King is wounded: Dark primitive impulses from within threaten the old ways. They must be realized consciously if there is to be a cure. The same impulses, if turned positive, have healing qualities. The conflict between opposing forces within, between archaic impulses and new

179

aspirations, tear the individual apart and threaten to destroy him. But the individual is also the vessel for their reconciliation.

The Grail itself: is that which preserves life, the inner idea of the *VESSEL*.

In the outside world the vessel makes for a major distinction between man and animal: man can conserve water and so save his life, where an animal would die because there was no water naturally available.

In the inner realm man can adapt to circumstances in contrast with animals who are struck down unexpectedly. The vessel is the mind of man balancing and reconciling the opposites, birth and death: it is symbolically like Mother Earth as womb and tomb giving birth and receiving back her dead. The Grail was the grave where death was turned into life, where inanimate wine was turned to living blood.

In the legend, the Grail was the cup used by Christ at his Last Supper, where he identified with the wine that was drunk, thereby identifying the one life with its many manifestations: Symbolically this points to the unending rhythm of life and death. And so is related to the myth of Osiris, as Emma Jung points out.

The Lance and the Grail, which must always be together: The One, and the Many, Essence and existence, the Enduring and the ephemeral, as well as the Masculine and Feminine, are all contained in this *UNION* of Opposites. The unity is no invention, but a human image of the true nature of one reality before it is dissected in parts by intellect and Ego.

Blue flames reveal where the treasure is: The conscious fire of the celestial spirit, which combines Feeling and Thinking, reveals what is of ultimate worth and value. (See *FUNCTIONS* of the Mind:)

Book:-

Jung, E. and Franz, M. L. von. *The Grail Legend* (1971). Excellent on the contrast between the classical Hero Galahad, and the more human Perceval, who has integrated some Shadow characteristics. Compare the *BROTHERS*.

GREEK MYTH
Sufficiently extensive, detailed and complex to reflect truly the complexity of different forces of life.

Symbolism reflects the anatomy of the psyche and its relationship with the outside forces of Nature. The meaning of each symbol often depends on the context. The relationship between the parts is often more significant than the isolated symbol, because such relations are a vital and integral part of life. And besides the symbol often cannot be understood in isolation because its meaning varies according to the context.

The great value of Greek myth, to anyone trying to understand the working of the psyche, is the extent of it. It has been passed down more or less intact. All the parts are woven, interwoven and sometimes, in later strands of tradition, rewoven to form complete patterns that reflect the patterns of the psyche and the patterns of life.

The feminine Archetypes in Greek myth, such as Goddesses (see GODS/Goddesses) and FURIES, or MUSES/Sirens: Particularly remarkable is the picture portrayed of the Feminine Archetype of Life, with its light and dark qualities.

For example, the Love Goddess, Aphrodite, is the secret lover of the God of War, Ares, and on her dark side is partly responsible for the Trojan war: Reflects the close underlying relationship between the positive and negative aspects of the single archetype of Feeling, which manifests as love or war.

Mount OLYMPUS/the depths of Tartarus; where a millstone could fall for nine days before it struck bottom: The upper realm reflects the lower, as the conscious world view reflects the unconscious world view. Consciousness transforms the same reality, from being menacing and alien to being radiant and positive.

Compressed symbols like the SERPENT and Pole of the God Hermes: Can only be understood when the rich variety of what is being compressed has first been fully grasped: the depth of Hades and height of heaven, as well as the breadth of human experience. So that for the Greeks the symbol would naturally rouse such associations.

GREEK MYTH
Particular Symbolism:-

i. For accounts of the Gods of Olympus and some of the other minor Gods: see Mount *OLYMPUS*; *ZEUS*/Hera, also *ATHENE* and *HEPHAESTUS*; *APOLLO*/Dionysus; *DEMETER*/Persephone; *EROS*; *HERMES*, who bears the *SERPENT*/Pole; The *UNDERWORLD*. Also the *FURIES*; *YOUTH*/Age; *PAN*; *SATURN*, for Cronos.

ii. For exploits and tasks of *HEROES*: *HERCULES*; *GORGONS*; *OEDIPUS*; *SCYLLA* and *CHARYBDIS*.

iii. Also see *JOURNEYS*, for their typical features in myth, as in the stories of Jason or Odysseus.

Books:-

Kerenyi, C. *Complete Works*.
Graves, R. *The Greek Myths* (1955).
Smith, W. *Classical Dictionary* (1872).

The GROUP/Individual
Achieving individuality involves both separating from the group as a distinct person, and then relating to the group, whether family or society.

This is further related to the inner process whereby the Ego must distinguish itself from the unconscious *COMPLEXES* (which resemble reflections of family and society) and then relate to the inner collective realm.

The formation of the psyche is rooted in animal instinct, and the Herd Instinct continues to play an important part in human life, more obviously perhaps in primitive communities as participation mystique. Whereas allegedly in more sophisticated societies, each Ego differentiates itself clearly from that of the group, and then relates freely to the group or society he lives in, as an individual, accepting personal responsibility.

However, there is a continuous tension between social disintegration and dissolution – symbolically linked with inner dissociation of the different complexes all ruling in opposition to each other – and the herd tendency, often unrecognized, gathers force in the unconscious shadow realm, till it erupts on the surface in any form of totalitarianism, tyranny, dictatorship or absolute monarchy. Each extreme justifies itself by being not as bad as its opposite, and the pendulum swings between those extremes. The individual dilemma varies according to the state of society at the time. Where the dominant conscious attitudes have become outworn, ageing and sterile, it becomes all the more important not to conform with them if the individual psyche is to remain healthy. It is in a sense easier (though not necessarily enacted) to break away from the social group and discover personal values in these circumstances. But it is not so easy to relate again. For this process is inclined to fragment society until the opposite reaction sets in. Where the society is well integrated, on the other hand, the individual is apt to slumber in a state of semi-consciousness.

The individual/The Human Race: The way you relate to society reflects symbolically the inward struggle of differentiating the personal psyche from the Collective Unconscious; and then relating to it consciously. Each person is distinct from the human race, yet related to the whole through his human nature. Although these two distinct phases in the process of achieving individuality take place automatically to some extent, they often do so in a blurred, confused way, if not clearly recognized.

The Symbols:-

The structure of symbolism is concerned with relations, values and wholes, which can be referred to the individual or the cosmos. But they can also, on the intermediate level, the mesocosm, be referred to the structure and interrelationships of society, of the city (see *BUILDINGS/City*) and so of politics.

For example the HERO in all his struggles represents the individual, separating his conscious Ego from the Unconscious and relating to it, and at the same time grasping his own particular personality and its relationship with society.

From the other end, all the particular symbolic initiations into the different stages of adulthood stressed especially the solitary discovery of personal identity:-

For example being thrown out of the group to weave an amazing head-dress sufficiently distinctive to allow readmission to the group as a mature individual capable of thinking for himself.

Or else stressed integration with the group on a wider level than before:-

For example, dying to the family and rising to a new life as one of the clan; Or being initiated with semen: to make the transition from the influence of the mother to the realm of the men.

In the same way for women the time may come to question the identification with 'modern woman', or whatever other collective dominant prevails.

Other Particular Examples:-

Chiron/the rest of the Centaurs: Chiron is distinguished among the centaurs as being far more conscious, more civilized. Although from the underworld, he represents the positive side of the Shadow realm. Living in a cave, with an animal body, he is also an educator. Wounded by accident, he comes to know the nature of the wound, and so can heal – this is like other *HEALERS*. The germs of light and of recovery are sometimes discovered in the darkest recesses of nature.

Polyphemus/the other Cyclops: By contrast Polyphemus stood out from the other cyclops for being more primitive. (See Kirk, G. S.)

A recent modern myth of standing out against the herd instinct is *Jonathan Livingstone Seagull* by Richard Bach.

Related Symbolism:-

The King is mediator between the individual and the group.

EGO, other *COMPLEXES* and whole *SELF*.

For the relationship of individual to Cosmos, see *Cosmic MAN* and *NUMBERS ONE/Many.*

GROWING/Shrinking
The forces of creativity and decay.

Especially related to the Archetype of the growing *CHILD* in relation to Mother Nature.

Related to phallic symbolism and procreativity.

GYMNASTICS
The attempt to make the body conform to the mind or spirit, or the ideal.

Hermes, whose limbs were beautifully and harmoniously

developed in the gymnasium, was the patron of the gymnastic games of the Greeks, as well as messenger of the gods, mediator of the ideal plan to man.

Related Symbolism:-

See *BODY*.

HAIR/Shaven Head
Like the rays of the sun:
Conscious thoughts, the Conscious Ego.

Hence every Sun Hero, for example Samson: Is symbolic of developing the conscious Ego in the first part of life; and so in the earlier stage in the evolution of man's mind, having one's hair cut off presents a threat to the natural course of inner development.

Yet even Samson, after a period in the dungeons of the unconscious, without eyes (i.e. without conscious vision) ends up stronger than ever before, and kills more Philistines at his death than in his life.

Shaving the head, from the time of the Priests of Isis: Is an ancient symbol of initiation, consecration, spiritual renewal – partly from cutting off conscious thought, in order to let the unconscious emerge, and partly related to the rebirth of the head, by returning it to the hairless state of the new-born babe. The two ideas are interrelated since the infant exists in a state of pure being without conscious thought, or consciously differentiated Ego.

Jung links this with the Hero losing all his hair in the belly of the monster on the night sea journey – all symbolic of the return to the womb, the unconscious, as the necessary preparation for rebirth. The rays of conscious thoughts must be eliminated to experience the unconscious.

It is furthermore symbolic of a ritual castration suffered willingly as a sacrifice: the individual (usually a monk) submits to the authority of whoever does the cutting (the Abbot still usually cuts the first lock), and sacrifices the outward enjoyment of manhood in order to seek the inner, spiritual creative power, the equivalent inner resources (*the winged horse* symbolically) which is thought to depend on inhibiting the sexual act.

HAIR

Negative Symbolism:-

Cutting the hair of slaves (in the past); also of convicts, soldiers and schoolboys: is symbolic of forcing them to conform, making them sacrifice their personal Ego.

Note:-

The irrational reactions, and exaggerated emotion generated at times by the length of people's hair indicates this symbolic aspect.

Baldness: Groddeck distinguishes between the baby-bald, where the body may be expressing symbolically the lack of virility, immature emotions and infantile sexuality; and the phallic-bald of erect mature men of an opposite type. One has failed to acquire a strong personal Ego, the other has shed it in favour of the true *SELF*.

Hair/serpents: Rays of conscious thought, light, in contrast with the rays of the unconscious mind, appearing in their first dark negative form; the writhing complexes, with their little eyes flashing in the dark (like the *FISH*'s eyes) depict in outward image a mind writhing with conflicting feelings and dark, erratic, uncontrolled intuitions that bring dread till transformed.

The beard.
Man's Feminine *ANIMA.*

The mouth and especially the lips (by symbolic association and displacement) symbolize the feminine sexual organs, and the beard, as pubic hair, often emphasizes this feminine feature of the man, his Anima.

But where the symbolic material is more concerned with the woman's fate: The outward show of femininity conceals the inner masculine Animus. Especially as the woman's erotic zone is related symbolically to her Animus. Physically it is her point of contact with men and so symbolically too (see *BLUEBEARD*).

HAND
The whole man in miniature.

Also the map or pattern of life and the psyche.

Symbolism derives partly from the fact that nature works from simple units and repeats them in continuously more complicated combinations. **The correspondence between the hand and the man reflects the correspondence between Man and the Cosmos.**

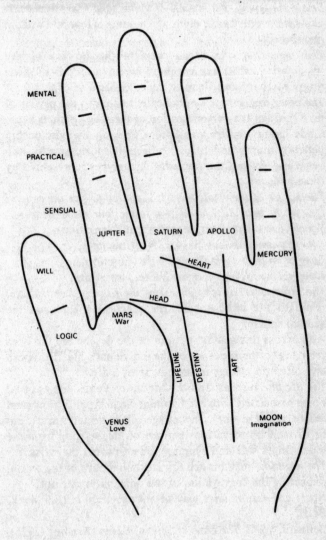

In Palmistry:-
The Thumb: depicts will and intellect (logic), i.e. the

Conscious Ego. Since many people identify almost exclusively with their conscious Ego, those palmists who read from only the thumb are justified, up to a point.

Below the thumb, the mounts of Venus, and Mars next to it: Consistent with GREEK myth, the mounts of love and war are juxtaposed.

The mount of the Moon: depicts the powers of the imagination, which express emotion and intuition – the little finger Mercury and Venus lying to either side of it.

The other fingers: are symbolically related to the psyche of man through the personification of the ruling planets in the Gods Jupiter, Saturn and Apollo. Possibly the relationship between thumb and fingers reflects the ideal relationship between Ego and the powerful Archetypes represented by these gods.

The nature of the whole hand is supposed to give the general type of the individual in relation to the four ELEMENTS:

Square palm with short fingers: Earth (Sensation).

Square palm with long fingers: Air (Intellect).

Long palm with short fingers: Fire (Emotion).

Long palm with long fingers: Water (Intuition).

The three divisions (phalanxes) of the fingers, from the tip: relate to the mind sphere, the practical sphere and the sensual sphere.

And across this general pattern of the psyche are the lines referring to the sequence of the individual's life. These can and often do change in the course of a life.

The life line runs around the Mount of Venus, life as usual being associated with the feminine archetype. If of normal length, about seventy years of age will be depicted and it can be divided up to various periods of life, starting from the index finger side and running down towards the wrist.

The head line may branch towards the mount of the moon, indicating the creative use of the imagination or not.

Heart and destiny lines may be strong, deep, red, or weak.

Book:-

Benham, W. G. *The Laws of Scientific Hand Reading* (1935).

HARE. Or Rabbit
The most widespread image of the *TRICKSTER* who effects *TRANSFORMATION*.

The HEALER/Sickness
Curing the body involves also healing the root of the affliction in the psyche.

Hippocrates/Asklepios: The contrast between the physical cure of the body, and the cure of the whole person, involving the mind and the destiny, which might include dying at the right time. To some extent, the contrast between conventional medicine and psychology.

Asklepian healing: Used symbols (i.e. the *SERPENT* of the *UNDERWORLD*) and specially induced dreams in ritual circumstances (*INCUBATION* dreams) and was otherwise mostly passive, waiting for the forces of the unconscious to manifest and effect the cure.

All such healers have a special relationship with the feminine forces of nature and the unconscious, the Moon or other goddesses, for example, Thoth with Isis, Eshmun with Ishtar, and Asklepios with Athene – and also in Celtic tradition: That is, the relationship with the feminine Anima. (Asklepios also used *the blood of Medusa*, i.e. the inner power of the feminine unconscious: from the right artery it healed, from the left, it killed.) The individual bore the elements of his own cure within; but the inner potential could only become operative in the right atmosphere of quiet, dark and sleep.

A small hooded boy, companion of Asklepios, completed the process of healing: Like the experience of *DISINTEGRATION* the sickness appears to have been used as a meaningful occasion for making contact with the unconscious via the Anima, and finally having some experience of the Self as *CHILD*.

Book:-
Kerenyi, C. *Asklepios: Archetypal Image of the Physician's Existence* (1959).

Sickness:
Sickness affects the body but also expresses symbolically the afflictions of the psyche.

Symbolism supposes, for example, that cancer is a physical expression of fear and sense of loss: so that to treat the cancer without curing the fear – of growth, maturity, and loss of EGO – means that the fear will only manifest again in some similar or new way.

Since the BODY is one of the most direct and intimately related symbols of the psyche, the body-functions and bodily diseases (though physical enough in themselves) may also refer to the psyche. An increasing number of illnesses are recognized as psychosomatic, i.e. arising from disturbances within the psyche, though the unconscious part.

The mind is related to the body through the Imaginary BODY, which mediates and filters direct experience. This idea of the body is sometimes called the subtle body, the psychic body, or the animal spirits. It is in any case a fantasy of the body, an image, somewhat gargantuan, and it is liable to take on large proportions, especially when giving trouble. It is somewhere on the way to Cosmic MAN gone wrong like the GIANT at times. The Body Image is the key to the symbolism of the body, the relationship of body and mind, and so sometimes the key to discovering meanings of illness, emotional needs that are being expressed in terms of sickness. Even though it may not be possible to effect a cure this way, it may be the only way to complete the physical cure, and prevent subsequent physical relapses, perhaps taking a different form next time. Furthermore with a growing subtle awareness of your own Body Image, through the use of the active or creative imagination, you may be able to anticipate its needs, and sometimes take the necessary precautions.

The relationship with this Body Image can be one of fierce conflict. There are times to give in and times to battle it out. On the whole the Body Image is demanding, overpowering, and lazy; it shares the inertia of the unconscious and is loath to change. In *Memories, Dreams, Reflections* Jung tells how he used to have fainting fits as a boy at the prospect of any studying, and when he overheard how worried his parents were about it he conquered it in one day by refusing to give in. But on the other hand it is sometimes even more necessary to befriend the body and value its impulses. The flesh is partly unconscious and feminine and needs to be treated as such. See also NURSE.

Some symptoms as Symbols:-

Headache: The head, the thinking FUNCTION, is aching (or crying) for attention. In women this often means paying attention to the Animus, the masculine side of their characters.

Backache: The back (spine) relates the mind (the cerebral world) to the physical and sexual sphere. The bridge, the link, may have broken down. Ideas may need to be put into practice. The 'spineless' fail to do this more than anything else. It involves the will, determination.

Stomach ache: The guts, the emotions, the Dionysiac side of life in need of conscious attention. (See *APOLLO/Dionysus*.)

General pains, nervousness: Energy which is not used turns back upon itself and attacks its own body. Women who neglect to use their masculine drives (their Animus) are especially vulnerable, as the primitive masculine is barbed with aggression.

The lungs: The spiritual realm. Sometimes just intellect.

Asthma: The spiritual realm threatened by the feminine realm of life, sometimes the mother. Factors which are moist (see *ELEMENTS*, Liquid) and smothering, which need to be distinguished as inner (projections on to the mother or woman withdrawn), a distinct part of the psyche, and then integrated; known and related to the rest of the psyche.

Stiffness, rigidity (lumbago, arthritis, rheumatism): Rigid mental attitudes, of an over-masculine kind. The lack of the feminine Anima or feminine qualities.

Epilepsy, fits: Intense fiery emotions breaking out of the dark unconscious.

Compulsive eating, greed: Known to be often emotional deprivation but the mind may even be off-loading other problems on to the body. A hunger for greatness, for fame, can be communicated to the body via the unconscious, and it complies by eating – without comprehending. Also see *ANIMUS*.

Vice versa, dieting, fasting: May be to subdue other desires.

Insomnia: Sleep is unconsciousness, and inability to sleep may indicate unconscious problems which the insomniac cannot face.

Skin troubles: The desire for transformation (like the snake changing its skin). The skin often erupts at particular periods of transition, like puberty.

Hay fever: a lack of due respect for the Feminine side of Nature. Not the flowers, but the inner feminine, the Goddess, or Anima, in a man.

Hormones, narcotics, insulin, shocks, convulsion therapy: Jung suggests that all these are symbols of quite different inner factors which the psyche is really needing and demanding. Particularly the great inner change (i.e. shock to the system) which allows the unconscious to manifest (see *DISINTEGRATION*). But the symbols are mis-taken literally.

In general, by noticing the reactions of the body and looking for symbolic meanings, it is often possible to discover the needs of the unconscious, of which the body is first aware. Even by noticing when suddenly tired or slumped, when particularly fidgety or sexy or hungry, you may be able to discover the pattern and the sense of it, the meaning behind it. So far as the psyche is concerned, becoming conscious of what is going on is the main thing, and the cure is only a by-product, which can be effected by any suitable or available means, once the root unconscious cause and meaning is understood. Recognizing the symbolism or unconscious meaning and value of disease does not necessitate becoming a Christian Scientist, or relying only on homeopathic medicine – though such movements may have preserved more respect for the symbolic aspect of medicine.

Mental problems, problems with work or even with the inner work, can all be transferred, unsatisfactorily, on to the body. Symbolically the 'body' (corpus) of work in progress may be identified with the actual physical body at an unconscious level. Overloaded with problems which don't belong to it, the body then reacts: acted upon inappropriately it then reacts inappropriately. And it becomes necessary to withdraw *PROJECTIONS* even from one's own body, and transfer or convert them back into the sphere where they belong.

The symbolic solution: When the body and psyche have become symbolically identified, a purely mental solution or symbol will not be enough. A physical symbol or symbolic action may be required to counterbalance (offset) the damage. But where the problem is primarily intellectual (to do with masculine conscious Ego or Animus), then a solution in the intellectual sphere is indicated. The same goes for the emotions and Anima.

Books:-

Grinnell, R. *Alchemy in a Modern Woman* (1973).

Jung, E. *Animus and Anima* (1957).

Also Jung, C. G. and Hillman, J. *Complete Works.*

Groddeck, G. *The Book of the It* (1969) and *Exploring the Unconscious*, where he says, '*Illness*, though certainly not a dream in the ordinary sense, may be described in a sense as a day-dream, a dream of that unconscious self which directs organic as well as psychic processes, and shapes the whole pattern of life.'

HELEN
The Feminine Anima in man, the source of erotic fantasy.

Fantasies launch many thousand ships towards the fortress of the unconscious. It is the sexual urge in conflict with the inhibition that rouses the imagination to new endeavours. This inner conflict between conscious and unconscious is highly creative.

She is the incarnation of the Love Goddess, Aphrodite. (Compare 'Aphrodisiac').

Her story of being retrieved from Troy is thought to be related to fetching the Moon Goddess back from the underworld – for example Dionysus fetching Semele from Tartarus.

The HELPFUL FIGURE
The Potential Self. The fulfilled Psyche.

The personification of a larger identity, a more complete person, first experienced as separate and other in youth, but later the youth may grow into that figure, who is related to his own potential.

This is an archetypal figure who appears in many myths, fairy-tales and other symbolic material. He is fairly easily identified, usually older than the hero, of the same sex and helpful. He is Jung's Wise Old Man.

For Dante, Virgil (though long dead) was just such a figure, leading him down through the underworld, i.e. the Unconscious. And eventually – partly on account of the relationship – Dante becomes the Virgil of his day and possibly even outshines his master and teacher.

The relationship of apprentice and master is based on the same typical pattern, whether in sorcery or carpentry. The apprentice hopes to acquire everything the master and teacher has, and then go his way.

For example, those who practise Zen revere the old teachers and patriarchs, but in the hope of rubbing eyebrows with them in due course; that is, treating them as equals.

Particular Examples of Helpful Figures:

HERMES and *Orpheus*, as guides into the underworld (i.e. unconscious) *Raphael* (in the Apocrypha).

The Daimon of Socrates.

Marpa, Milarepa's teacher, and spiritual guide. Milarepa was the greatest of Tibet's Yogis, already accomplished in black magic, before submitting to the ordeals which Marpa imposed on him.

Each Roman had his individual Genius, and the women their Juno, as Christians have their Guardian Spirit or Angel.

Also all such figures as Christ, Buddha, Krishna, Mithras (meaning friend, the Persian God of Light) who befriend the human spirit but are at the same time to be emulated, imitated. *Kidher in the Koran.*

Note:-

These few examples are enough to show that the figure can be entirely inner, a product of the unconscious, from the imagination, or dreams; or an historical figure; or an actual living person.

Personal Symbolism:-

This helpful figure personifies the hard core, the nucleus or central force of the whole psyche. If he or she should crystallize or constellate in the imagination or in life, then it's a question of keeping in touch. If in life, the actual person also corresponds to an inner figure who established the relationship.

The Ego and the Helpful Figure can gradually organize the *SHADOW*, the *ANIMUS/*A, and other complexes, building up the interrelationship of the whole psyche, the whole *SELF*, which is an individual carrier of the life of the Cosmos. *EGO* must sacrifice itself to the larger reality, or the Ego may get inflated with an unrealistic sense of importance and overwhelmed with responsibility.

HEPHAISTOS
The *ANIMUS* in women. Or *INFERIOR* emotion.

As the master-smith, craftsman god of the forge who controls the fire, but is deformed: He represents the fires of emotion, rejected, neglected in the unconscious.

Hera, his mother, rejects him at birth it is this unwantedness and neglect that is symbolized by his ugliness and deformity.

He is rescued and fostered by the Sea Goddess, and taught his craft under the sea: As a misfit, he is forced inwards by his circumstances, and has no choice but to find new ways, new paths via the unconscious. The neglect leads finally to inner compensations. This is the pattern of the *INFERIOR FUNCTION*.

He forges the original symbol: The symbol was a disc broken in half jaggedly, which enabled two parties to recognize each other. And this is still the main function of all symbolism, the bringing together of two halves, the reconciliation of opposites, the synthesis of experience; making whole what is broken, *SPLIT*.

Related Symbolism:-

Hephaistos assists at the birth of Athene, from Zeus's head. See *ZEUS/Hera*, for the relationship of man/woman, Animus/Anima in this ancient version.

He is also the craftsman of the beautiful *PANDORA*, to some extent the opposite of Athene: Her negative side.

HERCULES, or Heracles
A life cycle devoted to the Heroic struggle to integrate the forces of the unconscious, which ends in failure.

The failure may be the result of trying to graft these forces to his separate conscious Ego, which leads to inflation and subsequent defeat for all such Supermen. Compare the *TRANSCENDENT FUNCTION*, Supermen.

The twelve labours of Hercules: Are related to the twelve signs of the *ZODIAC*, the seasonal tasks of the year (see *SEASONS*) and the tasks through the different *PERIODS* of life.

But above all the inner symbolic task of coming to grips with the unconscious, and bringing unconscious content into the light of consciousness.

Hercules is a Sun Hero, symbol of Ego consciousness, but one who integrates much unconscious content, and gains immortality.

The madness of Hercules: He first cracks up (see *DISINTEGRATION*).

Then he is armed by the gods: With the special weapons required for doing battle with the inner unconscious realm.

He fights the Lion: which is the physical counterpart of the Sun, symbol of the Conscious Ego; therefore he does battle to subdue his own physical nature first.

Not far from the entrance to the underworld he does battle with the Hydra: as soon as he crushes one head with his club two or three more grow in its place: Trying to slay the monstrous negative side of nature in the outside world does not work. He has to withdraw *PROJECTIONS* and sever its immortal head, i.e. attack its essential nature in the unconscious.

The pursuit of the Hind, which has to be brought back alive: Possibly refers to the pursuit of archetype-of-life (feminine). His chase takes him to the land of the Hyperboreans, who were supposed to live exquisitely well, in accord with nature.

The fourth labour, the Boar has to be captured: sets the scene of spiritual rejuvenation at mid-winter. Snow drifts are mentioned. The Boar's tusk is related to the New Moon, and rebirth.

He diverts rivers in order to clean out years of accumulated dung: For a task quite beyond the power of the personal conscious Ego, he mobilizes the forces of nature. The cattle represent years (see *CATTLE*), and it is years of filth and pestilence, i.e. the collective *SHADOW*, which is to be cleared away, cleansed and purified.

The birds, the bull, the mares: refer to other voracious aspects of the animal instincts in man.

The girdle of the Amazon Queen: may be a manifestation of the Anima.

The Cattle: See CATTLE.

The Apples: See APPLES. Hercules is part TRICKSTER as he tricks Atlas in order to bring unconscious material to light.

The twelfth labour, capturing Cerberus: In coming to grips with the monstrous guardian at the threshold of the underworld, he becomes free to pass between the conscious and unconscious realms. He has destroyed the barrier between them, and restored nature, whole, of a piece.

Two aspects of the later career of Hercules both point to an uneasy relationship between the Heroic Conscious Ego and the unconscious feminine Anima (see ANIMUS/ANIMA.) In the one he is dressed in feminine garb, doing the feminine task of spinning, as slave to Omphale, Queen of Lydia. In the other his jealous wife gives him a tunic soaked in Centaur's blood, hoping to renew his animal passion for her, but he is consumed by inner fire and throws himself on his own funeral pyre: These depict two alternative fates for the conscious male Ego in the second half of life, if it cannot integrate the Anima. Either the Anima may take possession of the psyche. Or the Ego will consume itself, while projecting what is essentially an inner problem on to other women and thereby rousing the vengeance of the feminine powers.

HERMAPHRODITE (Hermes and Aphrodite)
The bisexual primal being. Life without distinction between masculine and feminine.
Or:-
> **The reunion of masculine and feminine, in a way that the two are so totally integrated that they form one being.**

If winged: Indicates that the union is of the mind – in the celestial sphere. ABOVE has been integrated with below, life with matter.
Note:-
Like the symbol of Incest, the Hermaphrodite startles, jolts, the conscious mind. This is typical of the way the

unconscious is diametrically opposed to conscious attitudes; and is out to shatter them.

HERMES
MEDIATOR. Part TRICKSTER.

The creative and inventive powers of intuition, partly confused and merged with conscious intellect. Hermes was the messenger God who moved freely between the three worlds, Heaven, Earth and Underworld. He was the Master Magician of the Greeks. Identified with the Egyptian Thoth, he is the inventor of such intellectual pursuits as astronomy, numbers, the alphabet; but invention is the work of flashes of intuition and creative imagination, rather than intellect itself.

Hermes also represents the centre and hub of the *SELF* which co-ordinates the different *FUNCTIONS*.

He invented lyre and pan pipe and carried dreams from Zeus. His hat is reminiscent of the halo (see CROWN) and he holds the CADUCAEUS.

He conducts the shades of the DEAD *into the* UNDERWORD: and so also initiates the living in the secrets of the unconscious. He was later identified with the Creative Word, the history of which goes back probably to the Old Kingdom of Egypt, and was revered as the inspiration behind that great body of symbolic work, the Hermetic Tradition (see *ALCHEMY*).

Book:-

Kerenyi, C. *Hermes – Guide of Souls* (1944).

The HERO/and Anti-Hero
Refers to the development of each separate Conscious Ego in the first half of life, Childhood and Youth. (See *CHILD. YOUTH* and *PERIODS OF LIFE*.)

Often with help. See *HELPFUL FIGURE*.

The Hero is basically the Sun Hero, and related to the symbolism of the KING, *and his task is to fight bulls, dragons and monsters and retrieve treasures or rescue damsels:* That is, he fights with the dark forces of the unconscious in order to discover the potential of his own masculine conscious Ego, which is a great prize, and also liberate the feminine treasure, his own *ANIMA*, which may be incarcerated, i.e. cut off and unrelated to the rest of his psyche, acting on its own volition, erratically and perhaps in conflict with the rest of the psyche. *The monsters and giants who guard the Anima:* Can be identified with the Anima, which is acting negatively in direct opposition to the hero, threatening to defeat his plans. As the sun casts the shadow, so the sun hero is partly responsible for all the dark monstrous forms that he encounters arising from his own unconscious. The heroes were close to their own shadow side and shared the double-edged qualities of the *TRICKSTER*. And the endeavour is all situated at the threshold of the unconscious, and their most difficult task of all is often bringing back the treasure, bringing up the content of the unconscious: for example, Hercules bringing Cerberus into the upper air.

The Events in the Hero's life:
   Portray the structure and SEQUENCE of your life.

It is often like a play within a play, a pattern within a pattern: the stages of the development of the Ego are described in different terms. The overall pattern can first be seen in the complete life; but the same overall pattern of life may be repeated in terms of a journey, or of twelve tasks.
The life sequence is basically fourfold: The birth of the Hero, the rise in power, the descent, and the death or disintegration: These four basic stages of life are common to all of us: it is your life being described. They can be related to the four stages of the work of *ALCHEMY*, which is also the life work. And can be further subdivided into eight or twelve, and seen as the stages of man's life reflected in the *ZODIAC*, for example.
The humble outward show of the birth is balanced by miraculous inner content: In reality, below the surface of outer trappings, something very extraordinary has happened with each and every birth of a separate conscious Ego. For symbolism this extraordinary event is comparable to the birth of a God, though in humble guise. Each individual child is the sole carrier of the treasure of the Gods, namely consciousness. See *ORIGINS*.

The child has super-human powers that triumph over the dark forces of adversity that surround it: Like the dawn, the birth of a new consciousness rises above the animal and vegetable realms and surveys the whole scene. The awareness of the little *ABANDONED* animal, the physical body, breaks bounds, transcends physical existence, has supra-normal powers. Each person, as he or she becomes *SPLIT* off from the whole of the rest of creation, takes with him a great prize, the prize of personal consciousness. Very often the Hero is depicted as the first to grasp this golden prize and bring it back for all other men: this light, this fire.

Whether a mythical figure, or an historical figure like Alexander or Napoleon, he must rise rapidly to his full power like the sun in order to be symbolically satisfying: Because this reflects the rapid development of consciousness in each individual from its faint and glimmering beginning, in the cot. It can only be depicted as a meteoric expansion and explosion, as the light bursts and spreads to the far corners of reality, illuminating them for man. In the short period of a lifespan, the whole slow process of evolution is recapitulated: from being dimly aware of day and night, we are each hurtled to the present zenith of conscious awareness in science, art, spirituality or nature. See *ICARUS*.

The Hero does not grow old, but he nevertheless has to face and grapple with the dark Shadow forces, and triumph over some of them: There are great gains in splitting off from the whole, in what is taken by the conscious Ego – but there are also great losses in what is left behind. Like the Hero, consciousness itself doesn't exactly grow old – it cannot be identified with the body – but it passes its zenith and must come to terms with Unconsciousness which lies ahead. Certain aspects of the vast unconscious area can be assimilated into consciousness, and the stories depict this.

For this purpose, the Hero is equipped with special weapons, the gift of gods, such as cloaks of invisibility or winged shoes – or other spectacular features not normally found in the outside world: Therefore these must refer to inner gifts, latent powers within the psyche, which are needed for the battle with the unconscious.

But eventually the Hero is BETRAYED, or passively suffers

heroic SACRIFICE: Ultimately consciousness must lose, must be dissolved back into unconsciousness. The old *KING,* an image of collective or communal consciousness, has to be replaced. The individual Ego is cut down, and turned into manure for next year's harvest. On the cosmic level, the process of *DISINTEGRATION* is only a step towards reintegration, with the next generation, who will take with them a slightly expanded consciousness.

The tasks of the Hero:
Often twelve in number:
   Reflect the twelve hours of the day and the twelve months of the year, the lifetime allowed for developing our consciousness, increasing the hoard.

The Journeys of the Hero:
   Mark the same progess. See *JOURNEYS*.

The inner development of consciousness between birth and death, which are the beginning and the end of the journey, and are related symbolically to dawn and dusk.

The relationships of the Hero:
   Consciousness expands through the realms of Feeling as well as thinking. See *MASCULINE/Feminine*. And *FUNCTIONS* of the Mind.

Particular Heroes: Every story has a hero of some sort, and many of them follow the symbolic pattern and throw light on the relationship of *CONSCIOUS* and unconscious.

For example the SPY *must enter alien territory:* Of the unconscious and retrieve something from it.

The detective must throw conscious light on the unconscious shadow realm of CRIME.

The Hero in white or light blue does battle with the villain in black: very often reflects the tussle between the conscious mind and the dark unconscious forces, whether in a Western or an Opera.

All such figures may be just as symbolic as the obvious Heroes like Perceval and Galahad (see the GRAIL). Or GILGAMESH and HERCULES. Or Jason and Odysseus (see JOURNEYS).

Conquerors: Are especially suited to depict the civilized conscious force triumphing over the dark barbaric territories of the Unconscious. The symbolic appeal is greater if very young like Alexander.

The Anti-Hero.
> **The embodiment of the forces of the unconscious struggling for its life against overblown inflated Ego-consciousness.**

For a long time there has been a growing lack of sympathy for the traditional hero, for the good reason that his day is done, his task is accomplished. Now the danger threatens from quite another quarter – though the pendulum may yet swing again, and in particular circumstances where the unconscious collective Shadow manifests in the old monstrous style, then the old heroic values could be needed once more.

Even the traditional hero extracted something of inestimable value from the unconscious forces themselves – the teeth of the dragon, for example, in the story of *CADMUS* or the blood of the monster. Whereas if the hero (i.e. the conscious Ego) rested on his withered laurels, so proud of his abilities that he neglected the treasures of the unconscious, then he had to be sacrificed and replaced because he was too old to battle with the forces of the unconscious.

Now there is less fear of being overpowered by the Shadow realm; the danger is in losing the treasures there. See *BROTHERS*.

The new anti-hero, who may save the situation despite the king, suffers rather than acts, is often crippled or deformed: May represent specifically the *INFERIOR FUNCTION*, but anyway the unconscious; the whole initiative is shifted from conscious to unconscious, from active to passive. Often it is his very twisted, complex, inner nature symbolized as his deformity, abnormality, which forces him to find another way, a way via the inner unconscious.

Other examples are the poor, deserters, refugees in the woods: all referring to figures in the Unconscious who, by resisting the dominant tyranny that is in power, save the situation.
Books:-
Jung, C. G. *Man and his Symbols* (1964), Part 2, by Henderson, Joseph L.

The *CHILD* in Grass, G. *The Tin Drum* (1962 tr.) would be an example of the stunted anti-hero, from modern fiction.

The HEROINE
Provides a pattern for feminine conscious attitudes, and Anima.

As the Hero does for masculine. The feminine Ego relates to the total potential and slowly grows into it. The typical heroine humanizes the brutish animal side of man, and provides a wellspring of emotion and unconscious life to soften his dry conscious purposes.
See also *ANIMUS/A*.
MASCULINE/FEMININE, The Feminine.
MAZE for Ariadne as heroine.
Books:-
Franz, M. L. von. *The Feminine in Fairy-tales* (1972).
Neumann, E. *Amor and Psyche: the Psychic Development of the Feminine* (1956).

HISTORY. Also Legend and Historicized Myth
Events and facts may be just as symbolic as products of the imagination.

Particular incidents may be selected and preserved, rather than others, because of their symbolic fascination or appeal. It isn't just the circumstances, and the way material is formed, that make it symbolic. Powerful experiences, arising spontaneously from the unconscious, are unmistakably symbolic. But ordinary everyday events or events from history may become symbolic, which can be assessed chiefly by the peculiar fascination they have, their power over the human mind. Wherever passionate interest is aroused in events which, on the conscious level, are of no particular concern to the individual, then it's worth investigating the possibility that there is some symbolic link via the unconscious, which accounts for the fascination.
The different periods of history: correspond to layers in the collective unconscious, and to some extent of life. Children,

or at least boys, go through a phase of being particularly interested in cavemen.

Jung had a dream about the different layers of the collective unconscious portrayed as different layers of architecture in Rome.

Later people are often attracted more by particular periods of history for reasons related to their own inner, partially conscious needs.

Historical figures: Figures like Alexander, or Napoleon can just as well be symbols of the heroic archetype (see *HERO*) as a figure of fiction or figures from myth and fairy-tale.

The French Revolution, Nazism, or the Bomb: Can be symbolic of the eruption of the collective Shadow, as much as Leviathan.

History is full of archetypal patterns: Symbolic considerations play a part in what material is selected and preserved, even if they don't govern the pattern of history as it unfolds.

Legend: Appears to be history which is not quite satisfactory enough from the symbolic point of view, so that facts are embellished to suit the symbolism.

Historicized myth: Is the opposite of legend. When people feel their mythology seems to be a bit up in the air, lacking in concrete and human situations, and they are beginning to lose interest in it for this reason, then they are inclined to turn the mythical figures – even gods – into historical people. Since the myths were often idealized episodes from history (see R. Graves), this can be in the nature of a return towards sources, and provide satisfying results in spite of distortions from the historical point of view. It represents the stage of withdrawing PROJECTIONS from celestial to the human (intermediate) sphere. Since symbolism is primarily interested in the value of the material for the individual now, all this makes very little difference to the symbolic meaning. See also *IMAGINATION, Fact/fiction*; *PERSONIFICATION*; *ANCESTORS.*

Book:-

Toynbee, A. *A Study of History* (1972). (Illustrated one-volume edition.)

HOMUNCULUS
The inner equivalent of a child: procreative power forced inwards.

This inner creative power is attained by a return to *ORIGINS*, the undeveloped potential before conscious *SPLITS* from unconscious. The symbol also relates to the *INFERIOR FUNCTION*, which is often the source of the reunion of conscious and unconscious.

The homunculus was born without recourse to woman. Urine, sperm and blood putrefied and after forty days the homunculus began to develop, according to Paracelsus. One of the aims of ALCHEMY was to get the homunculus to emerge from the vessel of transformation. In Faust he is a principal figure at the Witches' Sabbath: He is related to phallic power, sublimated in order to discover the secrets of life and the relationship of life to matter, one of the major concerns of symbolism as well as Alchemy.

Negative Symbolism:-
For man to ape God in an attempt to create a living figure has sinister associations.

Related Symbolism:-
Atum, the hermaphrodite Egyptian God, who existed before the world divided into male and female, masturbated to produce the primary elements of the universe.

The Golem, which grows apace and can get out of control: Like the unconscious.

The wax or clay figures used by witches and black magicians to inflict harm on others, presumably via the unconscious: Are often confused with the homunculus.

All figures brought to life, such as Frankenstein's Monster (in Mary Shelley's novel), zombies, VAMPIRES, even Pinocchio. See also *DWARFS*.

Book:-
Scholem, G. G. *On the Kabbalah and its Symbolism* (1965).

HORN of Plenty. Cornucopia
The abundant provision of nature and of life.

For those who know how to tap its resources, but this in turn requires inner resources.

HORROR FILMS. Vampires, werewolves, the undead, etc. **Stirrings of the unconscious, especially the neglected intuitive function.**

These manifest first in a negative and puerile form, but are full of undeveloped potential.

See also *VAMPIRES; DEATH.*

SCIENCE FICTION for the beginning of a positive and authentic use of intuition, which includes the prophetic faculty.

HORSE

Energy, on every level, from the energy which works the cosmos, down to the horsepower of a car.

The adjectives and attributes of the horse determine which particular aspect of that one universal energy is in question.

Positive/Negative Symbolism:-

Energy is either in harmony or conflict, so horses may be symbols of harmony and right relationship, or of war. Horses have in fact played a significant role in war for many centuries, and the facts influence the symbol – or, if you prefer, are an ephemeral instance of the archetypal validity of the symbol.

The 'lightning' speed, the swiftness of the horse, which is made available: Some instinct in man which can carry him to his goal faster than his own unaided intellect. This points to being carried along by instinctive intuitions. This type of horse often talks to its rider in tales.

In Greek myth, the Sea God Poseidon created the horse: Which indicates a strong association with the passions, which are the motivation and driving force in man. The sea and the horse are symbolically related and refer to these passions; for example waves are called 'white horses', and we speak of 'riding the waves'. Passions must be 'bridled'.

The sinister man-eating mares (or stallions) of King Diomedes: Seem to fit this context better than any other, as the devouring and time-consuming aspect of unleashed passion, which must be mastered by the Hero, Heracles.

Horses are also associated with Hades, the Underworld, death: Different qualities of the horse combine: its warlike quality, the dark unconscious animal instinct at odds with the conscious Ego, and the speed of the animal, all make it the ideal mount for the figure of death which suddenly and swiftly overtakes man on the road of life.

Riding the horse, where being carried by the horse is what is emphasized: The feminine libido, or energy, which starts by carrying a man in the womb, and later is the support of his inner life (see *ANIMA*).

Horse and Carriage: Different aspects of man's inner self, his energy, body, with the coachman as his conscious Ego, but the true master sits back inside the carriage, the Self. This is a striking image of the contrast between Ego and Self.

ICARUS

Symbolically describes man's life, the years that fly, as skimming between sun and sea – that is, between male conscious Ego, and feminine unconscious emotion.

Icarus is given wings of wax and feathers, made by his father, Daedulus, who warns him not to fly too high or the sun will melt the wax, but if he skims too low the feathers will get wet in the sea: Superficially it is just a moral tale which ends badly when the boy doesn't obey his father, who arrives safely on similar wings. Icarus flies too high, reflecting the typical pattern of meteoric rise and fall of the Ego in life. Symbolically, the story has associations with the flight into the mind realm, ignoring material factors as well as total identification with the conscious Ego. Icarus is in a state of elation as he flies up. See *ABOVE/Below*. The Ego has only a short reign.

Robert Graves links the story with the renewal of the King, who also represents the reign of the conscious Ego.

Related Symbolism:-

PROMETHEUS, who steals fire from heaven and is chained to a rock.

The PHOENIX (see BIRDS): Eats its own wings, and so returns to the earth.

In *ALCHEMY* it is necessary to dissolve (into the mind) and coagulate in relation to material existence.

In these examples there is a movement from angel to beast, but does Daedulus advise holding a course midway?

The I CHING
The most sophisticated *ORACLE* **ever devised, but also a complete system of symbolic wisdom arranged in playful form.**

As with other symbolic systems the I Ching, or Chinese Book of Changes, is an elaborate structure built from simple units, which reflects the structure of the universe itself.
Related Symbolism:-
ARCHETYPES; EGYPTIAN MYTH; KABBALAH; ZODIAC.

The Two Opposites.
    Originally the oracle provided the answer 'YES' or 'NO', like heads or tails when tossing a coin.

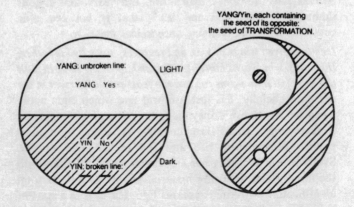

Gradually all the symbolic *OPPOSITES* accumulated around these two: the light masculine creative force of life in contrast with the dark feminine passive force of matter.
Related Symbolism:-
CADUCAEUS, with Pole as Yang, Serpents as Yin; *NUMBERS*, One/Many; *PATTERNS*.

The Four:
   Once separated, the lines could then be combined to produce
   new patterns.

Just as the Gods of *EGYPT* divide into male and female and
then produce offspring, so separating and combining
produces the symbolic patterns that reflect the pattern of
life. For the oracle this also produced new shades of meaning
in the answer.

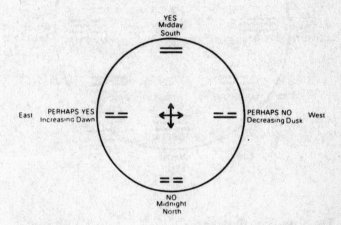

Symbolically the four signs, which result from combining
the two lines, are far more flexible and can be related to the
Four *DIRECTIONS*, the Four *SEASONS*, the human Family of
Mother, Father, Son and Daughter, as well as other basic
ELEMENTS and ingredients of the pattern of life with its
endless flux.

The Eight Trigrams:
   Even more flexible were the eight different trigrams or
   figures made up of three lines, arranged to accord with the
   Seasons from the time of the Chou dynasty, Twelfth
   Century BC.

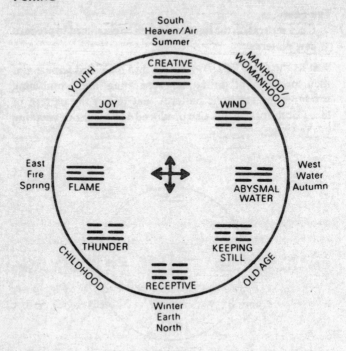

The Sixty-Four Hexagrams:

These reflect something of the complexity of the pattern of life.

By simply separating two sets of eight trigrams, and then relating them to each other in every possible combination of figures made up of six lines, you reach the final permutations of this extraordinary book of wisdom – arranged like an elaborate game.

The pattern of opposites: This is the basic pattern of life, of symbolism and of the I Ching. Starting with the simple contrast of Yang/Yin, it develops via the arrangement of the trigrams opposite each other, and is the continuous underlying theme of the final sequence of sixty-four hexagrams; for example, all are arranged in pairs of opposites, so far as the patterns of lines are concerned – where the pattern of lines cannot be turned upside down it is reversed.

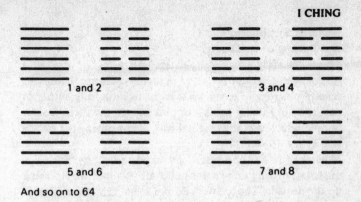

1 and 2   3 and 4

5 and 6   7 and 8

And so on to 64

The I Ching itself refers to the way the opposites combat each other like fire and water, or combine as sun and rain to germinate the seed and bring about the process of growth.
The continuous CHANGE and TRANSFORMATION, as everything turns into its opposite: Creative turns into receptive, active into passive, action turns into rest, yet there is equilibrium in the outcome which endures.
In the continual sequence of flux and change, the wind brings thunder, rain, then sun: The ELEMENTS take their turn: each turning into the next. Changing is the way by which the four persist.
The seed changes into the tree and back into its seeds: In the same way the past can be discovered from the traces it has left now, for example in archaeology, and the future can also be known in the present causes, which are like its seeds.
Union of Opposites in all three spheres:-
By following the archetypal pattern of nature – which divides and then relates – the I Ching remains close to the ways of nature and reflects the forces at work there.
In Heaven, Yang/Yin: Reflect the invaluable alternation of LIGHT/dark in night and day.
On Earth: They reflect the invaluable pattern of the firm alternating with the yielding, as in Ice and Water. See DISINTEGRATION/Integration; or the Dissolve/Coagulate of ALCHEMY.
In Man: The same symbols, Yang/Yin, reflect Love and Rectitude.

Personal Symbolism:-

The I Ching as an Oracle:

This is certainly a highly sophisticated oracle, but whether it works or not cannot be tested in theory, because there is no scientific theory to cover what happens randomly, either in nature or in tossing coins – or picking yarrow sticks from a bundle which was the original way of consulting the oracle (see *SYNCHRONICITY*).

However, it can be tested by experiment: by asking a question, tossing three coins in the air six times, and looking up the answer. The answers do not seem so vague and two-way as the Delphic Oracle appears to have been at times. Some are plainly more appropriate to particular situations than others.

Note on how to consult the *I Ching:* Toss three coins six times.

Three heads: give an emphatic 'Yes', or Yang:

———O———

Three tails: give an emphatic 'No', or Yin:

———X———

BUT, two tails and a head, give 'Yes', or Yang:

————————

and two heads and a tail, give 'No', or Yin:

——— ———

So in the last two it is the odd one out that counts, for reasons arising from the numerical value of heads and tails in terms of yarrow sticks.

The first throw gives you the bottom line, and the lines are built up from there. So in the section of the oracle referring to particular lines, the first line is the bottom line.

Finally in this section, headed 'The Lines', only the emphatic Yang and emphatic Yin – when you threw three heads or three tails – count. These emphatic lines then change into

212

their opposites, Yang into Yin and vice versa, which gives a new hexagram relating to the final outcome of the consultation: the seeds of future development.

Book:-

Wilhelm, R. (Trans.) The *I Ching* or *Book of Changes* (1951).

IDENTIFICATION
A natural process which relates man with Nature, *INNER* with Outer, as well as depicting an aspect of relationship between people, their empathy.

Identifying with the hero, heroine or other figures, is a completely natural unconscious process which we do automatically when we read a book or go to the cinema. We may also do it unconsciously when we look at an animal – our body may wince, if the creature's in pain – or even looking at a star or a flower.

Symbolism attempts to describe the relationship between the individual and the rest of the cosmos. This relationship neither exists inside the individual, nor regardless of him: it doesn't exclude him. In symbolism, the convention for describing this relationship is identification, which describes the feeling that relates or unites man with his environment. The relationship between the individual – who is the carrier of life – and the *COSMOS*, the dead material universe, is in fact very subtle, and not so easy to describe without a symbolic convention because it is hard, if not impossible, to assess exactly what matter is without life – without any particular organs of perception.

Note:-

This is why philosophy swings and veers between an idealist and empirical base and certain particular philosophers appear to switch base, such as Fichte and possibly Wittgenstein.

Symbolic identification is more primitive and childish, and concerns the living stream of direct experience only, which includes both factors.

So long as it's clear that the relationship between man and the Cosmos – or for that matter, man and the Divine Reality – is being described, all is well. The confusion arises from trying to pin what is essentially a relationship down to one end of it or the other, usually the human. The conventional symbolism of the microcosm, for example, which points to the relationship between the life force in man and life force in the cosmos – *atman* and *brahman*, which are then identified in Hinduism – if (mis)taken literally, is seen as a miniature cosmos somewhere inside the human being. It is as well to bear in mind there is no room for it there, however miniature, and there is no power to run it; the amount of power generated by the individual, as measured so far, is barely enough to light a dim bulb.

The positive side of identification: – the unconscious knows that it shares in the creation of light, of which trees are only dimly aware, and the sun not at all; it moves with the wind and the sea; and can change shape like a god or magician. For example, this is what *Taliesin, companion of Merlin* practises.

Negative Symbolism:-

This unconscious identification also has a negative side, normally called *PROJECTION*. Though the unconscious continues to identify naturally, it is the work of the conscious mind to discriminate clearly between inner and outer, between sun and eye, and above all between other people and unconscious complexes – to distinguish between the inner image of other people and the living reality.

The conflict between these two positions (identification v. discrimination) cannot be resolved lightly: it is part of the whole life's conflict between conscious and unconscious. But beyond primitive identification and conscious discrimination, there is a third position of integrated wholeness, when the meaningful process of identification is not unconscious projection, but conscious symbolism.

IMAGINATION
It is impossible to see the symbolic meaning of myths without using the myth-making faculty, namely the imagination, according to James Hillman.

At first glance the products of the imagination seem wild and arbitrary, but with a little more familiarity they begin to fall into shapes and patterns, which not only reflect (see *MIRROR*) the flow of energy within the psyche, expressing the emotions and intuitions especially, but also have recognizable associations with the patterns of archetypal mythology and symbolism. The images, like dreams, reflect the actual state of the unconscious; and the symbolic associations with traditional mythology link the personal unconscious with its wider context, the human imagination which works according to consistent patterns, with particular personal variations. These variations usually take the form of deficiencies – as with eyesight, short-sightedness and colour-blindness are the particular variations. When men's faculties are working at their optimum they can usually be assumed to work in accordance with each other. Hence it is no wonder that somebody of exceptional abilities and gifts is eventually widely appreciated. These are merely examples to emphasize the consistency of imagination, in spite of apparent discrepancies which arise from the fact that many people's imaginations have atrophied young or work in a limited field only, thereby creating the illusion of isolated fantasy unlike anyone else's.

Positive/Negative Symbolism:-

Like any other faculty the imagination can be used badly, which usually means not used enough. Faculties of the mind are much like limbs of the body, in that they wither if not used. Unfortunately people then become very intolerant of their crippled backward imaginations when those do begin to stir, usually with erotic fantasies or wishful daydreaming. Some people have been shamed into suppressing these, instead of urging the imagination on towards greater efforts.

Active Imagination (or Creative Imagination):

Imagination has been variously judged as an appalling deviation of the human intellect, or the mind's highest and most creative faculty (as Coleridge claimed.)

More often it is simply ignored, with the less said about it the better. Encyclopedia after encyclopedia may contain a paragraph on the subject, rarely a column. Only psychology is beginning to change this, and overcome the general embarrassment about the subject.

It is now over fifty years since Jung suggested making frequent active use of the imagination; and pointed to the fruits of it, in bringing together the different complex units of the psyche under conscious control, instead of pulling in different directions, and so consuming the individual's misdirected and undirected energy in inner turmoil and struggle.

Like the invisible man, the inner unconscious forces have to be clothed in images before they can be recognized by the conscious mind: once recognized, they are no longer unconscious.

How to start:

> **With imagination, as with a lot of other work, the greatest difficulty undoubtedly is in getting started.**

As with dreams it helps to know that dreaming goes on most of the night, but the difficulty still lies in capturing a few fragments in the morning, i.e. getting anything back across the *THRESHOLD*. So with imagination, which is the continuously active substratum to thought, the difficulty lies in getting hold of it. The greatest obstacle is probably the over-critical conscious Ego itself, which cannot tolerate any nonsense from the imagination. So the Ego needs to be set against Ego, and made intolerant of its own limitations instead, and set to guard the threshold like an obedient dog, ready to spring silently on the quarry and drag it in, rather than frighten it off. Then the patience of the fisherman or the deerstalker is needed, bearing in mind that what is being stalked is worth far more than a couple of meals. Even if nothing were sighted for a few years – not likely – it could still be reckoned a short cut straight across the mind to integrating inner unconscious forces; in contrast with the long way round via everyday life through projections and delusions.

Whatever crops up should not be despised, however ghastly, mad or flabby. Any imaginative content will gradually transform (become humanized) in relation to the light of consciousness. But first the imagination must be left quite free. Secondly it'll probably take on meaning and value in itself when related to other symbolic material. Compare Personal *MYTH*.

An alternative start: It is sometimes possible to choose a personal image from a dream, or any other symbol which has a particular fascination, and see what the imagination does with it.

Meditation: Most methods of meditating are forms of conscious deliberate dissociation, switching off the conscious Ego for a while, i.e. ways of contacting the Unconscious. See *DISINTEGRATION*.

Active imagination lies somewhere between free association and the undistracted attention of Yoga.

Book:-

Evans Wentz, W. Y. *Tibetan Yoga and Secret Doctrines* (1935) for a traditional disciplined use of symbolic imagination.

The Symbolic (Feeling) Mind/The Thinking Mind:
The unconscious expresses itself in images. By understanding the images we are coming to terms with the myth-making part of the mind; that is, working with the Unconscious itself, including the animal instincts. (See *FUNCTIONS of the Mind, Mythological/Logical*.)

The lack of imagination:
The loss of the inner unconscious orientation is just as disastrous as the loss of conscious orientation. That is to say, the loss of the imagination leads to neurosis as surely as lack of adaptation to the outside world. When neglected, it acts negatively and poisons life with unreal dreads and obsessions. But if contacted voluntarily, it won't take possession involuntarily.

Fact/Fiction: Symbols are not confined to products of the imagination. But because they refer to the psyche and life forces, it is simply irrelevant whether the symbolic *TREE, ANIMAL or human figure* exists or doesn't exist. It's like asking, 'Where is this rolling stone that gathers no moss?'

Hypnagogic visions, hallucinations: hypnagogic visions occur on the brink of sleep and hallucinations when the level of consciousness is otherwise lowered – by drink, drugs, exhaustion, lack of food, etc. – so both seem to be a breakthrough of the dream-mind into conscious, waking reality. The dream-mind projects vivid reality in contrast with the waking consciousness which seems to record reality (but see *COSMOS*).

Illusion (e.g. the fata morgana): On the whole the risk of confusing imaginative reality with substantial reality, images of a stone with stones, is slight, compared with the risk of failing to take seriously the very real emotional content of fantasy – of *the fata morgana conjured by the witch* – that reveals man's Anima, the source of all his feelings. But there is another commonplace and widespread illusion (see *PROJECTION*) which can only be dispelled through the sustained use of the creative imagination, as with *PERSONIFICATION* creating inner figures which can then be distinguished from outside people.

Book:-
Cobb, E. *The Ecology of Imagination in Childhood* (1977).

INCUBATION PERIOD
A period of time devoted to cutting off conscious thoughts in order to make contact with the unconscious.

This period may last between three and seven days, according to different traditions.
There is a certain amount of symbolism surrounding the actual act of turning deliberately to the unconscious in times of stress, or illness (see The *HEALER*). This is a deliberate act of self-isolation and turning inwards, sometimes remaining awake, especially at night, but with reduced (dimmed) consciousness. At other times it may be sleeping in temples, in circumstances intended to induce dreams. Sleeping in strange circumstances may in any case produce dreams. In the ancient world, Gubna was such a centre for incubation dreams (see the Egyptian Tale of Weni) and at Gibeon, Solomon had such a dream.
The Symbols:-
This is linked cosmically with the three days between the Old

and the New Moon, the three days of darkness, when there is no ray of conscious light in the night, but only the stars; symbols of the many eyes of the unconscious.

This is sometimes described as three days in the belly of the monster. The monster of Darkness has swallowed the moon as it swallows the conscious Ego. It is very hot in there and sometimes the hero loses all his *HAIR*. It is a period of regeneration and rebirth. It may actually be a significant minimum of time necessary for making contact with the unconscious. And a further three days may lead deeper into the vegetable and mineral layers of the unconscious, towards the preconscious totality.

Jonah spent three days in the belly of the whale. Also Pinocchio's period in a similar spot which marks a turning point in his career towards becoming human.

Christ's three days swallowed up in the dark tomb and under earth is also symbolic of this.

See also BIBLICAL SYMBOLISM, *Creation:* for seven days of sinking into the unconscious.

Sweatbaths: are part of ritual initiation for American Indians, and this is further related to the generation of heat (Tapas) in Yogic practices.

The expression 'sweating it out' refers to the difficult passive state of holding on through a crisis. Ordinary life is the ultimate reference point of all symbols. Extraordinary practices merely concentrate the normal processes of life: which enforce a certain growing awareness in any case. Here the symbols point to the long passive periods of life, formerly the winter months by the fire when the nights were long – and still the passive winter of old age.

The INFERIOR FUNCTION/The Main Function
The most neglected side of your potential causes many problems, but can be a valuable source of contact with the unconscious in the end and provide the means of integrating the psyche.

One – or maybe two – of the *FUNCTIONS* of the mind is invariably less developed than the others and lies dormant in the unconscious. It may be any one of the Four:

It isn't easy to work with a Function that operates slowly and badly. The Inferior Function has a random, erratic quality. Sometimes it works reasonably well and often it doesn't. It functions in its own way and cannot be summoned at will. This is the despised realm of the hobby, relegated to the shed at the bottom of the garden. In a specialized society, it is usually the exact opposite of what you do professionally, unless of course you have been forced into an unsuitable mould.

In terms of what is produced, it may be appalling, homespun philosophy for example, and better not shown. But around the mid-point of life (in your thirties) it can provide a second wind, bringing a new charge of emotion and energy from the unconscious, where it lurks: a concentration of new life just when the professional side was beginning to get worn out with over-use, starting to rattle badly. Curiously, by recharging life in general, the main function also picks up again. The conflict between the two – where should the time be spent? – creates new tensions which can be dramatic and exciting in themselves.

Because the functions are often distributed through a family, using the Inferior Function sometimes comes about very naturally through a child whose interests may be the opposite of one's own. But this distribution of functions can stultify the process if it has the effect of delegating all interest to the person who is good at it, whether spouse or child.

There are several hazards in getting to grips with the Inferior Function:-

One intellectual bored with his professional life was persuaded to collect wild flowers (after a dream) but soon turned it into a science, noting, naming and investigating the flowers; and so he was comfortably back in the rut with his main function again.

An intuitive might make one figure in clay which turns out rather poorly, so he begins working hard on all the possibilities for the next figure. But his actual contact with the material outside world is thereby lost. He is back to functioning intuitively, with only a pretence of clay involved. **The feeling type** may be all too aware of the value of thinking, without actually doing any thinking.

Or the Inferior Function may erupt negatively and be taken no further: for example **the sensation type** may be full of dark forebodings about sinister possibilities, which mark the time to pay more attention to his Inferior Intuition.

In general the Inferior Function is the cause of most of the problems in life and relates to the areas of greatest dread and suffering. It can't be raised to a higher level of consciousness, just like that – or quickly and conveniently guided along more rational lines.

On the contrary, the superior function has to sacrifice itself, and sink to the level of slowness and incompetence of the Inferior Function, without trying to force it but letting it come and go in its own random way.

However, in order to avoid the worst blunders, the two other functions can be called in, the two intermediate functions. The intellectual, who falls for the most idiotic tramp of a girl, can use his intuitive perception and sense of reality to get him out of the mess.

If allowed to develop in its own curious way and in its own time, the Inferior Function not only opens up new horizons – a new quarter of life, which also helps one relate to other people in that quarter – but even more important it is the source of uniting all four quarters, completing the process of integrating the psyche, conscious with unconscious, inner with outer, thinking with feeling,

Under more natural conditions we would not want to end up our lives one-sided, limited. And in due course extravert physical types are capable of extraordinarily deep, pure inner visions, which easily compensate for any naïvety, with their utterly spontaneous fresh authentic quality, that is the envy of the true (but jaded) visionary. And vice versa, the intuitive type may make a simple gesture – like drinking a glass of wine – into a magical festival. And the same applies to late developed feelings and thoughts.

The Symbols:-

DWARFS, MIDGETS and *CHILDREN:* Under-developed inner qualities. Most especially the youngest of four children whose incapacity is particularly marked: either he's intellectually a simpleton, or he's particularly incompetent in some other way.

Cripples, Deformities: Point to malformed inner functions of a dark unconscious nature.

Clowns or comedians who are especially naïve and gauche in their relationships with women: Inferior Feeling.

The FOOL. Tom Thumb. Cartoon figures e.g. 'Pluto': Inferior Sensation. *Donald 'Duck':* Inferior Thinking. *'Mickey':* Inferior Feeling. *Goofy:* Inferior Intuition.

The little Hobbits (Tolkein, J. R. R.): Inferior Intuition, full of dark forebodings.

The Hunchback of Notre Dame (Hugo, V.): Inferior Emotion. *A primitive figure, such as The Noble Savage* pointing to the primitive under-developed, uncivilized aspects of the Inferior Function. Especially if physical sensation is inferior.

Cavemen, or animals: It is sometimes best to treat the Inferior Function like an animal, placating, taming, and rewarding it. Also *menial servants, foreigners, barbarians, peasants.*

Figures like Dick Whittington and his cat (Anima). The god Bes in Egypt.

Also themes, such as the big being outwitted by the small, the strong by the weak. Compare Alice, who had to grow very small in order to cross the threshold into the Wonderland of the Unconscious (i.e. the author could only do so through the inferior transexual side of his personality).

The mouse that helps the lion, and *the tortoise that beats the hare in the race*, also symbolize the work of the inferior function.

Often the events in the story will follow the same pattern and sequence three times. And then there's a change, which only indicates that the story is now introducing the important theme of the Inferior Function and its reactions.

The Inferior Function is related to the Shadow (see *EGO/Shadow*). And the worst atrocities are perpetrated by it, especially collectively when thousands of Inferior Functions gang up together.

INNER/Outer
Symbolism is very much concerned with the inner realm of the psyche.

Most symbolic figures – *gods, monsters, fairies, giants, dwarfs, etc* – simply don't exist in the outside world as such. They can't be found there.

For direct experience, the difference between the inside and the outside world is very clear. What has become confused is the nature of the reality of the inner world, which is in fact a different side of consciousness, a different mode of experiencing reality, rather than another universe.

The nearest equivalent, which is used again and again as a symbol is the reflection in a *MIRROR* or in a highly polished shield. Though reflected in many puddles, there is only one moon. The reflection is merely a trick of the light.

So when we close our eyes we are not shut up inside our skins as if in a bag, zipped up the spine, cut off from the world. The so-called inner life, though experienced inwardly, is in fact in vibrant contact with the cosmos: what we experience is life itself.

There still remains a vast distinction between yesterday, which can only be contacted from within, and dragons or unicorns. These depict forces of life at work in the world, experienced through feeling and intuition.

Everything is in a permanent state of relationship between inner and outer. In terms of machinery, man is receiver and transmitter, cine-camera and projector. But this permanent relationship is established on many levels – of smell and taste as well as touch and sight; of creativity as well as receptivity; of feeling as well as thinking.

The primitive person or the child doesn't need to be convinced that his own inner experiences, of dream, and fantasy, are valid. It is more difficult to convince him that there are other things besides his moods, his feelings, which also matter: there is the whole of South America to think about, for example. But the pendulum can swing very far, and man is so adaptable that he can even be educated out of an intense awareness of his own subjective experience, and begin to live his life almost from the outside; if he sees himself objectively as the cog in the social machine, the struggling ant in the anthill, finally the hunt is on for his own subjective experience – but by then it's like looking for a needle in a haystack, and he hardly knows where to begin. Symbolism is subjective, and works from the inside— In terms of inward experience – or life from the inside – unicorns may be more valid than horses, and dragons of more central concern than hippopotamuses. Or they may not.

Given that there is no inner world – for lack of space – and that the human being is entirely taken up with different modes of experiencing the outside world, there are three main distinctions to be made.

   i. He may look out at it through his senses.

   ii. He may look out at it through his mind, with memories of it, thoughts about it, reflections on it.

   iii. He may look out at it through his creative *IMAGINATION*, picking up wings or spikes off swordfish and adding them to horses. This last is the source of change, growth and transformation in his own life; and in the outside world. It is closely related to the unconscious, but not identical with it. It can find images and symbols for unseen forces of life, the energy, the action that leaves no trace behind it in the air, life rather than substance. This may be the most intense way that man can be related to the outside world: by depth of feeling and insight.

But all three ways need to be related to each other.

The Symbols:-

MAYA, Samsara: In the East, where the people are more introvert by nature, substance is the delusion, while life is the essential reality. See *EXTRAVERT/INTROVERT.*

In stories, all going into caves, underground, under the sea: at least in part refers to trying to recover the personal inward experience of life, which may also be lost in unconsciousness. It then has to be brought back and related to the outside world: subjective to objective as feeling to thinking (see *UNION* of *OPPOSITES*).

Often the inner experience is gained at the expense of the outer. *The visionaries are blind (e.g. Tiresias).* The outer has been sacrificed for the inner.

Put another way this turns up as *the golden bird in the drab cage, or the golden horse in very dingy harness:* referring to inner qualities with no outward show – it is children who have to show everything.

The so-called Inner World is also the OTHER WORLD, i.e. the world of the unconscious. *The Hero is born of both worlds (his father is usually otherworldly, divine or whatever)* and so he has the potential for uniting the two worlds. Since the HERO represents everyone, everybody has that potential: the external situation can be reconciled with the internal reality. In Alchemy there were many symbols referring to the inward experience of life itself: *the Philosopher's stone, the permanent water*, etc. A number of symbols for the same thing indicates that it is something obscure and difficult to get hold of: the contrast between the symbols safeguarded the tendency to take the symbols literally.

Blood, especially, is a symbol of this inner reality, and so the *blood of the wind*, for example, is the inner reality of the breath of life itself. See *BODY*.

Anything *INVISIBLE*.

The mind discloses its own general nature and structure in symbols: therefore also see The *FUNCTIONS* of the mind which, when working in an inward way, perceive:

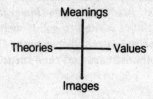

Book:-
Martin, P. W. *Experiment in Depth* (1976). Examines the work of Toynbee, Eliot and Jung in relation to a creative minority who turn inwards in a crisis and find a new way.

INSECTS
Precision. Meticulous thinking.

Insects are masters of detail and are often called in, in fairy-tales, to sort out things that have got impossibly mixed and muddled, such as grain and sand: Precision, detailed conscious thinking helps especially to sort out compulsions, obsessions, i.e. to discriminate conscious from unconscious content.

Analysing the inner psyche, especially sorting out values: i.e. discriminating between what is of value and what is useless.

Phobias about insects: Irrational fear of detailed thinking, clear differentiations.

See also *DIFFERENTIATION*.

INVISIBLE. Vanishing
Pure energy, in contrast with substance.

The *INNER* realm of life.

Action which leaves no trace.

Especially powerful, unconscious influences which aren't recognized by the conscious mind even.

If the hero (e.g. Perseus) puts on the cloak of invisibility: He enters the unconscious realm. He gives up his conscious Ego personality, with its appearances.

This is related to the symbolism of DEATH when the invisible last breath (symbol of the working-order of the man) leaves the corpse: The archetypal life process of dissolution and coagulation (see *DISINTEGRATION/Integration*). On the inanimate level this is related to solids melted into liquids and liquids vaporized into invisible gases. Or food broken down into the bloodstream and then turned into invisible energy.

Example:-

Wells, H. G. *The Invisible Man:* An attempt to distinguish between intuitive perception of the forces in man in contrast with the physical sensation of his material substance.

Note:-

Wells was highly intuitive but did not feel it was much use to him in the materialist society in which he lived. His intuitive side may have identified with his persecuted invisible man.

Personal Symbolism:-

Strong irrational outburst of emotion aroused by people who are not present, as if their invisible presence is felt long after they have left the room or are far away: this often means that what is really disturbing you is an aspect of your own (invisible) psyche buried in the unconscious, of which that particular person is only an image, representing the inner force. See *COMPLEXES*. The other person may be acting as an outer garment for the force to give it shape, just as Wells's invisible man bandaged and clothed himself in order to appear.

JACK and the Beanstalk
Climbing into the upper realms to steal that most precious of treasures, rational consciousness.

A popularized story version of the archetypal myth of man climbing the world tree to steal the treasure of the gods: Man mounts his unconscious *VEGETABLE* soul towards the light of rational consciousness.

The Giant's wife hides him: His *ANIMA* is his only ally against the hazard of being devoured by the giant forces of the unconscious, and in order to avoid that (having got a little treasure) the conscious mind is inclined to sever the connections with the unconscious, barricade the threshold, cut down the world tree (i.e. the Vegetable Soul, see *VEGETATION*).

Related Symbolism:-

See *PROMETHEUS*, where there are also gains and losses. (Note:- the children's version typically softens the end of the tale.)

See also *BIBLICAL SYMBOLISM, The Garden . . . and the tree of life; Cosmic MAN*.

JOURNEYS. Voyages
Your destiny described in terms of a journey which is through time, rather than space.

The course or direction of life as a whole.

As the sun marks the SEASONS and measures the years: So the typical or archetypal features of life are plotted and are represented symbolically as the conscious journey from Childhood to full maturity and on towards Old Age.

As the moon waxes and wanes on its journey across the night sky: So the dimmer course of the inner unconscious light also reaches a different but corresponding fulfilment before it ebbs away.

The events and encounters on the journey: The living experience of the archetypal features of the psyche, which appear in the images and forms provided for them by the creative imagination. But symbolism assumes that the nature and structure of the psyche and the forces at work there are of the same nature and structure as the forces at work in the cosmos. So these journeys don't consist of a fantasy voyage around the inside of the head, but the actual living surge of man's experience of life, expressed as accurately as possible in the terms available.

However, the symbolic journey need not necessarily be a product of the imagination, full of grotesque events. A perfectly ordinary trek can take on symbolic dimensions of value and meaning in reference to life in general. The encounters, the turning points, the crossings, the impassable barriers, reaching the destination, may all be as significant when referred to life in general, as the mythical voyages with all their monstrous encounters. For example, Hilaire Belloc's *Path to Rome*.

The fundamental mythical journey is the journey of sun and moon around the oceans of space, endlessly through time. In Egypt the Sun God sets out in the barque of millions of years and his crew has to battle with the monster of darkness at the prow, threatening to swallow them all. And the barque travels from East to West, and down through the gateway to the land of the dead. And rises again from the East: Through immeasurable TIME the life process continues, in cyclic fashion. The great battle – whether of gods or man – is for conscious light, life. But this cannot be conserved statically but only preserved endlessly by descending into the land of the dead, letting go into unconsciousness. Consciousness alternates with unconsciousness; death alternates with life; night alternates with day; the moon gets swallowed up and reappears.

The same archetypal features appear in the journeys of the Sun Heroes across the oceans of the world. They also have to fight off death-dealing monsters, and descend into the underworld.

228

Wandering:
   Is inspired by longing.

Man wanders in search of something lost. The monsters and obstacles may represent the contradictions and discontents involved in this search.

The Quest:
   Is a bit more specific.

But still the search in tales and myths is often for something elusive that exists beyond the edge of the world, i.e. an elusive part of the SELF lost in unconsciousness. Or it may be the living contact between man and nature that has been lost.

This is also a feminine task:
Isis has to search for the lost Osiris whom she finds inside a tree: In the inner realm of the unconscious vegetable soul (see VEGETATION), which had life without mind.
The goddesses also have to descend into the underworld to retrieve the male half of their psyche. For example Innini or Ishtar into Arallu. See also CLOTHES.
The desired goal, for example the Golden Fleece, has a fearful guardian: Longing is mixed with dread. Unity cannot be recovered without the sacrifice of the Ego: there can be no rebirth without passing through DEATH, whether symbolic or actual.
But the goal is also in the journeying, in the process of becoming: the culmination is in acquiring the qualities that are the products of the experiences on the way: completion, consciousness, wholeness. (See GOAL.)

The night journey – *the favourite theme for the inside of the lid of the coffin in Ancient Egypt – is related to the journey into the underworld:* The extinction of the Ego in order to discover the root of being: the living unconscious, vegetable root on which each new conscious Ego depends; by means of which conscious life keeps renewing itself, like the sun.
So long as these two, vegetable soul and conscious Ego, are SPLIT, the journey is torment, and ends in disaster. For the conscious mind they will always be opposite. They can only be lived as one by the whole being.

Walking:

Inner turmoil, conflict, confusion, leads directly to walking, even if only pacing up and down. Walking restores a balance and brings an inner calm. And is archetypally symbolic, in its mini-way: the left foot alternates with the right, the conscious side with the unconscious side, between heart (the emotional life, the feminine side) on the left of the body and reason on the right, and so between the opposing pressures which caused the turmoil in the first place.

The action of walking erect and balanced, like a vertical line, the world axis, can unite conscious and unconscious, mind and matter, in a way that thinking never can.

Particular journeys:-

The Odyssey; Jason and the Argonauts; The Ancient Egyptian Shipwrecked Sailor; The Voyages of Sinbad; Bunyan's *Pilgrim's Progress* and *Pilgrimages* generally; *Oedipus, Faust and Abraham all wander.* (See also *Eternal YOUTH.*)

Fairy-tales are full of quests to distant parts often for something which renews and restores life.

In Personal Symbolism:-

The point of these stories is to identify with the quest and know that there really is something worth searching for which can change and transform the experience of living. *The way of Tao; The Paths of TAROT;* also see *PERIODS OF LIFE.*

The JUMBLIES (Edward Lear)
The night *JOURNEY* to the distant shores of the unconscious.

Their heads were green and their hands were blue: The integration of thought with nature, or sensation, and the practical side of life. The head being green brings feminine substance of nature (green clothes the earth) into the mind realms, and vice versa the blueing of the hands brings the transforming power of the mind into practical matters.

They went to sea in a sieve: What it lacks practically as a boat, the sieve makes up for symbolically, for it lets in the sea of the unconscious – and even sifts it as it does so. It took them there and back all right, and they weren't 'all drowned' in the unconscious.

Compare 'The *OWL* and the *PUSSYCAT*', also by Lear and somewhat on the same theme. (Both mention 'owl', 'pig' and a boat with 'pea green' associations.)

KABBALAH. Or Cabala/Qabbala

Another complete symbolic system, wholly adequate in itself, for expressing the fundamental pattern, the archetypal structure of the cosmos, of society and of the individual psyche.

As in the most ancient symbolism known, this basic structure of life is depicted as a tree, The Tree of Life, with its fruit, the ten Sephiroth, or blazing spheres of consciousness, each with its dark Shadow side (the Shards).

The Tree of Life is to be lived rather than looked at. Since it is concerned only with the main ingredients of life, it is related to other systems which investigate the major concerns of mankind. But not in a precise way, but in a fluid, flexible, even playful way. This is not arbitrary or peripheral to the symbolism, but the very nature of it. Without this flexibility it cannot be applied to the particular situation, the individual life.

The Kabbalists rate intellect (8. Hod) lower in their scale of values than creative imagination (7. Netzach). They place intellect on the feminine pillar, making Knowledge/Theory purely receptive, while creative imagination is active and masculine, arising from the archetypes of Relationships/ Values. This is consistent with the fact that the Kabbalah was revived or developed in direct opposition to prevailing conscious attitudes in the West: Intellectual and Materialist. The *TREE OF LIFE* is a tree with three branches to either side, as found on Ancient Sumerian cylinder seals. (See Butterworth, E. A. S. *The Tree at the Navel of the Earth* (1970)).

Related Symbolism:-
The Tree of Life is probably related to, if not inspired by the *BIBLICAL* account of the Seven Days of Creation, which play an important role in the symbolism of the Kabbalah.
'Sephiroth' (derived from 'safar', to count) refers directly to

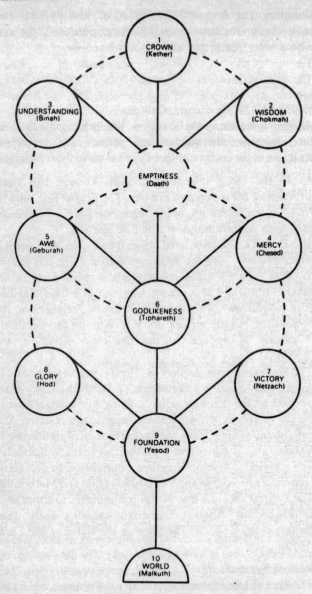

the ten archetypal numbers, on which depends the whole
multiplicity of creation in contrast with the One Tree. (See

NUMBERS, One/Many.) The *COLOURS* of the Sephiroth refer to experiences on the level of pure mind, pure life in contrast with matter. Compare with the intermediate plane in the Tibetan 'Bardo Thodol'. (See *DEATH*, Books of the Dead.) The Sephiroth can be compared to the *CHAKRAS* in Indian symbolism. The point of *ORIGIN* ('eyn sof', the Infinite) *SPLITS* into paternal power and supernal Mother, and these three form the upper Sephiroth. And the other seven form the offspring, that is, the body of Primordial Cosmic *MAN*, Adam Kadmon.

The myth of the divine Feminine Shekhinah, exiled on earth and waiting to return, expresses the recurring theme of symbolism: the break between *OPPOSITES*, such as *MASCULINE* and Feminine, *CONSCIOUS* and Unconscious.

The ten commandments will restore man's *UNION* with the Divine Man or *SELF*, which is the form in which God reveals himself to man. Just as the Gnostics thought of the infinite, the Transcendent, descending through many emanations to enter reality, and matter (like ripples in a pond), so the Sephiroth were thought of as similar emanations from *ABOVE* to below. But inevitably they also describe levels of consciousness within the psyche, first experienced presumably as an ascent, from below, upwards.

See also *PATTERNS; TAROT*.

Personal Symbolism:-

In childhood the outer world of sensation, which is the lowest of the Spheres, at the base of the Tree of Life, is at first poorly differentiated from the inner world of fantasy and dream, the Ninth Sphere immediately above. But when these two have been clearly distinguished and related to each other, they give birth to the Eighth Sphere, which represents the Conscious Ego.

Only when the Conscious Ego is sufficiently sure of its ground can it embrace once more the sphere of Imagination and Feeling – but in a new creative way. The Seventh Sphere is related to what Jung has called Active *IMAGINATION*. This is quite different from childish fantasy and marks a new relationship with the Unconscious which is as important as new relationships with the opposite sex in the outside world. Just as new relationships in the outside world can be

The same Sephiroth arranged as a *WHEEL*, as a *Lightning* flash from above down to earth, or as a *LADDER* reaching up from earth to heaven. Or as a single vertical *AXIS* with Twin pillars of *MASCULINE/* Feminine to either side. With other symbolic aspects of the Sephiroth indicated.

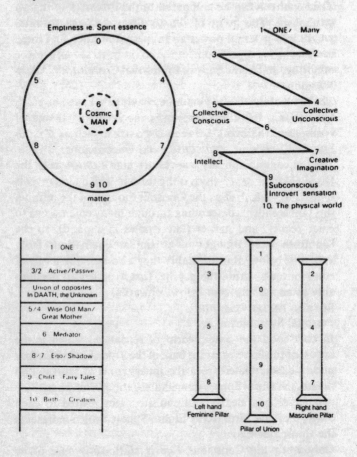

overpowering, so the unconscious can break in and break up the reality of the conscious Ego, if this is weak or malformed. But from this new union a *CHILD* may be born, that is, a new state of inner being, the Sixth, most important and most central of all the Spheres, from your point of view. This is the new-born, and as yet immature, *SELF*.

With maturity, the same process is repeated in the Upper

Spheres, but on the level of Collective rather than personal Conscious and Unconscious.

Once your mind has integrated all the different centres or Spheres of Consciousness, it extends towards an awareness of the undivided source of your own individuality. Or vice versa, this awareness may bring together disparate centres of consciousness within the psyche.

Book:-

Scholem, G. G., *On the Kabbalah and its Symbolism* (1965) (which contains excellent accounts of the Golem, see *HOMUNCULUS*); *LILITH*, and the Shekhinah.

Knight, G., *A Practical Guide to Qabbalistic Symbolism*, Vols I and II (1965).

KING. And his court

The dominant ruling power in consciousness whether individual or communal. Whatever part of the psyche is in control and directing the operations. The final arbiter of values within.

The ritual renewal of the king, either by replacement (originally with the sacrifice of the old king) or regeneration – linked symbolically with the regeneration of the mid-winter sun – gave rise to much mythology, which provided the ritual words for the occasion. The symbolism around the king remains valid whether an actual king was involved (representing his people) or the myth survived outside its context (transferred to eternity?) and was presented as fairy-tales. All deal with the state of the collective consciousness but this has a strong influence over individuals in the community.

The hero or sun king: The conscious Ego in command.

The weak, feeble king – often with a wicked vizier or prime minister in control: A weak conscious Ego and the psyche is possessed by the powers of the Shadow.

Often the king is in need of renewal; he may be sick or decrepit, for example, and his cure may depend on symbolic factors which point to the realm of the feminine: Like kings, dominant attitudes wear out, get dry and sterile. They become too abstract, meaningless and ineffective, and lose their emotional base. They fail to move. This is often for lack of relationship with the Anima, the inner feminine force. Which may just leave the king sad and moody – or worse. *Whether mythical or real, the King may combine the qualities of Hero and Wise Old Man, e.g. King Arthur, Charlemagne, and perhaps Barbarossa:* The Ego has integrated the other complexes (especially its dark shadow and dark feminine sides) and been transformed into the undivided *SELF*.

Note:- But of course somebody who is not a king can symbolize this too, such as Sophocles, turning from general into poet/playwright.

In this context, the Kings of Sumer and Akkad were masters of the four quarters (see DIRECTIONS). And at the Heb Sed festival in Egypt the King climbed a four-sided platform, with four stairways and also faced the four directions: As representative of the people, he was responsible for holding together the different ingredients in the fourfold structure of life, whether in the psyche, the community or the cosmos.

The symbolism around the king is closely related to the symbolism of Cosmic MAN: If the king can't be regenerated, the sun will never regain its summer power; if the king is impotent the soil will be unfruitful and the herds barren.

He is raised on a throne between heaven and earth, holding the orb of the earth, in a jewelled robe that represents the starry night, with the sun as his crown: The individual's life was projected on to the king. He identified with the king. The whole nation centred its life in the king, from whence life flowed back into man, animal and plant.

Note:-
The king was the focal point for the work and genius of the whole nation. His power to rule depended entirely on the people's consent to be ruled. His personality was hence of little significance compared with the corporate identity of the nation during that particular reign, which was great or miserable accordingly.

Negative Symbolism:-
King/Lion: The lion may be the dark animal side of the king, with wilder feelings, and great power. Also desires and passions.

The carnival king, usually a criminal, given one day's rule: Also, like the lion, represents the dark side of kingship. Or licence from conscious domination for a circumscribed period: blackout of consciousness. This is the tradition of amnesty for criminals. Compare *APOLLO/Dionysus.*

Mob rule, anarchy: The break-up of society is comparable with the break-up of the psyche, the autonomous rule of the separate *COMPLEXES.*

The Court.
Whether in reality, myth, drama or fairy-tale:
The epitome of the archetypal pattern of the psyche.

King/Queen: Masculine and feminine forces within, i.e. conscious intellect and unconscious feeling for life; or vice versa for a woman.

Usurpers to the royal throne or bed – the King's mistresses especially if scheming: Shadow elements in the unconscious, which have not been integrated and may take possession of the psyche, seize power there in the form of involuntary compulsions, obsessions.

The wise bishop/or scheming prelate (such as Richelieu and The Grey Eminence or Rasputin in the Russian Court): Intuition, positive or negative.

Chancellor/Dark Vizier: The material and physical side of life which, if in the wrong relation to the conscious Ego, may coerce it: and usurp control over the individual or nation from below.

The Fool: The *INFERIOR* Function. The unconscious child within, which if allowed free play can maintain the sanity and balance of the whole.

In Alchemy.
The King was the human personification of the work, the process of transformation, in four main stages, which were the equivalent of transforming base matter into gold:

Ego transformed into *SELF*, by stages.

1. *The decrepit king:* Limited Ego-bound consciousness.
2. *The king is dissolved or returned to the mother:* Ego is sunk back into unconsciousness.
3. *The king displays various symptoms:* In the raging conflict between conscious and unconscious.

4. *The king gives birth to an hermaphrodite:* The new
   dominant Self is born.
Related Symbolism:-
See *HERO; OSIRIS/Seth; SUN.*

Zen KOANS

**A set of powerful symbols continuously refreshed by the
practice of emptying the conscious mind in order to elicit a
direct and spontaneous response from the unconscious.**

The Zen Masters have devised a particularly vital and
physical system of symbolism, which may be partly designed
to combat the natural intuitive tendencies of the East, and
particularly those Eastern people who entered monasteries.
(See *FUNCTIONS* of the Mind.) Commonplace objects and
ordinary events are charged with symbolism; a silent empty
hand or a clean bowl, pointing towards life being meaningful
in itself without having to supply an added artificial
meaning: a union of meaning and event, of intuition and
sensation. There are some images of physical violence, such
as a finger cut off, a leg smashed between the doors, and self-
mutilation, pointing partly towards the symbolism of
physical sacrifice for the sake of inner enlightenment. See
BODY.

But symbolism that originally flowed from the unconscious
can quickly become a superficial conscious game. It is the
strong practice of sitting and emptying the conscious mind
till the symbolism receives its response from the depth of the
unconscious, or even the preconscious totality. In any case
experience from the essential being of the disciple has kept
this particular set of symbols alive for a thousand years, so
that Marie Louise von Franz, for example, can state that it is
the Zen Masters who have most demonstrated the complete
process of achieving human individuality, acting and living
from the undivided Self, i.e. the Jungian process of
individuation.
Books:-
Sekida, K. *Zen Training* (1975), or Kapleau, P. *Three Pillars
of Zen* (1965).

LADDER
The different levels of consciousness between man and cosmic MAN, between earth and heaven. (See *ARCHETYPES*.)

The ladder may have seven rungs and an eighth: Reflecting the layers of being, the levels of personal and collective consciousness unfolding through the different periods of life, in the course of its seventy or eighty years.

Related Symbolism:-

The World AXIS; The LIGHTNING Flash; ABOVE/Below.

The Cosmic TREE; KABBALAH. Tree of Life.

Note:- Fallen trees, with stumps of branches, may have formed the first actual ladders.

The seven or eight rungs, relate to the seven or eight circles of heaven – and are negatively reflected in the circles of hell – the orbits of the seven planets rippling outwards from the earth, into space, with ripples crossing. The seven stars of the Great Bear and the Pole Star. The orders of Angels and the Archons of the planets, representing the personified forces of the cosmos, to which man is related.

See *CHAKRAS.*

Horus set up a ladder to Heaven, in Egypt.

And in Mesopotamia *the Ziggurat was named the ladder to heaven.* It is a widespread symbol: there are Buddhist, Islamic and shamanistic ladders all fulfilling the same function. And later mystical ladders, for example, Hilton, W. *The Scale of Perfection* (1494).

LANDSCAPES
An inner landscape, or country of the mind.

Not actually situated inside the body, but the cosmos as viewed from the inside, with intuitions reshaping the contours of the mountains, and moods affecting the weather, whipping the sea to storms, in order to depict the value and meaning of the actual cosmos for man.

　i. *So in one context, the whole Earth is completely feminine:* Mother Earth and Mother Nature.

　ii. *But in another context land can be divided from the sea: Land/sea:* The conscious extravert outlook in contrast with the inner unconscious life. The male conscious, logical, thinking side of the mind in contrast with the feminine emotional side of the mind which expresses itself in symbols. What causes confusion with symbolism is when the symbols are isolated out of context. The vital factor is the interaction between the forces of nature which reflect similar life forces at work in the mind.

iii. *And in other circumstances: Different parts of the land can be further subdivided:* to bring out particular masculine or feminine features (see *MASCULINE/FEMININE*, also *ANIMUS/ ANIMA* for the way each human being, whether man or woman, shares masculine and feminine qualities, which need to be balanced within the psyche).

Particular Landscapes:
   Particular aspects of the psyche, such as the *MASCULINE/* Feminine sides. Or *EGO*/Shadow. Or the *SELF*.

Light familiar landscapes/Dark alien territory:
The contrast between the *CONSCIOUS* mind and Unconscious psyche.
As a layout of the pattern of the psyche, and the sequence of life, the territories described – or experienced – with symbolic associations, can usually be divided broadly between Conscious and Unconscious.
All the cultivated, tamed, civilized land – including buildings: The conscious realm.
The wilderness, the hinterland, the wild part of nature, all that lies beyond the borders of civilization: The unconscious, everything which surrounds the conscious, its edges, its limits, and which threatens death and extinction, can be a place of misery and exile, but may also be the occasion of new insights for the community or individual. See *ABANDONED*.
Note:-
But, as above, this symbolism is fluid according to the context. In the *GRAIL* legend (and others), the first glimpse of the unconscious may contain forests and animals (The Stag) but the supra-conscious powers there are represented by the Castle. Equally a building can be divided between conscious and unconscious parts.

240

Borderlands, outposts: the limits of the conscious personality and its points of contact with the unconscious. (See *THRESHOLD.*)

There are places for certain deeds, places for murders and ghosts, places that conjure fantasies or inspire the creative imagination: and this determines their symbolism.

Wide open country, especially if infested with male figures: The masculine mentality, the male conscious Ego.

So, for example, demon-filled deserts: Depict the situation where male conscious attitudes have created a psychological dust bowl – and possibly an actual one as well.

Woods, thickets, valleys, streams, especially if the haunts of witches or nymphs: The feminine realm. The nature of the figures there will show whether it's a problem area (*WITCHES* represent a problem). Or if all is well, so far as feeling is concerned, these places may be the source of vitality, relationships and values.

Caves, craters, crevices, ravines, and other dark sinister places: The Shadow realm.

Mountains, as the CENTRE of the world, the seat of the immortals, the place where the gods assemble: So the highest longings and aspirations of man.

But every hill, river, crossing, island or rock: Represents one of the forces of nature sunk into matter: or put the other way round, matter raised from chaos by insubstantial forces. These forces can be *PERSONIFIED*, i.e. related specifically to man, as nymphs, archetypes or gods.

The names of places, of rivers: Are often very ancient and also relate mankind with that particular natural pheonomenon (see, for example, Philip Cohane, *The Key* (1969)). The name is thereby deeply rooted in the collective unconscious of man, and so may strike a chord with the personal unconscious.

Personal Symbolism:-

Without this inward vision of the world, the earth itself is robbed of its significance for the individual. The inward visions may correspond accurately enough with the outside world – so long as the mind flies far enough for features that really matter to it. Or it may not: rocks may crash together, crushing boatloads of heroes for example. But the point, as always with symbols, is the relationship between man and cosmos – what the world and nature means in human terms. Compare also:-

JOURNEYS: UNDERWORLD.

LIGHT
Perhaps the most basic symbol of conscious life.

No doubt because the first and most immediate experience on waking from sleep or coma is of the light, which compares with a baby being born into the light.

Light/Dark: The darkness precedes the light, and forms the unity of the preconscious totality before there was any *SPLIT* – any light separated from darkness. This is described variously in myth as the abyss, the darkness that is brooded over, the void, the primeval ocean, etc. Then the light of consciousness appears in various symbolic forms such as the lotus (probably the moon in the night sky), the eye or whatever. The unconscious remains the ground and precondition of consciousness.

Day/Night: The movement, the cycles between conscious and unconscious, between waking, sleeping and waking again.

The light and dark personified: The contrast between light and dark, and what it means to human beings, is at the root of much mythology and symbolism. (See *GODS/GODDESSES*, for example, The Black Goddess.) The feminine earth gives birth to masculine conscious forces, but also like Isis robed in deepest black to swallow the sun, the same forces in reverse swallow up the Ego-consciousness.

Facing the dark, in the form of any dark region, whether under the sea or under the earth in caves: Turning to the inner dark of the unconscious, where forms dissolve and disappear. The dark is the place of depression; black moods and shadows. Searching into the mysterious unknown brings gloom. It is the place of mortification and sacrifice: the dark waters where the personal Ego drowns; the dark earth where the personal body decomposes.

Note:-
Striking dreams of young children under four seem to show some symbolic awareness of this aspect of the dark.

A return to the light, for example from the depths of the cave, the baptismal waters, etc., comparable or related to the symbolism of rebirth from the womb: Union of conscious with unconscious, bringing with it new insights, an increase of consciousness.

Related Symbolism:-
SUN. Especially *Dawn/Dusk* (e.g. *Shahar/Salem*). Or *the Asvins*, two celestial horses, in harness: one light, one dark; the eternal and the mortal.

Yang and Yin, see *I CHING.*
Also *COLOURS,White/Black.*
In Pictorial art, most especially the work of Escher, M. C. seems to be predominantly concerned with the interaction of light and dark, of conscious and unconscious.

LIGHTNING. Lightning/Serpent
Sudden flashes of intuition and deep insight, which can illuminate the night world of the unconscious for an instant, making it all stand out clear as day.

The lightning is a bright serpent in form, or a dragon's fiery tongue. It is full of creative energy, and symbolically brings the heavy rains that fertilize the earth, germinate the seed.
Lightning/serpent: The great serpents (a python, for example) are the dark unconscious form of the same force in nature – just as snakes instead of hair are the dark form of the sun's rays.

See *SERPENT.*
Related Symbolism:-
Quicksilver; The Messenger of God, HERMES; *The Arrow. See* BOW.

LILITH
Destructive feminine power.

Lilith was created before Eve, and rejected in favour of Eve:

LILITH

She is a more primitive side of the Feminine, that has been rejected and therefore repressed.

She was created from the mud at the same time as Adam: So psychologically she is man's Anima. See *ANIMUS/Anima.* It is especially in men that the Feminine forces lurk in the Unconscious, and from there act of their own accord, beyond a man's conscious control. This repudiated part of a man's own psyche can be very destructive. It may correspond to the Mother *COMPLEX.*

Lilith is thrust into the depths of the sea but returns to haunt men. She is the enemy and temptress of Eve. The Kabbalists have a ritual to expel her from the marriage bed: She acts like a succubus, motivating men and women from the depths of the unconscious. Like a destructive phantom, she is the enemy of family life and children. Powerful psychological forces are not subject to superficial conscious laws. Symbolic ritual is a more effective way of controlling them.

Book:-
Scholem, Gershom G. *On the Kabbalah and its Symbolism* (1965).

LION

A primitive or bestial side of the Ego personality: its Shadow. See *EGO/Shadow.*

Very often the Shadow of the *KING,* or Sun *HERO.*
Hercules and Samson, as sun heroes, must wrestle with their bare hands with the lion: This would refer to the tussle with one's own reflection or Shadow as the lion reflects the sun but on the earthly instinctual and more bestial plain. This is where Hercules starts his labours, i.e. symbolically struggling with his own character. The hand-to-hand fighting emphasizes the closeness of the two figures, which represent the one figure locked in inner strife, with the physical side of his own nature.

Related Symbolism:-
The *SUN,* simply because the lion resembles the Sun – especially in a child's drawing – with a mane like the golden rays of the sun.

LOOKING BACK
Turning the conscious attention back, sliding back, regression into the unconscious.

In the case of Orpheus and Eurydice, Lot's wife, and many fairy-tales, the fact that so much hinges on a mere backward glance: Reflects a very real situation in life, of the way an opportunity can be missed in a moment. One glance in the wrong direction, and a car crashes: life is swallowed up in unconsciousness.

And this is true of the difficulties of retrieving content from the unconscious, and getting it back across the *THRESHOLD*.

The content of the unconscious can never be seen directly with the eye of consciousness. The two are opposed. The individual must trust his intuition about what is there, just behind him, i.e. within.

Related Symbolism:-

There are many stories about losing human consciousness (i.e. being turned into an animal, on glimpsing a god or goddess, e.g. Actaeon).

EROS, Eros and Psyche.

GORGON, Medusa, for an instance of losing all conscious life – in this case by being turned to stone through looking directly at the unconscious form or the archetype of Medusa, rather than being satisfied with her reflection in the inner soul.

The real forces of the cosmos, whether light or dark, are too terrible to behold directly: man breaks up (into dust) in front of them.

The forces can only be observed as they manifest in nature or in images in the psyche (i.e. symbols).

Book:-

Otto, Rudolph, *The Idea of the Holy* (1968 Tr).

LOTUS (Water-lily, confused with ordinary lily)
The light of conscious life. The first movement of life in the primeval slime.

The importance symbolically attached to this Eastern species of the Water-lily derives from its resemblance to the *MOON*. It is the earthly reflection in the water of the celestial

moon – i.e. the reflection in human nature on earth of that
heavenly light which is like the original light in the ocean of
darkness, that swells with its fecundity and gives birth to the
daylight sun/son.

The different phases of the moon, which lie to either side of
the full moon in the month, relate to the petals of the water-
lily. It is the original Flower of Light ('Fleur-de-Lis') but in
the West this became associated with the ordinary lily.

*The water-lily, furthermore, grows from the mud and slime and
turns into a flower of exquisite beauty:* The forces of life that
can transform the mud of material existence (i.e. dead
matter) into paradise. The original emergence of this
wonderful white form from the mud leads on to the idea of
re-emergence, whether in the form of rebirth, resurrection,
or enlightenment.

Particular Symbolism:-

In Ancient Egyptian myth it was one of the first life forms to
grow from the abyss. And in Buddhism it is a supreme
symbol. In Yoga the opening or flowering of different levels
of consciousness, the *CHAKRAS*, are symbolized as opening
lotuses.

The child within the lotus: The true centre of life from which
the pattern of life – like the pattern of the lotus, which is a
MANDALA – can be discerned. See in Jung's archetypal
symbolism, the True Undivided *SELF.* The child radiates
petals, like the rays of the sun, each morning, every morning,
now as in Ancient Egypt.

Related Symbolism:-

The Lotus is the primeval plant, growing from the waters not
the land, as the *SERPENT* is the primeval animal. Thus it is an
even earlier form of the *ORIGINS* of life than the serpent.
See *VEGETATION.*

MAGIC
Including some psychic phenomena.

**A particular application of symbolism, which can become its
travesty, by confining symbolism to narrow materialistic
limits.**

Magic is the application of such basic symbolic ideas as the interaction between mind and matter. But magic lives in rather reduced circumstances. For the most part, it has been left only with the bits that didn't work very well: the rest, such as facts about contagious diseases, having passed into the realms of medicine or science.

Telekinesis, transporting objects by mind power: There seems to be some evidence for this – even Jung frightened Freud by making a cupboard bang as a result of concentrating power in his tanden or lower abdomen. And he found many cases of similar psychic phenomena, especially in adolescent girls. Note:-

From the point of view of symbolism, these rather freak – in the sense of uncommon – aspects are inclined to distract attention from the universal and fundamental significance of symbolism. So when people think of mind-over-matter, their views are narrowed to these few rare instances, and fail to notice that anything from the making of wine, the railway or a rocket is all mind ordering matter. It is even more important for symbolism that without mind, matter has no shape, colour, qualities, almost no existence.

See *COSMOS*.

Related Symbolism:-

See also *ESSENCE/Existence, and the ELEMENTS*. Like *ALCHEMY* magic is basically trying to reduce material existence to its single Essence and reconstitute it in new forms.

Book:-

Conway, D. *Magic: An Occult Primer* (1972).

MAGNET

The undivided *SELF*, attracting all the *COMPLEXES* to itself in a way that the Ego never can.

Related Symbolism:-

The *TREE*, in that the branches and twigs relate directly to the trunk, but not directly to each other.

Cosmic MAN

Man's Mind, which reaches to the limits of the universe.

Jung has called man 'the second creator of the universe', as a result of an experience he had when looking at the plains of Africa, and he saw the difference between Nature lost in unconsciousness, and all Nature as it is recognized and known to man. Each man is the individual carrier of this conscious life.

The limits of human nature coincide with the limits of the *COSMOS.* Mankind combines *CONSCIOUS* and Unconscious, *MASCULINE* and Feminine, *ORIGINS* and *GOALS,* and human nature has no existence outside particular individuals. Human nature comes whole, complete, in you.

Cosmic man is variously depicted, with arms and legs splayed to the edges of the universe. (See BODY.) His spine is the cosmic AXIS. His eyes are the sun and moon: All refer to man's inner experience. The individual is the carrier of life, and life lends light and distance to the cosmos.

Note:-

Falling asleep is a personal experience of the way light and distance, space and time collapse and disappear without life to maintain them. The idea of cosmic man hinges round the idea of the life forces which hold the cosmos in place while the individual sleeps. Cosmic man is therefore closely related to Jung's idea of the collective unconscious: the unconscious of Cosmic man is the stones and stars themselves.

The SACRIFICE of cosmic man: Cosmic man was divided into tiny morsels, and each individual man is a particle of the whole, capable of re-uniting with the whole.

Relating to Cosmic Man: The symbol of cosmic Man suggests the way that the unconscious is permeable to the light of consciousness, after all. Stars and stones were lost in oblivion for millions of years, without an eye to see them or a mind to grasp their form, till the eye and the mind evolved to survey the scene.

Experience ripples outwards on its way to permeate the whole. Thus the body of cosmic man is pure light which outshines the sun, sometimes pure *CRYSTAL*. It is the energy and brightness that has redeemed the sun itself, that was sunk in the dark void of unconsciousness.

In relation to the story of man, and the four Ages of Man: The life of mankind can be divided symbolically (see *TIME*): So can the life of the individual (see *PERIODS* of Life). The Childhood of man in this present phase of his story would cover the Age of the Pyramids and before, with man himself learning to read and write for the first time, and building with bricks, and large stones. Then reaching a zenith or climax of powers in mid-life, in the Classical Age of Greece and Rome. And now, after a somewhat eclipsed middle age, reaching out towards full maturity; completion to be followed by decline.

Note:-
This is a different aspect of cosmic man, which like all symbols is flexible.
The One Cosmic Man/many people: People are double in nature, made up of clay, mud and the pure invisible light of life, unstained and enduring.
One myth is explicit about how much the light of life disliked being crammed into the clay and it had to be forced in; this is variously expressed in other symbolic ways, as expulsion from the realm of light and descending through emanations down into dark matter, cosmic sacrifice, kenosis, etc.
This is not guesswork about events in the remote past but an expression of the very real current problem of relating mind to matter, the inward experience of reality to the practical side of life.

Negative Symbolism:-
This most fundamental of symbols concerning the right relationship between man and the cosmos, between the *EGO* and the *SELF* in terms of the psyche, can be experienced negatively in two ways. The first is when the experience breaks in as implosion upon the conscious Ego which is too small and brittle – with attitudes too rigid – to take it. In this context cosmic man is more like a destructive *GIANT.*
(Note:- Nijinsky, in his diaries just before he went completely mad, describes something of the shattering effect of this experience.)
Alternatively the symbol may be experienced as fantasies of personal omnipotence: in other words the personal Ego appropriates the experience to itself, and the result is megalomania of the worst sort, i.e. of cosmic dimensions.

Note:-

Since the aim and object of the more determined attempts to gain spiritual insight usually involve what can be symbolically described as union with Cosmic Man, the enormous importance attached to humility is at least partly if not wholly to counterbalance the above danger, of psychological 'inflation', that is, inflated self-importance, a sort of self-intoxication.

Particular Symbols:-

The Purusha of Hinduism who was three quarters in heaven (ie. thinking, feeling and intuition) and one quarter on earth (i.e. physical sensation).

Osiris (and his physical incarnation in the King of Egypt). Also *the Ba* (Self) in contrast with *the Ka* (Ego form) soul.

Plato's *Original Being; The Gnostic Anthropos;* also *Nous, or the One Man (Vir Unus).*

The Persian *Gayomard*; in Jewish mystical tradition, *the Spiritual Adam, Adam Kadmon.*

Buddha-nature, that pervades the whole universe; also *the Diamond Body* or *Body of Light.*

And *Christ as Pantocrator*; or as *the Spiritual Adam.*

Negative Symbolism:-

The great statue of bronze, silver and gold which falls because its feet are of clay.

The ancient world (Gnostics) also related this figure of Cosmic Man to the lewd phallic Hermes (i.e. Hermes as represented by the sign of the phallus), and to Korybas, the seducer of Dionysus, and the phallic Kabiri – thereby linking Cosmic Man with sexual fantasies of omnipotence.

Personal Symbolism:-

The life's work is to create and re-create the Cosmic *SELF*. Dissolve and coagulate it, *DISINTEGRATE* and re-integrate it until union with the enduring reality (that underlies ephemeral phenomena) is not just experienced in fragmentary glimpses, but becomes consolidated and permanent.

Self-emptying, as a repetition of the original cosmic sacrifice: The problem of adapting all life's energy to the particular circumstances, like forcing Cosmic Man into the small human frame, is not possible without emptying out Cosmic Man, throwing the experience away, leaving it behind. This is the typical movement of symbolism, and central to it: the symbol is a step on the way to an experience, and the experience is a step on the way to another symbol. Till there is no symbol left. But the symbols can only be dispensed with afterwards, not before.

MANDALA
Depicts the basic *PATTERN* of the psyche which spins from itself the web of life.

The circle and the square depict *INNER* and outer aspects of life: the watery fluid inner realm is round while the earthy world of substance is square.

The mandala is a summary of this whole symbolic realm with symbolic *PATTERNS, COLOURS, VEGETATION, ANIMALS,* etc.

The great example of the mandala in Tantric Art, in Eastern Temples, such as Borobudur, in Rose Windows, etc: Represent man's universal life from origin to end.

Less obvious mandalas in gardens, in kaleidoscopes, in patterns made with compasses. Or those toys children made – coloured discs of cardboard threaded with string to make them whirl: All have a fascination because of the symbolic appeal related to the mandala.

Personal Symbolism:-

Anyone can draw spontaneously the pattern of his or her life, all laid out on a sheet for him to see. Just draw spontaneously, occasionally using brightly coloured words within the picture, if you want. Some bits will be consciously devised and other bits may come from the unconscious and possibly lead to new insights.

Books:-

Jung, C. G. (and others), *Man and his Symbols* (1964).
Arguelles, J. and M., *Mandala* (1972).

MARKS. Seals. Branding
Either a mark of belonging to the GROUP (or herd), or a mark of distinction from it.

The individual set apart from the group – for example the mark of Cain.

MASCULINE/FEMININE

On all three symbolic levels, the typically masculine attitudes are in direct conflict with the typically feminine, and require to be reconciled.

This is true on the cosmic level of the hard resisting the soft and dissolving into it, and taking shape from it, for example. Or on the level of human society, the mesocosm, it is true of the battle of the sexes. But it is also true of a particular *SPLIT* into *OPPOSITES*, within each and every human being, whether superficially a man or a woman.

A man's feminine side is sunk in his unconscious, so the inner feminine figure is also the guide into the unconscious. And vice versa, because a woman's masculinity is buried in the unconscious, the masculine figure is the key to entry into her unconscious.

This makes the *UNION* of masculine and feminine of the widest possible significance in symbolism, as it may be the means of uniting *CONSCIOUS/UNCONSCIOUS.*

Because symbolism *IDENTIFIES* man and woman with the *COSMOS*, the cosmos shares the split in humanity between masculine and feminine. No doubt it is as a result of this symbolism that in many languages almost everything can be given a masculine or feminine gender.

It is fundamental to symbolism that originally there was no such split and that the rift needs to be healed, in an inner realm by means of love which amounts to reunion, or a union which amounts to love.

The Symbols:-

The union of the sexes is a recurring theme of symbolism, whether it's the blood of a figure of the opposite sex which must be drunk, or the happier chime of wedding bells: In the same way it is a recurring theme of Jungian psychology.

See The *'SLEEPING BEAUTY': EROS; WEDDING.*

ZEUS/Hera: For an ancient mythological example of the four-way relationship between Man/Woman/*ANIMA/ANIMUS.*

All masculine and feminine figures (see *PERSONIFICATION*) in symbolic material can be observed for their light and dark qualities, for their interrelationships, with reference to the light they cast on the inner situation. The number of male to female characters will probably reflect the balance of the communal psyche at the time and place of the story, whether about GODS/Goddesses, or KINGS/Queens, or brothers and sisters, such as 'Hansel and Gretel', or boy and girl as in 'FUNDEVOGEL'.

In the cosmic realm SUN and MOON, or sky and earth (see ABOVE/Below).

In the abstract realm Logos and Eros. Or the masculine and feminine pillars of the KABBALAH, with the central pillar as the pillar of union.

The phallic and yonic symbols that unite for procreativity and creativity.

Negative Symbolism:-

Much of the trouble (problems, conflicts) results directly from the interaction of masculine and feminine figures. Often a feminine figure stirs up the trouble – refuses to marry, sets impossible riddles and tasks in the hope of getting the young men's heads on spikes, etc. – but in the end the solution is happier than the original situation before she appeared.

Related Symbolism:-

In symbolism it's tempting to string together great lists of OPPOSITES under the titles: Masculine and Feminine. But each has different shades of meaning which should be kept distinct.

Masculine Conscious Ego.

See the HERO, for the main symbolism. Also the BROTHERS. For other aspects of the Masculine realm: see Cosmic AXIS; CENTRE.

The Feminine Realm.

Is closer to Nature and to Feeling.

The symbolism of male orientated societies tries to compensate for its dominantly masculine attitudes, but only in an unconscious – and therefore unsatisfactory – manner. It is an important and useful preliminary step, but a beginning only, and quite inadequate if left at that.

For example the HEROINE's role may show the Feminine side of life – but only as it affects men – and not so much as an entity in itself striving for development. The feminine realm

253

is not to be equated with the dark, but it is closer to the archetype of life, and the blind forces of nature, which makes women capable of saving a situation where men are helpless and ineffectual for all their well meaning. There is a softness of mood that makes for relationships, vital and vivid connections between individuals. But on the whole, symbolism, with reference to women, seems more to reflect man's turbulent relationship with the feminine Anima, and his own ambivalent attitude to women.

The Symbols:-

Whether in Goddesses, or love-goddesses of the cinema, there is a distinction between the ethereal and untouchable, celestial beings and the earthy passionate side of the feminine, and thirdly the dark underworldly aspect.

These are also related to the sequence of life:

i. The heavenly queen is often the young virginal maiden (Kore).

ii. The middle phase is nymph of life (Aphrodite) and mother goddess (Hera or Rhea).

iii. And in the last phase the Crone is related to the underworld.

Positive/Negative Symbolism:-

ATHENE/Medusa; Three GRACES/Three Gorgons; Artemis/ Hecate; Nine MUSES/The Sirens.

Medea gives HERCULES the poisoned coat: The Feminine power which should protect the man like a coat, can easily be turned to poison the male Ego.

Circe turns men to pigs: Although the power of the feminine may lead man to the fulfilment of his destiny via the Unconscious, it may also seduce him into the soft option of animal unconsciousness.

Orpheus is torn apart by women: He is destroyed by his own repressed raging passion.

MAYA

See the physical world of substance as so much deceptive phantasmagoria projected by the human mind.

The delusion of the outside world is more intense and therefore a more deceptive version of the inner delusion of dreams. See *INNER/*Outer.

The phenomena of forms, whether as in inner images, or with the apparent qualities of substance, acts as a veil between man and essential reality.

Note:-

The Yogis who proposed this extreme anti-materialist view of reality, aimed at being able to project an image from their mind till it was so solid they could reach out and touch it; and then dissolve it. This is an extreme example of creative *IMAGINATION*, creating and dissolving symbols, taking nature apart and putting it together in new combinations of inner and outer, as steps on the way to grasping the nature of reality.

Book:-

Evans Wentz, W. Y. *Tibetan Yoga, and Secret Doctrines* (1935).

MAZE Labyrinth, and Minotaur, plus Thread

Combines the pattern of the psyche, as in the *MANDALA*, with the path or *JOURNEY* into it; and out of it again.

The labyrinth on Crete constructed to imprison the Minotaur, the product of dark unconscious animal passions inspired by Poseidon, God of unconscious Emotion. The Minotaur, half-bull, half-man (usually a man with a bull's head) roved around the maze like a giant spider waiting for people to fall in, rather like flies: The picture is of repressed content in the unconscious. He is the dark, negative side of the relationship of *MOTHER* and son, which must be conquered in the depths of the unconscious.

The monster is symbolically like the original of the Beast, in '*BEAUTY* and the Beast'. His bull's head suggests that his bestiality dominates his human side: he is the victim of regressive impulses.

The Minotaur devours seven youths and seven maidens each year: This again is the dark, negative side of the psychic process of transformation, of the union of masculine and feminine in a sevenfold sequence leading to completion. Here the archaic and primitive aspects of the psyche consume the prospects of youth.

MAZE

Hero and Anima – Theseus and Ariadne – overcome monster and maze together. Ariadne supplies the thread: The routine fight with the monster ensues, but Ariadne enables Theseus to escape the maze. The maze is tricky as nature herself, and it is typical that a feminine figure, the feminine forces in life – nearer to nature, and nearer to the unconscious – can outwit it by a very simple device. The thread is as flexible as the serpent of the unconscious, it follows the twists of nature like the river which 'threads' its way to the sea. The feminine powers – whether in an actual woman or discovered within the man – are the subtle guide through the regions of the unconscious. This is an aspect of the thread of life and destiny spun by the *FATES*. It has to remain living and flexible as life to be useful rather than stiffen into law, i.e. become too rigid and masculine.

With masculine and feminine combined, the maze of psychic processes becomes the place of transformation: where the destructive tendencies of nature are overcome.

Related Symbolism:

See also *PATTERNS*, especially Spiral; *SEQUENCE*. When the flexibility of life –the archetype of life is feminine – is lacking, then the dead, rigid stone is left: see *STONES/Jewels*.

Compare Hansel and Gretel leaving a trail behind them as they enter the forest (of the unconscious).

The Koran is such a thread or rope through the tangles of the world and *GENEALOGIES* follow the thread from generation to generation.

MEAT
The animal and physical side of life. (See *ANIMAL*. Also *BODY*.)

Like blood: The inner reality.
Eating raw meat, e.g. the Centaurs: Near to raw nature. Not civilized.

The MEDIATOR
Personification of the *CENTRE*.

In physical nature it is the lightning which joins heaven to earth; or the vegetation which rises up off the earth and points towards heaven.

Torn between the conflicting ingredients of reality, between mind and matter especially, man looks for symbols of reconciliation which will help bring together the different aspects of his experience of life.

The Demiurge, between the one ESSENCE and the many appearances, the Storm Gods, like Baal Saphon (Lord of the North), and the Vegetation Gods, like Tammuz, Osiris, and the messenger Gods, all fulfil this function of Mediator: They are somewhere between the highest but most abstract conceptions of God or Gods, and the underworld. So they are closer to man's lot and predicament; more human, more popular, more able to help men 'in the gutters but gazing at the stars' (Wilde).

Shu: Whereas Atum is the Devine essence, he repeats himself as Shu, who is co-extensive with him but indwells in the millions of creatures, and is heard in their millions of voices: The divine immanence, of living reality, that is not subtle or elusive like the essence, but plain to see and obvious everywhere.

Finally the mediator is also the victim who suffers. Osiris, for example, is put together after being cut in pieces, but only to go to the underworld. He doesn't come back to life except in his son, Horus: This reflects man's intermediate position between the creative forces of life and the destructive forces of death.

Related Symbolism:-

The sperm-drop: mediates life, from one generation to the next.

And the serpent is related symbolically, especially the winged serpent with attributes of above and below.

Tiphareth is the mid-point in the Tree of Life (see KABBALAH). He balances all the other spheres of life.

Buddha, whose spirit rose up to the celestial sphere to greet the morning star, Venus; and the heavenly power poured down into the child, *Christ.* These two are the apotheosis of the Mediator figure for many. Compare also *Cosmic MAN.*

MEMORY
Like recurring dreams memories may haunt you because they are symbolically relevant to your present situation.

Personal Symbolism:-

Memories are stored in the unconscious, and may be used by the unconscious as symbols of the current situation that faces the individual. Especially if a memory haunts you or dogs you, it's worth just seeing if it could be in any way relevant to the current situation.

Regrets from the remote past: May be trying to say, don't make the same mistake again.

Negative Symbolism:-

Memory can be as involuntary and irrational as any other *FUNCTION* of the mind triggered off in the unconscious (perhaps by a smell, a tune, etc.) and often accompanied by overwhelming feelings, of depression, elation or whatever. If unrecognized, like other *COMPULSIONS* arising from the *COMPLEXES,* they become the tyrants of the mind. But if the moods can be given shape in images – even though the actual memories are not recovered – then they may serve to give access to the unconscious.

MESOPOTAMIAN MYTH

The roots of symbolism may lie here. If the *ZODIAC* is the prototype symbolic system, it may have been spread East through the Indus Valley, as well as West, from here.

In Mesopotamia, the mid-rivers region, between the Tigris and the Euphrates, from Old Assyria in the mountainous north down to the Persian Gulf, there seems to be some evidence for the roots of civilization. With the arrival of the mysterious Sumerians – so mysterious that there is one plausible suggestion that Sumerian was simply a ritual cult-language of the indigenous Semites there – around 3500 BC, this civilization took a leap forward with highly organized city states and the beginnings of undecipherable picture writing, not unrelated to the later hieroglyphs in Egypt – and with contacts with the Indus Valley (in India) which may have been a colony from this area. Since symbolism is itself a synthesis of human experience, with archetypal roots in the psyche, it is tempting to find these roots in a particular area of the globe. And many have succumbed to the temptation, choosing this particular area – the partly discredited Pan-Babylonianists – for the origin of certain fundamental constructions and names which sometimes bear a striking resemblance to each other. There still remains an historical possibility that the mythology of the world is related at source, and carried by such fine ocean going vessels, manned by more than twenty men, as are depicted in the pyramids, even as far as the Americas.

Meanwhile, the investigation of the mythology of this area is in a mildly chaotic state, partly because of the complexity of the subject. For example, the long lists of titles for one god or goddess, recited like litanies, later fractured and splintered into different deities, each of whom might further be written down six or seven different ways. But also partly because the pioneer work of men like Stephen Langdon, G. A. Barton and A. T. Clay, around the beginning of the century, has not been carried much further, but see also Westropp and Wake and E. A. S. Butterworth. Between them, they give fascinating accounts of the great early festivals, lasting eight days, during which all the statues of the gods were carried out of the city to the river, and guarded there through the night, and then brought back in. Also there were the New Year festivals and other annual events which formed the ritual background and context for the stories of the myths. We can trace the early symbolism of the *ELEMENTS*, of *TIME*, and the *ZODIAC*.

Much of the mythology has only been preserved in later, rewritten versions, but these contain fragments and vestiges of the most ancient wisdom yet discovered.

Note:-

Psychology, by discovering the reference point for all this ancient symbolism in the unconscious psyche, has shown a way of recovering its value and meaning for modern man. But anyone who has worked with his creative *IMAGINATION* will know that such material can arise spontaneously from the unconscious without any conscious grasp of what it really means. This increasingly widespread, conscious understanding of the emotional impact and value of these myths may be quite new. And it could make symbolism a treasured part of rational conscious life, instead of a compelling force of great power and significance, but beyond the control of will or reason.

259

Books:-

See Hawkes, J. *The First Great Civilization* (1973) for a readable account of this period, though not a great deal about the mythology.

Also Gaster, T. *The Oldest Stories in the World* (1958) and Gordon, C. *Before Columbus* (1972).

METALS
Valuable and enduring components of the psyche.

The extracting of metal from the ore, the mixing of metal alloys which combined their particular qualities into something new and sometimes better, was symbolic of the work of transforming human nature.

The metals were differentiated, purified and compounded. They were personified, had intercourse and offspring – copper had a love affair with iron as Venus with Mars (the Roman equivalent of the secret liaison that had always existed between Love and War, between Aphrodite and Ares in Greek myth): As visible equivalents of processes in the psyche, where dividing and relating the different components, such as aggression and sexual passion, is vital to the inner welfare.

Sulphur and quicksilver (like Gold/silver) were related symbolically to the sun and moon (see SUN/Moon): The masculine, conscious Ego and the feminine Anima; or the relationship between the feminine, conscious Ego and the masculine *ANIMUS*.

Anything made of metal: The symbolism of the conscious human spirit working (and reworking) upon inanimate matter, e.g. see *SWORD*.

The working of metals has always been closely related to the realm of the gods from ancient times – through the fire gods, and the men of spiritual power who were in the case of the Shamans, for example, originally the blacksmiths. So metals naturally lent themselves as symbols of processes in the soul – and we still talk (occasionally) of a person's 'metal', i.e. his fibre. See also *HEPHAISTOS*.

Lead, personified as SATURN: depression or Unconscious content, which once raised into the light of the conscious, rational mind, became gold. (See *DEPRESSION*.)

METEORITE
The world ABOVE showing signs of activity: solid messages from the celestial sphere.

MINERAL
The passive, the inert. Fundamental existence.

Mineral/Vegetable/Animal, e.g. STONE/TREE/SERPENT: Dead existence/unconscious life/conscious life.
But this interplay between different modes of existing reflects different layers of the psyche. And because of the contrary qualities of the unconscious (see *MIRROR*), by sinking (symbolically) to the mineral level, the individual can experience the most basic quality of existence itself – which may afford a profound insight (i.e. of the kind where the whole universe is discovered in a grain of sand, because both share the same manner of existing).
See also *STONES/Jewels.*

MIRROR
Or Looking Glass, including other reflections – which reverse the image, sometimes called 'inversion'. Also Shadows.
The *THRESHOLD* between *CONSCIOUS* and Unconscious, or between *INNER* and Outer.

The *EGO* confronts its own Shadow as a figure thrown upon the wall or reflected in the glass, projected into the outside world. Symbolism does not distinguish clearly between reflections and shadows – children sometimes share the confusion on this point. What is important is the way the glass acts as a dividing line between opposites.
Everything on the far side of the glass is in reverse, or in a lake is upside down, or in the case of the shadow is the same shape but dark, where the figure is light: And this becomes the perfect image for the opposing forces within the psyche – as it were either side of the glass.
Even to see our own face, our own appearance, we must look in a mirror: We can see everything except ourselves. This is even more true of the living organism, than of appearances – the face. We can see our own nature, as it is reflected in the

universe only. But so long as there is the glass between us and it, the split caused by the conscious Ego, then there is a distortion, a double image, the image of duality, with only a darkened reflection of the unconscious.

From this, we experience a world of opposites, which all arise from the one division (between the conscious Ego's world view, and the unconscious) of a single reality which has no split or seam, i.e. no pane of mirror glass to give the illusion of a separate reality. Clinging to the separate Ego-consciousness is like living in a world of reflections that are quite the opposite of reality, little personal moons underfoot in the puddle, rather than the single Moon, a shared experience. Or, in Plato's symbol, living in a cave and seeing only the shadows on the walls.

So long as the personal Ego interferes, everything from the unconscious (every image, every symbol) appears in reverse. And every action has to be done in reverse. From the point of view of the limited Ego-consciousness, regeneration appears as its opposite, the devouring monster – the maiden appears as the withered crone.

All actions have to be done in reverse in the looking glass land of the unconscious. To reach the desired goals it is necessary to regress to the *ORIGINS*; in terms of psychology, a positive regress, back towards infancy in order to move on towards maturity. The Hero must descend into Tartarus in order to arrive on Olympus.

All is counterbalanced, and extremes (even of love and calm restraint) tend to build up an *OPPOSITE* unconscious reaction.

By coincidence (or synchronicity) the mirror image that is reversed is none other than the reality. It is only a trick of the light which gives the illusion of duality, the illusion of a macrocosm and microcosm (or mini-universe in each puddle): And this becomes the perfect image of the *UNION* of the opposites.

Note:-

Wordsworth uses the image of the still lake of life, reflecting reality, perfectly and without distortion, and Buddhist tradition has the same image, polishing the mirror glass of the self till it reflects the world perfectly, without a single impurity to distort it. But Hui Neng became sixth Zen Patriarch by asking, 'What mirror?' i.e. there was no speck of dust to distort his personal view, but furthermore there was no longer any personal Ego left, no glass to divide his reality from reality.

Particular Symbolism:-

Lewis Carroll's *Alice through the Looking Glass* is packed with the reversed operations of the unconscious as they manifest contrariwise in images. Not least the entirely different centre of operations within the psyche, so that it is we who are being dreamed by the Self; just as Alice is told that she is a part of the Red King's DREAMS. The White Queen running and running to stay on the same spot expresses the way the earth is in a continuous state of upheaval, CHANGE and TRANSFORMATION in order to stay much the same.

Related Symbolism:-

An object and its mould, the picture and its negative: Point to the same idea of the way conscious attitudes are formed or moulded through the opposite in the unconscious. Only when the two are put together is their essential unity discerned. In the same way, the feminine is the mould for the masculine.

See WISH/*Fear* and SEX, *Desire/Fear*, for examples of the way this opposition can work in practice, and the way working on the conscious part can transform the otherwise inaccessible unconscious fear or compulsive desire.

Youth is the negative of age. Death is the shadow of life. Any one of these alone is threatened by its opposite. But standing on the broader six-pointed base where all the opposites are reckoned with, then the oscillations hardly show, as each transforms into its opposite and vice versa. For the conscious Ego the changes are no less dreadful and painful, but they don't affect the core of life, in which the individual also shares, wittingly or unwittingly.

Personal Symbolism:-

Further, we use each other as mirrors. Bound together as opposites in the family, etc., we slowly get to know ourselves through our relationships with others.

Note:-

In this context there is a very curious phenomenon about dreams which has never been explained satisfactorily; namely, that a long dream can ensue between the moment of an alarm clock going off – or a bell heard in the street – and the moment of waking presumably almost instantly afterwards. Attempts to explain this have centred round the possibility that the dream-mind works at an exceptionally rapid rate, unlike any other thought process. Only P. D. Ouspensky has suggested a plausible alternative, which was that we in fact dream in *Reverse*, working backwards towards causes and origins, and on waking our conscious mind turns the dream round automatically – just as our mind adjusts the image on the retina of the eye instantly. If this were so, it would confirm the way the conscious reverses the operations of the conscious even with regard to time-sequence.

MONEY
The archetype of Value, the Feeling side of life.

From being a useful intermediate commodity, that facilitated human relationships and reckonings, money – because of the contamination between symbols and reality – has all the symptoms at present of being an irrational compulsion, arising directly from the neglected feeling side in the unconscious, which therefore manifests negatively in a fairly widespread social way.

Whole societies are driven and compelled by 'economic pressures' that are involuntary and irrational. The symbolic solution is always the same and would require dissolving hardened conscious criteria, in order to assimilate and integrate the unconscious, in this case the feminine feeling side of life, including inward values, and extravert relationships.

See *COMPULSIONS*; the *FUNCTIONS OF THE MIND*; *OWL and PUSSYCAT*.

MONKEY
A potential source of renewal through the primitive _ANIMAL_ instincts and the Unconscious.
Positive Symbolism:-
Hanuman, the Monkey; or Wu Cheng En's novel, 'Monkey':
Both display the godlike strength and vitality of the animal powers in man, if consciously recognized and valued. Though such powers are never easy to control.
In dreams, as so far investigated in the West, the symbolism is usually negative.

Mythical MONSTERS
The embodiment of repressed Feelings and Intuitions in the Personal Psyche. But also the basic material of the universe, on the Cosmic Level.

Symbols are especially the spontaneous expression of intuitions and feelings, so the symbolic mind is in a sense describing its own fate in terms of such monsters, if left unconscious.
Unconsciousness is a feature of many aspects of creation, especially the feminine side of a man's psyche and the Forces of Nature, that are symbolically united in the symbol of Mother Earth, whose dark, negative side is symbolized as the Monster. Material substance nurtures, but also devours conscious life.
In the Babylonian Creation myth, Marduk slays the monster Tiamat, and divides its carcass into rain clouds and sea: Life precedes matter: the extent of the universe depends on the power or potential from which it derives its existence.
Note:-
Thomas Mann describes the cosmos as fungoid growths on the side of the dead God, which is a comparable symbol of the transformation from Life to Matter, from Conscious to Unconscious.
Composite monsters: Confused content of the unconscious, potentially destructive. Or content that has been successfully recognized and the parts related to each other in a living unity. See _ANIMALS_, Composite; _DRAGON_.
Mythical Monsters with many heads such as the Hydra,

SCYLLA, or Ladon: The one force has many appearances or projections in the outside world.

For every head that is cut off, two more appear: Symbolism points to the mistake of trying to tackle dark Shadow problems in the outside world without coming to grips with them inside first. However hard you try to eliminate a problem from the outside world, if it is at root a psychological problem it will recur later in life in another form, possibly worse. Thus the one problem of relating to the father, for a boy, may recur in all relationships with authority later in life. And a basically unsound relationship with the mother may affect relationships with many other women later.

MOON

The softer and more soothing light that welds relationships. Therefore the Feeling *FUNCTION* and the Collective Unconscious, both Feminine. Also imagination.

In contrast with the harsh light of the *SUN*, which insists on intellectual differences, this dimmer light of the night mediates between light and dark and so unifies scattered elements within the personality – the *COMPLEXES* – as well as in society.

The fascination of the moon as a symbol derives partly from the fact that it is seen as an intermediary between the heavenly mind world of consciousness, and the physical world of matter sunk in unconsciousness. It is, in fact, the planet nearest to the earth and, unlike any other heavenly body, shares in the flux of life, symbol of human suffering. *For example the Passion of OSIRIS, who was cut into fourteen pieces, which are related symbolically to the fourteen slices taken off the waning moon which then disappears – like Osiris. The pieces are then added to the New Moon, slice by slice, but joined perfectly without seam:* This reflects the inner work of analysing the psyche, differentiating the Complexes, and then welding together the whole.

Moonlight/Sunlight: The more delicate light reveals the whole universe of stars and planets – in contrast with the glare of the sunlight which blots it out – just as the Conscious

Ego, with all its more immediate problems, blots out the larger vision of life.

Negative Symbolism:-

The Moon as a rabid bitch: Portrays vividly the dangers of neglecting the Feelings, and the Feminine Unconscious.

Related Symbolism:-

The Moon is closely related to the *TRICKSTER*, full of magical transformations, in contrast with the Sun of the ordinary Conscious Ego, which never changes its shape.

Now it's there, now it's gone, because the moon rises an hour later each night, and finally performs its disappearing act at the end of the month: An image of the imagination itself, which gives partial and fluctuating expression to the flux of Feelings. And illuminates the endless night of unconsciousness. *The moon, like the MIRROR, is at the THRESHOLD of the Unconscious:* And may represent the feminine *ANIMA*, which guides men into the *UNDERWORLD* of their own minds.

The Phases of the Moon.

The phases of development of a woman's life, but also the Feminine soul, the *ANIMA*.

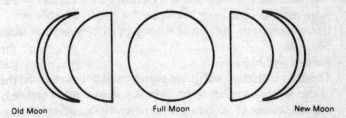

Old Moon   Full Moon   New Moon

Note:-

The waning moon fits into the curve of the left hand and is the left-hand side of the moon illuminated, and is a symbol of the decline and decay of life which precedes extinction. *The new white moon, the full red moon and the black empty moon:*

The white virginal maiden, the full-blooded maturity of love and pregnancy, and the darkness of old age.

But in the inner work of creative imagination the black moon comes first, symbolizing the depression that precedes the creative act. These three dark days between old and new moon refer to a period of inner *DEATH* and regeneration, and are related to the stories of Jonah swallowed by a whale, and Christ descending into hell for three days. The white new moon indicates the first rays of the imagination, and the red full moon, the full-blooded action of the scheme. Intuitive reckoning, and the evaluation of feeling, can only be fulfilled in the able handling of life.

The Month: Like the day or the year may be symbolic of a whole lifetime, with its phases depicting new birth, continuous growth, both physical and mental, up to the mid-point of life, followed by decline and finally extinction. See *PERIODS* of Life.

The New Moon, as boat sailing across the vast ocean of space: Also depicted the whole *JOURNEY* of life.

The Moon measures TIME on the Cosmic Clock: Which on the positive side causes growth, both in the realm of *VEGETATION*, but also of the deep roots of the life of the soul.

But on the negative side the moon symbolizes all that is fleeting, all that perishes.

The waning moon is shaped like a sickle or scythe, or the bow of the goddess of the hunt, Artemis/Hecate, with which to strike down mortals: The moon measures the length of a life and like a scythe cuts it down at the end of its days or months. See *FATES*.

Related Symbolism:-

The Two *MOTHERS*, which are positive and negative aspects of the Mother Archetype or Complex. And are two earlier manifestations of a man's Feminine *ANIMA*, before it is reborn as the young Maiden. And these may be depicted as the three phases of the moon, which govern the tides and therefore the tides of emotion, the Feeling side of life.

The Three Fates, or Three-Headed Hecate: Personifications of the Moon very often have a threefold nature, which referred to its three phases.

Moon Gods and Goddesses.

MEDIATORS, **and the source of creative imagination.**

The Egyptian God Thoth, identified with Hermes: Is the

creative inventor of all the arts and sciences, such as astronomy, medicine, music, drawing and geometry. He was the first of the magicians from whom men learned the secrets which govern the forces of nature. He instructed men in the ways of the gods, and, especially important, in the art of writing.

Thoth was sometimes depicted crowned with the full moon inside the crescent moon.

The Semite Moon God, Sin: Was also God of Wisdom. And the number of letters in the oldest alphabets were related to the stations of the moon. The very oldest, the West Semite Sinaitic Script, derived possibly from Egyptian hieroglyphs, developed directly into the later Phoenician and Hebrew alphabets and still later Greek and Western alphabets.

Moon deities were often depicted with horns: Which were emblems of power, as well as representing the new moon and the disappearing moon.

And could be embodied as CATTLE, *for example, Io metamorphosed into a cow.*

Croissants: May derive ultimately from the crescent-shaped breads offered to the moon goddess.

Negative Symbolism:-

The powers of the Unconscious are associated with the unconsciousness of death. Especially through the waning left-hand side of the moon, which may be why the left is often sinister symbolically.

Personal symbolism:-

The moon is inconstant, disorderly and even chaotic, more in tune with the lawless *IMAGINATION* than the orderly intellect. This is the primary substratum of the life of the mind, in a state of continuous unconscious activity. This unconscious life gives birth to conscious light, as the primary light of the moon swells and gives birth to the sun – or mother gives birth to son. But it is the *UNION* of the two, imagination and intellect, that is true wisdom.

The MOTHER Archetype. Mother and Child
Unconscious Life that gives birth to the Conscious Ego.
The Matrix of all symbolism. The first Mother Goddess, who gave birth to all mythology.

Similarly the revived interest in myth – by coincidence or synchronistically – centred on the incest between Oedipus and his mother.

Mother and child: depicts eternal self-renewal through many ephemeral forms. The relationship between the enduring and the fleeting.

The mother is the epitome of the vast potential lying behind the child: positively the strange mysteries of nature and negatively the cruelty of fate. This very force is often directly – and observably – responsible for making the child into a hero or rebel, a princess or a prostitute. She enthuses, or infuses, the larger dimension of life and death into the detailed destiny of the child. The possibilities of fate, hidden in the future, are given actual form in the child, the person with a conscious will of its own.

Note:- This may amount to overloading personal relationships with archetypal content, which is better transferred back where it belongs: on the broader shoulders of Mother Nature herself.

Mother and son. Incest: Not only are youth and maturity juxtaposed, endlessly transforming into each other, but also the masculine and the feminine, making a fourway opposition. Incest is the image of the reconciliation of this fourway conflict, but it can only be understood as an inward incest, taking place at the core of life; more real than the physical act, not less. This inward vision is entirely dependent on the incest taboo, the inhibition against physical incest, which is what makes the symbol so powerful. (See *FAUST*.) Because the physical act is forbidden, the desire for it is driven into the unconscious. And from there it may erupt spontaneously as an image of the deep, inner cohesion and unity of the whole universe. Whereas the physical act, by contrast, can only be depicted as a tragedy, which inevitably widens the already existing gulf.

The Symbols:-

Isis and Horus; Ishtar and Tammuz; Cybele and Attis. Aphrodite and Adonis, though not mother and son, referred to the same symbolic *UNION* of age and youth, feminine and masculine.

The Two Mothers.

Two aspects of motherhood, positive and negative: the natural mother who nourishes the body but not the spirit, and the dark, unnatural mother who fortifies the spirit often by means of adversity.

The natural mother is often contrasted with another maternal figure – usually a step-mother in fairy-tales – any foster mother or godmother, also sometimes an aunt, particularly the brother's sister: Are figures used to describe the dual aspect of the *ANIMA* within the psyche; or else accumulated wisdom concerning the changing role of the mother in the family; and on the Cosmic Level, Mother Nature herself, who gives birth, nurtures and protects all her young, but also *BETRAYS* them. As Dark Mother Earth, she stunts her offspring, smothers and devours them, as the earth digests their corpses. But in symbolism, as in life, everything is continuously changing into its opposite. In that the good natural mother turns into the primitive, dark force that nourishes the body and not the spirit; and the shadow mother who practises witchcraft in the forests of the unconscious, occasions an upheaval, which becomes the source of transformation and renewal. It is precisely what is needed to enable the child to break away from its natural mother, and leads directly to the discovery of the youthful Anima within.

The Mother turns into, or is replaced by the Dark Witch, and only the White Witch can help: The child's relationship with the mother is wholly beneficial, till quite suddenly there is the danger that the natural love between them will become a fixation, blocking the way to further development. The beneficial relationship turns menacing. In the inner realm the Mother Complex must be dissolved, and reformed as the Youthful Maiden. Whereas in the outside world young girls grow to maturity and motherhood, here in the inner realm the situation is reversed as in a *MIRROR* image. And the Mother Image must be transformed back into the Image of the Maiden. In everyday life it is the new love for the young girl which can oust the old.

Positive/Negative Symbolism:-

271

DEMETER, as Queen of living nature, pulsating and passionate matter, in contrast with her daughter *Persephone, Queen of the Underworld*, mistress of introversion, and spiritual insight, whom she initiates into the realm of ideas. The unconscious Earth Mother gives birth to the transforming *MOON*-mother.

Hera is the Matron who rejects her own Animus (*HEPHAISTOS*) and so remains the one-sided natural mother who nags her husband *ZEUS*.

Negative Symbolism:-

The Dark Side of the Mother: May be *a monster* or *wild pig*, with whom the hero has to do battle at the appropriate time, in order to avoid being castrated and devoured by her. Often the essence *or blood* of such monsters may be transformed into the youthful Anima.

The negative mother may also feature as *thickets, briars, hedges of thorns*, or *castle ramparts*, an *obstacle* or barrier which cuts off the hero, especially from his youthful Anima, the heroine. Often this symbolism is explicit when *the witch actually creates the barrier*, but in other cases she does so behind the scenes, as it were.

Related Symbolism:-

The *VESSEL* represents the inner womb, in which the ritual of *TRANSFORMATION* takes place. Here the values of the child are formed, whether false or real. If false only the dark, inner Mother is powerful enough to smash and remould them. The Father is a similar sacred precinct or temenos, in which the whole personality takes ritual shape. Compare *ANCESTORS*. See also *YOUTH*.

Personal Symbolism:-

Ideally in life the mother, by integrating her unconscious, and maturing other aspects of her potential besides just motherhood, plays the double role of the mother. But often it so happens that you do find 'natural' mothers who feed and nurture their offspring wonderfully well in childhood, and then become a drag on them later. In contrast there are the 'unnatural' mothers who can't cope easily with children, but nurture their spiritual adolescence and send them flying on their way into the world.

Books:-

Layard, J. *The Celtic Quest* (1975), for the psychological details of this theme, which recurs in so many fairy-tales and in more recent times, for example, in Eliot, T. S. *The Family Reunion* where the unnatural mother was the real love and passion of the dead father: and it is with this woman, who has lingered on in the house, a spinster, that the adult hero has an affinity, rather than the actual mother.

MUD

The basic material which life moulds and shapes to its requirements. Inertia, transformed into the *VESSEL*.

The great secret of Nature, and therefore the great search of man is to discover the relationship of life and matter. Which within the psyche is the attempt to relate Intuition, and the highest *FUNCTIONS* of the mind, with the Senses. On the middle human plain of everyday life, it is the great work of putting ideas into action.

In the Middle Ages there was a prolonged debate, lasting several hundred years, with many proofs offered on both sides, about whether life did spontaneously combust itself – which Pasteur settled with a bent glass tube. But for symbolism this remains the fundamental question: how the mud, a mixture of earth and water, ever produced life? Or else how did life ever reach this ball of mud? It is the same question as, Where did you come from? All the answer that Omar Khayyám got was, 'I came like Water – willy-nilly flowing – and like wind I go – willy-nilly blowing.'

In ancient myth man was made from mud and breath as he merged into the mud. His life was spun like clay on the potter's wheel. The ALCHEMISTS and others tried to inject life into the HOMUNCULUS or other dead matter. While Gnostics sought to liberate life from matter: Mud is the malleable substance of our being, full of potential for growth and *TRANSFORMATION*. This is symbolically achieved by *DIFFERENTIATING* the parts and then relating them, the 'Dissolving and Coagulation' of the Alchemists, or *DISINTEGRATION* and re-integration of psychology.

MUSES

MUSES/Sirens

The visions and inspirations of Intuitive Types are contrasted with the hazards arising from the *INFERIOR FUNCTION*, Sensation.

See also FUNCTIONS of the Mind.

The Muses were originally freshwater nymphs who sang at the Banquets of the Immortals. They were goddesses of song: Song is a combination of Intellect (words) and Emotion (music) and the relationship of these two gives birth to inspiration. Intuition (as the offspring of Intellect and Emotion), which is associated with fresh water symbolically, in this context.

The Sirens lure sailors to their death upon the rocks with their singing: The negative side of intuition is its disregard for material existence (the rocks). Lured by celestial songs men sometimes ignore practical realities. For example, the great idealists who massacre in pursuit of their visions are usually Intuitive types who ignore the actuality of the flesh, and seem unable to grasp the physical existence of other people.

When the Sirens challenge the Muses in a singing contest, the Muses win and decorate themselves with the wings and feathers of their rivals: This suggests a partial and somewhat superficial attempt to integrate the negative and fearsomely destructive sides of intuition, without ballast.

Related Symbolism:-

Other rivals of the Muses were turned into birds, and the above may be relevant to fairy-tales, where figures are turned into birds. But see *BIRDS*.

Note:-

The Opera is a medium especially suited to mythical and spiritual themes for these symbolic reasons.

MUSIC

Expresses Feelings, by which man grasps the value of reality, an ascending scale of values, and which relate the parts of nature in harmony with each other.

The whole *INNER* world bursts forth as sound, and the outer world bursts in as sound. People communicate through sound: the origin of language is Emotion, grunts rather than intellectual concepts; and, refined, this becomes music,

274

which for Tagore bridged the infinite gulf between two souls. Music also gives expression to the unconscious, the second Bardo plane. (See *DEATH*, Books of the Dead.) It is comparable to the riot of form and colour without substance.

The Pipes of PAN, the Trumpets of Death, the Pied Piper: Express the closeness of the Unconscious inner realm to the Kingdom of Death. The Pied Piper leads the children into the mountain that is both their inner realm and their burying ground, which are symbolically related.

Related Symbolism:-

COLOUR; NUMBER.

Book:-

Dunne, J. W. *An Experiment with Time* (1927) or the simpler version, *Nothing Dies*, uses the scales of the piano – or the *ALPHABET* – as a symbol of man's life from birth to death: the high-pitched cry of the baby to the last groan. But it's only when the whole scale has been learned, with the sombre dark notes included, that the infinite possibilities of music are opened up. If not quite so scientific as it claims, this is at least a modern expression of the claim of symbolism that simple units govern the harmony of the cosmos; and typical *PATTERNS* and *SEQUENCES* reverberate throughout it.

The MYSTERY CULTS at Eleusis and Samothrace
These provided the background in which certain symbols could have their most powerful impact, and regenerative effect.

The details were kept a fairly well-guarded secret, but they can be partially reconstructed from the shreds of evidence that do exist and partly may be surmised (i.e. guessed) from the typical reactions of man, which cannot have been so very different then.

Periods of fasting were followed by a cup of wine (or something stronger) in an otherworldly atmosphere underground, where sudden flashes of light gave visionary effects. In such highly emotive communal atmospheres, or alone in vigil, people can sometimes grasp the actual and real quality of life beyond the symbol. And go away refreshed from the core of life itself.

The symbols were of *MOTHER* and Child, *DEMETER* and Persephone as woman giving birth to herself forever anew, pointing back to the archaic origin of all, the nature of the Primordial Being, the germ of all existence.

And at Samothrace the Blind Old Man and the *YOUTH*, one gazing into the dark but endless night of the unconscious from the inside (the introvert) and the other the youthful extravert Ego – and the interplay of the two.

What looks like a terrible mess to the everyday Ego, in the right circumstances can be glimpsed from the core of life, and seen as an intelligible and glittering pattern radiating out.

Books:-

Kerenyi, K. *The Eleusis Mystery* (1967).
Hillman, J. *Loose Ends* (1975).

MYTHS, Universal and Personal

Myths could be defined as extended symbols describing vividly the typical patterns and sequences of the forces of life, at work in the Cosmos, in Society, and in the individual psyche.

Universal Myth.

Communal myths were the ritual words of the great cultic festivals of the ancient world, and the typical features of mythology gave symbolic form to man's life, his longings, his needs.

As products of the creative imagination, they mirror especially the unconscious: all that part of life which the conscious Ego, with its utility standards, ignores and rejects. As well as aspects of the forces at work in nature and in the psyche which the ordinary mind cannot grasp except in sudden flashes of inspiration, which myths attempt to communicate.

But because every myth has arisen straight out of the human psyche, each one is full of wisdom and understanding about the nature and structure of the psyche itself. Mythology is dramatized psychology. The experience of life from the inside, from its source in the mind, finds expression through the creative imagination. This uses anything that comes to mind, as the craftsman uses what comes to hand in order to give shape and provide images for the invisible pattern of the psyche, which is most closely related to the pattern of life, because it determines the whole quality of our experience of nature and of existence.

Myths don't operate like an arbitrary fantasy shuffling and reshuffling the facts according to whim. They are the product of a natural everyday process in the mind, which continuously selects and organizes the facts: just as the logical mind does this according to its specialized categories, so does the mythological mind whose chief criteria are value and meaning, as assessed by depth of Feeling and Intuition. The facts in themselves (objectively) are of no interest to the mythological mind: it is the facts as they affect the human condition that matter, the facts as they are experienced by human beings (i.e. subjectively).

Myths aim at bringing together man and nature, at synthesizing his experience rather than diversifying it; they strike through the chaos of detail for threads, patterns, currents that unify experience. And because of their success in doing this, they have been compared with Nature herself for profundity, permanence and universality, by Schelling. The psyche is partly passive and receptive, mirroring the world, but it is also dynamic and active, moulding the world. Most especially images from the roots of the mind – near to the supply of energy – that govern this prospective side of life. But it would be a mistake to imagine that man invents this future out of a void. It is the synthesis of the present experiences which can only be grasped as whole in their main, typical features (i.e. as symbols and archetypes) – and carried forward into the future. The loss of myth is a loss of orientation and direction, and is a catastrophe, affecting either the individual, or the whole society, or both. A slight deviation at the outset and a whole civilization could end up at quite the wrong destination.

Myth is a living reality which can and must alter, change and grow in vibrant accord with life. Too much looking to old stereotypes usually indicates that rigor mortis has set in. Secondhand worn-out symbols affect everyday life drastically, robbing it of value, making it utterly pointless and therefore utterly drab. The symbolic or mythological mind must continue to discover and express the actual meaning and value of life, or the mere clatter of symbols won't do much.

Everything has a natural meaning, a natural value for mankind, and this is what mythology expresses in the most dramatic images and beautiful language available at the time. But this, nevertheless, is inadequate, unless the symbols open the ear of man to the voice of the world, of the universe, speaking in the corn but also the volcano, in the sperm-drop and also the split atom. The pattern of myth, to be living and true, must absorb and relate the dark side of life. Not just the bottomless pit of Nature.

Trained porpoises with high explosives strapped to their backs. A Mother and Child shot from the torpedo hatch of a submarine: These also are symbols, and part of the mythology of modern man. Myth plumbs the irrational and the illogical, which matters because it exists. It is there. Book:-

Jung, C. G. and Kerenyi, C. *Introduction to a Science of Mythology* (1951).

The Personal or Individual Myth.

> **Your personal myth is the pattern of your psyche, conscious and unconscious, into which your past life – and the past itself – has flowed, and from which future life is spun.**

The inner pattern reflects outside life. Taken in, at a glance, it all looks still and formed, but take another glance and everything has moved a little. In the outside world the sun has moved round clockwise, and so in the inner world the pattern fluctuates, changes and revolves, and from its movement is spun the individual's experience of life.

This pattern can be drawn at any time: it is the *MANDALA*. It is always there, governing factors of our lives whether we notice it or not. And the creative imagination, the symbolic mind, is always ready to give shape to it. Only the creative imagination can express what life is like experienced from the inside.

Symbols form quite naturally in the mind: people and events are automatically fitted into the symbolic inner pattern, which selects and arranges everything according to its own criteria of what is relevant and meaningful, according to its own values of what is significant. This inner pattern, to a great extent, determines the behaviour of the individual, whether he's aware of it or not. To become aware of the pattern is, of course, an enormous advantage. So long as it is buried in the unconscious, the patterns conflict and grate with active conscious plans. But once you become aware of the Shadow side of the pattern, the Inferior Function that requires attention, etc., then a balance can be achieved without nearly so much loss of energy.

This inner pattern gives a direction and purpose to life (i.e. integrating the whole personality) relating the parts, *COMPLEXES* and welding them into an undivided whole *SELF* quite different from ordinary conscious aims. Not taken instead of ordinary extravert ambitions, but added to them, this inner purpose brings a whole new dimension to life. Whereas, if neglected, this unused, unfulfilled potential has a way of turning negative and destroying not only parts of your own life but other people's as well.

The Context of the Personal Myth:

> **The fragments of the personal myth which appear in dreams or in waking life are rather like pieces of a jigsaw puzzle, difficult to place without the overall picture.**

But because each individual is the carrier of life itself, the pieces can be set in the wider context of mankind's predicament, his lot, his position in the cosmos, as expressed through the mythology and symbolism of mankind.

Myths outline the fundamental patterns of the inner drama, against which the imaginative eye can discern its own mythical role. The myths and other symbolic material provide the context to what is going on in the psyche, and where it will lead.

Related Symbolism:-

The symbols in this dictionary have been selected with regard to their relevance to the problems and potential of the individual life now, but especially see:

PATTERNS, also *MANDALA; DISINTEGRATION/Integration*; *JOURNEYS*.

MYTHS

COMPLEXES; also *PERSONIFICATION; ANCESTORS; GOALS.*
Book:-
Martin, P. W. *Experiment in Depth* (1976), recommends keeping a record of symbolic inner experiences, which share something of the elusive quality of dreams, but become increasingly significant and valuable once recorded. Noting your most valued memories and then your greatest hopes, gives a framework from which the true mythical pattern may begin to emerge. Trying to visualize the future – which is unknown and so related to unconscious factors – activates the imagination, and reveals aspects of the inner potential.

NATURE
The unconscious. Nature is elusive to the conscious mind, without clear conscious aim.

Nature is the basis of mythology, which attempts to express the value and meaning of nature to man. With its personification of the elements, trees, rivers, etc. the symbolism of nature relates nature and man.

Nature/Human nature: The conscious Ego separates man from nature, and in distinguishing him from his environment tends to alienate him from it at the same time. Children, who are closer to their unconscious, feel the impact of nature much more strongly. It speaks to them more directly in a colourful three-dimensional language that defies interpretation.

The flux of nature: The continuous change in nature reflects the same fluctuation of cause and effect in the lives of men. Nature continuously breaks up, dissolves, flying into seeds, rotting down into the earth, etc., and then re-forming again, solid, fresh-built. In the same way conscious attitudes get stale, rigid, and then break up into bits, dissolve and reform. See *DISINTEGRATION/Integration.*

Nature/Culture: Reflects the inner conflict between unconscious and conscious. Everything in nature has values and meanings for man, from nature 'red in tooth and claw', the bloodthirsty survival of the fittest, to seeds waiting in a state of suspended animation for thousands of years. The difficulty is getting a complete enough picture to see any balance between the parts. For this reason symbolism tends to concentrate the whole overall picture in a single image, for example, the SERPENT/Pole and related symbolism.

Related Symbolism:-

PAN; APOLLO/Dionysus, for aspects of the conflict between Ego and Nature.

See also LANDSCAPES; VEGETATION; ANIMALS; etc.

PERSONIFICATION of Nature.

Book:-

Bleibtreu, J. N. The Parable of the Beast (1968), which manages to synthesize wide-ranging modern scientific data into a meaningful whole, which points towards a valuable modern relationship with nature in contrast with the contemporary alienation from it – even more pronounced and unrecognized in 1968 when the book was written.

NUMBERS

Another complete symbolism, no doubt originally based on a complete mythology of Cosmos, Society and Man, but expressed in a shorthand, or somewhat abstract form.

It is either a meaningful coincidence that we count up to nine and then start again, or sometimes in dozens, and that the gods were arranged in nines, or dozens; or else it may be supposed that the whole system of numbers derived originally from counting and numbering the Gods. Certainly from very early times particular deities had numbers sacred to them. It would also account for the symbolic masculinity of odd numbers while the even numbers may have been sacred to their consorts.

But whether this is so or not, the symbolism of numbers has since become so abstracted from what roots it may have had, and so complex, that it seems to have become more of a construction by the conscious mind. So it has lost much of its immediate impact. The symbolism is more consistent (and interesting) where the links are still obvious with other aspects of symbolism. For example, seven is related to the planets (or Great Bear) and therefore the celestial sphere, and twelve to the Zodiac and Olympian Gods.

NUMBERS

The sequence of numbers in general: The sequence of time. On the cosmic level the sequence of evolution or creation. The process by which one splits into two, who have offspring in the third.

Odd/Even numbers: Odd numbers, apart from being the creative male principle, are related symbolically to the idea of unity, the *UNION* of opposites, because they can't be divided by two, while even numbers refer to the duality and conflict of everyday earthly existence.

NUMBERS symbolize the basic *PATTERNS* of the *PSYCHE*, which determine the *SEQUENCE* of Life in *TIME*.

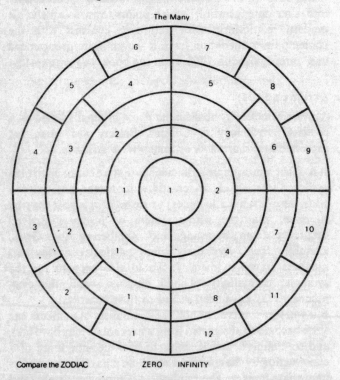

Compare the ZODIAC   ZERO   INFINITY

Multiplying the numbers together: may refer to the relationship of husband and spouse – because productive of more offspring than mere addition of the numbers.

Adding: may refer to relationships like brother and sister.

Particular Numbers.
   As with colour it is helpful to try to think of actual obvious associations with the numbers.

For example certain numbers can be directly associated with *TIME*, and may occur quite frequently with that significance: seven, the week; and, building the units from there, symbolism likes to work in terms of seven periods of seven weeks each, to complete the year as $7 \times 7 \times 7$ days, even though the results are not quite accurate. Twelve also refers to time because of the twelve lunar months which may have determined the smaller unit of the twelve hours of the day.

Zero.
   The void. The empty abyss before anything existed.

Note:-
This abyss is also described with four ingredients, rather like negative elements: nothing, nowhere, infinite and dark.
Also *INVISIBILITY*.
On the personal level this refers to self-emptying, especially of the personal Ego, or symbolic *DEATH*.
Zero/One: The infinite gulf between non-existence and existence: or between the unconscious existence of a stone and conscious existence.
Because of this context, zero is closely related to infinity symbolically (i.e. zero goes into one an infinite number of times: if you divide anything by zero the answer is infinity). Zero is then symbolic of the infinite value of existence by contrast with non-existence. It becomes the circle of preconscious totality, the serpent that encircles the entirety of all things, eating its tail, living off itself perpetually, as does the universe, a closed system.

One.
   The essence of all phenomena, which is a single unity, before being divided and redivided. (See *SPLIT*).

The *ORIGINS*, often personified.
On the personal level this refers to the undivided *SELF*. There is a direct correspondence between Self and origins: the individual Self is traditionally seen as a reflection of the origins of all phenomena. But modern man is inclined to

turn this on its head, and see everything in terms of projections from his own psyche.

Note:-

This is partly the result of taking symbols literally and then dismissing them because they are not verifiable facts: which fails to take into account the way symbols can reach beyond the facts. See *UNKNOWN*.

ONE/Many.

The contrast between Essence and existence; the enduring and the ephemeral. Unity in diversity.

This contrast is the core and key to symbolism. Symbols are basically all of the same nature: they are symbols of *UNION*. And once the whole pattern of life has been glimpsed as a unit, then all the parts are inevitably related. There is an inherent cohesion, especially pronounced because of the underlying relationship between *OPPOSITES*, which are mutually dependent on each other.

Just as light and dark throw each other into relief – light would lose much of its splendour without its opposite – so the *MANY* is inconceivable without the nature of the *ONE*, on which to build. But if there was only one, it would not be the same sort of one, it would lose part of its essential character, as one in contrast with many.

On the personal level it is the contrast between the conscious Ego, which experiences everything in diversity, that is, in bits, and the unconscious, for which there are no distinctions, no differences, for all is merged. This merging, or submerging, is experienced most often in sleep. But it is the aim of most mystical disciplines to experience it when awake; and from then on to know the interplay between conscious and unconscious which is reality itself. Whereas sleep is a regressive fusion of the two – and not very interesting – the waking experience is integration of the unconscious unity, with the living diversity.

This contrast between the one and the many is the key to the broad pattern of number symbolism – which is a complete system of symbols by itself, encompassing the *COSMOS*, the *ELEMENTS, TIME*, etc. It sums up, in a highly compressed form, the contrast between Cosmic *MAN* and Men, *CENTRE* and circumference; the difference between life and lives, between sound and words, or, for example, between one indivisible truth and many theories. The one reality, which corresponds to Plato's realm of Ideas, in contrast with many objects.

This symbol, more than any, illustrates the way symbolism is a process of simplification, unification, discerning cohesion and order in the relationship between man and the cosmos.

Related Symbolism:-

Because symbolism is intended to heal the rift between conscious and unconscious, and because the unconscious responds to pictures more than philosophizing, this concept of One/Many usually appears in more picturesque symbolic garb, such as:

UNICORN/Stag; SERPENT Pole/Serpent; SACRIFICE of primordial man.

Or for example: *one-footed creatures:* the one foot implying the many (which are more normal), e.g. *the One-Footed King*, or *the Sun God (Rohita) appearing as a one-footed goat* in the Atharva Veda. Or *the blade of the SWORD* in contrast with *the Tree* with its proliferating branches.

Personal Symbolism:-

Everything (the Many) is related to Life (the One) of which, as Jung points out, the individual is the sole carrier. The physical image of this is the way one couple could re-populate the whole earth – as perhaps one couple originally populated it? Although the individual is born whole and well integrated with the cosmos, in his pram and till much later he is quite unconscious of it; and what he doesn't know is of little value to him. The inner symbolic work (of individuation) consists of realizing this unity, becoming conscious of it, and so making it real. In practical, everyday terms it is living the contrast between a magnificent, unbroken light, and the particular taste of a juicy pear on a sunny day.

Infinity. (∞)

Is symbolically an extension of the Many above: and the one can be contrasted with the numberless as above: One/Many.

It refers to the sum total of all that is known and unknown. Whereas Zero may be the preconscious totality, infinity is the integrated totality of collective conscious and unconscious.

See *CADUCAEUS* for a more vivid image, with the same significance.

Two.
> Duality of OPPOSITES. Also see *SPLIT*.

One, Two, Three.
> The one splits into two and the two join in their offspring, who re-unites their qualities as the number three combines the numbers one and two.

As in Triads of *GODS*. See also *ORIGINS; SPLIT; UNION* of *OPPOSITES*.

Four.
> Completion, actuality in the realm of matter, with its many fourfold aspects: see *DIRECTIONS; ELEMENTS; SEASONS*.

This fourfold division recurs again and again in mythology, symbolism and dreams. Other more elaborate divisions are often related to it. Thus eight may be the same fourfold division, with four further subdivisions in time and space, which may appear as four gods and their four consorts. Nine – as in the Aenneads of Gods – may be these same eight plus a central original one. Twelve can be two subdivisions instead of one. So all these numbers can be related to the basic pattern of time and space; which reflects the pattern of the psyche as much as the pattern of the cosmos, and the sequence of life, rather than just the movements of the cosmic clock. See The *FUNCTIONS* of the Mind.

Related Symbolism:-

The Four Suits of the TAROT which correspond in Celtic legend to *the Unconquerable Sword, the Magic Spear, the Cup from which an entire army could be sustained,* and *the Stone of Destiny* – on which Kings are crowned to this day. Or again: *the Candelabrum (Menorah), Aaron's rod, the stone tables of the Law, and the Urn that held the Manna from Heaven*. All these different sets of symbols are loosely related by their fourfold nature, and Jung throws light especially on the way the psyche reveals its own fourfold structure in symbols: intuition above, sensation below, with thinking opposed to feeling.

Book:-

Jung, C. G. *Psychological Types*, in *Collected Works*, Vol. 6 (1971).

Five.

ESSENCE and Existence.

Relates to other fivefold patterns in nature such as the HAND, the BODY, and other five-pointed symbolic structures, like Pentacles in TAROT or the pyramids: refers both to nature, the natural physical life, and the nucleus of energy and life, the fifth *ELEMENT*, or quintessence.

There's a story that somebody once dreamed he had discovered the whole secret of life, and leapt out of bed in time to write it down. In the morning he went – full of excitement – to see what he had written:

$$'2 + 2 = 5'$$

Logically it's rubbish, but mythologically it's a very ancient symbolic truth about the structure of the psyche and of nature. Once the fifth element of the cosmos is found it enables man to discern the underlying unity of nature. And the four different ingredients of the psyche combine into something completely different: the undivided Self.

Seven.

Seven periods of time required for transforming consciousness. The lunar (inner) way.

Like twelve (3×4), seven ($3 + 4$) is a basic unit of time, and *TIME* is the dimension of the spirit, and is the essential ingredient necessary for *CHANGE* or *TRANSFORMATION*. So it is the symbol of energy and movement in contrast with matter or substance; or rather, the combination of static substance, the four-square block of reality, and dynamic movement, the three-pointed triangle, like Fire which transforms the other *ELEMENTS*.

Seven is often the last step before completion. But completion is related to the complete circle which is both

Zero and Infinity. Seven resembles the Many, and is closely associated with the seventy years of man's life, while the eighth step completes the cycle in *DEATH* and the *UNKNOWN*.

Seven days of the week: Are still named after the five major planets plus Sun and Moon, binding Time to the Cosmic clock and the movement of the spheres. See *ZODIAC*. The week symbolizes the whole course of man's life – as with Solomon Grundy.

The Sun's Day: Marks the birth of a new separate Conscious Ego. See *SUN* and *HERO*.

The Moon's Day: Marks the relationship of *MASCULINE* with Feminine. *CONSCIOUS* day with *UNCONSCIOUS* Night (see *MOON*).

The day of Zeus, identified with Tiu, or Mars in France: The warring *OPPOSITES* are more a feature of hot-headed youth, in the first half of the week, as preserved in France. Whereas Zeus would be better placed beyond midweek, beyond the crisis and turning point in the middle of life, with Jove.

Mercury or Wotan holds sway over the middle day of the week: Mercury especially is the *MEDIATOR* who accomplishes the *UNION* of warring opposites above.

The day of Jove (Jupiter) or Thor: the full power of Manhood. See *PERIODS* of life.

The day of Venus or Fria: The perfection of Womanhood.

Saturn's Day: Decline and disintegration into the dark realm of the Unconscious. Completion. See *SATURN;* the *UNDER-WORLD;* and a similar cycle in *ALCHEMY.*

Related Symbolism:-

It is the *UNION* of 3 and 4, of heaven and earth, of life and substance, of mind and matter which makes seven such a significant number in symbolism. On the Cosmic level the Great Bear pointing to the one fixed star, the pivot of the universe – besides the planets – was the other important celestial manifestion of the principle of seven, which is in a sense *the MEDIATOR* between the one and the many (see above *ONE/Many*). *The creation took seven days (see BIBLICAL SYMBOLISM)* and *the stories of the Flood refer to seven days* – linking the ark with the Moon boat, as well as with more local floods. In Gilgamesh *Humbaba, the monster, wears seven cloaks* and *Innini strips herself of seven garments*, to enter the underworld. At the command of Ea mankind was re-created in sevens, seven male and seven female. As with the flood story, there is a dark side to creation, to the relationship between heaven and earth, man and nature, which also manifests in sevens: *seven years of famine* in different traditions. For this – purely symbolic – reason, the plagues of Egypt may originally have been seven, but it's known that two different accounts have been put together which could have swelled their number. And there are often seven (or eight) days of feasting or fasting.

The seven-branched *TREE* of life, the seven-branched candelabrum, the *CHAKRAS*, the *LADDER* (or ziggurat) to heaven with its seven steps, are more personal aspects of the same symbolism which refers to the unity of matter and spirit, transforming each other in the course of time.

Eight.
Completion. The Solar (extravert) way.

There is the same interplay of three and four (underneath) but with the original one added. In this way seven, eight and nine are all closely related in symbolism.

To emphasize (pictorially) this more ancient symbolism, the numeral '8' is sometimes said to represent the two spheres, heavenly and earthly, joined, touching.

But the symbolism is more to do with the cycles of time, the four seasons marked by the two solstices and equinoxes, and subdivided once more. Eight is the year, and the eighty years of a lifespan, in which to complete the life's work of relating earth and heaven.

Related Symbolism:-
This same pattern of eight manifests on many levels, cosmic and personal, and in society its essential cohesion made it a symbol for cohesion in the middle realm (mesocosm) of the city which often had eight gates, etc. See *PATTERNS*; also *BUILDINGS, City*. In Ancient Egypt Knuhm was the city of eight. Also see *LADDER* and *I CHING*.

Personal Symbolism:-
These periods of time and life become personified as young, mature and old gods, figures, etc., and are related to the four *FUNCTIONS* of the psyche. These determine the different ways

of experiencing reality, by sensation or intuition, or by thinking or feeling. And these get doubled because each can be experienced in a typically masculine or feminine way, or alternatively extravert or introvert manner because, for a woman, her male side is inner and opposite; and vice versa for the man.

Nine.
   The eight steps as we are whirled around the cycle of life, plus the still centre.

Related Symbolism:-
The still *CENTRE* is Ra, Lord and Ruler of the Nine Gods at Anu in Egypt. See *EGYPTIAN* Symbolism.
The Nine Muses who may number in accord with the nine months of pregnancy – which can be taken as a suitable period of preparation for inner creative work as well.
There are also nine orders of heavenly powers, like Seraphim, Cherubim, Archangel, Angel.

Ten.
   The end of one cycle begins another.

Ten starts the above cycle of numbers again in the decimal system, and is completion, beginning and end, inclusive of all other numbers (i.e. the One and the Many).
Related Symbolism:-
The Ten Sephiroth of the KABBALAH.

Twelve.
   The twelve months of the year, symbolically related to life and the life's work.

Serving a central shrine on a monthly basis, as at Delphi, was also known long before in Sumer as well as among the Hebrews. It relates men's lives to the movements of the Heavens so that the two should be in accord.
Related Symbolism:-
The Twelve signs of the *ZODIAC* – sometimes eight, which illustrates the symbolic relationship between eight and twelve: the difference only lies in the number of partitions, divisions within the entity, i.e. the year, the life.
Also the *Gods of OLYMPUS.*

And *the Knights of the Round Table, or Paladins of Charlemagne.*

Other Numbers.

Must usually be divided, broken down into smaller units to discover the symbolic significance. Where symbolism prevails, the numbers are not always exact. For example, the numbers referring to the days, weeks, etc., choose a basic symbolic number where a pattern can be discerned, then add the necessary extra days outside the calendar.

NURSE. Wet nurse/Sick nurse
The figure who protected and nourished the baby may be the object of a confused unconscious desire later, when the Inner *CHILD* **wants to be pampered or nurtured. Possibly with dire consequences.**

Because the unconscious is the source of symbolic material, and sees in pictures rather than clear concepts, it fails often to distinguish between the child's nurse (i.e. the wet nurse) nourishing, protecting and strengthening the growth of the individual – and the sick nurse. This confusion can have the very undesirable results of people making themselves ill – via the unconscious, see *HEALER/Sickness* – when what they actually yearn for is protection and nourishment of their inner selves, which they could provide for much better in other ways.
Related Symbolism:-
These two nurses correspond in many ways to the Two *MOTHERS.* And the *ANIMA.* in white.
In myth the Nurse may be symbolic of Nature herself looking after the *ABANDONED* hero.
See also *DIFFERENTIATION*, for the value of clear, conscious discernment of unconscious content.

NURSERY RHYMES
Contain much symbolic material, aimed at integrating the psyche, *MASCULINE* **with Feminine,** *CONSCIOUS* **with Unconscious.**

Like so much material which seems nonsensical to the conscious mind, yet exerts an irrational fascination, nursery rhymes are crammed with symbolic themes which appeal especially to children, who are much closer to their unconscious – their individual conscious Ego is only just beginning to emerge from it.

Circles, for example, pennies, hot-cross buns, rings: usually refer to integrating the whole psyche. (See *PATTERNS*, Circle.) The four farthings in a penny, or quarters of the bun, may indicate the four quarters of the psyche, i.e. the conscious Ego and three Unconscious *COMPLEXES*, or *ARCHETYPES*.

Bells: Like pestle and mortar, are especially a symbol of the union of Masculine and Feminine. Bowl and clapper complement each other to make the sound that gathers people together.

Black animals, which were sacrificed to the gods of the UNDERWORLD in ancient times, such as black sheep, black hens, black birds: point to unconscious content.

Male and Female figures, such as king and queen, often with an inferior figure such as a little boy or maid or servant: may refer to Father, Mother and Inferiority Complexes.

Pigs, are a recurring theme: because, as in other symbolism, they are womb animals, and represent the Mother and Mother Complex.

Mice, also occur often: representing a primitive aspect of masculine inner forces, for example, the Ego, Animus or Father Complex. Like the Animus mice are associated with spinning. And women who are frightened of mice may also be frightened of men.

Bed, sleep: unconscious attitudes or content.

Particular examples:-

'*Baa, baa, black sheep*': the depths of the imagination is where wool is gathered as an offering to the three major complexes, Master, Dame and Little Boy – in order to appease them and so prevent them erupting dangerously or negatively.

'*Ding dong bell, puss is in the well*': describes the fate of the Anima (see *ANIMUS/A*) repressed into the unconscious and then retrieved.

'*Hickory dickory dock, the mouse ran up the clock; the clock struck one*': refers to the male conscious Ego striving to attain its identity on which the unity and cohesion of the personality depends – through the movement from unconscious to conscious, below to *ABOVE*, from the Many to the One (See *NUMBERS*, One/Many).

'*Higgledy piggledy my black hen, she lays eggs for gentlemen*': out of the chaotic and disorderly imagination, which is a product of the unconscious, comes potential new birth. But be respectful, and gentlemanly with her.

'*Hot-cross buns, one a penny, two a penny*': symbols of *UNION* (see *PATTERNS*). Relationships are bound by the feminine feeling function (daughters) rather than sons.

'*Little Bo-Peep has lost her sheep*': describes the attempt to differentiate the different content of the unconscious imaginings, which flit across the sky of the mind like fleecy clouds, and are quickly lost to sight.

'*Little boy blue . . ., under the haystack fast asleep*': his animal instincts have strayed into the meadows of the unconscious, and are devouring his substance, his life. The horn could refer to the horn of abundance which he must wake up to enjoy.

'*Little Jack Horner*': appears to discover his Conscious Ego, his 'I', which is an important part of growing up.

'*Little Miss Muffet*': the spider is often the Mother or Mother Complex, which appears to be frightening away the Youthful Anima. (See *ANIMUS/A*.)

'*Mary, Mary, quite contrary*': the feminine unconscious feeling side of life, which is often contrary to conscious masculine attitudes. (See *MIRROR*.) Shells especially are attributes of the love-goddess.

'*Oranges and lemons . . . you owe me three farthings . . . but when will you pay me . . . I really don't know . . . here comes the candle to light you to bed*': three quarters of the psyche are still in the depths of the unconscious – owing, not known – and need to be brought to conscious light before it's too late.

'*Ride-a-cock-horse*': a full acount of harmony with animal instincts, and the feminine Anima – clothed all in white – at Banbury Cross, where *OPPOSITES* meet.

'*Sing a song of sixpence*': the content of the unconscious is opened and four-and-twenty blackbirds begin to sing – they exult day and night, one for each hour. (See *TIME*.) But all is not entirely well. The maid, or *INFERIOR FUNCTION*, gets her nose – symbol of her intuition – pecked off by a blackbird – or swallowed in unconsciousness.

'*Twinkle, twinkle, little star*': a glimpse of personal destiny and the True *SELF*.

Note:-

Dorothy Parker woke up in the night with what she thought was the solution to the problems of the universe, and wrote it down. To her disappointment, it turned out to be:

'Hoggimous higgimous, men are polygamous;
Higgimous, hoggimous, women monogamous.'

Like a nursery rhyme this contains many symbolic themes: 'hog' and 'mouse' would be *MOTHER* and Son, i.e. the union of *MASCULINE* and Feminine, *YOUTH* and Age, emphasized in the polygamy and monogamy which further suggests the movement between One and Many (see *NUMBERS*). But such a dream can only be understood as a 'super dream' or important dream – which is how she experienced it – when placed in the wider context of symbolism, which chooses to depict important truths in a flippant, nonsensical or startling manner.

Book:-

Vries, A. de. *Dictionary of Symbols* (1974), includes interesting nursery rhyme material.

Inanimate OBJECTS — including Sex Objects
Basic passive existence, without any consciousness of being.

Where more life, vitality, is appropriate, this may mean life has been robbed of its most vital essence, perhaps its value, its meaning. This is precisely the result of reducing subjects to objects, i.e. of looking at individuals objectively, analytically, statistically, with man devalued as a cog in the social machine.

The false, limited form of 'objectivity', which is confined to the masculine, logical *FUNCTION* of the mind, is the direct result of excluding the Feminine feeling realm – as well as the supra-sensual intuitive realm. So in myth – because there were the same problems in the ancient world as now – it is, for example, the feminine figure of Medusa who withers the sap of life and turns to *STONE*. (See *GORGONS*). In fairy-tales it is sometimes a bird, again symbol of the feminine.

Objects/living creatures: The same point may be made more subtly – or more realistically – without any magical activities in modern fiction, etc., by people valuing inanimate objects, such as metals, coloured stones, etc., above life.

For example, the miser Silas Marner: who, in the end, turns his affections from the gold to the golden-haired child (George Eliot).

Depersonalizing/Personification: The process of depersonalizing can be extended upwards even to other human beings, whereas the contrasting process of *PERSONIFICATION*, which is a major element of symbolism, can be extended downwards to inanimate objects, in order to describe the mutual interdependence of life and matter, and back again. Note:-

There is a necessary balance between Feeling, which relates the Archetype of Matter with the Archetype of Life, and Thinking, which divides life from matter to the point of alienating one from the other. See *SPLIT.*

This balance could be achieved more easily if recognized clearly, as the contending needs of two equally important Functions of the mind. Unfortunately, ambiguous words like 'subjective' get bandied about and cause a lot of confusion. (N.B. Subjective, as meaning a deep appreciation of life through the Feeling Function, must be clearly distinguished from Subjective as meaning ignorant, limited and Ego-centric.)

The sex object: Negative sides of the personality, neglected or repressed, often manifest in a particularly clear form through sex. What could be called 'the cult of the sex object' manifests in this case the neglect of human Feeling. See *SEXUAL* Symbolism.

Also see *COSMOS; Cosmic MAN; APOLLO/Dionysus; RUMPEL-STILTSKIN.* But contrast *MINERAL*, symbolic of the level of pure existence and the insights it may bring.

OEDIPUS

The dark shadow side of the relationship between Mother and son. See *MOTHER*, Mother and Son.

Turned negative because ignored and neglected in the unconscious, instead of being integrated and transformed through life.

This is a recurring theme in myth and other symbolic material and the Oedipus story is a particularly popular version of it, worked and reworked by the poets and dramatists of the ancient world. Again in this century the Oedipus story has become a hub of interest to psychology. And through it, the interest has spread to other myths and symbols.

Oedipus's father is told by an oracle that he will die at the hands of his son, so he abandons his new-born son with his feet threaded and bound so they swell up: Oracles or divination give utterance to the unconscious side of life, which the father then seeks to evade by killing his son – which corresponds to remaining in a regressive, unconscious state. The swollen feet may symbolize a lack of proportion between the lower, unconscious side of life and the upper, rational side.

Oedipus is rescued and brought up by foster parents, but when he's grown up he consults the oracle at Delphi which tells him that he will slay his father and sleep with his mother. He flees from his foster parents for fear of this; and does just this with his real parents: The dark compelling force of the unconscious is manifest. It is what is not known, not consciously recognized, which determines the action.

There is no conscious decision involved except perhaps the fatal decision to flee from fate rather than stay and confront it.

Related Symbolism:-

There are links between Oedipus and other Sun HEROES. He kills his Father, which resembles the ritual SACRIFICE of the Old KING, in favour of the New, just as the old weakening SUN is replaced by the New-born Sun after the Mid-Winter Solstice. Like Samson he is left blind, in the dark of the Unconscious; like OSIRIS in the UNDERWORLD, he is also in exile: All these incidents tie the story to the *JOURNEY* of the *SUN* which measures the lifespan of everybody, and is symbolic of your life struggle, the battle of conscious and unconscious forces. The whole story is not a chance event, a piece of bad luck for Oedipus, but describes man's predicament, as psychology has shown with abundant clarity.

Oedipus gives the answer to the riddle of the Sphinx: it is Man, in the course of his lifespan, who walks on four legs, two legs and finally, with a stick, on three: Another strand in the symbolism tending to tie the story more closely to the life cycle of all men.

See also *FAUST* and *SEXUAL SYMBOLISM*, for more on the symbolic significance of Incest.

And COMPLEXES, the Mother Complex.

The ANIMA: It is not so easy to resist the pull of the unconscious and the past; and as a result many people remain childishly dependent upon them. It can only be achieved through an heroic struggle which differentiates and transforms the mature Mother Anima into the youthful Anima, which can then be absorbed and related to the rest of the psyche.

Personal Symbolism:-

In investigating personal problems – clearing out our own blocked drain – the profound relevance of this myth is rediscovered in terms of ordinary everyday life. In various degrees, a man may have an all-consuming passion for his mother, which may undermine his whole life. Thus the tragic fate of Oedipus – variously described when he finds out what he has done – is by no means exaggerated.

The story represents a typical or fundamental human dilemma. Seen positively, it is the first stirrings of the dark side of the Anima which devastated the whole inner landscape with plague – which in the story was what brought to light the patricide and incest.

Mount OLYMPUS

The pattern of the psyche and the sequence of life. The archetypes, or most typical features of life, and especially the life of the psyche.

OLYMPUS

The gods and goddesses who reign there are all descended directly from the God of Time. The clouds form a wall around them and the gates are the hours. Furthermore, the deities who rule in assembly, range from the younger ones like Hermes, Athene, Ares, Apollo, through fully mature figures like Zeus and Hera, to the more aged figure of Poseidon: All indicates something of the close original relationship between the gods and the process of time, measured by the sun and moon, planets and stars.

The deities are also symbolic of the *ELEMENTS* with which they are associated: Poseidon and Aphrodite are from the sea and therefore personify the emotions, Poseidon being symbolic of the more introverted unconscious and animal passions, as he lives under the sea.

Zeus/Hera: Sky and earth, life and matter, *ABOVE* and below, as well as *MASCULINE* and feminine.

Ares, who exulted in the din of war for its own sake: Animal instinct and aggression.

The Gods of Mount Olympus arranged in one of the various possible symbolic *PATTERNS:*

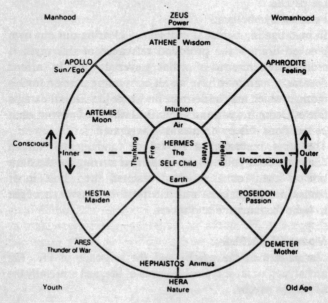

298

Apollo/Hermes: The conscious Ego in contrast with the Self.
Hephaistos: The transforming power of the forge, of fire.
See also GREEK MYTH.

Note:-

The way the Elements manifest may change their significance: Fire manifests as Sunlight, flashes of lightning, the warmth of the Hearth. Water as rain or sea. So the above pattern is not fixed but flexible. It can be adapted to express changes and transformations within the psyche.

Personal Symbolism of the Diagram p 298:-

The left side of the Pattern, represents man's Ego and inner *ANIMA* – within the circle – with its threefold nature of *Hestia*, the Virgin (or Inner Mother) Artemis, the Dark Moon Mother, and Athene the redeemed, conscious, celestial Anima, ever youthful. Opposite, on the right of the pattern, stands Womanhood, with inner *ANIMUS*, as Father, *POSEIDON*; as Inferior or dark, unconscious. Masculine force *HEPHAISTOS*; and Messenger Guide to all the Complexes and parts of the Self, *HERMES*.

But the pattern also shows features of the clockwise development of consciousness. In a man from the seed at the centre, that is, the seed of the Self from which the Ego is later born, *HERMES*. To *HEPHAISTOS*, who is like the primitive older *BROTHER*, ancestor of the Ego, the Shadow from which it evolves. Then *APOLLO, ZEUS,* and finally turning inward after the mid-point of life, to integrate unconscious Feeling, *POSEIDON.* And in a Woman, a similar developing consciousness, which leaves behind it the permanent pattern of the psyche traced from younger Goddesses to older, each personifying different aspects of the psyche: *Hestia, Artemis, ATHENE, Aphrodite, DEMETER, Hera.*

But processes within the psyche can be speeded up independently of the actual lifespan; and centres of consciousness can be activated beyond the bounds usual for a man or a woman. For a human psyche to be complete in its response to life all the twelve latent powers personified as Gods and Goddesses would need to be under conscious control of the mature Self.

ONION

The layers to the core and *CENTRE* of life, which is *ESSENCE* not substance.

Or the other way round, the essence which gathers substance (or image) around itself in layers to manifest its power. The ripples or emanations between the origin and source of life, and ordinary everyday existence.

Personal Symbolism:-

The layers of persona and encrusted attitudes may, on occasion, have to be peeled or shed, for direct experience without the Ego acting as a barrier between *INNER* and outer.

The OPPOSITES

In the typical sequence of creative activity in the cosmos or in man, the magnificent variety is the outcome or product of an intermediate tension between opposites.

Symbolically there is an underlying unity about the cosmos which, when experienced inwardly through symbols, is experienced as the *ORIGIN* and seed of the many-branched tree. The seed *SPLITS* into two: and these two are symbols of duality itself, the nature of opposition, and therefore encompass all opposites. When the opposites can be united, their union bears fruit, in new origins, new beginnings and new wholeness, unity. This is an archetypal pattern, a typical pattern of nature which operates on many levels from the positive and negative wires of an electrical current producing new energy, to the union of masculine and feminine producing a child.

This pattern also operates within the psyche where the conflict and tension between the opposites causes considerable distress, as well as galvanizing energy.

What causes some confusion is that one symbol – such as a circle divided in half with one side shaded – can cover every sort of opposition, e.g. the opposition between male and female, as well as between active and passive. But this doesn't mean the masculine force can be equated with the active or the female with the passive. Though there may be some overlap, each pair of opposites needs to be clearly differentiated from the others.

Which, in the form of a diagram, might look like this:-

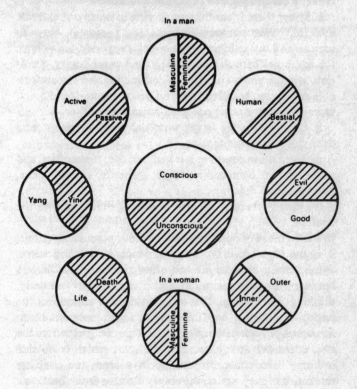

It would take a complete galaxy of such circles to include all the opposites we are confronted with in ordinary, everyday life. The practicality of symbolism is that it expresses the underlying typical pattern in a way that can then be applied – with the discrimination of intellect – to many varied particular situations.

However, the distinction between conscious/unconscious is central and dominant to all other pairs of opposites, because invariably we bring our mind to bear on all oppositions, and the conscious usually identifies with one side and leaves the other side ignored and neglected in the unconscious. From there, typically, the neglected side begins to cause difficulties and problems, and then erupts in open conflict. The personal conflicts viewed against the background of social conflicts reveal a certain pattern of possible reactions.

i. Either there is continuous veering between one extreme and the other: between classical/and romantic, between logical/and mythological (symbolic); the pendulum swings, for example, between puritanism/and promiscuity, tradition/and progress, and there is continuous and uncomfortable oscillation between war/and peace, turmoil/and quiet. Over-emphasis on the one pole poisons the other.

ii. Or it is possible to get worn out with indecision, and drop dead from the tension.

iii. Even more common is it to evade the true conflict, and settle for a compromise that amounts to an inner, psychological death.

iv. Finally there is the true solution, which resolves the conflict.

In such a maze of opposites, with various possible reactions, it is the *TRANSFORMING SYMBOL* which guides and helps. Symbolism is close to life and offers the living middle way between, for example, mind/and matter, spirit/and body, thinking/and feeling. This solution doesn't cancel out the opposites, but is a new third thing, which embraces both, flows out of both, is born of both. It can be grasped by the *TRANSCENDENT FUNCTION*, and the *SELF*, which is outside ordinary Ego consciousness. So in a sense the conflicts remain, but they are continuously flowing into their own solution and out again into new conflict – unlike the dead end. The struggle continues but in harmony with nature, at one with cause/and effect. Nevertheless the differences remain perfectly apparent to the conscious mind: in fact, there is no consciousness without perception of differences. See also *UNION OF OPPOSITES*.

The Symbols:-

The conflict between opposites is an exceedingly powerful element in life, and therefore the opposites appear personified as gods: *The God of Wrath/The God of Love*. *The Stem of Jesse* by which Israel flourished; *The rod of Assyria* which devastated the nation. *GOD/Devil; Heaven/ Hell; UTOPIA/Chimera*; Or *Tiger/Lamb*, in Blake's poem.

The Right-Hand/Left-Hand Paths
Two Worlds, which are really two modes of experiencing the one world, by a mind which is split; sometimes four ways. See *COSMOS*.

Much of the dictionary is arranged in opposites with their symbols because they are so fundamental to symbolism and life. For example,
CONSCIOUS/UNCONSCIOUS; INNER/OUTER; LIGHT/DARK; MASCULINE/FEMININE.

On the particular contrast and conflict between thinking and feeling, expressed in mythological or symbolic terms (i.e. between *Logos/Eros*): *The Straight Sword* (which is with the *Word*, even etymologically) in contrast with *the tree*. The Sun/Moon (but a curved sword may be lunar). *A long fish/Frog, see FUNCTIONS* of the Mind.

ORACLES
Divination is applied symbolism, which stands or falls on the dependability of what Jung has called 'synchronicity' – a pattern of related chances and meaningful coincidences.

Symbolism derives from the premise that the archetypal patterns of nature recur on many levels. Patterns found in the hand, or in the body (of man or animal) or in the stars, will be related to patterns within that most complex of all structures in nature, the psyche or life of man.

But even though very real correspondences can be found between the hand or the position of the planets at birth, and the character of the individual, this doesn't amount to divination.

The next step is crucial to the whole affair. Jung describes it very simply (in his introduction to the *I Ching*) as doing something random in order to discover something random: namely your chances in life. By a law that has nothing to do with cause and effect, there may be some chance correspondence between the pattern of stars, pennies, cards – and the pattern of events in the future. If there is any link it is via the unconscious. If there is a dependable law of striking coincidences, nobody has succeeded in formulating it, or regulating it.

Unlike the law of cause and effect, in control of the conscious will, this law is a typical manifestation of the unconscious: irrational and involuntary (see *CONSCIOUS/Unconscious*). Anybody who attempts divination is at its mercy. It is not wholly dependable in every instance, and it can be, for some people, wholly unreliable on every occasion.

Nevertheless, people who are attuned to their unconscious and perhaps slightly intuitive, if they approach these 'arts' in the right way – i.e. empty of all conscious design, vacuous as the crystal ball – do seem to get results that are beyond the run of ordinary odds. Confucius felt that the *I Ching* had only let him down once in his life, and that seems to have been the occasion when it accused him of being a bit of an old pedant.

Conscious design is directly opposed to the aimlessness of the unconscious, hence people who started with an extraordinary flair in this direction often seem to have ended up cheating, having lost all contact with their in-born capacity, because conscious aims and designs have been allowed to interfere.

Divination can keep alive the structures of symbolism in the form of a game, and in a way that leads on to further investigation. Or it can act as a barrier of idiotic superstition, that brings every other aspect of symbolism into disrepute with it.

However, like symbolism it is basically listening to the voice of Nature, and besides, it lays the foundations of symbolism open to a kind of testing, without which it can easily get lost in realms of fantasy.

The Symbols:-

Originally divination was listening to the sound of the wind, through the leaves of an oak tree; or in the case of the Hero of the Flood, it was the sound of the wind in the reeds and wattles of his hut, that warned him of the approaching deluge in The Epic of Gilgamesh. In Mesopotamia Shamash, the sun god, was god of Divination. *APOLLO/Dionysus* had their respective oracles at Delphi and Thrace. The *SERPENT*, symbol of the Unconscious, usually bestows the gift of divination or is associated with it.

It has been practised in almost every society and seems to be ineradicable even in the most sceptical of times.

See also *ZODIAC; I CHING; TAROT*.

Related Symbolism:-

The possible correspondence between unconscious pheno-mena and Nature relies and depends on the correspondence, or symbolic identity of *INNER* and Outer. The life of the mind determines the nature of the *COSMOS* in ordinary, everyday living rather than in *MAGIC*.

ORIGINS. Origins/Rebirth

The infinitely small origin of life and consciousness, which fits into seed and sperm-drop, and grows to pervade the infinite variety of things in the Cosmos. Like the Cosmic *TREE* or Cosmic *MAN*.

i. *On the cosmic level:* The symbols of origin refer back to an unlikely fact which took place long ago: life emerged from the gloom and endless death of billions of years.

ii. *On the individual level:* Origins are not merely in the past but now: the roots and depths which underlie temporary existence and surround it on all sides, just beyond the puddle of light in which we live, i.e. just beyond the range of the conscious Ego.

iii. *And on the middle landing – the level of the mesocosm, or the corporate identity of mankind:* There are the pairs of ancestors doubling and redoubling back down the generations, till the whole race of man is involved, flowing into and out of the birth of a single child.

And the three realms are interdependent, interlocked in ordinary, everyday life: one human being could not exist without the others, the others could not exist without the cosmos. And the symbols of origin compress the three realms quite simply, as life does.

This is the archetypal matrix, or mother of all, before the opposites came into existence, before there was any consciousness to make distinctions. But once distinctions have been made, the conscious Ego then lives in a shattered fragmented world.

In order to restore the original unity, it's not a question of returning to origins, which is quite impossible, as well as quite useless, but of recovering them, grasping them consciously through the symbol, and bringing them into the immediate present. We become conscious of what was achieved unconsciously – just as, for example, in watching another child being born we may recover something of the experience of being born.

The Symbols:-

The symbols can be divided (for convenience) into i. mineral, ii. vegetable, iii. animal, and iv. human/divine.

i. The *CENTRE*, the *dot*, the *scintilla*. The *Centre of the Earth*, for example.

Also *The Omphalos*, or primeval mound; *The Obelisk*, a petrified ray of the sun; *Sunrise*, *The Spring* (as the beginning of a year) or *a spring* as the source of a river; *The Atom*, a concourse of atoms produced the gods, elements, and all things (Epicurus, fourth century BC); *NUMBERS*, One.

ii. The *seed*, to which the whole Vegetable Kingdom traces its origin. And *the Lotus*, the very light of life.

iii. The *Cosmic Egg* and the *SERPENT*. And with animal life, the first sound symbolically breaks the endless silence. (The noise of eruptions, etc. is not counted as meaningful sound because they were not heard – the concern is with the sound of life.) E.g. *In the primeval beginnings the breath of life emerged from the throat of the Phoenix*. The Phoenix is also depicted bringing the Vital Essence or Spark of Life from the Divine Isle of Fire, in Egyptian myth.

The childish conundrum of 'Which came first, the chicken or the egg?' is also a powerful symbol of origins for a child. And it may be related by a long chain of oral tradition to the mythical goose which laid the Cosmic Egg, as well as to the tale of the goose that laid the golden egg, till its neck was wrung.

iv. Finally there are the many human/divine figures, either unborn, or born in extraordinary circumstances, that reflect symbolically the extraordinary unlikelihood of ever being born into this world at all: who can reckon how he came by this 'hard to attain' human form?

Such as: *ATUM, ATMAN, ADAM, ADONIS, ATTIS, TAMMUZ, DIONYSUS, ODIN*.

Also *the Sperm-drop* and *the blood-clot*, used as symbols of Origin in the Koran.

Atum, the Egyptian ancestor of man, is described as Master of the Castle of Primeval Forms, and unnamed creatures. He contained all potential existence within himself and gave birth to it by masturbation.

Atman is the Divine Spark in man for Hinduism and can be identified with Brahman; i.e. it is of the same essence as the life of the Cosmos.

Adam, the Biblical ancestor of mankind, names all the creatures, i.e. distinguishes them consciously. He's thought to be related etymologically to Adapa, an early Hero King of Mesopotamia.

The Divine Child, of the Greek and Semite world, Adonis, Tammuz, etc., was often symbolically linked with the Spring and the growth of Vegetation.

Odin was the ancestor of man in Nordic tradition.

Books:-

Arberry, Arthur J. *The Koran Interpreted* (1964).

Larousse, *Encyclopedia of Mythology* (1965), for more detail.

Origins/Rebirth

The symbols of origin were a favourite design for the coffins of Ancient Egypt (see *JOURNEYS*). And the great rituals for recovering the link between man and his source or origins are fundamentally connected with the idea that if we ever emerged once from 'nought, infinity, darkness and nowhere' we may be able to manage it again. And anyway, in the meanwhile, the established connection with the symbolic origin is a source of strength, stimulation and unity, inner as well as social.

The Symbols:-

As a symbol of origins *the PHOENIX* is also a symbol of rebirth. He is consumed in the very fire which he brought, i.e. the fire of life gives birth and destroys. And then from ashes, first a kind of worm or maggot emerges, which grows into a chicken, and only gradually back into the full fledged magnificence and splendour of the Phoenix. Again the Phoenix is partially identified with the Sun: a sun's ray strikes the pillar just as the Phoenix alights. And the sun is

strongly linked with life symbolically: it also sinks into death and is reborn at dawn; weakens and sickens towards mid-winter when the days get shorter and darkness predominates. This is also a favourite theme of fairy-tales where the old king is getting decrepit and somebody has to find the source or origin – represented by various symbols – and return with it.
Book:-
Darwin, C. *The Origin of the Species* (1859). This substantiates with scientific data the ancient symbolic premise that all life-forms are a unity, deriving from a single source.

OSIRIS/Seth
The Conscious Ego and the Unconscious Shadow. (See *BROTHERS*.)

Osiris is the light of the world, both sun and moon, but personified because related to the light of conscious life, which perceives the light: Just as the sun has to sink into the Western sea, and be dissolved in the darkness, before it can reappear in the East, refreshed, so the Conscious Ego refreshes itself by letting itself dissolve into the dark realms of the unconscious; and the *IMAGINATION*. (See *DISINTEGRATION/Integration*.)
Note:-
One of the difficulties about symbolism for people today is that the logical thinking faculty objects to the old-fashioned cosmology. Such modern scientific data as the fact that the earth is spinning can be dismissed, along with a lot of other conscious attitudes, so far as symbolism and the unconscious is concerned, which remain backward in this respect. But symbolism also remains close to life: for ordinary, everyday experience the sun also rises in the East and sinks in the West. And its symbolism remains unchanged.
Osiris is cut into fourteen pieces – just as the waning moon disappears slice by slice – by his brother, Seth, who is the personification of darkness: This is another image of disintegrating into the night of the unconscious. Seth (who broke violently out of the womb) is blind, unregulated,

animal instinct and force. (He became Satan.)

Isis searches for the lost Osiris and finds his body (which is only later cut into pieces in this sequence of the story) enclosed within a tree: Symbolically the tree is the very root of man's unconscious life. And here Isis acts like man's Anima, his female guide and guardian through the realms of the unconscious, above all helping him to get out. (See *MAZE*, where Ariadne performs a similar function for Theseus.)

Isis manages to piece together the body, just as the moon reappears piece by piece, till it shines in the sky whole without seam: In psychological terms this reflects the process of seeing the difference (i.e. *DIFFERENTIATING*) and relating the parts of the psyche: the *COMPLEXES* and the *ARCHETYPES* which form the whole *SELF*.

Seth, the 'Great Magician', a dark TRICKSTER figure, is reconciled and used as guardian of the Sun Boat (the light – to ward off evil, Apep): It is typical that the dark Shadow figure, who is familiar with the ways of the unconscious (once he has been brought across the threshold between conscious and unconscious), is of the greatest service to the Ego. Osiris is no longer naïve: he is now conscious of his brother's treachery, and so can use and transform it.

Related Symbolism:-

Vishnu the Creator and *Shiva the destroyer.*

The MEDIATOR Gods, of which Osiris is one: he is the godhead, immanent, close to human life and experience.

The Fisher King in the GRAIL legend has been compared with Osiris. The latter rules in the underworld, the Halls of the Dead, just as the Fisher King rules in a lifeless Palace. Both are wounded in their sexuality, symbol of their creative life. And the attendants don't know what is wrong with them. In any case the tales are symbolically related, in depicting the quest for immortality via the unconscious.

Orpheus was another such 'Fisher King' before he became acclaimed as the 'Good Shepherd'.

Book:-

Rundle Clark, R. T. *Myth and Symbol in Ancient Egypt* (1959), who points out that Ancient Egyptians were not unaware of the psychological value of this myth which was 'useful to man here on earth, as well as when he has died', for the 'lasting vitality' which it brought, as well as its comprehensive understanding of existence.

'The OWL and the PUSSYCAT' (Edward Lear)
The integration of MASCULINE and Feminine, of ABOVE and below. The owl signifies the mind, and the cat the body; and the two are united.

'*They went to sea*': This integration can be accomplished only via the sea of the unconscious.

'*In a pea-green boat*': Within the context, may have a sexual reference, but probably turned inwards (sublimated) and become creative fantasy and IMAGINATION.

'*They took honey and money, wrapped up in a £5 note*': The inner realm of spiritual ESSENCE is related to the practical necessities of existence, within the outer wrappings of physical nature (see NUMBERS, Five).

'*The owl looked up to the stars above and sang to a small guitar, "O lovely Pussy"*': The sexual imagery complements references to the unconscious psyche. Sexuality is another aspect of the Archetype of Matter, which must not be left neglected in the unconscious by people with an introvert or intuitive character. (Yet the implication is that any lack of physical prowess was compensated with fantasy and song.)

'*They sailed away for a year and a day*': Both periods symbolize a lifetime.

'*There in a wood, a Piggy-wig stood, with a ring at the end of his nose*': The wood is the unconscious, and the pig normally symbolizes the dark side of the MOTHER whose treasure (the ring that leads to union with the youthful Anima) has to be extracted, in order to transfer the affections to a mate – or in order to achieve inner wholeness.

'*The (gold?) ring is bought for a shilling*': May symbolize the exchange of silver for GOLD: thereby transforming unconscious content by making it conscious.

'*They dined on mince and quince, which they ate with a runcible spoon*': They made appropriate use of everything in the universe, animal, vegetable and mineral.

Note:-
This shows something of the penetrating simplicity of

symbolism: quite generalized statements are endowed with the particular flavour of life, which accurate logical statements of the same category miss completely. But see *MINERAL*, Animal/Vegetable/Mineral.

'On the edge of the sand, they danced by the light of the moon': They move between earth, sea and sky: thereby integrating the physical, the emotional, and the intuitive.

The action takes place in the land where the Bong tree grows: The land of the *IMAGINATION* – for Bong trees don't grow anywhere else – which expresses Feelings and Intuitions about life. When these are presented in vivid images, unconscious content becomes conscious and the inner rift between the two·can be healed (see *UNION* of Opposites). See also *'JUMBLES'; WEDDING.*

PAN, the Goat God of Nature

The demonic force which manifests both as attraction, in rape, and repulsion, in panic. Throughout nature, fear and desire are related. See also *WISH.*

Fear, whether of wild places in nature or of the strange inner compulsions, brings man closer to nature in a way that is denied to the person whose defences are too formidable. Pan is the embodiment of the living, creative force of nature, the connection between the psyche and nature.

'Great Pan is dead': This connection is lost: nature is robbed of life.

The cloven hoof: The irreconcilable *SPLIT* in nature.

He always inhabits wild uncivilized places: The unconscious parts of the psyche, untamed by the conscious Ego, where impulses and instincts reside.

Dionysus especially is attracted by him, though all the Gods are fond of him: Pan comes from the Dionysian side of life. See *APOLLO*/Dionysus. Including lechery, wine etc. Nevertheless, he personifies natural behaviour beyond the range of conscious Ego purposes, and so is the source of relationship with the divine realm of Mt. Olympus. And is the authentic spontaneous seed of the *SELF.*

His nymphs: The soft mossy side of nature.

Book:-

Roscher, R. W. H., and Hillman, J. *Pan and the Nightmare* (1972).

PANDORA. Pandora's Box
The dark, shadow side of nature and of the Feminine.

When Man, Prometheus, stole the fire of conscious life, he left behind the natural, instinctive, animal existence, and from this dark, neglected side comes inherent affliction: the tension between mind and body (the human and animal sides) of human nature. Pandora was the first woman made by the craftsman Hephaistos out of the mud of the earth, i.e. out of Nature herself, who is rich in gifts. Pandora means 'All-gifted'.

Pandora either found a jar in the house of Prometheus's BROTHER, *or brought a box from heaven with all the ills of the world in it. Either way she opened the box and all the afflictions of mankind escaped and spread across the earth; only hope was left in the jar or box when the lid was slammed down:* Psychologically this describes the way the unconscious projects its own negative complexes, attitudes and dreads on to the reality. Much of the inner work consists in withdrawing these projections: the fantasy of opposites which arises from a split mind. Hope, in this instance, may be allied to Pandora herself, the sweet cheat, the beautiful temptress: it robs the moment by postponing life; the will to live is projected into the future.

Related Symbolism:-

MAYA, which also described the way man projects the reality around him from within. Unconscious passion and folly, when it's contained within the individual, causes great affliction.

Also the episode where *Shiva* is tempted away from asceticism, back into the dance of life by *Shakti.*

Many fairy-tales about female figures bringing gifts are fundamentally related to this same theme of positive, conscious gifts and the negative backlash from the unconscious side, the neglected fairy.

PANTHEONS. The Assembly of the Gods. All-Gods
The *PATTERN* (which governs the sequence) of the forces of life,
on Cosmic, Social and Individual levels.

These pantheons distinguish the particular forces in nature
and human nature and relate them to each other, not all that
harmoniously. Rather, they show the sources of their
quarrels, etc.

Within the psyche they refer to the archetypal pattern of
forces at work in human nature, as well as the typical pattern
of personal complexes, (e.g. it is possible to offload the
personal Father and Mother Complex on to Zeus and Hera,
which would leave personal relationships less burdened with
universal problems).

*The circle of the gods forms a unit in itself, with interacting
parts: and certain recurring features, often a remote ruling god
and more powerful intermediate god,* reflect the relationship
between the Self and the Ego.

*The NUMBER of Gods, such as the original one, plus four gods
and their female consorts, or twelve:* Relates the Gods
symbolically to the four quarters of space, the seasons in
TIME.

Also the four *ELEMENTS* and the four *FUNCTIONS* of the
psyche.

Particular Symbolism:-

Enlil (later *Marduk*) and his pantheon in Mesopotamia.

Ra and his Aennead in Egypt.

Baal Saphon and remote Father El, and their assembly on the
Mountains of the North in Canaanite myth.

The Vedic Gods. (The Vedas are hymns to individual gods of
Fire, Storm, etc., but an assembly is presupposed.)

See also *OLYMPUS; PATTERNS.*

The Knights of the Round Table, may be an historicized myth,
and in any case exhibits the same symbolic structure, related
to the Cosmic Clock and the movement of the universe,
which is reflected in the cycle and patterns of men's lives.

PARADOX

Expresses symbolic truths about the existence of the
OPPOSITES in nature, in an apparently illogical and

contradictory manner, to indicate the way to the reconciliation of opposites.

The *UNION* of opposites cannot be achieved by the Thinking *FUNCTION*, or the Conscious Ego, which always stands opposite the Unconscious, where everything is reversed as in a *MIRROR*. Paradox expresses the two sides of life and nature, which are double-sided, double-edged, both conscious and unconscious. These two sides can only be reconciled through will and action, when Conscious and unconscious work in unison, with the Ego related to the higher *SELF*. Paradox is despised by the intellect, but prized by the whole person. By holding both sides of the truth in conscious opposition, paradox can become the agent of their union. It stays close to the feminine archetype of Life, rather than the masculine archetype of Logic. It has a value in expressing intuitions about the Future and in relating to the *UNKNOWN*.

Paradox was of particular importance to the ALCHEMISTS, who used it to describe their Philosopher's Stone, the goal and product of their labour: Their work was to heal the *SPLIT* in consciousness first by clearly differentiating the opposites and then by expressing both sides in one breath.

The stone is base and noble, immature and perfect, cheap and precious, volatile and solid; it is both the basic substance of life and the transformed essence, it is one and many (see NUMBERS): This is the plain double-sided truth about life, ordinary everyday life, which is of enormous value to those who find the value, and cheap enough to throw away for those who count it cheap. In related biblical paradox, we are made little less than God with all creation at our command, and we are like grass, the wind blows over us and we are gone – all is vanity.

The principle of the art of Alchemy is a raven that flies without wings night and day. Or seek the moon and you'll find the sun: The true value of life can only be found through the dark, hidden way of the unconscious – and it may be costly. Plunging into Shadow reveals the true nature of light even more than the other way round. Plunge into *DEATH*, or symbolic death, in order to realize life. Nothingness is the foil for existence, against which existence shows the brightness of its colours. Man responds or corresponds to Nature only when he is as double-sided.

Related Symbolism:-

The double-sided *TRICKSTER* is a key figure on the border of *CONSCIOUS* and Unconscious, almost the *PERSONIFICATION* of the *SPLIT*, and of Paradox.

Paradox also expresses the way everything *CHANGES* into its Opposite in the course of life and action. The Son turns into the *FATHER*, the *YOUTH* into the Old Man. Beauty turns into Ugliness, and out of the Beast comes the Prince. See *TRANSFORMATION*.

Book:-

Abelard, P. *Sic et Non*, brought together the contradictions in the Bible, pointing to the truth that can only be expressed through paradox. But it was misunderstood.

PATTERNS. Shapes
The pattern of the psyche, which determines the pattern and sequence of life.

The mind imposes order upon the chaos of sense impressions from Nature. The question of whether this order really exists in the outside world doesn't arise for symbolism, which identifies Nature with the creative mind – Nature's masterpiece. All experience of reality springs primarily from the nature of life, and not from the nature of matter.

From the most ancient times very basic, almost geometrical abstract patterns have been valued as powerful symbols, and especially as symbols of immortality, unity, balance, cohesion.

There are traces suggesting that the patterns were originally three-dimensional objects revered from before writing was known, and it is easy to guess how, with the introduction of writing, which started as a stylized attempt to produce convincing pictures, the patterns became formalized, and simple enough for anyone to scratch on to stone, soft clay, leather, or paper. Anybody can draw a matchstick man, though not many can paint a portrait. So, for example, the great prehistoric standing stones, which retain some of their powerful symbolic impact to this day, would be represented by the vertical line – which hasn't got much impact left. And the circle of the horizon, the whole earth abundant in food, might originally have been represented by a great circular slab raised on top of two others; or the massive doorways, through which the rising sun sometimes poured its light, might later be represented by the simple horizontal line, pointing from horizon to horizon and onwards endlessly.

Personal Symbolism:-

To recover something of the flavour of pattern symbolism, it may not be necessary to go quite so far back as the childhood of man. The excitement of early childish scribbles may well be far enough.

But to lose all touch with the symbolism of patterns is to risk letting the psyche, society and even the universe fragment. Trying to live without some symbolic grasp of the overall picture or pattern of life would be like trying to play chess without a board or trying to do a very difficult jigsaw puzzle without the master picture.

Pattern symbolism is particularly compressed, like *NUMBER* symbolism, which lends it the power to balance the psyche when confronted by a welter of conflicting data. To this day, people dream in geometric patterns when the psyche is cracking up at the wrong time in the wrong way. Drawing *MANDALAS* has proved effective in the same circumstances.

The Vertical Line.

Time.

i. Joins above and below, mind and matter. It is man erect, who is the sole *MEDIATOR*, in charge of gardening the earth with his mind.

ii. It is his phallus, and the sperm-drop, just as it is the lightning that brings the fertilizing rain.

iii. It is the Cosmic *AXIS*, and the World *TREE* with its roots in hell, and fruit as light-giving and life-giving, moon and sun (like the silver nutmeg and golden pear), and the stars.

iv. In other words the vertical line can be applied symbolically to everything vertical in the world: it combines and relates them through their vertical nature.

The Horizontal Line.

Everything lying along the horizontal plane of life. Man with arms outstretched pointing towards the *OPPOSITE* extremes which lie to either side of him.

He is the focal mid-balancing point: the *CENTRE*.

The cross.
   The *UNION* of opposites.
   The whole psyche.

The cross is simply the combination of the vertical and horizontal lines. But adding a completely new factor, the cross is a single unit (a whole), yet it includes the fourfold division of nature – into *SEASONS, DIRECTIONS, ELEMENTS,* mind-*FUNCTIONS*. It also has a specific central point (see *CENTRE*). It joins and balances all aspects of man's precarious existence. It is also closely related to his shape – especially if the cross has a shorter, upper stem, as it

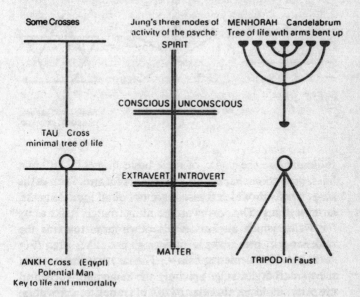

Some Crosses

Jung's three modes of activity of the psyche:
SPIRIT

MENHORAH   Candelabrum
Tree of life with arms bent up

TAU   Cross
minimal tree of life

CONSCIOUS UNCONSCIOUS

EXTRAVERT INTROVERT

MATTER

ANKH Cross   (Egypt)
Potential Man
Key to life and immortality

TRIPOD in Faust

Note:-
It is hard to tell whether the Tripod in *Faust* should be considered a cross with three arms dropping down to the unconscious; or three triangles pointing up like fire to heaven; or perhaps the ambiguity is fortuitous.

sometimes does, or a small circle as in the Ancient Egyptian Ankh Cross. Indeed, in the ancient world it was so much considered the ideal shape of man, the blueprint of his existence, that criminals were tied or nailed to it so as to make them conform to their ideal, inner nature. (See *CRIME/Punishment*.)

Other arms can be added to make it into the wheel or the tree of life. See *KABBALAH*.

The three-dimensional cross (like a weathercock) or the two crosses superimposed on each other: Are particularly apposite symbols of everything there is in the universe, up and down and all around. And are related to the sacredness of the symbolism of seven and eight. (See *NUMBERS*.)
e.g.:

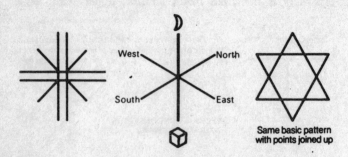

Same basic pattern with points joined up

By joining up the points of these basic crosses by different lines, then other shapes and patterns are formed. Such as the *six-pointed star* which is also a symbol of all four elements, i.e. everything. The downward pointing triangle is like a cup for water which always travels downwards towards the underworld; the upward pointing one like fire. (See *PATTERNS*. The elements, below.) The fact that the centre of the two triangles is in precisely the same spot (if drawn properly) indicates that the *UNION* of Opposites takes place only from the centre, i.e. the *SELF*.

Unity/Duality

The vertical line of the cross would normally be considered unbroken in symbolism, whereas the horizontal – on the physical plane – would be considered broken, a world split between duality, rife with conflict. Compare *SPLIT* and *OPPOSITES*. This relates the symbolism of the cross with the unbroken and broken lines of the *I Ching*:

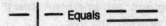

i.e. Unity rising through duality, the *ESSENCE* within existence. The *ENDURING* within the ephemeral.

The Circle

Whereas lines (and crosses) only depict the static pattern of existence and of the psyche, the circle adds the dynamism of movement, the cycle of *TIME*.

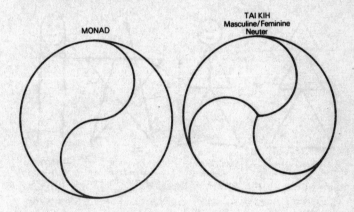

MONAD

TAI KIH
Masculine/Feminine
Neuter

The equal-armed cross is set in motion and the circle is formed.

It is time which completes every process, so the circle is also a symbol of completion, including the completion of a lifetime. See also *WHEEL*.

360° of the circle correspond (roughly) to the days in a year: and symbolize a lifetime. In China the circle had 365°.

Other patterns and shapes.

Just as everything in symbolism relies on the premise that everything in nature and life is a vastly complex structure built out of simple units (see *NUMBERS: ARCHETYPES*, etc.), so with patterns which are complex combinations of vertical, horizontal, slanting and curved lines. *The upward spiral* combines the idea of the circle, the cycle of time, movement and change with the idea of the vertical *AXIS*, the enduring and unchanging principle: in other words, it's a simplified diagram of the *SERPENT* and pole.

Because all symbols are a product of the psyche, very often the results in pattern symbolism may be profitably referred back direct to man. Even the wonderful and complex temples in the New Empire in Ancient Egypt are discovered to be based on human proportions (see R. A. Schwaller de Lubicz *Symbol and the Symbolic*, (tr. 1978) and as quoted in West, John A. and Toonder, Jan G. *A Case for Astrology* (1970)).

Christmas Tree

Man in Lotus position

Pentangle or five-pointed star related to man's five limbs

The fingers as heads bodies and legs (See HAND)

The elements

Square: Earth. So the Sensation *FUNCTION* of the mind which perceives matter and image, and asks the question, 'WHAT is it?'

Circle (or downward pointing triangle): Water. As sea water, normally the unconscious feeling *FUNCTION*; the emotions, passions. Working extravertly it makes for relationships, inwardly it establishes values, and asks, 'WHICH do we want?'

But fresh water is often The Unconscious Intuitive function, as a source of life, meaning, wisdom.

Upward Pointing Triangle: Fire, which as light is the thinking function (which asks, 'HOW?') and as warmth is the emotions, the soul. But also may symbolize the transforming fire of conscious intuition.

The crescent moon: Air, breath, the breath of life (without which there is no life), and therefore the life spirit itself. The horns of divine power are related to this symbolism. In the psyche it may signify intuition which asks, 'WHY?'

The Stupa (Tibet) which piles these symbols on top of each other: Everything in the universe:

Related Symbolism:-

See *MANDALA*, as well as *WHEEL*.

The four-armed Krishna is symbolically equivalent to a living three-dimensional cross.

For the dark and the light in patterns: *OPPOSITES.*

The circle (related to the circular horizon here) *and the wand* are the basic weapons of magic, just as *the sword and shield* are of battle, whether by significant coincidence, or because shapes and patterns are so basic there are no alternatives. *CADUCAEUS.*

321

PATTERNS

See also *RELIGIOUS SYMBOLISM:* although the symbolism of patterns puts man at the centre of the universe, bringing order to the psyche, to society, and even to creation, this tends to become man-*CENTRED* or worse: that is to say even more egocentric, rather than life-centred, if torn from the context in which the symbolism arose. It is only when the many different centres of each individual can themselves be given a centre, that the life pattern of Nature can be related meaningfully to the life pattern of human nature.

Just as symbols are concerned with the interrelationship of Mind and Matter, and not with one or other on its own, so they are concerned with the relationship between the individual and the whole.

PEARL
The incorruptible product of the life's work.

The soft flabby oyster makes the pearl which is revealed at the death of the oyster: Man's flesh completes the cycle of life, and then disappears, leaving behind the enduring work, often formed from the grit of suffering. The *ESSENCE* of Life.

Related Symbolism:-
Like Silver and the *MOON*, the pearl may signify the *ANIMA* or the Feminine principle of Life. It emerges from a shell like the Love Goddess.

PEER GYNT (Henrik Ibsen)
The relationship between the Ego and the Self.

Aase and Solveig. As Anima image, both are mother, bride and wife to Peer. Solveig slowly takes over the role of the actual mother (Aase). The whole play of life takes place between Peer and the never-ageing Mother. The rest is peripheral. The mother gave birth, shapes his life, forces him to wander, and is not unrelated to the eternal earth, the grave. She is the background of Peer's fantasies, the rich and self-sufficient life of the mind.

The green-clad troll: The negative mother image, which prevents him transferring his love to Solveig, leads him to flee into projections and promiscuity. By her he begets a child which tries to slay him, presenting the dangers of inordinate thoughts, desires, wishes.

Peer's visions are full of women and riding: Symbol of loving and the power of Eros. (Man rides in the body of his mother, his first horse, according to Groddeck.)

He drowns his thoughts with lies: His conscious logical thoughts are subjected to his unconscious fantasies, which is the opposite of repression.

He refers to himself usually in the third person, as children sometimes do: He speaks from the universal self, all life.

The trolls: Represent the illusory Ego realm. (Compare *MAYA.*)

His wanderings: Are negatively the flight from anxiety, and positively the search for the will of his Master, that is, his true Self. (See *JOURNEYS*.)

The Ego abdicates so that the Self can be crowned: In becoming the Self, Peer becomes 'anything you like, a Turk, a criminal, a troll of the mountains'. An *'ONION'*, with nothing at the core, although the essence is in every layer.

The Button-moulder: The negative side of the Self that melts down the Ego. (See *DISINTEGRATE*.)

Book:-
Groddeck, G. *Exploring the Unconscious* (1949).

PEOPLE as Symbols

Other people can play a symbolic role in your life, supporting and confirming your Ego by their similarities; or confronting and opposing you as Shadow figures; or they may appear as the successful fulfilment of your true *SELF*. See *HELPFUL FIGURE*.

Just as people play symbolic roles in dreams, so they do in life. We select friends, and even husbands or wives, for symbolic reasons. And people we loathe correspond to neglected aspects of our own personality.

Distinguishing between actual people in our lives, and the symbols they represent, can bring to light how archetypally and symbolically based the everyday mind is. This is especially so in the case of people, because the emotions and intuitions – the mainsprings of symbolism – come into play so much more forcefully and necessarily here, than in any other sphere of life. The imagination is suddenly and inevitably put to work, wondering what goes on inside the other person. Inevitably we use for material, like any good novelist, what goes on inside ourselves, and project it on to the other person. The more unconscious (and poorly differentiated) this process is, the more catastrophic it can be.

People are sometimes afraid that the vivid and active use of the imagination will only increase the hazards in this direction. But the evidence is all to the contrary. Once the imagination is recognized as an active force, always at work, it becomes easier and easier to distinguish images from facts. It's only when it's unrecognized, at work in the unconscious, that it causes confusion.

The inner *COMPLEXES* need to find suitable and appropriate Archetypal material – whether arising spontaneously from their own unconscious, or found ready-made on Mount Olympus or in fiction – in which they can recognize clearly the whole inner world of the human psyche.

But if this is not done, then it is usually other people who get roped unwillingly into the fantasy instead. Others are lumped together into types. Especially dreaded is the type who represents one's own *INFERIOR FUNCTION* – whether ghastly intellectuals, dreaded handymen with their little screwdrivers, moody emotional types, or stuck-up prigs who think they're better than everybody else.

Whether you're aware of it or not, people do play a symbolic role in one another's lives. The point about withdrawing *PROJECTIONS* is to know what is going on.

An actual child may prompt a response from the child within, and so on.

An older wiser person may temporarily be a valid and valuable figure of the inner Self, and represent the potential towards which you are moving: somebody further along the same road.

Contrast *PERSONIFICATION*.

PERIODS OF LIFE

Your life can be divided and subdivided into different periods of growth or refinement in the psyche. And in between each period is a crisis or turning point which requires a change of attitude in order to adapt to the new conditions ahead. See *TRANSFORMATION*.

The Symbols:-

All similar processes of growth, transformation and decay which take place in Nature, in the course of *TIME*, may be symbolic of corresponding invisible, inner processes taking place in man.

The Year, with its different Seasons, with appropriate tasks of sowing and reaping, as the sun grows stronger up to the midsummer solstice and then declines: Is a clear symbol of the phases of man's life which recurs persistently throughout symbolic literature, as well as dreams.

The different phases of a JOURNEY, with particular encounters and events on the way: Often reflect the phases of life and indicate appropriate action at the turning points. In this context life is not unlike four marathons, each of twenty years rather than a bagatelle of twenty miles. And – as in all-rounder competitions – each stretch is across a different terrain, requiring different skills and stamina.

For example, moving from land to sea, from horse or car to ship: May indicate a turning point from extravert Sensation, which is now having to take into account *INNER* unconscious factors in order to survive or thrive. See *FUNCTIONS* of the Mind; *LANDSCAPE*.

SACRIFICE: The turning points and crises sometimes demand drastic changes.

Two halves of Life: Youth/Age.

The whole life can be *SPLIT* in the middle into two *OPPOSITE* periods, which reflect each other as in a *MIRROR*, where all the images are reversed.

Life falls dramatically into two halves, Youth and Age, and, sometime around the late thirties or early forties, everybody reaches a turning point of the greatest significance, both psychologically and symbolically. If it is not marked by changes of attitude – which may involve in particular paying attention to the *INFERIOR FUNCTION* – the second part of life may become increasingly painful, difficult and vacuous. If this has almost come to be expected, and if the really wonderful old person is now the rare exception, then it only goes to show how widespread and acute the problem is.

The Symbols:-

Summer/Winter: The first part of life is for preparing, planning ahead, sowing and planting. (See Personal *MYTH*.) There is also the flowering of physical beauty and of the Emotions. But the second part of life is for the Fruit and the Harvest, and then sitting still and feeding on what has been produced.

The SUN reaches its zenith, the height of its power, and then declines. The waxing and waning of the MOON: The important relationship between *CONSCIOUS* and Unconscious, which is the theme of so much symbolism, has to be worked out in the course of life. The second half of life especially is the time for the Conscious Ego to shrink, decline, like the sun sinking into the Western sea, to make room for the greater vision of the Cosmos at night, symbol of the Unconscious. After the mid-life crisis, all the basic assumptions of the Ego need to be reversed, turned completely upside down, to accommodate the Unconscious *SELF*. Relating truly to the Unconscious culminates naturally in sinking into the corresponding unconsciousness of actual *DEATH*.

Related Symbolism:-

DISINTEGRATION/Integration: This is the process whereby the Conscious *EGO* splits like an acorn and re-establishes its roots in the depth and breadth of the Unconscious.

See also *OSIRIS/Seth*.

The Interrelationship of Youth and Age:

Youth transforms into Age – psychologically as well as physically. But Age also transforms into Youth – in its progeny, in the fruit it bears.

Whereas, in the first half of life, the flow of energy may be profitably directed to the growth of the personal Ego, at the mid-point the flow of energy naturally changes direction as if the tide had turned. In the *INNER* realm it now flows towards the *SELF*, or *CENTRE* of Life. In the Mesocosm the energy flows towards family and society. And it pours out into the Cosmos. The process culminates in physical dissolution: giving back the bread and potatoes – borrowed temporarily and now returned – to their original source in the earth.

But whereas the Conscious Ego separates these two halves, the Unconscious *SELF* can be identified with both at once, the one turning into the other, in a continuous process, pulsating endlessly as the tides.

The Symbols:-

This is another major instance of the habitual *SEQUENCE* of Symbolism: the one whole life forms a unity in its *ORIGINS*, but is experienced by the conscious *EGO* as *SPLIT* into two halves which are quite *OPPOSITE*. These two halves can only be related to each other at the deeper level of the Unconscious *SELF*, which accomplishes the *UNION* of Opposites. Whereby the intricate *PATTERN* of life is experienced as a single whole with the glittering threads going back and forth, like half-lives.

This is a recurring theme at the very hub of symbolism.

For example, the MYSTERY Cults at Eleusis and Samothrace, where YOUTH/Age were contrasted, and then revealed to be related, as in the case of Pothos/Tiresias, DEMETER/ Persephone: Demeter held a piece of corn for which the movement is archetypally the same: from the dark under earth up into the sunlight and back into the earth. Within the psyche it is the movement between conscious and unconscious; a cyclic movement, emerging out of the unconsciousness of the womb and early childhood into full consciousness at the zenith of life; and the returning towards unconsciousness, but with a deeper and deeper awareness of all that lies beyond the range of the conscious Ego.

Incest between MOTHER and Son: Was also a striking symbol of the everlasting Union between the two halves of life.

See also *SATURN*. *YOUTH*/Old Man.

The Four Periods of Life: Childhood. Youth. Manhood or Womanhood. And Old Age:

There is a loose – but valuable – archetypal relationship

between the fourfold division of life and the Four *FUNCTIONS* of the Mind, which can help discover appropriate attitudes and behaviour at a particular period.

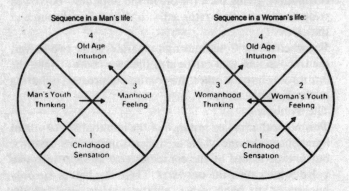

Note:-

But this correspondence between the pattern of the psyche and the sequence of life cannot be applied in any rigid, intellectual way. Symbols and images are much more fluid and flexible than intellectual concepts and words. See the *ZODIAC* for a more complex, and therefore more lifelike, pattern and sequence.

The Symbols:-

The Four Seasons, but with early heat waves in Spring and cold wet spells in August: In spite of a certain flexibility there is appropriate behaviour for each season as for each period of life, and anyone who tries to carry old attitudes forward too long will experience increasing strain.

The Archetypal Shadow, Ego, Animus/Anima and Self: In this scheme there are two further subdivisions of the first and second half of life. In the first quarter the personal *EGO* slowly emerges from the more primitive Shadow or *ANIMAL* instincts, and then in the second quarter, when the Ego is fully differentiated, it relates to this Shadow as to an older *BROTHER*, or sister.

Turning back towards the Unconscious in the second half of life, a woman encounters her Thinking *ANIMUS*, and a man first encounters his Feeling *ANIMA*. Traditionally a man pursued his career first, and didn't marry till his mid-thirties when well-established; then he married a much younger woman who might later develop her intellectual capacities as her children matured – in conformity with the archetypal pattern.

Finally, only in the last quarter of life could attention be devoted to Intuition and the Self, embodied as a Wise Old Man or Woman. In India it was the appropriate period to throw up everything and become a hermit or contemplative. Intellect and Emotion have accomplished what they have, and with life nearing completion it is time to discern its meaning, perceived by Intuition. Part of the wisdom of age is the stripping away of irrelevant details, paring down to the fundamentals, and simplicity. What James Hillman calls qualitative refinement in contrast with the earlier growth. The wisdom of Age is selfless and close to the Unconscious. Unfortunately in the West the *FUNCTION* of Intuition has often atrophied, which may be why old people often become an increasing problem and nuisance.

The Four Ages of Mankind: Gold, Silver, Bronze and Iron: Referring respectively to Childhood, Youth, Man or Womanhood, Old Age. But the order could be reversed, see *AGES* of Man.

The Four Suits in the TAROT or ordinary pack of cards: Pentacles or Diamonds, Wands or Clubs, Cups or Hearts, Swords or Spades: The thirteen cards in each suit refer to the thirteen weeks in each season, and therefore to a quarter of life.

ZODIAC, for Four Ages in current cycle, of Taurus, Aries, Pisces and now Aquarius.

The GODS, were also used to depict the periods and development of life:

For example, *The Divine CHILD, the YOUTH (Adonis, Apollo, Hermes). The Regal Figure of Middle Life, like Zeus, and the Old Grey Beard (Lord of the Sea, i.e. the Unconscious Realm), Poseidon.*

The Same is true of the Goddesses, though less completely, less well-differentiated. There is The Maiden, Kore, the Mature Woman and Mother, and the Crone. Consistent with the symbolism of Sun as Masculine and Moon as Feminine, the three phases of the *MOON* depict the periods in a woman's life – in contrast with the seasons marked by the sòlstices and equinoxes of the *SUN*. Again, the third period has become nearly always negative: even Jung perpetuates this with his Wise Old Man but a Great Mother – a truer match would be a Wise Grandmother.

In life Wise Old Women seem to be just as rare as Wise Old Men, but no rarer. The Sufis (Islamic Mystics) have a tradition of women Sages and there was the female oracle at Delphi. But otherwise they are left merely to happen every so often, in spite of a lack of tradition, or symbolic guidelines. When they do feature in myth or fairy-tale, they usually give an air of familiarity with the dark and sinister side of the unconscious and of nature (the so-called left-hand path) if they are not just witches outright – which would result directly from the social neglect of mature feminine wisdom.

A Diagram of the Four Periods of Life, with some of the Symbols.

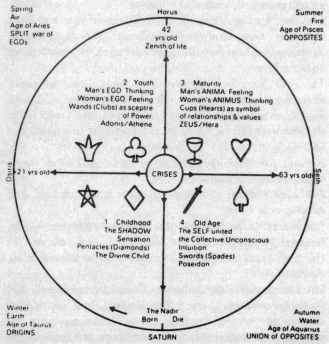

Spring
Air
Age of Aries
SPLIT war of
EGOs

Summer
Fire
Age of Pisces
OPPOSITES

Horus
42
yrs old
Zenith of life

2 Youth
Man's EGO Thinking
Woman's EGO Feeling
Wands (Clubs) as sceptre
of Power
Adonis/Athene

3 Maturity
Man's ANIMA Feeling
Woman's ANIMUS Thinking
Cups (Hearts) as symbol
of relationships & values
ZEUS/Hera

Osiris

CRISES

63 yrs old

Seth

21 yrs old

1 Childhood
The SHADOW
Sensation
Pentacles (Diamonds)
The Divine Child

4 Old Age
The SELF united
the Collective Unconscious
Intuition
Swords (Spades)
Poseidon

Winter
Earth
Age of Taurus
ORIGINS

The Nadir
Born Die

SATURN

Autumn
Water
Age of Aquarius
UNION of OPPOSITES

Note:-

The tradition that the soul was circular may have referred originally to its course through time – the dimension of the spirit, rather than its globular appearance.

In Hinduism there are traditionally four stages of life. The first two, in the first half of life, involve developing the Conscious Ego. But then there is a significant break in attitude: a turning inwards and towards the unconscious.

i. Discipline and Education.

ii. The Active life of the householder.

iii. The Loosening of the bonds of life. Reflection.

iv. The life of the Hermit.

Further Subdivisions of life into twelve periods of seven years each:

May help with more specific shorter-term aspects of inner development and transformation. •

Because symbolism discerns (or creates) units and patterns which recur, a favourite subdivision of life is to break the four main periods down into three phases of seven years each, thereby turning life – always roughly – into twelve periods of seven years each, corresponding to units of time such as the twelve months of the year, or the seven days of the week. This works up to a point, especially in childhood where fairly drastic changes take place at Seven (The Age of Reason) and Fourteen (Puberty) and Twenty-One.

The Symbols:-

The twelvefold division of the ZODIAC.

The Tasks traditionally ascribed to each month of the year: Refer also to the twelve tasks of life.

The twelve Labours of HERCULES.

Note:-

The cells of the body renew themselves in seven-year cycles.

Personal Symbolism:-

The archetypal *PATTERN* and *SEQUENCE* of life, with its typical division, only provides the background, against which to view the infinite variety of personal experience. But the background may exert a valuable influence on personal endeavour. For example, born intuitives may still be struggling to integrate the practical and physical side of life

331

at the end of their days; nevertheless, they may feel more at ease in the fourth period of life and come into their own.

PERSONIFICATION
A device of the imagination to give pictorial form to the valuable relationship between the forces of Nature and the forces of Human Nature.

To the modern intellect with its interests devoted mostly to facts and theories about how the facts operate, the personification of a river as an old River God (like Yam or Father Thames) is a trifle ridiculous. With hindsight, had there been a little more feeling for the symbolic personalities of the rivers, there might have been a little less pollution.

Nor is treating a river like a human being devoid of meaning; once the device is understood it is by no means irrational, because symbolic relationships work in many directions. For example, by respecting the river like a person, you respect the people to whom it brings life.

Purely inward desires and aspirations, arising out of emotion and intuition, could also be personified, which gave them a vivid form. Without such figures, it is much harder to realize a vague and wishy-washy potential.

Personification of the Cosmos – Cosmic MAN: Relates man to the Cosmos; brings the Cosmos, so vast in scale, to human proportions, so as to make vivid the very real connection and interplay between man and his environment.

Personification of Nature: The symbolic mind, the imagination, personifies all the time (quite naturally), so long as the human experience is sufficiently intense. This intensity is inclined to diminish with age, and the conscious thinking function quickly dismisses minor irrational glimpses of the living nature of the universe from which it gets its share of life. These glimpses remain irrational so long as they are at an unconscious level. But once experienced intensely enough, there is no other way to describe the ineffable workings of Nature, except as the workings of Life itself. So to give many lives to sun, sea, stars, trees, is only to endow them imaginatively with the Life that is already theirs, the continually transforming Life which flows through them, Conscious and Unconscious.

Nature is the physical existence of the Life force, its body. Modern man tends to limit his faculty for personification to the Inner Figures which lack substance as a result.

Of course personification can be the result of primitive confusion about where I end and it begins. But once life is clearly differentiated from matter, and my life is distinguished from Life itself, then the personal share in Life – of which each person is the temporary carrier – places the individual in such a close relationship with the Natural Order of the Cosmos that he can become at one with nature. This experience has been clearly formulated since the time of the rituals for becoming an *Osiris* in Ancient Egypt.

The Inner Figures: Again from Ancient Egypt there is a text describing the inner dialogue of a man discussing the pros and cons of suicide, with himself, that is, a dialogue between his Ka and his Ba soul, which corresponds roughly to the Jungian Ego and Self.

Active *IMAGINATION* brings to light the inner drama, the battle of personalities within. Every complete psyche is a theatre of figures with a story unfolding. The figures represent the *COMPLEXES* personified. Indeed, the most convincing or useful picture of the way the psyche works, with its different centres of energy, is in terms of this imagery of the interior community, and the interaction between its members.

The Symbols:-

Personification plays an enormous part in myth, fairy-tale and other symbolic material. See *PROTEUS.*

Talking-animals, for example, or *animal Gods* (theriomorphic Gods) express the relationship between man and animal, not just inwardly, but physically as well. The physical presence of the Bull, the Serpent, etc., distinct from man and opposite to him, is meaningful. (In contrast with dream images which are inclined to be Egocentric and concerned primarily with the person's animal nature.)

Myth relates man to the actual physical universe, depicts his encounter with it, his experience of it. It is futile to try to understand the Figures in Symbolism in any other way except as personification of forces, whether masculine or

feminine. The imagination provides these valuable images –
quite spontaneously – the action and interaction of mind and
matter, which would be difficult to grasp otherwise.

Related Symbolism:-

*COMPLEXES; PROJECTIONS; GODS/GODDESSES;*The *HELPFUL
FIGURE; ANCESTORS.* Contrast *OBJECTS,* Depersonalized.

Personal Symbolism:-

These inner Figures of themselves are nothing but helpful, so
long as they don't get projected from the unconscious and
contaminated with real people. If somebody plays a large
part in your life when they're not there, it's worth trying to
work out if he or she is merely being used to represent some
factor of your inner personality. (See *PEOPLE* as Symbols.)
This is one way of coming to recognize these inner figures,
who are valuable constellations of the forces at work in the
unconscious. For example, the Child Figure, Male Figure,
Female Figure, Power Figure, Inferior Figure, The Dark
Figure, Older Figures of both sexes, etc.

PIG. Boar and Sow

Brute resistance to change or transformation.
  Refusal to adapt.

Often the *ANIMUS* or Anima, which are especially primitive in
this respect. For example, they are very likely to resist the
kind of transexual changes that are demanded at the mid-
point of life. In other words, in the face of problems
concerning the opposite sex, people may turn out to be pigs:
male chauvinist pigs – and their female equivalents.

*The white tusk of the boar determines its association with the
moon,* which is in turn a symbol of change and
transformation, because of its waxing and waning, marking
the passage of time which effects all change and
transformation. This association, coupled with the fact that
the pig is a striking image of all that is most sub-human,
combines to give the idea of resistance to change. (See
CHANGE.)

The sow breeds in 'litters', and is voracious: Which further
associates the pigs with time, that gives birth, transforms and
devours.

The Hero has to overcome the boar: That is, he has to overcome his panic fear at the prospect of change.

Circe turns Ulysses's men into pigs: The negative, stuck, atavistic side of man is contrasted with the progressive, evolving side. The tale goes on to suggest that only the forward-looking intuition with its plans and visions of the future can evade this brutish conservatism in man. *Hermes*, the personification of the Self or the intuitive faculty *supplies the flower*, by which the life sentence of unmitigated brutishness can be reduced to a year of stagnation on the island.

Consistent with this symbolism the pigs are the worst backsliders in the Island of Dr. Moreau (H. G. Wells) and Animal Farm (George Orwell).

The solitariness of the old Boars, like the rhinoceros (in Buddhism): Solitude, in the fourth and last period of life, devoted to the intuition and contemplation.

Book:-

Layard, J. *The Celtic Quest* (1975), for a detailed study of this symbol, which in the context of his inquiry referred mostly to women and their Animus.

PROJECTIONS. Psychological Projecting
The inner *COMPLEXES* **sometimes get unconsciously projected on to other people who are used like blank cinema screens.**

From being negative and destructive, once clearly recognized as part of the *INNER* realm, the same inner forces can be transformed into positive *ARCHETYPES*, a valuable part of conscious rational life.

The overcrowded unconscious generates projections. Confusing the inner realm and the outside world, the person who is limited to his conscious Ego keeps making the mistake of foisting all his unconscious complexes on to other people. Because the unrecognized and neglected complexes (centres of energy) invariably manifest in a negative way at first, he may have a negative attitude to anyone except the few whose conscious Ego is a carbon copy of his own. If his own *INFERIOR* side is inadequate with regard to material existence, then loathsome bank managers will dog his personal path and the Gnomes of Zurich will be held responsible for the downfall of Europe – where the great feasts of Christendom have been turned into Bank holidays, etc. See *DWARFS*.

But if, on the contrary, intuition is the weak Inferior side of his character, then it will be the priests, with hypodermics full of heroin, who will be held responsible for the troubles of the world.

The process is exactly like cinema: the other person is ignored, turned into a blank screen, a container for all your own fantasies and symbolic life. Others are merely there to provide flesh for the complex, and in them the inner complexes become incarnate. This is particularly true of figures of the opposite sex, who are turned into embodiments of the Animus and Anima. Relationships become burdened with characteristics and needs deriving from the inner Mother complex.

Positive Symbolism:-

The Complexes are experienced exclusively from the point of view of the Personal *EGO*, the ordinary everyday 'I'. From this limited vantage point, they are part of an independent, unconscious realm. But from the point of view of the *SELF*, the same centres of energy are conscious, rational, functioning parts of the whole integrated psyche. And are then normally called the *ARCHETYPES*. In other words, *ARCHETYPES/Complexes* are the Positive/Negative sides of the same symbols for inner forces, on the individual level, the microcosm.

And the positive side of projections is that they are nature's way of confronting us with our own complexes and forcing us to come to terms with them. These projections are Nature's *PERSONIFICATIONS* – in flesh and blood. And the actual relationship between a man and woman, in the long run, can ensure inner union of masculine and feminine forces, the integration of the Animus/a. But the process is very much helped along when the individual begins to distinguish between fact and fancy; recognize that emotions aroused by other people (the disgust, the fear, etc.) come from the *INNER Realm*. In the same way, the value we place on gold is a projection from inside man, and not part of the soft bright metal itself. This is the activity of withdrawing projections, which is simply becoming conscious, becoming aware of what is going on, getting to know reality. Instead of being driven by impulses unwittingly, we begin to have voluntary control over the circumstances, which are in themselves neutral.

The Symbols:-

For a man, My Lady Soul, who in traditional symbolism sits spinning: She spins webs of fantasy, involving moods and feelings arising from the unconscious. She is the source of all the delusion, a large portion of which consists of flattering the vanity of the conscious Ego. In a more modern idiom, she works the cinema projector – which by coincidence looks rather like a spinning wheel. This is the Lady Anima, who animates an edited cartoon version of life which she throws between the individual and reality.

For a woman, My Lord Soul: Who projects more a barrage of words, that in the fairy-tales turn into reptiles. Pointless secondhand opinions, that defy any further thought on the subject. The Power complex, which women haven't had much opportunity to exercise in the past, can become very negative and destructive in the hands of the Animus, without the conscious Ego even being aware of it.

Note:-

For Jung the Archetypes are not man's projections. Man is, on the contrary, the projection of the Archetypes.

PROMETHEUS
Is primordial man, and his story depicts man's position, his lot, his predicament.

He steals fire from heaven: The treasure of the Gods is the conscious rational mind, the divine spark which raises man above the animals, and the rest of creation.

He is chained to a rock or pillar and an eagle or vulture pecks at his liver by day, only to be restored at night: The conscious mind flies up, spreads through the universe, but then becomes aware of its pathetic physical nature, its helpless dependent body. The eagle – so golden – is symbol of the sun of consciousness, but the vulture is the dark, shadow side of the same symbol. The drawback is that conscious Egos divide, discriminate, gnaw at the natural, animal feelings, (in the guts); by picking and choosing, man gnaws at himself, destroys the wholeness of the experience of living, which is only restored in the unconsciousness of sleep. This is a very vivid image of the torment of human life, not unrelated to the *SERPENT* and pole: *the pillar* being the unchanging world *AXIS*, all that endures in man's life, transmitted by the phallus, from generation to generation. While man himself – not just his liver, which contains his life-blood, see *BODY* – decays and is made whole again. A lifetime of decay that is miraculously restored and made whole again through the unconscious; on this level the symbolism of the night refers to death itself. Without this process, the youth of mankind would never be restored. He would have been getting more and more decrepit for thousands of years, as in one episode in *Gulliver's Travels* by Jonathan Swift.

Prometheus can do nothing but suffer: This refers to the fact that the Ego must be passive, must dissolve, disintegrate, and hope for a solution in due course from the more central core of the Self – in this case symbolized by *the mature Hercules who rescues him.*

See also *PANDORA*.

Note:-

The name *Prometheus* means 'forethought', which is the particular quality of intuition, and it is the intuitive type who has special abhorrence for material and physical existence, i.e. feels chained to the rock of material existence, or 'tied to a dying animal'. In this context the myth, as a whole, can symbolize the suffering and sacrifice involved in spiritual (or artistic) striving, in trying to transform the human condition into something more exquisite, more refined, more godlike, or genius-like.

In terms of evolution it's a question of mud into energy, monkeys into Dante and Shakespeare, slowly.

PROTEUS
The *CHANGES* and *TRANSFORMATIONS* of life, in Nature. The

personification of the unconscious, in the psyche; see the *TRICKSTER.*

He is shepherd of a flock of seals (belonging to Poseidon) which he brings up on to the rocks to bask at midday: Seals are like fish, but warmblooded and can exist on land, and therefore refer to unconscious content, which is capable of becoming conscious.

He was a wise old prophet, and anybody wanting to learn the future had to catch hold of him at noon: Prophecy is linked with the faculty of intuition. The midday hour suggests the mid-point of life which is particularly favourable for turning to the unconscious, and paying attention to the *INFERIOR* Function. Quite often this is intuition, neglected in the earlier part of life in favour of more pressing conscious aims and plans.

Once seized, he changed into every conceivable shape: He represents those truths that are difficult to grasp, are presented in different images and symbols. But he divulges the truth in the end to those who hang on through all the *TRANSFORMATIONS.* So he represents the underlying truth beneath the changing appearances, in the depths of the mind; or *the depths of the sea to which Proteus then returns.* See *CHANGE; TRANSFORMATION.*

RELIGIOUS SYMBOLISM
Religion and psychology have been the chief means of preserving and communicating symbols, which must first be experienced spontaneously, erupting from – or breaking into – the individual psyche.

Symbolism was the traditional religious language of mankind, and most symbols can be traced back to their use in ritual. But ritual, as the creative expression of the psyche, reflects the pattern and structure of the psyche, and of life. Myth was originally the words that accompanied *RITUAL* actions, which together formed an ancient drama, a dramatic compression of the drama of life. And fairy-tales are for the most part a recognizable (though degenerate) version of ancient myths – considerably distorted by a process of oral transmission. Or else they express, in story form, the symbolism of alchemy or other unorthodox religious groups, dedicated to the work of inward discovery. Although symbols arise spontaneously from the unconscious, for them to be preserved, transmitted, grow, and become of collective value, some form of organization was needed. This was so especially before the invention of printing, which partially accounts for the religious monopoly of symbols – now taken over to some extent by psychology.

Symbolism does just about as well – or as badly – whether preserved and transmitted through a religious context, or a psychological one.

Within the religious context there were festivals, vigils and night processions, the slaying of bulls or the sacrifice of horses and formerly of kings, all calculated to induce intense experiences of a symbolic nature – though not necessarily all that desirable in themselves. And in the face of this the symbolism was all too likely to crust up into flat formulas devoid of feeling or meaning for the majority.

Re-opened to personal investigation, there is a certain lack of support, lack of corporate growth. The atmosphere in which symbolism can flourish was limited till recently to a small circle of psychologists who attended the Eranos meetings and suchlike, rather than the public. It is true that groups are springing up everywhere, and rapidly changing the situation, but there is still a lack of cohesion. Although individuals may benefit enormously, society as a whole is still starved of the fruit of symbolism.

The religious establishments have often lost touch with their own symbolic roots. As F. D. Maurice put it in the last century, before the cracks had become so apparent, religion was crumbling chiefly because those entrusted to transmit it didn't understand what they were talking about. And in turn psychology makes little effective provision for the majority of individuals.

And yet there is a growing background of literature which has enabled many people to rediscover the source of living symbols within, the true spontaneous products of their own unconscious. For many, this provides the main beam of interest thrown on the symbolism of the past.

But there is no reason why the three very different disciplines – individual, psychological and religious – should not complement each other in the long run.

The problem of God: On the supra-human level, the problem for symbolism is to account for the large proportion of symbols which point beyond human experience. Or, to put it another way, the danger of the psychological approach to symbolism is that it may be missing the most important point by tending to become too man-based and man-centred. For example, the fact that Jung calls the highest totality in man, 'the Self', does little to dispel this feeling of uneasiness. His elaborate definitions of the word – which has its background more in Hinduism than in the West – do not always get through. Without a firm grasp of man's dependence upon the processes of life, of which he has a share, people can get inflated with an unpleasant self-importance, which could become a widespread social catastrophe, as well as a personal one.

But it takes great trust, as well as great scepticism, for anyone to try to reach out into the *UNKNOWN*. Only by dissolving all rigid intellectual concepts of the conscious Ego – whether for or against the God idea – can the individual let Life speak for itself. This is the symbolic solution. Only then can a person compare his own authentic, spontaneous and inward experience with that of others, as expressed symbolically down the ages. Then the objective validity of such inward experience becomes apparent. The difficulty lies in creating the time and the circumstances in which to accomplish this.

ONE RELIGION/Many religions: In the framework of symbolism, all the different religions can only be viewed as varied human expressions of the undivided Truth. Because life cannot be divided from life, so there is only one *TREE* of life with many branches. The human psyche, mankind, the energy of the Cosmos and whatever lies beyond the limited range of human perception, is all-there-is for symbolism to refer to, in a partial or complete way. The differences in religion arise from the differences of symbolism, but not in what the symbols refer to: man and the Cosmos, from which man can deduce something of the nature of conscious life and unconscious existence; and the relationship between the two.

The Symbols:-

ORIGINS; NUMBERS. One/Many; UNKNOWN; GODS. Mono-theism; BIBLICAL SYMBOLISM. The God Image; CHRISTIAN SYMBOLISM; SACRIFICE.

Books:-

Huxley, A. *The Perennial Philosophy* (1946).

Happold, F. C. *Mysticism* (1963).

Fromm, E., Suzuki, D. T., and Martine, R. de, *Zen Buddhism and Psychoanalysis* (1960) points a way to the value of relating the religious and psychological approaches.

RITUAL

Is the dramatic enactment of myth, designed to make a sufficiently deep impression on the individual to reach his unconscious.

Myth is extended symbolism, and aims to put human life within the context of the living Cosmos. The year with its seasons and feasts, long processions, night vigils, singing and dancing to arouse emotions, fasting to induce intense inner states of awareness, descending underground, flickering lights that reflect the stars, initiations, immersions, are all symbolic *ACTIONS*. They are common to many varied rituals and spiritual disciplines used to transform the psyche, and see it through the main periods of transition and crisis in life, such as birth, puberty, marriage, and death.

For example, the KABBALISTS used symbolic action to unite ABOVE and Below, Man and Cosmic MAN, microcosm and macrocosm.

Repetition of words and phrases is used in most ritual: Not because it can add anything to the meaning, but because it adds intensity of Feeling, which is so important to symbolism. See *FUNCTIONS* of the Mind, Logical/Mytho-logical.

Related Symbolism:-

MYSTERY Cults; *SACRIFICE; PERIODS* of Life.

ROMAN MYTH
Follows Greek Myth, but with its own set of names.

The God of Time, *SATURN*, an Italic divinity was identified with Cronus, or Kronos.

The twelve great gods of the Graeco-Roman *PANTHEON*. See also Mount *OLYMPUS:*

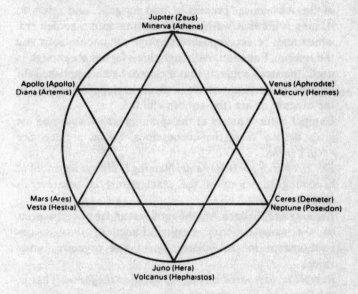

Jupiter (Zeus)
Minerva (Athene)

Apollo (Apollo)
Diana (Artemis)

Venus (Aphrodite)
Mercury (Hermes)

Mars (Ares)
Vesta (Hestia)

Ceres (Demeter)
Neptune (Poseidon)

Juno (Hera)
Volcanus (Hephaistos)

See *APOLLO, DEMETER, HEPHAISTOS, HERMES* and *ZEUS*, for the symbolic significance of these particular Graeco-Roman Gods.

The God of Love, Cupid, was identified with *EROS*.
Bacchus was the Roman name for Dionysus. See *APOLLO/Dionysus.*
The Roman *FATES* were Parcae, Greek Moerae.
The Roman Gods of the *UNDERWORLD* were Pluto and Proserpina, for the Greek Hades and Persephone.
The Roman *HERCULES* was the Greek Heracles.

RUMPELSTILTSKEN (Brothers Grimm)
The *PERSONIFICATION* of the *INFERIOR FUNCTION*.

RUMPELSTILTSKEN

Like other DWARFS: But in this particular case the story concerns the Inferior Feeling *FUNCTION,* especially negative values which are compulsive. The miller puts self-importance before truth, the king is avaricious and puts spun gold above the life of the girl, and the girl exchanges her unborn child for the help of Rumpelstiltsken.

Spinning straw into gold: Is in itself symbolically equivalent of the Alchemical process of making gold, and refers to turning a life that wasn't worth a straw into a golden era: which may be accomplished through the unconscious and the Inferior Function. Although this is legitimate enough in itself, the story suggests that it cannot be accomplished for ulterior or exterior motives (a theme in alchemy) and not at the expense of life (the unborn child).

Rumpel is the Animus at the spinning wheel, spinning the girl's destiny from the unconscious, but at a price. See *PROJECTIONS.*

The girl has to guess his name: Naming is always a symbol of becoming conscious of the exact nature of whatever is named.

The king and Rumpel: Are the extravert and introvert aspects of the same Inferior Feeling Function, that creates relationships in the outside world and organizes inner values.

Rumpel is discovered singing his name in the forest: That is, the forest of the unconscious.

When his name is known he deflates to half his size or disappears: The sexual symbolism of the deflated phallus, which is also stuffed with emotional compulsions when erect, can be applied inwardly as well as physically. In the *INNER* realm it refers to the impotence of that particular complex to dominate and disrupt life. The union of masculine and feminine, in the potential life of the child, is no longer threatened by that compulsion once the compulsive instinct has been named, i.e. made conscious and brought under rational control.

SACRIFICE including suffering
Exchanging the primordial unity of Life for the individuality of the many lives. And vice versa, sacrificing individual separateness for the sake of social and cosmic cohesion. See *NUMBERS*, **One/Many.**

All sacrifice refers back to or is symbolically related to the primordial sacrifice of Cosmic MAN: The division of life into parts and segments. The *SPLIT* of the *ORIGINS* that divides and subdivides the One into the Many: the primal sharing out of life between root, serpent and man.

The original unity of the one man (or divine being) had to be sacrificed for the many men to pour from his phallus, down through the generations. Symbolically this is illustrated by the overthrow of an original ancestor or god, his castration and posthumous generation via the sea of the unconscious (i.e. Uranus and the Furies). But however it may be expressed, the facts don't change: the method of life's renewal is through the older generation making room for the new – by departure. In one way, the single ancestor flows out into the many offspring; but the other way round, four grandparents and eight great-grandparents, quickly doubling back into billions of ancestors, make for the birth of the one child.

This is celebrated through sacrifice. That is, the division of the one life – originally presumed to be human and probably the life of the ex-king – into many parts, which are consumed and integrated into the life of the new generation.

Conscious life is sacrificed by one generation (the dead) in order to be bestowed on the next (the living): it can only survive by being passed on.

Animal sacrifice: Animals were substitutes for man in the ritual sacrifice, possibly chosen unconsciously for their symbolic significance: the bull for the physical side of procreation, the dove for the transmission of the powers of the feminine soul, whether the Love Goddess of relationships to whom the bird was sacred, or the sacred feminine Sophia – Wisdom.

The sacrifice of bread: The fact that all life is one and that corn has to be threshed and broken up before sowing and regenerating in the many, related it to the ancient primordial sacrifice. Personified vegetation gods – like the Canaanite Mot – were cut to pieces and scattered.

Furthermore the grinding of grain into flour reflected the same archetypal process in Nature. Sometimes flour was then kneaded into man-shaped cakes to be consumed and so transformed into the energy of the man. Which demonstrated the unity of all life, vividly and solidly – not just in words but in food – to the ancient mind.

In this context the sacrificial stake: Represents the world *AXIS*, the enduring principle, to which the ephemeral physical sacrifice is tied.

Particular Symbolism:-

The sombre dismemberment of Dionysus, is the background, not just of Greek Tragedy, but of life, whenever we are being torn apart ('cut up') by outward suffering or inner conflict. It is not civilized: it is inevitable. Then ritualized, in order to off-load the burden of it from the lonely person, to the central core – the primal sacrifice of man.

In Hinduism, the slaying of the PURUSHA to make men.

In many myths, the blood of the first Victim – the inner life essence – is mixed with the clay in order to make men.

OSIRIS who is cut up by his brother Seth.

In some instances, the Victim is explicitly cut into two, and then four: Reflecting the division and subdivision by which *The Many* proceeded from *The One* symbolically. (See *NUMBERS,* One/Many.)

The story of Isaac has the same symbolic significance even though the sacrifice did not take place.

Christ. See *CHRISTIAN SYMBOLISM*, The Crucifixion.

Orpheus was torn apart by women: That is, the feminine unconscious which is also the life process.

Prajapati, Mot, Tammuz and Adonis were also victims of symbolic sacrifice.

Note:-

Saul cutting up the Ox with which he was ploughing, and distributing its bleeding parts in order to muster the tribes of Israel is related to this same symbolism on the level of society: the reintegration of the divided parts is what brings back life and power – too late for the Ox – but not for the clans.

See also *DISINTEGRATION/Integration.* Integration – in the psyche, on the social, and on the cosmic level – is the reverse process of disintegration, that is, death.

Personal Symbolism:-

As with all symbolism, the symbolic Sacrifice can be applied on many levels. The archetypal movement to which it refers operates on all three symbolic levels of reality, which reflect different layers of consciousness:

i. On the Cosmic level, the single Life Force is shared out into many different parcels. And these parcels have to rip themselves open – as it were – if they want to experience their share in the unified life of the Cosmos.

ii. On the social level, individuals sacrifice their separateness in order to form a group. But groups also sacrifice much of their efficiency in respecting the individual. See also *GROUP/*Individual.

iii. Sacrifices take place within the psyche, for example, at the transition crises between the different *PERIODS* of life: first the *CHILD* and childishness have to be sacrificed on coming of age. But as with other sacrifices, the *ESSENCE* is extracted and related to the next period of life. Ideally later, Old Age should exchange vigour for refinement.

On the personal level the sacrifice of the animal: Man's giving up the animal compulsion to act, animal drives, animal instincts, in exchange for human consciousness and will.

Individually DEATH is the major Sacrifice: In terms of exchange, the conscious personality is changed back into the unconscious life of the Cosmos, for the sake of the next generation of conscious personalities, in a two-way movement of giving back what was originally taken.

Personal Suffering, Illness, Misery: The Ego can never tolerate suffering, nor its own dissolution. It is only at the level of the core of the Self where intellect can dissolve back into the flow of the river of life that suffering can be integrated into the meaningful pattern of life, with forms shattered into the whole, so as to revitalize the force of nature.

SACRIFICE

In the context of sacrifice, suffering remains exactly the same, except that meaning is added – a creative Intuition of the meaning.

Whereas it was noticed that the intellectual spirit of poetry (aesthetics) could not transcend the horrors of a concentration camp like Auschwitz, Jews and Christians (Bonhoeffer, for example), with an Intuition of the meaning of suffering (related to a tradition of this) as part of the process of transition and transformation, were able to appropriate 'this waistcoat of flame' for purification.

Note:-

Hellfire in myth is not different from the fire of purification so far as the suffering is concerned. But symbolically the difference lies in man's creative power to transform the suffering into sacrifice, as part of an archetypal pattern that pervades Nature and is the very means by which the Cosmos renews itself. Once related to its archetypal source any individual sacrifice becomes meaningful. The particular significance can be discerned against the larger meaningful pattern.

SALT

The incorruptible *ESSENCE* of life, which is discovered through *DISINTEGRATION*, decay, and suffering. The Wisdom that comes from the bitter experiences of life, especially disappointment in the Feeling realm.

Positive/Negative Symbolism:-

Purification through suffering. See *SACRIFICE*. Through the taste of gall, the bitterness of (salt) tears, man gains insight, especially understanding and discernment in questions of human Feelings. Being plunged into the sea of emotion often involves deep *DEPRESSIONS*, which open the individual to the dark unconscious side of life. Reflection upon the experiences may bring to consciousness all the layers of Feeling within, as distinct as separate *COLOURS*. Such reflection leads to the union of thinking and feeling, which is wisdom. For the individual, the suffering involved may be seen like salt thrown into a wound in order to heal it.

Salt preserves, conserves and has in itself indestructible

qualities. In contrast with this, as the body decays at *DEATH*, its salts are the last residue, the leftover. This contributes to the meaning of salt as the enduring essence, in contrast with the decaying phenomenal world. It is the decay which is so repellent to the phenomenal Ego. But no duality is implied in the symbol: duality is a product of thinking, not symbolism. The salt is essential, material substance. Like the thread which makes the pattern and the pattern which is the thread, so the essence is conserved through ephemeral *TRANSFORMA-TION*, not apart from it. Because soda salts are used in the process of making Glass, this adds to the invisible yet material significance of salt, which suggests a *UNION* of spirit and matter, as in *CRYSTAL* Glass.

Related Symbolism:-

The Salt seas, with their Gods like Poseidon, and tumultuous monsters like Leviathan, or Tannin or Typhon: Referring to the depths of unconscious Emotion.

Also the Ouroboros SERPENT, and EROS: Like the Oceans the Feeling Function encircles the world mythologically, and binds it together.

The Dove that is in the lead in Alchemy: Which is just another symbol for saying that it is ordinary basic experience which contains all the spiritual beauty, or alternatively all the flavour, the salt.

The Tear of Kronos.

SATURN or Kronos

The lowest and darkest stage of any process of *TRANSFORMA-TION.* **The terrifying aspect of losing your** *YOUTH.*

But at the same time this nadir of life, this mood of worst *DEPRESSION*, liberates what is essential from the dross and affords the chance of transformation.

In the case of the Youth, Saturn is the stumbling block which confronts him. He is the terrifying aspect of the Old Man in front of whom the Youth is helpless, incapable, immature. The Youth dreads maturity yet is driven relentlessly towards it.

Kronos castrates his father: He *SPLITS* or severs the point of contact between male and female in his fierce struggle to be born, to achieve individuality.

SATURN

He devours his own children: In his fierce struggle to avoid extinction at their hands. It is in this guise that he is the Sinister Old Man, holding Youth a prisoner in the dungeons of his own unconscious. See *YOUTH/Old Man.*

But in the end, even this Titan is transformed, to rule over distant idyllic isles of a Golden Age: In this Saturn becomes the focal point of opposites, each changing into the other in the course of life: the moment of depression being also the moment of 'hitting bottom' and therefore being on the up again.

SATURN
Nadir of Time

Related Symbolism:-

The moment of low ebb: Is also the turning point of the tides.

Saturn may carry the sickle or scythe of DEATH, which is shaped like the sinister waning MOON just before extinction.

The SUN at the mid-winter solstice, bereft of power.

Lead and ash: As referring to the leaden and ashen experiences of life.

Books:-

Vitale, A. *Saturn: the Transformation of the Father,* in *Fathers and Mothers* (1973), with other contributions by Neumann, E. *et al.*

Also Green, L. *Saturn* (1976), for the astrological significance of the symbolism.

SCIENCE FICTION

The product of Intuition, the neglected *INFERIOR FUNCTION* of Western Society at present.

The popularity of science fiction indicates a swing of the pendulum away from the archetype of matter, towards the

revival of the neglected intuitive function, with its interest in prophecy, foresight, insight, plans and visions; synthesis.
Outer space: Inner space.
Sci-fi: Psy-Fi.
It is a contemporary example of the use of the mythological mind, with its concern for the potential of mankind and the future. It is studded with mythical themes and allusions to myth. If it is sometimes rather childish, this reflects the present position of intuition as the *INFERIOR FUNCTION* of society, neglected in the social unconscious where it has been withering for some time.
Related Symbolism:-
The HORROR film is on the whole the purely negative eruption of dark unconscious intuitions, while Science Fiction is the authentic but as yet inadequate expression of the same function experienced positively.
Book:-
In *Dune* by Herbert, F. (1966) the materialist establishment is threatened by the lean desert fringe – that is, figures in the unconscious wilderness – who have mastered the giant worm of corruption which always threatens the conscious Ego.

SCYLLA and CHARYBDIS
Unconscious content, neglected within or *PROJECTED* on to the material world, but either way manifesting negatively and destructively.

Man has to steer his course between being swallowed by the inner unconscious world (the whirlpools of the seas and the mind), and being devoured by the many-headed projections of the unconscious in the outside world.
The crew sail nearer to the many-headed Scylla, and most of them get devoured: People still prefer the enemy they can see. They project their shortcomings on to other heads; they blame and battle with other people, and many perish in the process.

The SEASONS of the Year
Man recognizes the *PATTERN* of the Cycle of *CHANGE*, and

TRANSFORMATION. **He discerns a bolder shape which in turn shapes the activities of his life.** See *ENDURING/Ephemeral.*

Everything seems, at first glance, to be a continuous flux of ephemeral existence, with everything disappearing, rusting, dying, corrupting. This is the immediate impression, the close view. But seen in perspective the very same process of *TIME* seems to be one of continuous renewal. Whether this is on the scale of day and night, activity and rest, leading to another day, or life and death leading to another life, or the creation and destruction of universes or galaxies. The Seasons are an intermediary symbol of any such process, being sufficiently complex to be near to the complexity of life, yet sufficiently simple to grasp directly – almost physically.

The Two Main Seasons: Summer/Winter.
    Youth in contrast with Old Age. See *PERIODS* **of Life. Extravert in contrast with Introvert.** *CONSCIOUS,* **with Unconscious. The** *OPPOSITES.*

In Winter man lives more indoors, and Nature's powers lie underground, both symbols of the *INNER* unconscious realm of the *UNDERWORLD.* As always it is the *UNION* of the Two that makes for the whole cycle, the whole life process, the whole grasp of reality. Not that there was ever any real division, except for the Conscious Ego which adheres to half the truth only – the half that suits it, and so *SPLITS* reality. Related Symbolism:-

The winged lioness with serpent's tail at Thebes: The lion was the summer sun and Serpent the dark of Winter, and the two were joined.

In nature the nesting of birds and their migration, especially of swans, geese, quails: Marked the transition of the two major seasons. The birds were thought to be the carriers of *APOLLO*, and reminded man of the flight of time.

Summer lasts from the scattering of seed to the harvesting of the crop – whereas in winter the harvest is brought into the barns: The first part of life is for extravert activity, while in the second part you live off the Inner store and reflect upon it. It is more contemplative.

The Four Seasons:
>The Fourfold division of the Sequence of time is related to the Fourfold pattern of the psyche, and of life: Childhood, Youth, Manhood/Womanhood, Old Age. (See *PERIODS* of Life.)

From the Mid-winter's Solstice, with the New-Born SUN gaining in strength for thirteen weeks: The Mid-winter solstice was the oldest New Year, and is still the time for celebrating the birth of the Infant Christ. Childhood is the period of Sensation, tasting and touching for the first time. See also *FUNCTIONS* of the Mind.

Spring: Youth, the emergence of the fully conscious Ego. Man reaches the height of his power with the Summer Solstice. For man it is loosely related to the development of his Thinking Function, for Woman the flowering of her Emotions.

Summer: Manhood/Womanhood. Men should ideally get less ambitious, softer and warmer, and develop their emotions, while women have the chance to develop – often neglected – intellectual capacities. It is as if, for men, the light of the Spring sun turned to the warmth of Summer, whereas for women the early warmth of Spring turned to the full light of Summer. This is typical of the flexibility of symbolism, in that the *SUN* gives both light and heat and can be applied to the Thinking or Feeling Functions.

Autumn, when the power of the Sun declines towards the mid-Winter Solstice: This is the fourth and last period of the year and as a unit shapes or reflects the last stage of the *JOURNEY* of life which is symbolically closely linked to the Journey of the *SUN*. It is a period of the decline of Conscious power, which allows for the refining and perfecting of what has been wrought in the psyche.

Related Symbolism:-

The Seasons can be loosely related to the Four *ELEMENTS:* the bare Earth to Winter, the Spring rains germinating the seed to relate Water to Spring. The heat of summer relates it to Fire. And the Winds of Autumn to Air. With variations for climates, where the rainy season comes in the Autumn, for example. But because the pattern of the psyche and shape of man's lifetime are the main concern of symbolism, the meanings often remain firm, though the symbols change. So Water can refer to Intuition in the fourth phase of life, just as well as Air. And Intellect can be depicted as air, i.e. light without heat, as in the symbol of moonlight.

These two, the *ELEMENTS* and the *SEASONS*, form the very basis of all other symbolism. In *PATTERNS* the Elements would correspond to the grid of vertical and horizontal lines, while the *SEASONS* add the ingredient of *TIME*, the circle – from which combinations all other spirals and patterns derive.

Major systems of Symbolism, such as the *I CHING* and *ZODIAC*, are derived directly from consideration of the basic units of Matter and Time, that is, the Elements and the Seasons – their interaction, and effect upon men.

Mythology is plainly based upon the same fundamental insights about reality, but primarily concerned with man-in-the-cosmos, not separate from it. So these products of the psyche are of greater interest to psychology than to any other branch of science. Much of mythology appears to have grown up around the great festivals that marked the Seasons.

Personal Symbolism:-

It is difficult to imagine how symbolism could ever be truly effective again in helping to shape the course and destiny of man's life without returning to some form of annual cycle of festivals. Time is the most amorphous of all the ingredients of life, if left to itself. Without any shape, even a day can become boring and begin to drag. At the moment it often seems as if mere circumstances are allowed to shape men's weeks, that slip into months and years till a whole life is gone, piecemeal – without the inner needs and patterns of the psyche having any say whatever. But the natural patterns of the psyche can hardly be discerned at all unless they are realized to be interrelated with outside patterns of Nature, which can then help determine the style and quality of life.

SEESAW
A simple image of the duality of the world and the way it operates.

Any form of dynamism similarly requires two poles, two *OPPOSITES*, in order to operate. But by standing in the centre, the Self can control the operation, between *EGO* and Shadow, or the individual and the other person.
See *SPLIT*.

The Archetype of the Undivided SELF
That which is of highest value to man, regardless of delusions. It links the personal *COMPLEXES* to their background in the universal *ARCHETYPES*.

The core of Life itself, which the individual shares. The personal Ego divides life from Life; and many Egos *SPLIT* up life. But with the *SACRIFICE* of the Ego, contact is re-established with the undivided Self. My existence, as a share in Existence itself, can be returned to its central core without loss.

In terms of *PARADOX*, the whole undivided self is both inside and outside the individual. The phenomenon of life is double-edged, involving both conscious and unconscious content, so cannot be summed up in a simple one-sided intellectual formula.

The Symbols:-

In terms of symbolism the Self is both *SERPENT and pole: the myriad wheeling constellations and the One Pole Star.*

Round the other way, it is the unity of the whole, the interrelationship and interdependence of all the parts (of every individual Self) which are like pieces in a jigsaw or mosaic. From the point of view of the Egos involved, the separate pieces are in a chaotic jumble. Yet from the point of view of the Self they form the complete picture in which all share totally.

As with other obscure entities, there are many different symbols, which combine in an attempt to pinpoint precisely the meaning, and at the same time avoid the mistake of taking any one symbol literally and so missing the reality

completely. For example, all *MEDIATOR Figures.*
In the first half of life *the HELPFUL Figure. A radiant animal, a tree, a star, or simply a golden ball.*

But the undivided *Cosmic MAN* is probably the most consistently helpful symbol, in that, if understood properly, it is not easily reduced to personal proportions and projections. This is the figure who is the personification of Life itself, in a person, in mankind, in the cosmos, and beyond.

The Buddha's nature reached up and out to pervade the universe at one with the cosmic figure. And *the Christ* emptied himself of this cosmic figure at birth.

Because the Self has been split up, it is often symbolized as a reunion, whether as *homecoming* or return to Paradise, or *reunion of the sexes* as in the case of *the union of the one-legged King and the one-legged Queen*, or *MOTHER and Son* (see *UNION*). *Or the union and transformation of substances* in the retort or vessel of the Alchemist. See *ALCHEMY.*

Negative Symbols:-

Instead of a guiding force which stands behind the personal Ego, the Self can turn negative, like any other content left to moulder in the unconscious. When ignored it turns into a driving compulsion, projected on to *the tramp* in *Molloy* (Samuel Beckett) or *the white whale* in *Moby Dick* (Herman Melville). In *Molloy* the negative Self absorbs the Ego, which is related to the dread of being mixed back into the *universal human porridge* of the Button-moulder in *PEER GYNT* (Henrik Ibsen), whereas Captain Ahab wants to appropriate the Whale for his Ego.

Contacting, and integrating the Self:

By integrating the Ego back into its framework in the universal Self, you are then able to move as freely and as lightly between *CONSCIOUSNESS* and unconsciousness, between life and death, as between waking and sleeping.

The conscious personality is not particularly concerned about letting go of itself in sleep – and just as a night of sleep is soon gone, a million years wouldn't take long for the dead. See *ORIGINS.*

The idea is simple. All the difficulty lies in contacting the Self, not as a wordy concept, but as a true living experience. This sometimes happens spontaneously by chance, in a vivid life-giving experience. Otherwise it may be done at the borders of consciousness and unconsciousness, on the threshold, with the intellect in a state of abeyance. Alert, yet relaxed and empty, like a cat watching a mousehole, or a frog waiting for a fly.

This is the goal or aim of Yoga which means union with the core of life, a long-standing concern of man.

Book:-

Butterworth, E. A. S. *The Tree at the Navel of the Earth* (1970).

The Archetypal, or typical SEQUENCE

Symbolism is primarily concerned with the dynamic flow of life and energy. And although it may describe this continual movement in terms of patterns or substances, these are only static charts and images to depict the invisible flow of energy in the universe, society and the psyche.

Just as there can be a chart of the tides and currents in the ocean, so symbolism suggests that great movements of the cosmos, of history and of the psyche all conform to the same fundamental sequence.

The Twofold Sequence. As in Two halves of life: Youth/Age. Uniting and dividing, separating and joining, dissolving and coagulating, in *ALCHEMY;* the oscillation between one and two in *NUMBER* symbolism: *DISINTEGRATION* and Integration in the psyche, this is the very simple fundamental movement of life and symbolism.

It is so obvious that the intellect is inclined to be sceptical. Yet for symbols to be truly effective, they need to be as simple as breathing in and breathing out, simple bodily movements that integrate Conscious with Unconscious, Thinking with Feeling. For example, see *JOURNEYS*, Walking.

The Symbols:-

All the symbolism of *OPPOSITES* is never static, but refers to the essential ingredient, namely the dynamic flow between the two, between *ABOVE* and below, between *CONSCIOUS* and Unconscious, between *MASCULINE* and Feminine.

Symbols refer to the continuous transformation of one into the other, as *LIGHT* turns to dark, War into Peace, and *YOUTH* into Age.

The Fourfold Sequence. As in *CHILD; YOUTH;* **Man/Woman; Old Person.**

> **The** *ORIGINS SPLIT* **and form the** *OPPOSITES,* **which unite in the** *UNION* **of Opposites.**

This is only a subdivision of the twofold sequence, making the movement clearer, so that it corresponds more closely, for example, to the *PERIODS* of man's life.

The Symbols:-
The Four stages of the Work in *ALCHEMY.*
See the symbols for the four stages of the movement:
   i. *ORIGINS.* ii. *SPLIT.* iii. *OPPOSITES.* iv. *UNION* of Opposites.
See also *NUMBERS*, Four; or *TAROT*, The Four Suits.
Personal Symbolism:-
There is a symbolic sense in which the *CHILD* is *HERMAPHRO-DITE.* Sexuality splits in *YOUTH*, and the rift widens till the *OPPOSITES* relate with the maturity of Manhood and Womanhood – causing many conflicts and problems – which are resolved in Old Age, when each integrates its opposite.

The Seven or Eightfold Sequence.

> **This is most especially related to the seventy or eighty years of man's life, and most closely corresponds to the seven or eight steps in the process of integrating the psyche in the course of a lifetime.**

The Symbols:-
These steps between the different levels of consciousness are like the giant steps of ten years each up the *LADDER* to heaven – like the big stone steps of the Ziggurats, or the Step Pyramid, or the Mayan altars. As layers of consciousness they open like *LOTUS* flowers, more and more petals opening to the sun, as life goes on, as with the system of *CHAKRAS.* As

the flower opens in response to the sunlight, so your mind responds to the light of universal Life. This response is the dynamic core of symbolism and all the systems depict it, in different ways. The *ZODIAC* displays the Seven Major planets moving over the carpet of fixed stars, each planet ruled by a God, a life force. In the Aennead of *EGYPTIAN* myth, it is Eight Gods who live in response to the light of consciousness, symbolized by Ra. Even the seven days of the week with their ruling Gods depict the same movement of life and consciousness (see *NUMBERS*, Seven). Or again, the Seven Stars of the Great Bear or Plough depict the Archetypal Forces, mediating between the still *CENTRE*, the Pole Star, and the multitude of stars like many individual lives. In the case of the *I CHING*, each of the eight steps, symbolized as trigrams, contains or is related to all the other eight; thus each giant step has eight intermediary steps, making sixty-four smaller steps.

These systems cannot be aligned exactly: nor are they entirely consistent. But there is a pattern that emerges, of Seven or Eight facets of the psyche which are cut and polished during seven or eight phases of man's life. It is the typical pattern of Human Nature, the basic chess-board with eight symbolic squares, on which you play out your individual destiny and *MYTH*. As in draughts, the pieces can become Kings; man can gain new levels of consciousness and be reborn as Universal Man. As in chess, pawns that were once confined to moving one square at a time can suddenly become queens and move freely, anywhere, anytime.

Most especially the Tree of Life in the *KABBALAH* discloses a sequence for the development of life and consciousness, with its sevenfold Fruit related specifically to Man. Also see *SEASONS, JOURNEYS* or *PERIODS* of life, or the *HERO*, for the *SUN*, symbol of consciousness, also marks the stages of the development of that consciousness.

The Steps.

Left/right, no/yes, conscious follows unconscious, like breathing in and breathing out. This is the dance of life – and of Shiva.

The First Step: All the *OPPOSITES* are contained together in the Preconscious totality of the sperm-drop, and other symbols of *ORIGINS*. Then the first, dark, unconscious step is taken, with birth, that is typically all physical, all body Sensation, groping. See *FUNCTIONS* of the Mind. This is archetypally the step of the Primitive elder *BROTHER*, the *ANIMAL* Man, the Shadow that precedes the Ego. And lasts very roughly a decade. But it potentially contains all the other steps in embryo form, more highly evolved in some than in others. Particular variations in individuals mean that this step will manifest their Main or Superior Function: the different Psychological Types can already be distinguished by the age of Ten. See also *CHILD*.

The Second Step: Is symbolic of the birth of the Conscious Ego, the Age of Reason, the everyday 'I' emerges. It is the age or stage for relating to the symbolic *HERO* or *HEROINE*. For men it is typically related to the development of their Thinking Function, and women their Feeling Function. Origins are *SPLIT* into *EGO*/Shadow, *MASCULINE*/Feminine, Thinking/Feeling. *Or to put it another way, the second step is strewn with images of Feeling and Thoughts, or with pottery figures of Samson tussling with his animal nature, the lion and story books of Heroes.*

The Third Step: Is archetypally one of dynamic oscillation between the *OPPOSITES:* that can only be resolved through a third factor, the *INFERIOR* Function in the psyche – that in the outside world is like the Child, offspring and Union of man and woman. Archetypally this Inferior Function is Intuition, which can grasp the whole picture, and has the foresight to begin to grope towards the *CENTRE* in an Unconscious way, and the relationship of opposites.

The Fourth and Fifth Step: Which is reached symbolically around the mid-point of life, is the *SELF*, the *CENTRE*, the *MEDIATOR*, who relates man to Cosmic or Universal *MAN*. What was guessed intuitively, is now realized consciously. The Personal Psyche is completed with all its parts functioning: your whole life responds to Life itself.

There is some close connection between fully Conscious Intuition at the top of Personal Consciousness, and Universal Sensation at the base of the New-born Cosmic *MAN*. What was once glimpsed in flashes and seemed far removed from personal experience – such as remote periods of History – are experienced with almost physical, bodily sensation by the more developed Creative *IMAGINATION*. So the Physical Sensation of Cosmic *MAN* can almost be identified with Personal Intuition and as Conscious and Unconscious sides of the same Function. This links the Fourth and Fifth step: the *UNION* of Opposites and new *ORIGINS*.

The Sixth Step: Although the shift from *EGO* to *SELF* is achieved in an instant, it is like a sudden conquest of Unconscious territory. Symbols are like Towers, or the Great Wall of China, to mark and hold the territory gained. They remind the ordinary everyday Ego of the vaster territory that is now the domains of the Self. The Towers with their *FLAGS* are watch-towers, as well as landmarks for others travelling that way, and so a means of communication, which gives conscious objectivity to personal experience.

Again there is a Split, but this time on the collective level between the archetypal Masculine Conscious Thought or Justice, and the archetype of Eros, all relationships, Feelings or Mercy. The scale is different from the second step, the horizons are wider.

The Seventh Step: Jung's Collective Unconscious – which he saw going back in time like the layers of Ancient Rome – stands opposite the Collective Conscious of Mankind which could be symbolized by an enormous library, like the British Library with its domed central room. And all of it would be uselessly collecting dust, but for the Individual, you and me, the living carriers of this Archetypal life stream.

The Eighth Step: Completion. The two feet come together again, at a standstill, the standstill of *DEATH*, which has to be faced whole, and symbolizes the final *UNION* of Opposites. Traditionally there is no symbol or image of this last step. The *UNKNOWN* cannot be filled with man's delusions and *PROJECTIONS*, especially not projections of emptiness.

Related Symbolism:-
BIBLICAL SYMBOLISM, The Seven Days of Creation; and *CHRISTIAN SYMBOLISM*, The Seven Miracles of John.
Personal Symbolism:-
This basic sequence is more concerned with the psyche than

361

with everyday life, but it can be applied in many ways on many levels, if suitably adapted. But the adaptation must not be rigid or formal – it must be applied with Intuition and Feeling, not Intellect. Then it may throw new light on the typical, basic significance of particular practices in concentration to develop higher consciousness, or the sequence of Annual Festivals which in turn reflect the

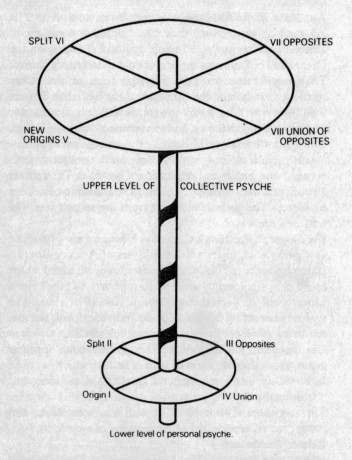

One out of many possible ways of visualizing the eight stages of the *SEQUENCE*. But all such patterns miss the main point, the movement which is more like dance step: feet together – apart – apart – together. Compare *CADUCEUS*. *Hopscotch*.

broader cycle of life, with ancient initiation ceremonies at particular crises, and turning points.

For example, for Christians, the Seven Sacraments: Baptism celebrates Origins, Penance the Split, Marriage the Opposites on a personal level. Communion is the central sacrament of the Union of Opposites. Confirmation (or adult Baptism) corresponds symbolically with New Origins or the birth of Cosmic Man, Priesthood to the Opposites of *ABOVE* and Below on the collective level, with the Last Sacrament to celebrate Death, the eighth and last step.

For Buddhists, the eight levels of Dhyana or Jhana: Eight centres of concentration or absorption are the core of Buddhist practice for attaining higher consciousness. They are a subtle and highly sophisticated account of the workings of the psyche, describing eight stages in the process of cutting off personal sensations, thoughts, feelings and even intuitive bliss in order to reach the centre of being, and so discover man's relationship with unlimited space, consciousness and peace, and finally in the eighth stage the aim is to reach a sublime state which is neither perception nor non-perception. But this concentration or mindfulness is only a preparation for insight into the nature of reality.

SERPENT Snakes

A primitive form of animal life, and therefore a deep layer of the unconscious.

The different *FUNCTIONS* of the psyche have not been differentiated: symbolically the serpent combines reptile and bird, animal and fish. It is close to the *ORIGIN* of life, the primal underlying unity of all life forms.

Primal instincts, stirring, and therefore demanding to be transformed.

It is a symbol of the *UNION* of opposites in a primitive, animal way. Its serpentine way of moving, both on land and in water, emphasizes this a little further.

Particular Symbolism:-

The Kundalini serpent: Is the serpent-power residing at the base of the spine – or in the prostate – which is related to the power of sexuality. This may be transformed into the inner

363

life force (prana), or ritually discharged as semen. Kundalini is feminine and related to the archetype of life.

If the person remains in a state of passive submission, the white light of the other world can integrate the Ego from its side, and bring a life to maturity.

The (Gnostic) Ouroboros serpent, with its tail in its mouth: The All, which renews itself by devouring itself: the waters, or the oceans of space that encircle the cosmos, making of it an enclosed self-supporting system, endless through its changing forms. On this cosmic scale the rule of nature changes from, 'Eat or be eaten', into, 'Eat and be eaten.' It is the binding force of the universe, which interrelates the parts. It also signifies the cyclic process of *TIME.*

The winged serpent: The triumphant *UNION* of *ABOVE* and below, mind and matter. The emerging animal life form rearing up from under its stone is joined with the winged creature (divine spirit) swooping down from above.

Apollo's cult, the Ophites, the Nassenes and other serpent cults: The evidence suggests that live serpents were involved, and that the rituals took place at night or in a cave or in the unfathomable depths of the forests, thereby leading the initiate down into his own inner depths. In such circumstances the other-worldly magnificence and terror of the serpents could be experienced. This experience is associated with new insight into the nature of the movement of life, and arouses intuitions about the future, from the life of the unconscious.

In Egypt the eye of God was turned into a cobra and became the crown (the Uraeus): Indicating the inner eye of the unconscious like a third eye. See *BODY,* Eye.

Atum took the shape of a serpent at the beginning of time; and at the end of time he will take the shape of a mongoose and devour himself.

Lotan (Canaanite) or Leviathan, the great sea-serpent.

Ladon (Greek), who was set to guard the golden apples of the Hesperides, till Hercules slew him.

Apep (Egyptian), serpent of darkness that threatened to swallow the sun: Like animals and men, the Gods had to fight against the darkness of the unconscious.

The Serpent is frequently related to the feminine, unconscious force: For example, in Egypt the Slippery One turned itself into a curly headed maiden in order to win the world from Ra.

Lilith (an earlier and therefore darker form of the feminine than Eve) was associated with the serpent on the Tree of Knowledge.

The power of prophecy of Apollo's Serpent Oracle at Delphi was bestowed on women, indicating that it was a feminine force at work.

Positive/Negative Symbolism:-

The snake inspires both awe of the sublime and fear of the inhuman. As an independent life form, the serpent surprises and fascinates. But it is also cold-blooded, with its unrelated fixed stare. It leads to what is beyond and outside the human orbit, high and low. It has the peculiar wisdom of the instincts, but is also the enlarged worm of corruption.

Different animals wrestling with the serpent: Every animal (or human *FUNCTION*) has had to fight for its own particular form of consciousness and differentiate it from the unconscious background. The two can only be related if they have first been clearly differentiated.

Often it is a bird which tussles with the serpent (e.g. Garuda) or the dove is contrasted with the serpent: The contrast between man's higher and lower nature and the conflict between them.

Related Symbolism:-

The Serpent is like the root of all animal life, and is connected with the symbolism of the roots of the TREE of life.

In BODY symbolism it is connected with the spinal column, which joins the physical nature (the genitals) to the spiritual nature (the head).

ANCESTORS, who might appear in serpent form, symbolically their root form. The Serpent was the oldest of the Old, the ancestor of time and form.

See also *LIGHTNING/Serpent*; and *The GORGON, Medusa for serpent hair.*

The CHAKRAS, as wheels or coils up the spine, are related to the Kundalini serpent.

Book:-

Krishna, G. *Kundalini* (1970), with a psychological commentary by Hillman, J.

Serpent/Pole.

> **The pole is the rigid, *ENDURING*, masculine principle with the serpent as the soft, feminine principle of life coiled around it, like the spine and the Kundalini above.**

It is the world *AXIS* and the changing phenomena.

See *ESSENCE*/Existence, or *CADUCAEUS*.

The serpent and pole are opposites in every way, Alive/dead, coiled/straight, etc.: And together they symbolize the *UNION* of all *OPPOSITES*, which is, in the first instance, realized at a very primitive level. The bright, conscious Ego has to allow itself to be pulled down into the lower depths or back thousands of years towards its *ORIGIN* – in what is termed, psychologically, a positive regression.

Related Symbolism:-

The Healing Serpent on a stick (e.g. of Asklepios): The healing qualities of the serpent are normally attributed to the fact that it changes its skin, but symbolically it refers to the return of man to the depths of his unconscious Self, which heals: in the same way as the cosmos renews itself, via the unconscious.

See The *HEALER*.

The Pole/Serpent symbolism is related to the *One/Many* (see *NUMBERS*.) Or the still *CENTRE* of life, of being, the hub from which activity emanates: like the Pole Star.

The pole is also the Dharma (truth, teaching) which continues straight, while the Sangha (relationships) complete their cycles. See also *PATTERNS, Spiral*.

The rods which Moses, Aaron and the Egyptian Magicians turned into serpents, may have originally shared this symbolic significance; also the healing serpent they erected on a pole in the Wilderness.

SEX

Sexual Symbolism.

The creative force in the universe.

The creative life of the mind, especially creative imagination, which expresses man's feelings and intuitions about the physical world.

Sperm-drop and ovum: The *ORIGIN* of man and life, which as energy is the source of reality.

The sexual fluids: The flow of psychic energy.

Extravert sexuality, whether in the form of masturbation or promiscuity v. introvert retention, inhibition, taboo: James Hillman suggests that the tension between these two creates enormous psychic energy, and could be responsible for much of our evolution from animal to man. It develops internal heat – tapas – and leads to vastly increased imagination, because it switches the base of reality, which is energy, from substance – the flesh – to magical fantasies that are in excess of nature.

For example the Song of Songs, much Sufi poetry, and the works of St. John of the Cross: Sexuality has been driven inward – sublimated – and flowers in works of creative imagination that are full of sexual symbolism. But contrast *SEX*, Impotence, below.

Sexual repression: Is too extreme a reaction to sexuality. Instead of turning the desire inward – with accompanying introspection and psychic development through the use of active imagination – repression excludes, or obliterates, any mental manifestation also. The energy, instead of flowering inwardly, turns negative and festers in the unconscious. The opposite of repression is conscious attention which may need to be extended over a period of years – to compensate for the years of neglect.

Positive/Negative Symbolism:-

Sexual compulsions/phobias: These arise from sexual repression, and like other *COMPULSIONS* erupt from the unconscious as independent forces, beyond the control of reason or will.

Desire/fear: As in other departments of symbolism desires and fears are related as positive and negative workings of the same psychic energy. In this case the conscious fear is often repressed and manifests as unconscious desire. Many sexual compulsions arise from displaced fear of the opposite sex, which is related to the fear of maturity and its responsibilities. See *ANIMUS/ANIMA, MASCULINE/FEMININE, YOUTH/Age, SATURN.*

In the unconscious everything turns into its *OPPOSITE*. See

MIRROR, also *WISH*/Fear. When unconscious desires are repressed distortions of conscious fears, it is sometimes easier to tackle the fear, which is nearer to the surface of conscious life and easier to cope with.

For example fear of growing up and of responsibility may manifest as sexual arrestedness, whether in the form of infantility, homosexuality or masochism: The problems of maturing well are in any case more important than the sexual problems.

The same applies to growing independent of Mother and Father *COMPLEXES*: Which may have a devastating effect on personal sexuality.

Note:-

The unconscious irrational response to the whole issue of sexuality, so charges it with subterranean emotional currents, that the subject is robbed of all natural simplicity, which would be the conscious rational response to sexuality. This most precious *INNER* joy is too often made to look ridiculous in the cold objective light of the logical thinking *FUNCTION*.

But contrast *SEX*, Shame, below. (See chart of the Compulsions as they relate to *ARCHETYPES*.)

Related Symbolism:-

Sex is related to the Sensation and Feeling *FUNCTIONS* in the mind, and failure to use either of these functions well may cause sexual troubles – so as to attract the necessary attention.

For example, bungling the physical side of sex: May be calling attention to the much wider problem of the Sensation Function as a whole: the need to relate to the material substance of life – the flesh, the blood, the skin of it – but also the inner image – the fantasy. The unconscious reacts in order to extract a more balanced attitude from the conscious Ego. If its excesses are in the direction of ignoring the material nature of existence, then these may cry for attention through sexual frustration.

But, for example, mishandling the emotional needs of yourself and others – which leads to similar frustrations: Points to a lack of attention – this time – to the Feeling Function; which outwardly secures relationships and inwardly creates values.

Earnest conscious attitudes of self-importance may be exaggerated at the expense of play, joy and creativity, which causes the neglected Feelings to react. Women are traditionally closer to their feelings, and have a truer sense of proportion.

The SHADOW: Sexuality may provide early glimpses of neglected unconscious sides of your personality, which can become valuable if worked upon meaningfully. Failure to integrate other aspects of the Shadow – besides the Sensation and Feeling Functions – may attract attention through sexual impulses. For example the desire to play menial parts, like the maid, in sexual fantasy, could be symbolic of the need to pay more attention to the *INFERIOR FUNCTION*.

Equally *ANIMUS* and *ANIMA* may manifest in fantasies that involve identifying with the opposite sex.

The Symbols:-

Standing stones and prehistoric circular slabs: Megaliths and Menhirs: Early monuments to the creative power of masculine and feminine sexuality.

Atum created the world by masturbation: This myth alludes to the fantasies of omnipotence that accompany masturbation, and are connected with the mentality of the Eternal *YOUTH.* The individual has a primary devotion and responsibility towards his own psychic processes – and whatever fosters and furthers their continuous development. But there is always a danger of getting stuck in one phase if this is not related to the general pattern of human development.

APOLLO/Dionysus: Apollo represents the heroic struggle to direct sexual impulses. The desire for mastery is as spontaneous and natural as the sexual desire itself, according to James Hillman. And does not depend on outside social restraints. In contrast Dionysus is the symbol of the relaxation and play of sexuality. Sexuality is an objective power – symbolized as Archetype or god – coursing through the individual, and whether the individual decides to resist it or play along with it, it does not like to be ignored. But tussling with your sexual vitality – in order to refine and educate it – is also a different kind of play. Although this is the play of the gods themselves, the individual cannot evade his personal responsibility, his share. This is the *PARADOX*, the two-sidedness of life, its depth.

Atum/Apollo/Dionysus: The balance between these three is the source of controlled freedom: they are the powers but you hold the balance. By cultivating a conscious relationship with these powers, you gain a measure of control over your own sexuality – instead of being unwittingly driven by impulses, compulsions and phobias.

The gods revel in human sexuality, or transform into animals and enjoy sex in that guise: Reversing the *MIRROR* image, this points to the sacredness of human sexuality and the animal instincts. Sex is a direct manifestation of these animal instincts which are in turn related to the *COMPLEXES*, which are personal primitive forms of the *ARCHETYPES* or the gods themselves. As a primary manifestation of the unconscious, sexual drives deserve considerable attention: they provide a main route to experiencing and understanding the whole range of inner reality.

In myth there are many phallic gods: for example Hermes in phallic form (the hermae), the Kabiri, or Priapus, the red one (ruber). The gods rape and seduce. Korybas is a pederast who seduces the child Dionysus. There are Androgynes or Hermaphrodites. Virgin goddesses were also whores who turned men back into animals: All these figures remain as relevant today, showing the ingredients of sexuality, and its relationship with the unconscious *COMPULSIONS, COMPLEXES* and *ARCHETYPES*. As with all symbolism the solution lies in a balanced tension of *OPPOSITES*, rather than swinging between extremes.

In myth this balance is suggested by heroic gods who subdue the animal passions, and chaste goddesses who punish inappropriate sexuality: As in life, so in symbolism there is a necessary and profitable inner conflict.

HEPHAISTOS, was born of masturbation (virginally) from his mother, was addicted to pleasure and also forged the symbol: In mythical language this states the close connection between sexual fantasy and symbolism. This close association of the two has sometimes – in recent times especially – led to the suppression of both. For empirical evidence of the relationship between sex and the creative

CHART of Sexual compulsions as they relate to the *COMPLEXES* and *ARCHETYPES*.

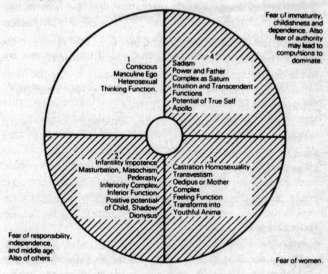

In a man's psyche:

Fear of immaturity, childishness and dependence. Also fear of authority may lead to compulsions to dominate.

1
Conscious
Masculine Ego
Heterosexual
Thinking Function.

4
Sadism
Power and Father
Complex as Saturn
Intuition and Transcendent
Functions
Potential of True Self
Apollo

2
Infantility Impotence
Masturbation, Masochism,
Pederasty,
Inferiority Complex,
Inferior Function
Positive potential
of Child, Shadow
Dionysus

3
Castration Homosexuality
Transvestism
Oedipus or Mother
Complex
Feeling Function
Transforms into
Youthful Anima

Fear of responsibility, independence, and middle age. Also of others.

Fear of women.

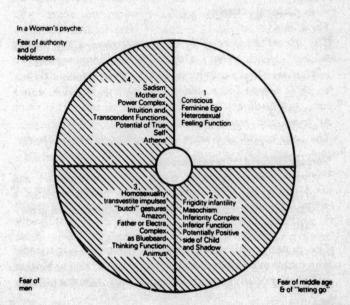

In a Woman's psyche:

Fear of authority and of helplessness.

4
Sadism
Mother or
Power Complex,
Intuition and
Transcendent Functions
Potential of True
Self
Athene

1
Conscious
Feminine Ego
Heterosexual
Feeling Function

3
Homosexuality
transvestite impulses
"butch" gestures
Amazon
Father or Electra,
Complex,
as Bluebeard
Thinking Function
Animus

2
Frigidity infantility
Masochism
Inferiority Complex
Inferior Function
Potentially Positive
side of Child
and Shadow

Fear of men

Fear of middle age & of "letting go"

SEX

Note:-
Particular sexual compulsions may resolve themselves if the individual attends to the wider context of the *COMPLEXES, FUNCTIONS* of the Mind, *ARCHETYPES*. Conscious Fear, and other symbolism to which they are related. Trying to cope with the unconscious directly can be counter-productive as in looking glass land. See *MIRROR*.

imagination. See *SEX*. Impotence, below. Sexual fantasy is the seed of the symbolic life, which if cultivated properly flowers in the discovery of the Complexes and bears fruit in the inner relationship with the Archetypes, or the gods themselves.

Books:-

Hillman, James, *Loose Ends*, especially the essay, 'Masturbation'.

Layard, John, *The Celtic Quest* (1974).

Chang, Jolan, *The Tao of Love and Sex* (1977).

Particular features of Sexual Symbolism:-

Heterosexuality.

Family life.

It's no accident that ordinary family life reflects the inner Archetypes, and all deficiencies or inadequacies in the family circles affect the inner realm which usually manifests in personal sexuality.

For a man:

The life experiences of being a son/having a son; having mother/wife/daughter; having a father and becoming a father; are outward living counterparts of the inner dynamic flow of energies personified as the *ARCHETYPES* of *SHADOW, ANIMA* and *SELF*. Ordinary family life gives ample scope to develop all three, both inwardly and outwardly.

The same applies to woman, as Daughter, Wife and Mother.

Variant patterns of sexual behaviour.

Present inner symbolic needs are misunderstood and projected on to the physical plane, which provides a substitute compensation – rather like a consolation prize – rather than a true solution.

The present symbolic need arises from past experiences which cannot be altered, and is frequently related to Mother and Father *COMPLEXES*, deriving not only from the physical presence or absence of parents, but also their inner unconscious development. Parents seem to give actual physical birth to rejected fragments of their own inner unconscious life.

The past cannot be altered and sexual habits are deep-rooted in the past and are the product of many generations. But the present and future are open to change through the symbolic work of creative imagination. Relating to the complexes and archetypes inwardly prepares the ground and sows the seeds of future rationality even with regard to sex which often remains beyond the reach of reason or will because ignored and undirected: therefore erupting negatively from the unconscious.

The Symbols:-

Only a vital inner relationship with particular symbols of Shadow, Animus/Anima and Self, such as God, Goddess and Infant Deity, can restore the inner balance which is even more important than whether the outward circumstances are affected or not.

Castration.

Including 'castration complex'.
Inability to mature. Or being possessed by the ANIMA.

Fear and desire are mixed as conscious and unconscious reactions to the same impulse. This may derive from an ANIMUS-possessed Mother, whose unconscious male side emasculates the potential rival in her son – keeps him childish or feminine.

Castration as SACRIFICE: The natural animal libido may be sacrificed for the sake of inner creativity. Outward sexual restraint is practised for the sake of inner union with the Anima, as muse and female figure of wisdom. But this is a vivid instance of the way the symbol must not be (mis)taken literally. Symbolic castration – becoming 'a eunuch for the kingdom of Heaven' – is concerned with the relationship between sexuality and spirituality which is still obscure. According to many accounts men of spiritual power were more highly sexed than average not less: potential Shamans were chosen for masturbating more frequently, for example. On the other hand Abelard's genius doesn't seem to have been impaired by his physical castration. As a symbol, castration points to inner creative powers.

In myth, the Amazons broke the limbs of their male offspring so they could not fight: As Animus-dominated women render the male limb – member – ineffective.

Related Symbolism:-

Impotence. See *SEX,* Impotence below.

Homosexuality.

Is symbolic of an inadequate conscious relationship with a woman's *ANIMUS,* or a man's *ANIMA.*

This may have arisen, in the past, from an overpowering figure of the opposite sex – father or mother – instilling fear of that sex, or an inadequate figure of the same sex – again often the parent of the same sex – giving insufficient support for the dominant physical characteristics to gain equivalent hold in the mind. When the Ego is arrested in its development and remains immature, then the Animus or Anima can take possession of mind and body – resulting in 'camp' and 'butch' mannerisms.

Von Franz suggests pushing the Animus or Anima out to work in this case: let the Anima work as Muse on appropriate tasks involving feeling and imagination, and set the Animus tasks of thinking and discernment.

Related Symbolism:-

Integrating inferior female qualities and gestures for a man, or inferior male aggressiveness for a woman, is similar to integrating the *INFERIOR* Function in general. Animus and Anima manifest negatively as problems from the quarter of the psyche containing the *OEDIPUS* and Electra *COMPLEXES,* which are partially dependent on relationships with the parent of the opposite sex. See *SEX*, Incest, on page 375.

Impotence.

Inwardly all contact with the powerful drives and energies of the unconscious has been severed.

Creativity and sex are the *INNER* and outer products of the same driving force. When one is blocked, it affects the other. The *BODY* is the symbolic manifestation of the human psyche so there is a close relationship between fantasy and erection – as in dreams. The same force, the same energy manifests as image or action: so failure to use the creative imagination has been found to result in impotence, which was only overcome by means of making contact with the unconscious through free play of the imagination.

Incest v. Incest-taboo.
The forbidden nature of incest has borne great fruit in terms of human development.

Whereas incest within the family represents a closed system which excludes the possibility of change, the taboo generates expansion and transformation. Considering the strength of the desire for incest, John Layard wonders how such a valuable taboo could have arisen and speculates that it was the jealousy of the father rather than any conscious or unconscious ingenuity that brought it into being.

Once outward expression is forbidden the strong desire is driven inward. If left to fester in the unconscious it may then cause much misery. But if transformed into the youthful *ANIMA* or *ANIMUS*, it becomes the source of understanding the opposite sex – as well as the inner reconciliation of *CONSCIOUS* and unconscious, *MASCULINE* and feminine, age and *YOUTH*.

See also:- *MOTHER* and Son. *FAUST*, the Mothers.

Brother/sister: If forbidden satisfaction in the outside world, can also become the means of discovering the unconscious figure of the opposite sex within.

Infantility.
The *INFERIOR FUNCTION*. A neglected immature side of the personality, often inferior feeling in a man, cries for attention this way.

The desire to be a dependent infant is related symbolically to the fear of responsibility, maturity and independence: possibly because the inner *CHILD* is in danger of being smothered by these. The social demand for mature adult behaviour, if it becomes oppressive, can have a similar reaction on the level of society – as in the case of the Punks.

Masochism/Sadism.

Are symbolically related as fear and desire for maturity, independence, responsibility. They are negative by-products of unconscious complexes and archetypes.

They both arise from the same unconscious background, the relationship and balance between the archetypal *SHADOW* and *SELF*, which also manifest primitively as the Inferiority Complex and the Power Complex.

Like the Power Complex, even sadistic impulses if understood, once refined and transformed, may become the source of discovering the True *SELF*.

And in the same way masochistic impulses can be seeds of transformation, enabling the mature crusty person, burdened by life, to rediscover the carefree vigour of the inner *CHILD* and *YOUTH* and relate to them where and when appropriate.

Related Symbolism:-

Masochism is loosely related to being dominated in the first half of life, and Sadism to dominating others in the second half. See *PERIODS* of life. Fear of the second half of life may manifest as masochism, particularly in the form of being restricted. Desire to be punished may relate to a lack of will power, insufficient *EGO*, which needs the support of external structures in order to avoid extremes, excesses. See also *CRIME*/Punishment. The desire to be demeaned may be the *INFERIOR* Function taking possession. Whereas fear, originally of the Father or Mother, may get projected on to other people, overcome in a temporary and negative fashion through sadism. See *PROJECTION*.

Necrophilia.

Fear of women and repression of the inner *ANIMA* has resulted in everything feminine being lost in unconsciousness: that is, dead.

A man's lack of Feeling robs other women of life for him. And in extreme cases his dead feeling gets projected on to the dead in an unconscious compulsive way. It would require great devotion and attention to bring the Anima back to life: and a long time, a hundred years in the case of '*SLEEPING BEAUTY*'.

Pederasty.

Fear of maturity or SATURN. **Or the inner Archetype of** CHILD **or** YOUTH **is demanding attention for other reasons.**

The former CHILD may have been rejected in the Unconscious, with his positive childlike qualities as well as his negative ones. And from there he signals or attracts attention in the guise of other children who seem utterly desirable because of their spontaneity and joy.

Shame.

Helps keep inner problems confined to the psyche where they can be resolved, rather than projected on to the outside world.

Shame provides a useful inhibition against trying to satisfy inner symbolic needs in an exterior or material way, which would be ineffective as well as embarrassing. The realms of fantasy need to be clearly distinguished from the physical facts.

SHADOW See EGO/Shadow

'SLEEPING BEAUTY' or Briar Rose (Grimm Brothers)

The Feminine Unconscious, which has a prickly as well as a beautiful side. Here the alternate titles immediately give the gist of the story.

When the feminine, feeling side of life (Eros) is lost in unconciousness, life is nothing but thorns for a hundred years. *Beauty is pricked by the needle of the spinning wheel which puts her to sleep and she is roused by the youthful figure who penetrates the barrier of thorns:* Any spike or prick may represent the penetrating phallus, and be a symbol of the masculine side of life. This is unconscious, unrelated, negative throughout, and so Beauty's negative Animus puts her to sleep, turns her off, just as she reaches puberty. And also discourages young men.

The whole castle sleeps too: The castle represents the MANDALA of the psyche, which is in a state of stagnation, sterility, because its masculine and feminine halves cannot relate.

What is true of the psyche is also true of society, which is all thorns and no bed of roses, so long as it is stuck to limited, masculine attitudes – that are too rigid, too logical.

The hedge of thorns grows so high, that even the flagpole of the castle is hidden. The skulls of youths who attempted to penetrate it are impaled on the thorns: Even the symbols of the unconscious (see *FLAGS*) have been lost to sight. Cut off from its source of vitality the masculine element is also doomed.

After a hundred years the right youth comes, is not discouraged by the fate of the other youths, the hedge parts for him and he enters and brings life, without difficulty: It seems he has done nothing very exceptional to achieve such wonders, except come at the right time, as von Franz points out. Because symbolism embodies the Forces of Nature and the unconscious forces at work in the psyche, as in tragedy, so in other symbolic material there is often nothing man can do about his birth, his death, his fate. It happens or it doesn't. It is talking about forces beyond the control of the conscious Ego, which have to be accepted. But this passive acceptance has to be related to continuous striving.

The trouble arose in the first place because of a neglected corner or complex in the unconscious – there were only twelve golden plates: That is, only twelve spheres of consciousness, so one of the feminine powers – *personified as thirteen Wise Women or Fairies* – had to be neglected.

From the beginning there is always a part of the pattern of the psyche which is excluded in the unconscious, and this causes misery or trouble at some time in life, in one *PERIOD* of the sequence of life. In the same way the solution often comes from outside in an unexpected manner.

Related Symbols:-

Themes of Tragedy, e.g. *Romeo and Juliet.*

Persephone in the underworld, while the world above is barren.

Adam expelled from Eden, guarded by a flaming sword which turned every way.

Book:-

Franz, M. L., von. *Problems of the Feminine in Fairy Tales* (1972).

Note:-

But for an older version of the tale see Nizami (twelfth-century Persian poet) from an era and an area where symbolism was better understood. Here the difference is that the youth can only save his head from being added to the other spiked skulls by acquiring wisdom from the greatest sages. It would therefore seem that the easy walkover for the youth – after a hundred years have elapsed – is a travesty of the original story. But the distortion indicates that there are two solutions to problems arising from the unconscious: either to tackle the symbolic work in a deeply inward way (the Eastern short cut) or to wait and rely on nature to heal in due course.

SPHINX

TIME, which also devours those who can't answer its riddle, which was concerned with the *TRANSFORMATION* of man through the different *PERIODS* of his life.

It has been suggested that the Egyptian sphinx was a monument to the year when the summer solstice fell at the cusp of Leo and Virgo. If so, this provided the particular instance or occasion to visualize and depict the awe-inspiring quality of Time, the God of Time, the Father of Gods for Classical Greece.

See also *OEDIPUS*.

SPLIT Duality

The symbolic split can be applied to the psyche as the Conscious Ego picking and choosing, or to a seed splitting to let out the taproot and trunk, or to the taking apart of an engine in order to put it together again, mended. Or to the splitting of the atom.

The *ORIGINAL* unity has been shattered, which allows for new individuals, separate conscious personalities, but if these fail to relate to each other then there is Inner *CONFLICT*, and outer strife of all kinds.

Symbolism is very basic, fundamental. The Split refers to any split which, if perpetuated, becomes an evil, something

379

that is broken. But the idea is that if it can be put together again, made whole, then something is gained, a new consciousness or a new stage of evolution. See *SEQUENCE*.

In the *SEQUENCE:* As male and female parent produce offspring, the next step, the *UNION* of *OPPOSITES*, produces something new. For example, *CONSCIOUS* and Unconscious can only be reconciled at a new level of consciousness.

In the psyche:-

The split has already taken place. The conscious Ego has already appropriated its half of reality. The work of differentiation consists of assuming – and then slowly discovering – the other lost half in the Unconscious. This is the creative work of the active *IMAGINATION*. Like a work of fiction, it has to create out of nothing the other half of the personality, which is lost in unconsciousness. All it has to go on is the fact that the unconscious is diametrically opposed to the conscious half.

Therefore for woman the unconscious part is masculine and vice versa. See *OPPOSITES*. Once an aspect of the conscious Ego has been matched with an equal and opposite force of the unconscious Shadow and Self, then the two can be related. This restores the original unity but with an added awareness and conscious control.

The original unity is a state of unconsciousness as experienced in early childhood. When the conscious splits off, crystallizes, it cannot manage to take with it more than part of the whole psyche. The rest has to be regained piece by piece – from fragments of dreams, through active imagination, or by other ways of dimming or dissolving the conscious personality. Part of the paradoxical nature of symbolism is precisely because of the movement from union to split and back again to new reunion – akin to rebirth. This is clear enough when lived, but may sound contradictory to the logical mind. It can be better expressed by symbols appealing directly to the mythological mind, and closer to the living processes.

The Symbols:-

The One seed splits into two: and from its centre comes the offspring: the fulfilled inner potential of the original one. For example, the avocado stone is a dramatic instance of this, because it is large and egg-shaped before it splits to put roots down and stem up.

Two of anything, can refer to this archetypal rift: as in *two worlds.* See *COSMOS; Two GIANTS; Two CASTLES; Two Animals; SCYLLA AND CHARYBDIS.*

The family triad of GODS (or men) is one of the oldest examples of this primary movement of nature. Human nature, originally conceived as one, is split into its two halves, male and female, which must dissolve back close to the origins of being, as semen and ovum, in order to give birth to the third, the offspring of both.

In CREATION myths the narrative often centres round the activity of separating the parts, i.e. splitting, cutting, as in the primordial *SACRIFICE. The monster Tiamat* is cut in two, one half to form the lower ocean of primordial chaos – subsequently ordered by further separation – and the upper portion to form the oceans of space, and its clouds from which the rain pours. In the same way in the Biblical account the waters above are separated from the waters below, night from day, land from sea. *CREATION* itself is a symbol of the most fundamental root processes in nature, projected back in time – rather than an historical account, without eye-witnesses.

In the psyche the primary split is between *EGO* and Shadow or in traditional symbolism the *BROTHERS,* such as *OSIRIS/Seth.* This duality of conscious/unconscious is the basic structure of the psyche and so manifests as the basic pattern of all mythological material, which reflects the pattern of life as man experiences it, two-sided, double-edged.

Other examples:-

Mercury Duplex, half male, half female; *Geb and Nut* (Egypt) are torn apart – earth from sky, matter from mind; and so are *Shu and Tenut*, life from order (form).

The SYMBOL itself, as originally forged by *HEPHAISTOS,* was a disc, broken jaggedly, so as to be able to ensure recognition of the other party. This is symbolic of the whole work of symbolism: the conscious mind shatters, breaks the whole in its function of selecting, while the symbol enables re-union of the two parts which reflect each other in equal matching but opposite ways, like object and mould, like negative and photograph, or like the two jagged edges of the symbolic disk.

See *MIRROR*.

In the *SEQUENCE*: The Split is a necessary intermediary stage on the way to the *UNION* of the whole on a more evolved and highly conscious level.

But the Split itself is the source of inner conflict, rivalry in the social sphere, and alienation from the cosmos, which is undesirable, if unduly perpetuated. The breach, the rift itself becomes the source of the perpetuation of evil. And in this context the binding force holds together the whole, re-establishes unity, whether in the psyche, for humanity, or for the cosmos, and becomes the highest good. This binding force is quite the opposite of intellectual discrimination; arising from feeling which establishes relationships and values, and from intuition which perceives wholes and which is expressed in symbols taken from nature and life itself.

The SPY Story
Alienation

This is an especially relevant myth for modern Western Man who is alienated from Nature, as well as from other people, and his own Unconscious. Like a paranoiac spy, he skulks about in his own world hoping to get by, hoping not to be recognized. His environment has become hostile, the Ego must be particularly alert and fit to avoid the snares and bugs that may be anywhere. The Unconscious is the enemy territory which he cannot come to terms with, or conquer, and so he must live in fear, relaxing little, even when making love.

STAMPS
Like *FLAGS* are packed with symbols.

Even the simple head of the *KING* is such a symbol. Or Cross of Lorraine, see *PATTERNS*.
This may account for part of their fascination.

STARS

The lights in the unconscious. The myriad or legions of figures who inhabit the collective unconscious: like fish's eyes under the sea.

The Pole Star and the wheeling constellations: The Pole Star in the North is the still CENTRE of the universe; all that is enduring and permanent. In contrast with the changing phenomena of time and the seasons: the year marked by the signs of the ZODIAC which also measure the ages of man in thousands of years. See NUMBERS, One/Many.

The Pole Star was probably the celestial manifestation of Gods like the Lord of the North, Baal Saphon, identified with Seth in Egypt. And may be related to the heavenly Shepherd at the centre of his roaming flocks, of stars or clouds.

The Great Bear of seven stars: Symbolically the feminine serpentine mother of the Pole Star. See SERPENT/Pole. Part of the significance of the numbers seven and eight is these particular stars, these lights on the cosmic tree which lead the eye to the enduring ESSENCE, the Pole star which orientates man in his journey across the sea of the unconscious, and shows him the pattern of his destiny from the seed at the still centre.

Artemis (in Greece), Diana (in Rome), Neith (in Egypt), Anath (in Canaan): Are associated with these seven stars, which represent the mother Anima, the guide of the unconscious. Shamans dressed up as bears, in order to contact their inspiration. It is thought this may derive from the customs of an earlier matriarchy with shamanesses.

The six-pointed star of Ishtar with its centre may refer to the seven points of light, re-arranged into a symbolic pattern. These seven were the seven oxen that turned the mill of the sky, the driving force of TIME itself.

The night sky after the sun has set: Reveals a much more extensive universe, as does the unconscious, when the conscious Ego is dissolved (see DISINTEGRATION). Jung saw the night sky as the most suitable region for man's projection of unconscious content, which is neither just inside the psyche nor unrelated to the psyche. The complex of the individual *SELF* is like one star, related harmoniously to the Archetypal Self, the Whole Universe.

STATUES
Substance and form without life. Unconscious matter.

Unconscious matter needs to be assimilated or integrated with life, before life gets assimilated into the *STONE*. It is this relationship between life and matter – or mind and matter – which is the basis of many myths and stories.

Statues brought to life: Is the perfect integration of mind and matter, equivalent to resurrection of the dead or the production of the Diamond Body. See also *HOMUNCULUS*. It is related to the creation of the world or the making of birds out of mud that then fly away. It also refers to the first life that broke into or emerged from the cooling mud and gases of the earth. How to relate life to mud is the secret of the gods and makes man godlike if he can discover it. And it is close to the secret of immortality.

The Ka statues in Ancient Egypt, like the statues in squares in London: Combine the enduring qualities of wood or stone, with the form and appearances of the man. And the expectation that the two ideas will stick together and the man will endure.

STONES/Jewels. Being turned to stone/Finding treasure
Dead matter/Living matter.
    What is worthless, in contrast with what is most precious to man.

Male order (in excess) in contrast with female life.

Although jewels don't actually have any more life than stones, they sparkle and reflect the light – symbol of living spirit – like life, as a result of man's working upon them (cutting the facets) as with his work upon the material world and his own physical body: And this in itself becomes symbolic of differences between mere physical existence, robbed of all joy, and the perfect accomplishment of life.

The cutting of the jewel: is symbolic of distinguishing between the different facets of the one psyche – the different complexes, etc. Although the jeweller cutting the stone would hardly be conscious of this connection, nevertheless, via the unconscious, it is only the man living in a highly differentiated society who has the tools – also produced by the psyche – to project the facets of his mind into the stone. The jewel becomes the symbolic vessel of his life, energy, and time.

Treasure: But the jewels remain only the symbol of what is truly precious, a great proportion of which is buried in unconsciousness: The treasures of the unconscious are placed symbolically underground, in caves, or under the sea.

Aladdin: Because of the continuous hazard of people mistaking the symbol for the reality, symbolism itself often provides contrary symbols to make the point clear. The old, insignificant lamp with its inward power (partly phallic; it has to be rubbed – see *SEXUAL SYMBOLISM*) is symbolic of the creative power of the mind. Which was worth more than all the treasure in the cave.

Note:-

In this connection there is a story in which anyone who found the treasure was punished by having his eyes replaced with large rubies and his tongue with a large diamond, and then pushed back out into the desert with his eyelids and mouth sewn up.

The Philosopher's Stone: Similarly, one of the symbols in *ALCHEMY* of the highest good was related to the ordinary stone, the ordinary, earthy, physical reality of life, just what was lacking at the time: the spirituality around had failed, rather dismally, to integrate the physical reality of nature. *To fix the volatile* (i.e. to give substance to the potential) was a major concern of the Alchemists, which was why they worked so long with actual material substances, easily ignored or dismissed but really very significant. At the time, sensation was the *INFERIOR FUNCTION* through which the union of the whole was achieved.

The Megaliths, the Standing Stones: Probably raised in honour of Baal Saphon, i.e. Seth (according to Westropp and Wake), these stones are the epitome of conscious life working upon inert matter, and raising it towards the sky (i.e. transforming matter into the energy and life of the mind.

See *AXIS: CENTRE*). The obelisk as a petrified ray of sunlight suggests the same enduring relationship of energy and matter.

The value of the stone as a symbol is related to the specific life context of the time: As representing the Archetype of matter, it is the physical substance of the world (see *COSMOS*), which is then impregnated by the living spirit. Matter is totally unconscious by itself and is symbolic of the depths of unconsciousness. When worked upon, it represents the union of spirit and matter, of *ABOVE* and below, neither of which are intrinsically masculine or feminine, but the feminine is often associated with unconsciousness and the earth.

Negative Symbolism:-

It is usually Feminine figures who are associated with turning people to stone, as The GORGON, Medusa, or a bird in fairytales, also symbolic of the Feminine powers: Medusa is the antithesis of the Sun *HERO* in every way, as well as the dark shadow of the Feminine archetype of life. She is a writhing picture of the negative, deadly side of unconsciousness. The conscious Ego is petrified of the unconscious – and so is petrified by it.

This emphasizes the fact that the integration of unconscious content can only take place at the level of the *SELF*, the core of being, and not at the level of the Ego which remains terror-struck by death and disintegration.

Gravestones: In ancient myth stones ruled over the dead.

Particular Symbolism:-

Ninurta (Mesopotamia) was involved in a battle of Nature in which the stones took sides: those which fought for him were rewarded and made to shine with the brilliant light of jewels.

All the tales, stories and myths of *statues coming to life, clay mixed with the life essence*, etc., are symbolically related to this theme of the curious relationship between unconscious existence and conscious life – and the way one turns into the other.

Gilgamesh shattered stone, and the fragments went off to seek life, whereas the people of yesterday are turned back to clay (like fishes they fill the sea, i.e. of unconsciousness).

In Greek myth, Lichas was hurled into the sea and turned to

386

rock by the Sun Hero.

In Stephen Langdon's *Semitic Mythology* (1932) *the Love Goddess turns a girl to stone for gloating over the jealousy and feuds aroused by her beauty.*

The stone, wrapped in swaddling clothes, was given to Cronos, the God of Time, to swallow, instead of Zeus – and other related nursery tales of sewing up stones inside the wolf: Again refers to the distinction between the life force and the material substance: the enduring energy which travels on through many metamorphoses, rather than through stagnation and remaining the same. See *CHANGE; TRANS-FORMATION;* or *ENDURING*/Ephemeral; or *ESSENCE*/Existence.

The wolf is the dark, negative aspect of Time, which devours. More recently in *The King of the Golden River* (Ruskin, John (1851)) *two of the brothers are turned into black stones* for trying to appropriate the treasures of the unconscious for their personal egotistic use.

STRUWELPETER (Heinrich Hoffman)

'Perhaps the most important textbook ever written on the workings of the Unconscious,' according to Georg Groddeck.

SUN

Masculine Conscious Ego. The Ego is the dominant factor in the psyche as the sun is the dominant light of the sky.

It is the force which brings light, form and order out of chaos and dark: discriminates, separates as, for example, in marking the seasons.

For personification of the sun: The relationship between sun and man. See *HERO.*

The black sun, often Saturn: The masculine forces trapped in unconsciousness, often the woman's unconsciousness when it represents her *ANIMUS.*

Sunlight/moonlight: The logical mind versus the mythological mind. The moon is the primary light symbolically which swells with pregnancy and gives birth to the sun. While the sunlight insists upon differences, the softer moonlight welds creation into a unity. The archetypes of Knowledge and idea versus the archetypes of relationships and value. Or law and justice in contrast with love and mercy. But also see *MOON*.

Particular Symbolism:-

Ra, Osiris, and Horus (Egypt) were related to the Eagle or falcon as the rising sun, and the lion as the devouring heat of the sun. The Sun God was lord of the two horizons, and the eye of God. The sun boat was the barque of millions of years, i.e. measuring *TIME*.

Also *Asshur* (Assyria).

The sun gods and heroes are forever fighting off the dark of the unconscious, or death, though often, in this, they are gods of light itself, including lightning – the Intuitive *FUNCTION* – and sometimes the Moon – the rational, conscious, feeling Function: compare *Indra v. Vritra*; or *Apollo v. Python*.

Shamash or *Mash*, another Semite sun god – after whom Samson and Gilgamesh are named.

Related Symbolism:-

BLUEBEARD is symbolically related to the negative side of the sun, slaying the dawn, as youthful maiden.

HAIR, like the rays of the sun, may symbolize conscious thoughts.

SWORD

The thinking function which discriminates, divides, separates. (See *SPLIT*.) Or the Intuitive *FUNCTION*. Or both.

The Intuitive Function penetrates below the surface, thrusts to the core (or centre) of the matter, indicating insight. This applies especially to swords with magical powers, such as Excalibur. And in the Tarot suit (see *TAROT*). Or if golden (e.g. Chrysaor, with Pegasus the treasure or essence of Medusa, see *GORGON*).

The fact is that intuition and intellect are not always clearly differentiated in symbolism as in life.

The knight's sword: His conscious intellect has won the mastery over his brute passions.

The shattered sword: In certain circumstances old hand-me-down conscious attitudes are no longer valid and must be reforged afresh by the individual. For this work the blacksmith, the master of fire (symbol of transformation) is required.

Forging the sword: The human spirit of life at work transforming nature.

Pulling the sword out of wood or stone: In terms of sexual symbolism is freeing the male conscious Ego (the phallus) from the state of being mother-bound. Which is the physical equivalent of freeing the consciously forged spirit from the ordinary physical existence of animal nature. For universal Man, it is the distinguishing and relating of the enduring One with the many proliferating branches of the tree, or of matter. See *NUMBERS, One/Many*, or, for example, *UNICORN/ Stag*.

Sword/distaff: MASCULINE/Feminine.

Related Symbolism:- The Word (see *ALPHABET*) 'Sword' and 'Word' are thought to be etymologically linked.

LIGHTNING.

SYMBOLS

Describe pictorially and vividly what is of greatest concern to man: his own inner being and its relationship with the universe around.

Some symbols are taken direct from Nature – for example, snakes, bulls, trees – but are used to describe the symbolic effect that they have as they break into man's psyche at moments of intense value and significance. Other symbols – such as dragons and gods – erupt from the psyche. But at best symbols shatter this distinction between *INNER* and Outer. For example, the *ELEMENTS* combine bone, breath, energy and blood, as well as Earth, Air, Fire and Water, and so are like four pillars of the one bridge between man and nature.

Inner visions seek expression and outer facts seek meaning, for man, and at best symbolism mediates and combines these two.

Symbols mostly work on three levels: in the psyche, traditionally called the microcosm; in society, traditionally the mesocosm; and in the universe, in Nature, formerly called the Macrocosm or Cosmos.

In the psyche: As Coleridge put it, 'symbols give form to forgotten truths about my inner nature'. Symbols cannot be fabricated. They are products of Feeling and Intuition and erupt spontaneously from the *IMAGINATION.* They are very often riveting and fascinating even though their sense eludes you. Symbolic *ACTION* may be socially embarrassing and personally inappropriate yet meaningful. The aim is to bring to light other centres of your own personality, to make them conscious and from there get them under the control of the will. However primitive the impulses, these can be transformed and either made rational or allowed for, once brought to conscious light. Symbols have the power to galvanize great sources of energy within, when deep, unconscious impulses are related to conscious plans, and no longer in conflict with them.

In Society: Symbols can bring together the shattered fragments of society. For example, see *KING* or *BUILDINGS.* Also *FLAGS.*

In Nature: Symbolism is the language of Nature and of the Universe in solid objects, the language of food and oceans – not mere words. As truths about the Cosmos which are too vast to take in, the overall vision of reality can be digested by man and therefore be of value to you, the individual, only when compressed into a symbol.

Note:-

There is great profit in scientific analysis, specialization, different compartments, disciplines, but ultimately man cannot live in sections or little bits. He must live his life whole, and the parts need to be related for him meaningfully. This appears to be the primary work of symbolism. And where symbolism is lacking, there is inevitably disintegration and dissociation.

See also *SPLIT,* for the origin of the Symbol forged by *HEPHAISTOS*, which is relevant here.

SYNCHRONICITY

Meaningful coincidences, significantly related patterns of chance.

This is Jung's word for events which are plainly related, but not according to the ordinary laws of cause and effect. His suggestion is that the laws of cause and effect, though adequate for many aspects of life, are too limited to cover every form of relationship between phenomena.

By positing the Archetypes, which are neither mind nor matter, but at the roots of both – and can manifest in either realm or both, quite independent of strict chronological sequence or the ordinary rules of cause and effect – he gives a hypothetical base to his theory.

Meanwhile the coincidences continue, for those who notice them, regardless of whether there's a theory to cover them or not. And as the notion of the unconscious gains ground, the idea of interaction via the unconscious – outside time and space, beyond cause and effect – seems plausible.

The Symbols:-
The Gods intervening in human affairs.
Also see *ORACLES* and *I CHING*.

TAROT or Ordinary Playing Cards
Pictorial images of the forces at work in the world. The Trumps represent the more powerful unconscious forces associated symbolically with the Lunar Way, while the rest of the pack corresponds to the extravert Solar Way of everyday conscious life.

Like the *I CHING*, the Tarot is a complete system of *DIVINATION*, which means that its cards claim to represent all the fundamental forces at work in nature and human nature. The infinite variety of life results from the different combinations, *PATTERNS*, and *SEQUENCES* of these forces, reflected in the random patterns and combinations of the cards.

Trumps: The twenty-two trumps major correspond symbolically to the twenty-two letters of the alphabet, which in turn represent the stations and phases of the moon. The moon stands between the single enduring essence of life, and the multitudinous variety of this world. Just as every single thing under the sun (and much else besides) can be

The *TRUMPS MAJOR* of the Tarot, as symbolic paths, leading to the integration of the whole psyche.

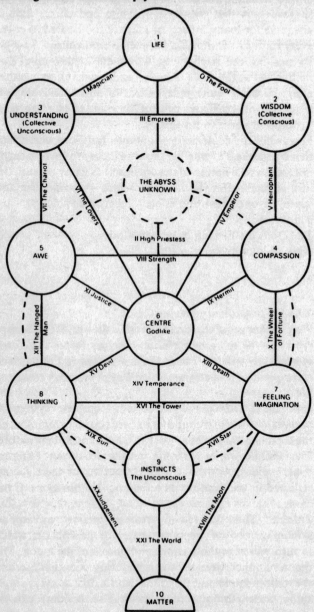

Note:-
There are three separate realms of activity. Cards I to VII depict the realm of
the Mind, the Spirits, the Gods. Life force. VIII to XV: the realm of Man.
XVI to XXI: the realm of Matter.

represented by the letters of the *ALPHABET*, so the trumps
major of the Tarot represent the archetypal base, the typical
ingredients of reality.

By themselves, they can adequately depict the main features
and forces at work in the world. Whether their casual
arrangement, when used without the rest of the pack, done in
the symbolic *PATTERN* of a simple cross, in any way
corresponds to an individual's life and destiny can only be
tested by experiment.

They have been related to the spheres of life, fruit of the tree
of life in the *KABBALAH*, as paths between the spheres (or
Sephiroth). Whereas the Tree of Life represents the dynamic
pattern of nature, the Trumps are closer to man's actual
journey, his destiny.

Note:-

But symbolism is always relative – in its concern with
relationships. So in relation to the *ONE Cosmic Axis* (symbol
of the One Essence) – *the Ten Spheres or Fruit of the Tree of
Life* become symbols of the *MANY*, the beginning of the
movement of life. See *NUMBERS, ONE/Many*, and *KABBALAH*.

But in relation to the *One Tree of Life* (which takes the place
of an elaborated Cosmic Axis) – *the Twenty-Two Trumps
Major* represent symbolically the moving paths of destiny:
the Inner Lunar way – the introvert path of the twenty-two
stations of the *MOON*.

Whereas finally, in relation to *the Trumps Major* (which now
become the flying buttresses of the Tree of Life and so a part
of the enduring world Axis or, if you prefer, the equivalent of
the Platonic realm of Ideas) – then it is *the rest of the Tarot
Pack, the other Fifty-six cards*, which come to represent this
world of change and transformation: the Extravert way of
the *SUN*, symbol of the Conscious *EGO*, the fifty odd cards
corresponding roughly to the weeks of the Solar Year.

Because inner Unconscious processes are opposite to
conscious processes, it is typical that the ascending order of
the Trumps in importance, from the *World* to the *Magician*

TAROT

who is like the *TRICKSTER* or *HERMES*, is inverted or reversed,
XXI to I. See *MIRROR*.

The Four Suits,
in the rest of the Tarot Pack or Ordinary Playing Cards.
The Four *FUNCTIONS* of the psyche that determine the
course of life.

The typical fourfold division of everyday life, especially the
four *SEASONS* of the year, which symbolize the four *PERIODS*
of life between birth and death, as well as the four Functions
of the psyche.

Note:-
The Fifty-two cards of the ordinary pack are more obviously
related to the fifty-two weeks of the year, than the four suits
of fourteen cards in Tarot. With symbolism, however, other
factors, such as the fourteen days of the waxing or waning
moon, may carry interesting associations that far outweigh
any concern for meticulous accuracy – since the interest was
never in time-keeping but in the destiny of man.

More disturbing for symbolism are the number of factors
that affect the date for celebrating the New Year, which
marks birth. At root it is the Mid-winter Solstice when the
sun is reborn (c. December 22), but in the north this marks
the beginning of the real winter cold, more often associated
with old age and death. Nevertheless, the symbolism of the
Tarot suits reflects a mid-winter start to the year and to life –
even though the pictures don't always keep to this.

Pentacles, or Diamonds: Childhood. Sensation. Earth. The
beginning of the year from the rebirth of the sun when the
days begin to lengthen: or the first seven days of the new-
born waxing moon.

Pentacles depict a five-pointed star, symbolic of the night of
unconsciousness from which childhood slowly emerges with
its five animal senses.

Wands, or Clubs; Youth. The thinking Function of the male
conscious Ego.

Spring to mid-summer; or the second lunar week ending in
the full moon. The flower of life.

Wands symbolically relate to sceptres of power. See *KING*.

Cups, or Hearts: Womanhood/Manhood. The feeling

394

function. Feeling is here the heavenly water that nourishes life.

The Summer of life till the Autumn Equinox (c. September 22). The cup is the vessel, the container that relates the forces of the cosmos and binds them together like the great encircling serpent *EROS*. See *VESSEL.*

Swords or Spades: Old Age. Intuition. Air, as wind, the breath of life, the spirit.

Autumn equinox to mid-winter; the feeble and diminishing power of the sun – that is, the conscious Ego and the waning of the moon to extinction. The nights get longer: the unconscious is on the increase again. The sword points up and down. See *ABOVE/Below.* And is akin to the world *AXIS*, joining spirit and matter, and is a sign of mastery. The spade on the contrary points only down, towards the unconscious in a negative form, death. But see *SWORD.*

Note:-

Because in life Intuition and Intellect are poorly differentiated, they are frequently confused in symbolism also. So the identification of Wands with Creative Intuition, and with inspiration and will, is also valid if the Swords are made symbolic of Intellect and Order.

The compression of symbolism which combines different factors and different insights, layer upon layer, means that different interpretations may be significant and complement each other. Marie Louise von Franz especially has been at pains to show how changes in symbolism often reflect new circumstances in the outside world: but the interaction is not easy to trace. Certainly the above – rather schematic – guideline to the symbolism of the Tarot needs to be contrasted with other, differing views, for example, Aleister Crowley's *Book of Thoth* (1944) or Alfred Douglas, *The Tarot* (1972).

Books:-

Waite, A. E. *The Pictorial Key to the Tarot* (1910).

Knight, G. *A Practical Guide to Qabbalistic Symbolism* (1965).

THIEF

Within the psyche there seems to be an allocation of property.

THIEF

Some gifts, powers or qualities are proper to the Ego, and others to the unconscious complexes. And judging from the myths, the two sides, conscious and unconscious, are continuously perpetrating border raids upon each other and carrying off trophies. And then they are being subjected to counter-attack and punishment.

The inner conflict between *OPPOSITES* means that one is forever gaining at the expense of the other.

The conscious mind, the Hero, forever seeks the treasures of the unconscious: Which are ferociously guarded and when the theft is accomplished, it is fearfully punished whenever possible.

But on the other side the Shadow, the Animus and Anima, are also thieves: Robbing the conscious Ego of its vitality, its source of fantasy, which is the nourishment of the psyche.

The robbers' den: The unconscious, full of all this stolen treasure.

Note:-

Whether Conscious steals from unconscious or the other way round, both are forms of self-robbery – which can only be avoided by relating the *OPPOSITES*. See also *UNION*.

Or else Time is the thief: Stealing away the greatest of all treasures, your lifetime. And it gets lost in unconsciousness, if hoarded in some dark, underground cave – if you are unaware.

Particular Symbolism:-

The SERPENT, who steals back the treasure of immortality from Gilgamesh. *Eve*, the Feminine Ego or Man's Anima, steals the fruit of the Tree of Knowledge, i.e. consciousness.

PROMETHEUS; HERCULES; Jason; and *Jacob*, all steal on behalf of the evolving Male Conscious Ego.

Autolycus and *Cacus*, represent the thefts of the Shadow from the Ego. *Hermes*, is the thief, Time.

Related Symbolism:-

See also *The TRICKSTER*.

THRESHOLD

Including Menhir, Barrier, Doorway.

The border between *CONSCIOUS* and Unconscious, *INNER* and Outer.

This appears in symbolic material in many guises, but it is recognizable because difficult to cross and sometimes even harder to return. See *LOOKING BACK*. Entrances to caves, castles, the underworld, and the underworld of crime (the robbers' den). It can be river boundaries or mountain ranges in the country of the mind. Or forbidden doors, forbidden because the unconscious content is in a dangerously repressed state. However, if the prohibition is ignored, it may work out for the best after an initial series of catastrophes.

The menhir: The sun itself crosses the threshold to dispel the night of the unconscious (as at Stonehenge).

Figures may have to change shape or sex in order to cross: It may be necessary to give up identification with the conscious Ego, and instead identify with the *SHADOW* or *ANIMUS/ ANIMA*, in order to cross.

The laws that operate either side of the threshold are often reversed, the processes in operation are different, as on either side of the *MIRROR*.

It is also the threshold of time between past and future. The dark, unconscious future pours into the present, gets filled with conscious light. And vice versa, the dark, unconscious past swallows up the conscious moment. In this context *Janus* is the doorkeeper with one head looking back and one forward – guardian of the first month of the year, January.

Particular Symbolism:-

Ulysses clinging close to his animal nature (i.e. the ram) in order to escape across the threshold of the cave of Polyphemus.

Other Guardians of the Threshold: Charon; Cerberus.

See also *TRICKSTER*. And *the BROTHERS* who personify the two sides of the threshold.

Book:-

Streatfeild, D. in *Persephone* (1959) shows convincingly that a barrier in a cafeteria – which is the entrance to the underworld of crime – may be as symbolically significant as the Gates to the Underworld.

TIME
The whole of time is divided and subdivided, in correspondence

with the pattern of the psyche. But Time also unites the opposites: Birth to death, youth to age, night to day, work to rest. See *UNION*.

All time is symbolically a unity, without seam or split, which is then divided into two times: the split between conscious and unconscious in man is projected on to time itself as time known and time unknown, past and future, for example. Or, put another way, the archetypal split, the bifurcation of life, which manifests in human nature, also manifests throughout nature itself. As with the other archetypes, the unity of time is divided and subdivided.

   i. On the cosmic level, the cosmic clock of sun, moon and stars marks and measures the divisions and subdivisions of time.

   ii. On the intermediate level, evolution and the story of mankind mark the passage of time.

   iii. On the individual human level the transformations from youth to old age, from birth to death.

All three levels are products of the same single process.

Eternity/Time: Eternity expresses the essential unity of time: as both *the-origin-of-time* and *all-time.* The measuring stick of time (whether by sun or clockwork) leaves no trace or mark on time itself – anymore than does writing in water. The chronology of time, the magnificent variety of time, divides and subdivides the surface only. In exactly the same way as the continuously shifting moment cannot put a lasting wedge between past and future – it is like a wheel whirling along the endless unbroken expanse of time.

Compare *NUMBERS, One/Many*; and related symbolism.

The Symbols:-

All *Sky Gods* are symbolic of the life force, energy, mind, and are also closely related to the processes of time. This is the dimension of the spirit, the working order, the movement of cosmos and man, in contrast with the static dead, three-dimensional substance of the world. In Greek myth, the Sky God (*Uranus*) specifically gives birth to the *God of Time (Cronos)* who is the Father of Gods and Goddesses.

Sun Gods (like *Ra* in Egypt) and *Moon Gods* (like the Semite, *Sin*) are close to the roots and origins of myth, as the moving parts of the cosmos which are related to the movements of man in that they measure his days, and appear to govern the fluctuations in his food supply. See *SUN; MOON.*

PATTERNS, The Vertical Line, The Cosmic *AXIS,* which both unite *ABOVE* and Below, symbols of the *UNION* of all opposites, effected in due course – to which the unavoidable personal response is patience.

The Two Times,
as Before/After, Past/Future, or Youth/Age.
> **Conscious time, in contrast with unconscious time. But these *CHANGE* and *TRANSFORM,* one into the other in conformity with the pattern of *CONSCIOUS*/Unconscious. The unknown future becomes the known present, and then fades into the forgotten or repressed past.**

As with the *ESSENCE* of the different material substances, there is no real distinction between the unity of time and the apparent divisions. The unity is the thread flowing on through all the parts of the pattern of time. Symbolically it is the ridge-pole of the *CADUCAEUS,* between the two writhing serpents, twined and intertwined, of day and night, of youth and age, of summer and winter, of death and life, of past and future, stretching away back to the first man and before: and on and away beyond the last man.

The Four Times:
> **Reflect the fourfold order of the psyche.**

The two main divisions can be further subdivided into four, as in Dawn to Midday, Midday to Dusk, Dusk to Midnight, and round to Dawn again. Compare *The SEASONS; The PERIODS of LIFE.*

Time divided into Seven.
> **Reflects the seven levels or centres of consciousness, that are loosely related to seven – or eight – stages of man's life. See *NUMBERS,* Seven; and The *SEQUENCE.***

All these divisions are arbitrary if you think about them yet they are deeply satisfying symbolically because they correspond to patterns in your life. The complete cycle of the *MOON* was quartered to make four weeks of seven days – just as the complete cycle of the sun was quartered to make four seasons – and both reflected the four periods of man's life. But the seven days were especially significant, and formed a basic unit of time, and of life: seven days, seven weeks between festivals, and seven periods of seven weeks, with three weeklong festivals completing the cycle of the year. Then there were significant Seven-Year Periods, and Jubilee Years every Forty-Nine Years in the Ancient Near East, where much of the symbolic tradition originated.

Such cycles would specifically relate man's life to the *INNER* unconscious way, the way of the *MOON*, and the moon gods, Sin or Thoth, who was identified with *HERMES*. In contrast with the extravert way of the *SUN* and the *HERO*, symbolized by the Solar divisions of the year into Eight. See also The *TRICKSTER*.

Further subdivisions of Time:

    Reflect different ways of ordering life into a *PATTERN*, where parts can be seen to be related and significant – rather than fleeting, ephemeral and pointless as they appear when the psyche breaks up and the pattern fragments – as a result of the loss of creative power.

Twelve is especially common as in twelve hours, and twelve months of the year, see *ZODIAC*. Roughly 50 weeks or 360 days occur frequently in symbolism, as the number of the Gods on Olympus, the number of tasks for *THE SUN HERO* Hercules, or degrees in a circle. All of which indicates that the mysterious quality of time, and man's relationship with it, is the continuous and abiding concern of symbolism, as of life.

The Twelve Lunar Months in the Solar year relate *SUN* with *MOON*: the *INNER* Pattern with the outer *SEQUENCE* of life.

Time in relation to the psyche:

    The sequence of life and destiny is spun from the pattern of the psyche, but the sequence of life also moulds the psyche, and the interaction of these two reverberates outwards through the cosmos.

So that whole cycles of evolution have their final product, their culmination in a species (dinosaur or Dante), from

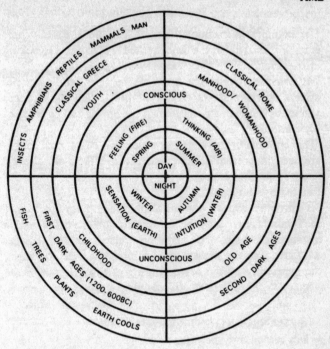

The CYCLES OF TIME
Which correspond symbolically and are related to the life of
the psyche. The Self, from the still point at the centre, is aware of
the whole pattern in perspective. While the individual Egos rattle
round the edges.

which is spun the next phase of development. So the Ages of
Man, or the periods of individual life, can be loosely
connected with the development and refinement of inner
qualities. (Symbolism is very flexible and so can establish
connections where rigid intellectual attitudes would fail.)
On the level of fairy-tales, etc., late Autumn: is the time when
darkness is on the increase, the power of the Shadow realm is
gaining strength: a time for witches to celebrate (*Halloween*,
etc.).
Whereas the mid-winter solstice, as the turning point when
the nights are at their very longest, yet the light is on the
increase, is the time for the Shadow Figures (such as *the
Devil, Seth, Pan*) to make a last assault and be driven out.

401

Note:-

For example, in traditional Jewish folklore, the mid-winter feast of Hanukkah is the time for the Devil to come knocking at the door.

The crucible of time: The cycle of time (as a binding circle) affects the *TRANSFORMATIONS* of life. Often the changes cannot be hurried, any more than the Spring can be brought forward.

This crucible brings together cause and effect: past causes are seen in present effects; and future effects are already latent in present causes.

Related Symbolism:-

As with other aspects of symbolism, the primary function of the symbol is to reunite the shattered fragments of life; in this instance of time. The symbols relate *YOUTH* to age, *ANCESTORS* to the present generations, etc., and so restore the experience of the original unity of time. See *UNION OF OPPOSITES; The SERPENT, Ouroboros.*

The TRANSCENDENT Function
Man's response to the *UNKNOWN*.

The idea that Wisdom lies in realizing what we don't know, grasping the limitations of the Senses and ordinary, everyday attitudes, may arise from a very intense experience that is like looking behind the scenes of ordinary life, and opens up vast vistas of potentiality – unformed and indescribable according to all accounts, symbolically like a million other dimensions not yet perceived, and a million other worlds as complex as this, but not yet created. In other words the Infinite. See also The *SEQUENCE*, or the *CENTRE* or *TRANSFORMATION*, Deification.

The Symbols:-

Superman – as in the comic strip: The most powerful experiences of the Transcendent often come in childhood, as if the Function atrophies for lack of attention after that. So figures who embody the Function appeal very much to children.

Nietzsche's Superman: The Function is appropriated by the Ego, and fails to relate man to what is beyond his grasp, and therefore fails as a symbol to relate *INNER* with Outer.

Ether, among the ELEMENTS, the centre of the LOTUS, or Onion; or the Holy of Holies which is empty: Nothing, No-Thing which is also the invisible nucleus or *ESSENCE* determining the shape of all things. This pure life, pure being, can only be experienced by dissolving into the nothingness, self-emptying, or contemplation. As if the Transcendent Function can only operate when all the other functions are in abeyance.

For Christians the Rule of God, and for Buddhists the Buddha Nature, which pervades the whole universe: Both symbolize the Transcendent realm that awakens man's response. See also Symbolic Goals.

TRANSFORMATION
The transformations in Nature – the way everything changes into everything else – reflect inner processes of growth and transformation within your own psyche.

The *PERIODS* of life and transitions in the psyche: particularly the major changes of attitude required in order to face the second part of life.

When the conscious Ego is dissolved in the unconscious, it can re-emerge in any shape, can identify with anything in the universe. Life and matter are inextricably bound together. This process of *DISINTEGRATING* and rising in a series of different forms, as beetle, sun, plant, star, is depicted on ancient Egyptian coffins (see Rundle Clark, R. T. *Myth and Symbol in Ancient Egypt* (1959)).

Conjuring tricks and magic: Are a physical caricature of this inner spiritual process.

Growth, puberty, menopause, old age: The outward appearance of the inner transitions and transformations, as they affect the body.

For the same archetypal force at work in nature, in the cosmos: See *CHANGE, Flux.*

Animals turned into humans: Blind moods and passion, compulsive entanglements, transformed, humanized.

Humans turned into animals: The animal instincts are in control in the forests of the unconscious.

The Symbols:-

403

TRANSFORMATION

Figures like *PROTEUS*; also *Nereus, Glaucus,* and other figures who hover on the borders of sea and land, and move from one to the other.

FROG/axolotl: The frog makes the transition from water to land, from unconscious to conscious, and back. Whereas the axolotl (seemingly almost by choice) remains newt-like in the water, while its relatives become the land-going salamanders. Hence the axolotl is a symbol of refusal to mature. See *YOUTH*, also *SATURN.*

Most Gods, goddesses, witches and wizards have the power to change shape: sometimes specifically from maiden into crone and back; also from human to bird; from count to vampire-bat, etc.: All reflecting the different modes of operation of the conscious and unconscious psyche.

Caterpillar/butterfly: The transition from physical, earthbound sensation to the flight of the mind experienced inwardly. See *INNER*/Outer.

Also compare *Symbolic DEATH; DISINTEGRATION/Integration:* The basis of change is to separate the parts and reassemble them in new combinations.

Note:-

'Transformation and again transformation is the eternal entertainment of the eternal spirit.' (Goethe)

Deification, apotheosis, transfiguration, i.e. men turned into gods: is the final goal of all such transformation: discovering the true nature of life, and of the *SELF.*

TREE

Life without consciousness: the unconscious life of man. His vegetable soul.

A tree may be dimly aware of the difference between day and night, summer and winter, we don't really know. Even so, for man it is a symbol of the bare processes of life, growing and dying; processes that continue at a deep level.

Living several hundred years, the older trees span ten or more generations of man, so they become a symbol of the family tree branching outwards, generation to generation. *In the scale of evolution the tree is intermediary between inanimate matter (the earth) and the conscious mind:* And it is a symbol of the intermediary force which binds these three realms together.

The roots, sunk in the earth: Are symbolic of bare existence, but they also plunge into the *UNDERWORLD*, where the *DEAD* and the past are buried layer upon layer. Roots are related to *SERPENTS* and other primal forces.

The trunk: All the tangled roots flow into the One trunk and then spread into the Many branches. See *NUMBERS*, One/Many. This contrast between One and Many is emphasized if *UNICORNS* are sitting to either side of the trunk of the tree.

The branches: The rich variety of life with its abundance of provisions. *BIRDS* in the branches may be man's conscious thoughts.

The tree of life: The tree points upwards to the sky, and is the most primitive means of ascent (i.e. climbing trees). So it is a very ancient symbol of the upward ascent, step by step, stage by stage, whether for the race of mankind or for the individual. See *LADDER* and related symbolism. Also the *SEQUENCE.*

The Cosmic tree: May have preceded the idea of cosmic *MAN.* It is related to the ridge-pole of the world over which the beautifully embroidered star-spangled sky is thrown. It is related to the World *AXIS* and is a symbol of *UNION.*

Like a tree reflected in the water (see *MIRROR*) this same tree is reflected on earth, where the light of consciousness in man forms the glittering fruit, matching the stars.

When the roots are in the sky: The roots then symbolize the permanent *ARCHETYPES*, which manifest in a transitory way on earth, coming and going, like fruit and leaves, with the seasons.

The evergreen trees, including mistletoe and the Christmas Tree: The everlasting side of life – all that *ENDURES* in contrast with whatever *CHANGES,* with the changing seasons. The cypress, being also tall and straight, is particularly symbolic of the enduring unity of the essence of the material world. Hence cypresses (and yews) are planted in graveyards. The phallic shape of the cypress complements this because man endures through the creative power of his phallus.

TREE

Christmas Tree, lit up at midnight of mid-winter: Especially, is deeply symbolic of continuity through all the cycles of change. The lights reflect the stars on the cosmic tree.

The sacred oak: Was anciently connected with the gift of prophecy. The noise of the wind in the leaves was the breath and voice of Nature. If listened to, in a passive state, it might still reveal depths of unconscious wisdom, accessible to intuition only.

In the realm of vegetation the twisting oak was the equivalent of the forks of lightning from the sky – both attributes or manifestations of the storm gods.

The rings in the trunk of the tree: Are like the storehouse of the past, rippling outwards from its core, with good and bad years marked. Here is a clear instance, on a simple level, of life as the end-product of *TIME*, the culmination of the process, the storehouse of history.

Sap of tree: Sap of life.

The fruit: May be the source of the Water of Life (Eau de Vie); also Soma; Ambrosia (i.e. the life-giving *ESSENCE*).

Related Symbolism:-

KABBALAH, Tree of Life.

Spring-green and evergreen is related to the significance of *the emerald* and possibly *the scarab.*

VEGETATION and the Gods of Vegetation and therefore resurrection.

PATTERNS, The upward-pointing triangle.

See also 'JACK and the Beanstalk'.

The TRICKSTER

A figure who hovers on the borders of conscious and unconscious, where the light and shadow plays tricks.

The personification of the tricks played on the conscious mind by the emerging content of the unconscious, like tricks in the *MIRROR* that reverse the image of reality. This figure is closely associated with Intuition, though not confined to Intuition. He is a messenger of the potential wholeness of the psyche, by crossing the *THRESHOLD* between conscious and unconscious.

He is also associated with the *MOON*, the mirror of the sunlight, which transforms, changes its shape – now it's there, now it's gone.

The Trickster is also associated with the weak but cunning *INFERIOR FUNCTION* which is familiar with the threshold between conscious and unconscious.

He is an ambivalent figure, the embodiment of both sides, both attitudes, not either/or but both/and: i.e. both conscious and unconscious; the stable world which *ENDURES* through continuous flux and *TRANSFORMATION*. He is the *PERSONIFICATION* of the live truth, expressed in *PARADOX* (in contrast with the dead concept).

He is the Lord of Phantasmagoria. See *IMAGINATION*.

Symbols:-

Brer Rabbit in the Uncle Remus Tales *(Harris, J. C.):* The rabbit (i.e. small hare) is especially the symbol of Inferior Intuition and Brer Rabbit is always facing death (the unconscious) and is snatched from it.

All magicians, wizards, e.g. Merlin: MAGIC attempts to cross the border of conscious and unconscious, of form and essence, dissolving forms into underlying fluid state and pulling them out again in new shapes.

The Devil, and most demons: are part tricksters appearing in the conscious realm with the reversed qualities and values of the unconscious. For example, the devil tricks God into plaguing Job.

Former Gods: represent an older and darker layer of the mind, and are often turned into demons as above, or they are the recognizable background of stories about magicians and sorcerers. For example, *Seth, the 'Great Magician'* of Egypt, who tricked Osiris into climbing into his own coffin, identified with Baal Saphon, is the background figure of the crafty Satan. *Cronos, Pan, Wotan*, after being banished to the unconscious, reappear similarly. Or *Orpheus*, god of the unconscious (dead), the older layer of the mind, which is also closer to the animals which he can tame with his lyre.

Nereus – or Thetis, the feminine version – are like PROTEUS who comes up from below the sea on to the rocks, and cannot deceive with his prophecy, once he has been made to speak; first he changes into lion, snake, panther, boar, water, tree.

TRICKSTER

With his flock of seals is the epitome of the slippery side of the truth, not accessible to the simplistic – one-eyed and one-tracked – conscious Ego.

Many oracles can be read either way. Prophets and prophecy always display something of the double edge between conscious and unconscious, when only partially integrated into the rest of the psyche, e.g. *Cassandra*, as the feminine version of the Trickster, who always spoke the truth, but nobody believed her. In the same way, Edward Lear's verse speaks profound truths about the unconscious, masquerading as nonsense.

The Sun HEROES: in order to cross the borders of the unconscious and back, have to learn a trick or two on the way, e.g. the 'wily Odysseus' (see ULYSSES), and Hercules who tricks Atlas. Gilgamesh plays tricks to outwit the guards of the heavenly realms in order to get the secret of immortality from the hero of the Flood. In the same way Jacob tricks his older, more primitive (i.e. less conscious) BROTHER.

Hermes, identified with the Egyptian Thoth, a moon god: Is the personification of the creative *IMAGINATION*, the most positive side of the Trickster.

Book:-

Radin, P. *The Trickster* (1956), with introduction by Jung, C. G.

ULYSSES, Odysseus
HERO **and** *TRICKSTER*

His line of descent is from HERMES via Autolycus, the cattle THIEF. He pretended to be mad to avoid going to Troy. He forged a letter and planted money in order to get Palamedes stoned to death. Throughout his story he is continually threatened with extinction (i.e. unconsciousness). He tricks Polyphemus, the Cyclops, with his name 'No man'. He tricks Circe with a charmed flower and he tricks the sirens by being tied to the mast. He claims credit for the Trojan Horse, and, disguised, he tricks the suitors: All of which establishes him as a figure at the *THRESHOLD* of the unconscious, like all Trickster figures.

He outwits the unconscious. He learns its secrets and returns with them.

Related Symbolism:-

The MOON, and its voyages across the oceans of the night sky:
The Odyssey may be an historicized myth about the twelve new moons of the year; their voyages and adventures till only one is left, destined to be extinguished also.

The UNDERWORLD. Arallu, Hades, Sheol, Hell, etc.
The unconscious. (See *CONSCIOUS/UNCONSCIOUS.*)

For mankind as a whole, this is where the residue of the past has settled, the sediment of the living world. For the individual, all the unlived fragments of his life lie there, distorted, disfigured, misunderstood.

The river of forgetfulness (Lethe) flows there: This is an image of the nature of the unconscious, which is sunk in oblivion. It is the reversed side of the image of the waters of life.

The descent into the underworld and the return, as part of the journey of life, and task of the hero: For the extravert – especially if he is of the Sensation/Thinking type – the difficulty is to get into the unconscious at all. For the introvert – especially if he has a powerful *IMAGINATION* based on his dominant Feeling or Intuitive functions – the difficulty is getting out again, and making contact with the outside world.

This is the movement of withdrawal and return. In symbolic language, the difficulty of withdrawing into the inner realm is expressed by the problem of *finding the entrance*, which may lie far to the West, where the sun sets. Being the land of the dead, and partially concealed, guides are needed. There are often *barriers and obstructions* to crossing the *THRESHOLD*, doors and gates which may be opened only with magic formulae. And there are *the fearful guardians of the underworld*, like *Cerberus*, or *Aker, the monstrous Sphinx*.

The particular figures who make the descent may represent the INFERIOR FUNCTION.

For example, when a child (Aladdin), or the youngest brother in a tale is selected. Or may represent the Anima, as goddess or heroine: Each major transition in life from one *PERIOD* to the next is experienced as loss of the former self. This is just part of the content, the treasure, that gets buried in the unconscious. The transitions are experienced (i.e. felt) as times of *DISINTEGRATION*, whether this is consciously recognized or not, and are normally accompanied by intense depressions. These are times of great loss, and foreshadow the final loss in *DEATH*. The descent, the journey down into the underworld, is a journey of recovery, to restore and relate the different parts of the psyche, the different periods of life. But it requires facing up to the monsters that devour the years, and going back across the periods of transition, with their accompanying gloom.

Some figures get stuck below in the underworld, such as Theseus and Pirithous, who grew fast to their rock thrones: The theme of failure in relation to the unconscious is usually associated with outrageous schemes and plans of the Conscious Ego, which wants to grasp the content of the unconscious without giving due respect to the powers which rule there. It is a question of relating conscious and unconscious on an equal basis, rather than trying to manipulate the unconscious realm for the benefit of the conscious Ego. (See also *LOOKING BACK*.)

The return, usually with something of inestimable value, such as a treasure or a figure of the opposite sex, is related symbolically to the new growth of Spring crops, beyond the death and the dearth of winter, e.g. Ishtar retrieves Tammuz: From the most ancient times, via the imagination, the psyche has provided a picture of its own structure, conscious and unconscious, and symbols that unite or relate the two; and which give a strong intuition and feeling for the value of this relationship.

Particular Symbolism:-

Alice, falling into the underworld, guided along tunnels by the white rabbit (Inferior Intuition), *experiencing difficulty getting across the threshold into Wonderland*, is as much an image of this same two-part structure of the psyche as any ancient myth. It is typical that for the dry, conscious, masculine Ego, it is the small, feminine child that enters this realm. The Wonderland described is full of the vitality of the unconscious, where the one stream of life animates all the plants and creatures in a vibrant, wondrous relationship. Integrating this content with ordinary everyday life is not so easy, and the return is, partially at least, a let-down.

It is via *the dead OSIRIS*, of Egypt, dwelling perpetually in the underworld, that the link between the individual soul and the rest of creation is achieved. Plant life and conscious life are the two halves of life: life looks at its own reflection in nature. (See *VEGETATION*.)

For Dante and for Christendom in general, the underworld (hell) was drastically segregated from the upper realms, indicating a rift between conscious and unconscious, which may have served a purpose but in the long run has proved non-viable (see *The BROTHERS*). Even so, Dante's journey to the upper sphere of pure enduring light is accomplished by first descending into the underworld. Symbolically hell, *DEATH, DISINTEGRATION.* The unconscious is a source of life in that it breaks down the nature of existence till it is in a state where the *ESSENCE* can be distinguished from the dross, the ashes, i.e. the mere substance.

TARTARUS, by one account, is as far below HADES, the underworld of Greek myth, as Heaven was above earth. And it took a falling millstone nine days to reach the bottom of it. This shows a balance in which the worlds of the conscious mind are reflected in the depths below. The tiers and levels of underworld and upper world have been subdivided – usually in relation to each other.

Related Symbolism:-

The struggle of relating to the Unconscious – or getting trapped there – can be expressed in many ways, such as *the battle with the Monster*, and *being swallowed by the Monster*, or *being trapped in the STONE, or wood of unconsciousness.*

But also *PROMETHEUS*, and his theft of fire, and his punishment.

Note:-

In terms of evolution, every gain in consciousness, every increase in awareness, in areas of Feeling and Intuition, as well as Thinking, has been achieved in the teeth of this dynamic struggle with the inertia of unconscious matter. So it is not those who venture into the unconscious who are in most danger of being trapped there, but those who fail to recognize its existence. Restricted to their conscious Ego, the other half of their own nature is lost to them in oblivion, or is asleep (see *SLEEPING BEAUTY*) or dead to them (see *DEATH*). Book:-

Streatfeild, D. *A Study of Two Worlds: Persephone* (1959).

UNICORN
The One. See *NUMBERS*, One/Many.
  The *UNION* of Opposites.

The spirit which unifies in contrast with the flesh which diversifies.

Inner creative power in contrast with the phallus.

It is either white or many-coloured: It is the principle which unites the spectrum of colours, the white ethereal light which contains all the colours of the rainbow. The one is the *ESSENCE* of the many and vice versa. Also see *CATTLE*.

Unicorn/Stag: Emphasizes the symbolic meaning of the one horn in contrast with the many and ever increasing proliferation of points on the stag's antlers. The mythical embodiment of the inner realm of the mind is contrasted with the actual creature of the woods, brown like earth, symbolizing the relationship between mind and matter, *ABOVE* and below.

The great rutting ceremony of the stag with its herd of females emphasizes this idea of its proliferation in the material realm of nature.

Unicorn/Lion: The inner world of mind and imagination, contrasted with the ordinary extravert life of the Ego. The King was traditionally a mediator between these two realms.

The lion beating the unicorn round the town: Depicts symbolically the fairly common situation, where society tries to get rid of tension, not by finding balance and equilibrium, but by repression. In the nursery rhyme the whole conflict is *drummed out of town*, i.e. into the unconscious, where it has been causing no end of social problems ever since.

Lady and the unicorn: The relationship between the Feminine soul, or Anima, of man, and the spirit or Self. As the story goes, the soul cannot capture the essence of life, or realize its inner unity, by running hectically from activity to activity, but only by sitting quietly, which is how the lady Anima catches the unicorn. This refers to what can only be achieved by passiveness, openness, receptivity in the inner work.

Unicorn, as attribute of Artemis, who turned Actaeon into a stag which was torn to pieces: In symbolism each man is only a fragment of the One divine man, yet he contains the possibility of being reunited with the whole. (See *SACRIFICE*.) Artemis was one of the Virgin goddesses, which may have led to the association of the unicorn with chastity.

The unicorn transforming into the dove in Alchemy: Sublimated Matter becomes volatile. Withdrawing from immediate sensual experience, gradually the nature of life itself – which can be identified with the cosmic Self – puts man in touch with all parts of the cosmos through all periods of time.

Related Symbolism:-

The SWORD. And the sword of the swordfish.

The World AXIS; or *PATTERNS, Vertical Line.*

The unbroken line, Yang, see *I CHING*.

The UNION of the Opposites. Conjunctio

The key to symbolism, and the most important function of all symbolic material, is to relate the opposites in such a way that they form a unity – two very different halves of one complete whole. See *SYMBOLS*.

On the Cosmic level the fundamental opposition is between life and matter.

On the human level, between life and death.

Within the psyche, conscious opposes unconscious.

See *OPPOSITES*.

In the Sequence:-

The original unity of life has split itself up into many parts. See *ORIGINS; SPLIT; SACRIFICE*. Within the psyche the Conscious Ego has broken off, with considerable effort and suffering, from the preconscious totality.

This emphasizes the fact that the ultimate union of the opposites has nothing to do with sinking back into the original state of unconsciousness, where the end would be the same as the beginning and all the struggle between would be totally pointless, just a mad swelter of misdirected effort. Although a deliberate dissolution of consciousness takes place – a determined return to the origin – it is as a step across the threshold, a step on the way, which is only completed when the individual, or the group, has stepped back again, with a deeper knowledge, a firmer grasp of the double-sided nature of life, and of the psyche; and of the relationship between the two sides.

The great prize of the conscious Ego, which distinguishes between the opposites, would be valueless, if the opposites did not continue to remain opposites. All the rich variety of life would sink back into drab uniformity; potential only, without particular form.

But nor would it be possible to relate the opposites, if they were not already opposite parts of a larger whole, arising from a single origin; and remaining at root single in nature, in *ESSENCE*. And many symbols continuously refer back to this essential truth.

The *UNION* of particular opposites:-

Life/Death: Life and death cannot be merged or confused. They are utterly opposed to each other, locked in combat. But symbolism relates them to each other, as dawn is opposite dusk, East opposite West. On the symbolic level (of the Self, of the Cosmos) the balance remains the same throughout. The balance between life and death is no different from the first cry of the new-born infant to the last gasp of the old person.

The balance is kept steady by the two-way process of continuous transformation: if the young only grew old, then there would be no balance, and the symbols of union would be rightly rejected as worthless. But, in fact, the symbols point to both sides of the truth – death also makes room for new life. Note:-

The Ego may be able to see both sides, which are fairly obvious, but it cannot live them (i.e. feel them, experience them) as part of its very own life. And instead of broadening into the symbol, the Ego is inclined to tailor the symbol to its requirements.

The union of conscious and unconscious; of Ego and Anima, or ANIMUS in a woman: The physical union of man and woman is the vivid illustration of the nature of the union of all the opposites, whether within the psyche, or in human life, or in the cosmic life of Nature. The man and woman lose themselves in their origins – which is a form of ecstasy – and by sinking back to the origin, the offspring is conceived.

Within the psyche, there is a similar movement back to the preconscious totality, where the Ego is merged with the Anima, or in the case of a woman the Animus, and from the two is born the Self, which is neither one nor the other, and grows slowly to maturity. But it doesn't wipe out Ego or Animus/a, any more than the child eliminates its parents. The Ego can never quite accept both sides of the picture. Supposing it manages to identify with the unconscious, even then it can't tolerate the particular irritations, sufferings and humiliations of everyday life. Whereas the Self is both sides of the picture and can't help the joy of containing both, of knowing the centre, between origin and end, whether long or short; i.e. having reached the centre it can move quite freely to any point around the circumference between the birth and death of its Ego, and back before and on beyond. See Cosmic *MAN*.

The idea is easy enough to follow, and is a central theme of symbolism. To live it requires being mastered by the force of life itself. It is the action, the flow, the dance of life that unites.

The Symbols:-

The SELF, and its symbolism: e.g. *Cosmic MAN.*

PATTERNS; MANDALA; WHEEL.

MOTHER and Son, as symbol of the *VESSEL* which contains the whole.

The WEDDING at the end of the fairy-tale. Or *Lingam and Yoni.*

The MEDIATOR: HERMAPHRODITE.

Water and fire (warmth) both acting upon the seed to swell and ripen it.

FIRE melts, vaporizes, which may facilitate union or transformation (see *ELEMENTS*).

The encircling *EROS*, the force which binds together, and is related to *the Sacred precinct, the Magic Circle*, as well as *the Vessel*, e.g. *the Retort of the Alchemists*. Or *the Ouroboros SERPENT*. Both Tao and Zen value the Original Whole, the preconscious totality, as the foil to ethical or cultural consciousness, which are products of the Ego.

Book:-

Jung, C. G. *Mysterium Conjunctionis* [Jung's masterpiece], in *Collected Works*, Vol. 14 (1963).

The UNKNOWN. The Imago Ignota
The Unconscious. Or the *TRANSCENDENT*.

Without relating to the unknown and the unconscious, it is impossible to extend the boundaries of what is known, or to gain new consciousness.

Once particular speculations have passed into the sphere of knowledge, then they become redundant. But the capacity to speculate through symbols, through the imagination, shifts its ground, extends its bounds – or atrophies. Only a particular attitude of openness, emptiness, can liberate the individual from his personal confines and limitations.

The Symbols:-

The top platform of the Ziggurat, with no image.

The Living God of Judaism, without image.

In Tibetan Yoga, imagery is carried so far that the adept is supposed to be able to reach out and touch the images he creates with his mind. Nevertheless, he must know that these are only figments of his imagination, and sweep them aside if he is to confront reality itself. A recent Zen Master pointed out that nobody who imagines he's a millionaire actually thinks he's got rich. In the same way to have visions of all the Heavens, Buddhas and Patriarchs, is not the same as arriving in heaven. Symbols are concerned with the Reality, not the image, the vision nor the words, except as signposts.

In the KABBALAH, Eyn Sof: Is the hidden root of all the Sepiroth – or Divine Emanations – which are the invisible life forces, or archetypes. There is no symbol for Eyn Sof: it is without form and nothing can be said about it. It is the Opposite of all finite forms – the Infinite.

Man's response to Eyn Sof, also in the Kabbalah, is DEATH, *without a number:* Is the abyss, the gulley of emptiness: without confronting it, without taking it into account – in a vibrant, living, everyday way – man is trapped in his illusions whether of the senses or the mind. See TRANSCENDENT FUNCTION. Similarly in Christianity, *self-emptying (kenosis)* – not only of the Ego, but of the Cosmic Self (see Cosmic MAN) as well – is the way to avoid inflated smugness, but also of grasping the quality of reality. In mysticism this is related to the Apophatic Way.

For the Greeks the wisdom of knowing that you know nothing: knowing the limits and limitations of human knowledge.

Not this, Not that (Neti, neti), of Hinduism.

Note:-

Although No Symbol is the final GOAL of the symbolic quest, this doesn't mean there is any way of by-passing the intermediate stages of MYTH and personal myth. See also IMAGINATION.

Book:-

Evans Wenzt, W. Y. *Tibetan Yoga* (1935).

UTOPIAS/Chimeras. (Paradise/Hell-on-earth)
The extreme OPPOSITES **on a global scale.**

The boring aspect of most descriptions of Utopia or Paradise tends to illustrate the point that something vital is lacking, which needs to be integrated from the other dark side.

The ideal is imperfect because it is only one half of life: it is one-tracked and limited. Furthermore, it is dangerous because it builds up an increasingly powerful, opposite tendency in the unconscious.

Whereas life favours the muddy as well as the clear, the dark as well as the light, the night as well as the day: and Wisdom celebrates life's chequered carnival.

The Hyperboreans, among whom Apollo spent his idyllic childhood, and who dwelt beyond the North Wind; Apollo returned to them once every nineteen years: The North is the region of the Unconscious and 'beyond the North' would suggest the preconscious totality beyond the split of

Conscious and Unconscious. This is the place of Wholeness which is always a Paradise before the Conscious Ego – in this case as Sun God Apollo – separates, or, in an equivalent tale, eats of the Tree of Knowledge.

The return every nineteen years may be an oblique reference to the crises and turning points, especially in midlife at about forty. The crises also arise at twenty-one, and sixty-odd, between the four major *PERIODS* of life when it is necessary to turn inwards (also symbolized by the North) and recover contact with the Unconscious, in order to make the necessary *TRANSFORMATIONS*.

Utopia/hell-on-earth, as for example in Huxley, A., *Island* (1962) and his *Brave New World* (1932); or Orwell, G., *1984* (1949); *or man eating man till only the crabs are left, in* Wells, H. G., *Time Machine* (1895): Karl Popper argues rather convincingly that Utopias, dreams and visions of a better future are the cause of the greatest miseries inflicted by man on man. Nevertheless, this is partly the result of taking the symbolic goal literally and placing it in the remote future, which leads to the rigidity and bigotry of some political idealists. To take away the goal altogether, the ultimate vision, is to rob life of direction and meaning.

The *GOAL* is often more powerfully felt and more effective in its negative form of the hell on earth. Negative goals may be of greater value, afford greater impetus and so work better as signposts for direction. But the unconscious forces at work are particularly unwieldy and difficult to direct at the best of times.

Note:-

People, whose main *FUNCTION* is Intuition, have sensation as their *INFERIOR* Function, and so have difficulty in relating to the material and physical side of reality. It isn't their visions and ideals in themselves which cause the trouble: but their inability to integrate them with material reality.

VAMPIRES

Either repressed, unconscious content which is manifesting destructively, or the negative *ANIMUS* in women – the Sinister Old Man. See *YOUTH*/Old Man, also *SATURN*.

i. Repressed content of the unconscious rising up to sap the life blood – drain the energy – of the individual or the community.

If they can find no outlet, the animal instincts start to devour themselves.

Unlived fragments of life which have become negative and obsessive. Irrational aspects of the unconscious, which have not been recognized, so can't be transformed.

The living dead, the living death, is above all the opposite of *TRANSFORMATION*, and in the stories *DISINTEGRATION* becomes highly desirable, but can only be achieved passively through the active intervention of the living, i.e. the conscious mind.

They are *PERSONIFICATIONS* of forces that have failed to make the necessary transition. They are stuck in past archaic forms and clinging to them, and it is this which terrifies, and drains the living of their vitality. They are old attitudes that refuse to transform.

Or:-

ii. In particular instances, the negative Father Figure; that is, the Animus in women.

The Sinister Old Man – the negative aspect of the Wise Old Man – who represents, within the psyche, rigid forms of male consciousness, without any real (feminine) life: cold and frozen solid, formulas carved in granite.

The interplay between male and female vampires: The interaction of Animus and Anima.

They crave for blood: They long for life. *Neglected COMPLEXES* that desire to be used.

Changing shape, into a bat, or the same applies to werewolves, etc.: Emphasizes that the unconscious is the place of transformation, but this is a dark, negative change, of no value.

The idea of unending change has been grasped at an unconscious level, but arouses only the deepest horror of not being able to die, of there being no possible escape from the unending process.

The *UNION* of Above and Below has taken place, but from the depths, dragging conscious rational life down, into the caves and darkness of the unconscious: instead of integrating the extremes from the centre.

The old soul stuck forever in the processes of decomposition, decay – without ever coming through and out the other side. Like all images or figures of archetypal reality, it applies to the personal psyche and to the cosmos; as much to a period of depression, when blocked and unable to find a way through, as to cosmic processes of flux, and continuous recycling from which there is a need to be liberated that extends beyond personal death.

The ray of sun: As always it is the union of the *OPPOSITES* that saves the situation. The continuous nightworld of the unconscious is shattered, and disintegrated in the light of consciousness. Just as the other way round, consciousness dissolves and drowns in the unconscious.

The two are mutually exclusive, yet only together do they form the whole pattern. One is the reverse image of the other.

The stake in the heart: And here the phallic force of creativity is reversed. See *MIRROR*. The forces of destruction (see *DISINTEGRATION*) are necessary throughout nature, in order to make way for the next phase of development.

Related Symbolism:-

DEATH; UNDERWORLD; HORROR FILMS.

See also *SATURN; CONSCIOUS/UNCONSCIOUS.*

VEGETATION. Plant life

The base of life itself: or the Vegetable Soul. The earliest phases in the evolution of life, and therefore the deepest layers of man's own unconscious life.

Man, looking at nature, is life divided from life: and one part is now contemplating other aspects of its own nature. The vegetable soul corresponds to the feminine archetype of life. In men, this is related symbolically to the Anima – also to the involuntary nervous system.

The Lord of Life, whether Dumuzi, or the feminine Demeter, Lady Life; or Dionysus, of the Vine: Manifests physically in human form, as well as in the crops. Life feeds off its own body, supplies its own needs, existing partly above and partly underground, in both human and vegetable forms, i.e. part conscious and part unconscious.

Seed: The spark of life, which swells into actual living forms and contracts back into the seeds. It is related to the spermdrop and to *ORIGINS.*

The smell of flowers and the stench of graves: The invisible forces of creativity and destruction at work in the world.

Related Symbolism:

TREE; also *LOTUS.*

The VESSEL

The Feeling *FUNCTION* **that forms relationships, and holds together the content of life.**

Without the vessel, the different ingredients of life cannot be mixed together, so there can be no *UNION* of opposites, and no *TRANSFORMATION.*

The body itself is such a vessel holding spirit and matter in union.

On the cosmic level, the cosmos is the vessel of life and matter.

The womb/the witch's cauldron: The vessel of creativity in contrast with its negative aspect.

Barrels, bottles, etc. – conscious inventions holding liquids which could not otherwise be held: Become symbols of anything which can contain the flowing forces of nature, which are not easy to hold. For example, when they contain *DJINN.* See also *PANDORA's* box.

Negative Symbolism:-

The container: may also be a trap, a closed system, old unsuitable attitudes: unconscious repressions.

Pandora's Box/Deucalion's Ark: Are the negative and positive aspects of the same symbol. As usual with symbolism, the negative manifests first through Prometheus, and only later does the positive life-saving quality of the symbol become apparent, through his son Deucalion.

Particular Symbolism:-

The Ark; The GRAIL; The sacred precinct (Temenos); The magic CIRCLE; EROS.

WAR
The rift between Conscious and Unconscious: the great, inner struggle between Ego and Shadow, between the Collective Ego of the Nation and its Collective Shadow.

The inner war – sometimes called the The Great War – is then projected out across the face of the earth – the Little Wars – in symbolic language.

WATER
Without water there is no life: so water is not an image or simile, but a symbol of life.

The intermediary between solid but dead substance and the volatile spirit of life. See *ELEMENTS*. The precondition of life, its *ORIGIN*. An even older form of existence that precedes and sustains life. The potential realm: the Primeval Waters in Egyptian myth contained the seed of millions of beings.

In terms of the psyche: The feminine unconscious moistens the dry, hard, conscious realm of the male Ego, and brings life to it. Vice versa, the too moist, the too emotional and unconscious, may need to be dried out in a fiery male domain (hellfire).

In the sequence of life, it is related both to the uterine and seminal fluids, into which life dissolves and from which it regenerates. (See *DISINTEGRATION*/Integration.)

The permanent water (aqua permanens) which cannot be found, but must be produced, created: Man's creative faculty produces the sense, the meaning of life. Only life itself can comprehend life – the nexus. This water corresponds to the enduring quality of life, which is forever purifying itself; becoming clearer and clearer. Water is symbolic of the flow of the life force, the underlying essence. All the life forms drink of it, yet it remains distinct from them. They come and go, but it flows on.

The deep water abyss under the surface of the world, that wells up in springs – the waters beyond as in the inundation of the Nile, on which life depended – and the fresh water from above as rain: Combine to symbolize the mysterious source that spawned creation, and sustains it still. In the human psyche, contact with this mysterious essence is possible through Intuition, and is the source of wisdom, meaning insight into the course of life, and therefore into the future.

The river is related to *the SERPENT* and *the LIGHTNING.*

Negative Symbolism:-

Floods, drowning: Water kills and give life: destroys as well as creates.

The river of forgetfulness (Lethe): Water brings oblivion, as well as wisdom.

Particular Symbolism:-

Apsu, in Mesopotamian myth was the fresh water *ABYSS* under the world that was the source of that wisdom, which is also profound and deep, and not immediately accessible to the conscious Ego, which apprehends the forms and appearances only.

Related Symbolism:-

The Water of Life, the Living Waters, were also related to other vital fluids such as Ambrosia, Amrita, Mead for the warrior, Soma, Wine, Blood: All of which symbolized the surge of the libido, the feeling of being alive, the continuous flow of vital interest, to and from the unconscious.

Because this vitality arises partly from the animal passions and drives, the fluids may be guarded by monsters, etc., indicating that the bestial side needs to be mastered before the pure, uncontaminated, animal vitality – possibly the blood of the monster – can be enjoyed.

Spider's WEB

The potential of life spun from within, which forms the pattern and sequence of actual existence (primitive mandala).

Or webs of illusion, whether inner illusions spun by the Lord and Lady Soul (see *ANIMUS/A*) or outside facts as illusion (see *MAYA; PROJECTIONS*).

WEDDING, Marriage

The *UNION* of the *OPPOSITES*.

As the typical ending: It is the true symbolic *GOAL* of life. *When it takes place on a mountain, whether the marriage of Zeus and Hera on the heights of Gargarus, or the OWL and the*

PUSSYCAT married by the Turkey who lived on the Hill: Emphasizes the union *ABOVE* and below: the point where the world *AXIS* holds up reality. The union of life and substance, spirit and nature.

For the hero: The discovery of the Feminine side of his own nature, the refined aspect of life in contrast with heroic quests and adventures.

For the woman: The most significant of all her initiations into life.

She submits her left hand only to be ringed by the man: She keeps entire and for herself the conscious right-hand side of her personality and submits only with the unconscious subliminal side of her nature – including her primitive masculine Animus – to be tutored to maturity by the man.

Monogamy/Promiscuity: The union of Ego and Anima (or Animus) leading to the attainment of individuality, the undivided self, in contrast with the hydra-headed projections of promiscuity.

Note:-

Mere practical issues alone would not have been enough to account for the strong tendency towards monogamy in the human species.

Related Symbolism:-

ZEUS and HERA: for the fourfold relationship of marriage, man, woman, Animus and Anima.

The marriage of King and Queen in ALCHEMY and the *Chymical Wedding of the Rosicrucians.*

WHEEL
The movement of life. The cycle of *TIME.*

The *PATTERN* of the psyche set in motion. This is the means by which inner potential becomes the actual *SEQUENCE* of events in a person's life.

The spokes, which may be six or eight: The parts of the pattern as well as the different stages of life between birth and death.

The hub of the wheel: The centre of life. See *CENTRE.*

Related Symbolism:-

ZODIAC for the wheeling constellations around their still

centre, the Pole Star: as they relate to the wheel of birth and death.

The compulsive attraction of *the Roulette Wheel* may be partly because it is symbolically charged. Red alternates with black, as conscious with unconscious. The numbers refer to the year and so to the life of man. Zero is birth, death and rebirth. It is the wheel of fate that fascinates.

See also *MANDALA; PATTERNS, Circle.*

'The WIND in the Willows' (Kenneth Grahame, 1908)

The overall landscape of the book is divided between the tamed known land along the river, and the wild wood beyond. The main figures are animals. All except Mr Toad live underground: Would suggest a concern with the instinctual animal level of the psyche, which has a wild intractable side as well as a more amenable aspect, though all the creatures that live underground would refer to the unconscious.

The Badger lives in the depths of the wild wood, but is not threatened by it. He is entrusted with the ancient traditions: He represents the *SELF*, the principle of unity within the psyche, of which the nucleus is often the neglected powerful forces of Intuition. These forces can only be reached through braving the terrors of the wood, the terrifying negative aspect of the unconscious.

The God Pan presides over all: The specific mention of the god *PAN* emphasizes the concern for man's relationship with nature.

While Toad is plunged in the dungeon the wild-wooders take over Toad Hall: This reflects or echoes other symbolic material of dissolving conscious into unconscious. See *DISINTEGRATION.* In the first phase of the process the complexes break in, causing havoc and disorder.

Toad only escapes with the help of a washerwoman and her daughter, and dressed as a woman: That is, he escapes with the help of the Anima. See *MAZE.*

United, the main figures recapture the Hall and Toad is transformed: The different forces of the psyche are brought into union, and gain the mastery of life, overcome the terrors of the unconscious. The Ego is transformed.

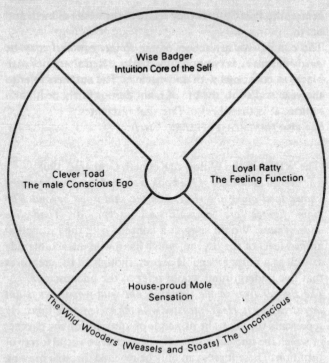

The WISH. Wishing Wells, etc
The well-springs of feeling: desire.

Wishes are normally granted by female figures, e.g. fairy godmothers, etc.: The realm of feeling, of the erotic, of relationships and values, is usually designated as Feminine. For a man it is the domain of his Anima, who projects a world of fantasy which instils longing and makes goals attractive.

But as with so much in life, this is only a necessary beginning, a means to an end. The wish (the desire) leads on to discovery. (See *PROJECTIONS*.)

For a woman, the wish god is her ANIMUS.

Negative Symbolism:-

If left in a dark, flickering, semi-conscious state these wishes turn negative and destructive. They become delusions to pander to a wishful picture of oneself and the world.

*In the stories this situation is depicted when the wishes abort,
e.g. frogs and toads come out of the mouth or the bag instead of
treasures. Instead of the river transforming to gold, the person
is transformed to stone, etc:* These stories are usually
depicting the Ego's attempt to exploit nature or the
unconscious for its own utilitarian purposes.

Note:-

As usual with symbolic stories, the time is drastically
shortened. The desire and the granting of that desire needs to
be spread out over a normal life span. And the little obstacles
and difficulties on the way to getting the wish fulfilled are
seen as so many years of struggle, and then the story can
usually be seen to depict a very real life situation. For
example, with really determined effort, much gold can be
acquired – or could in Victorian times – but the joy of it may
vanish away.

Wish/Fear: The positive and negative sides of the same
impulse. Once desire is seen to be the cause of the fear, it can
be rationalized and so brought under conscious control.
Some detachment becomes almost inevitable, once it is
grasped that the outcome of the desire is so undesirable.

It is the conscious wish or desire that has to be modified:
because man cannot easily manipulate his unconscious – in
this case the dread.

See also *SEXUALITY*, Desire/Fear, where repressed fears turn
into their *OPPOSITE* in the Unconscious, namely compulsive
desire.

MIRROR and *UTOPIA*/Chimera give further examples of this
type of relationship between *CONSCIOUS* and unconscious.

WITCH

**The destructive, negative side of Nature and the goddesses of
nature. The Mother *COMPLEX* of the Dark *MOTHER*.**

The side that resists being brought into the light of
consciousness and being directed by the rational will.

*Like some women – witches – prefer not to be seen too clearly.
They prefer the night-world where the lights glow and flicker
dimly. The depths of the forests. The end house:* They inhabit
the border region, the *THRESHOLD* that leads to the

427

unconscious, which is why their help can be so necessary at times. They often represent the man's Anima. See *ANIMUS/A*.
They are skilled in magic: They often represent the *INFERIOR* neglected faculty of intuition – which may be the source of the elixir of life.
Their love-potions: The unconscious Feeling function.

WOTAN/Odin
The fury of the night.

The unconscious Dionysian qualities (see *APOLLO/* Dionysus). The Shadow side of Christian values: the dark instinctual nature which is father of the Anima.

The YOUTH/Old Man
Including the Eternal Youth – occasionally referred to in Latin as 'Puer Aeternus' and 'Puer/Senex'.
Symbol of the rift between the two halves of life. See *PERIODS* of Life. Also *MOTHER*/Child.

When these two – Youth and Age – are related to each other – which is only possible via the unconscious, and in particular the Anima – it becomes a source of creative energy, which is lacking when the two oppose each other.
Cronos devours his children, Oedipus slays his father: The rift between the generations (in the family) manifests as the typical conflict between father and son.
Within the psyche, this recurring mythical theme of the raw youth confronted by the Sinister Old Man refers to the inner rift between the formless potential of youth – unlimited possibilities still closely related to the mother and the formless ground of the unconscious – and the concrete facts of a particular life. To each, the other side looks like death.
The Eternal Youth Figure, e.g. whether Adonis, or Peter Pan, the Little Prince: As with the Romantics, this figure prefers actual death, to the solid, frozen forms of old age, which seem all too concrete, petrified in their conscious, material systems and structures. For him, the Old Man is the epitome of law and order, lacking spontaneity or life. Many such

figures – e.g. Alexander the Great or St. Exupéry – actually failed to live the second half of life.

Though others survive into old age, they often do so as pickled boys, without ever reaching true manhood. They may become wanderers.

The Sinister Old Man: The process of transformation is stultified, out of dread of the process of life, which includes decay, disintegration. The youth becomes his bête noir, threatening to usurp his power.

The Union of the Bearded Figure and Boy, e.g. Tiresias and Pothos, on Samothrace: The fruitful and creative flow of life through all its periods and transitions can only be achieved by overcoming the major obstacle between: by attacking it from both sides. Youth integrates age and transforms into it, but age also has to re-integrate youth.

From both sides the intermediary figure is the *ANIMA* (see *ANIMUS*).

For the youth the Mother Anima has to be transformed into the youthful Anima. In so doing the Youth transforms himself from son into mate and father, facing what for him is the greatest *SACRIFICE*, the death of his own youth.

The old man has to risk regeneration by abandoning himself to dissolution in the formless unconscious, the womb of nature. And thereby recovering his creativity, his adaptability, at one with the flow of life.

The union of these two figures is no superficial handshake in the mind, and can only be achieved after crucial testing. The symbols of *UNION* and transformation are of considerable help.

Once achieved the union of Youth and Age amounts to the union of conscious with unconscious, as well as the integration of the pleasure principle with the power principle – e.g. of *APOLLO* and Dionysus in myth – or the integration of Id and Super-Ego in Freudian language.

Related Symbolism:-

SATURN; The HELPFUL FIGURE; DISINTEGRATION/Integration.

Books:-

Franz, M. L. von. *Puer Aeternus* (1970). Vitale, A. 'Saturn: The Transformation', in *Fathers and Mothers* (1973).

ZEUS and HERA. The Sacred Marriage. (Hieros Gamos)

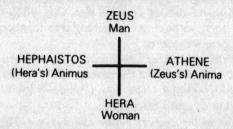

This was the only true marriage among the Olympian Gods. And true to the conventional old-fashioned marriage, Zeus was continuously unfaithful with his many loves, and Hera nagged him.

But they also follow the typical (or archetypal) pattern of marriage in another, more interesting, way. They illustrate Jung's hypothesis that the ordinary marriage is a fourway relationship, as above. And from the shadows of the unconscious, the Anima and *ANIMUS* (inner figures of the opposite sex) can make or sabotage the marriage, just as Athene is the successful rival and even the annihilator of Hera. And the crippled Hephaistos is the opposite of the powerful Zeus, but with Hera tries to overthrow him.

In this fourway relationship, particular attractions and antagonisms may be set up between the man and his wife's male Animus, or vice versa between the woman and her husband's Anima. And this may affect relationships with the children.

But if brought to conscious light, it provides the basis for a much richer and more varied relationship, in which both partners fulfil the whole of their own inner potential, rather than depending too much on the other: thereby forcing each other into extreme positions.

For example, many men are puzzled by the way that, as they become more and more crisply logical, their wives get increasingly scatty and emotional, almost in inverse proportions. Which tends to make the man get even more entrenched in his position, in order to introduce a bit of sanity. Whereas this really indicates the time to concentrate on the development of his own Anima: a little emotional and irrational behaviour from his feminine side is found to ease the situation.

The ZODIAC
The whole pattern of the psyche and the potential sequence of man's life.

In spite of some anomalies (from the point of view of symbolism) the Zodiac remains probably the most magnificent of the wheels of *TIME*: it links the pattern of the cosmos with man; and the cycle of the year with his destiny.

The whole Zodiac: Universal or Cosmic *MAN* to which each individual is related, in the particular way which his birthchart indicates.

The planets: The Archetypes. The typical human characteristics that are distributed in different combinations for each person.

The Sun: The male conscious Ego, which is the seed of the Self. The *HERO*.

In a woman's life the position and relationships of the Sun to other planets may throw light on the masculine side of her character (see *ANIMUS*) and thereby on her relationships with men. See *SUN*, the symbolic significance of which may derive ultimately from astrology.

Note:-

This is the only aspect of the birth-chart considered in the 'Sun-sign' columns in newspapers, etc.

Moon: The feminine unconscious realm. In a man's life the Anima. (See *ANIMUS/ANIMA*.)

Saturn: The dark Shadow (see *EGO*/Shadow) side of the personality which is also the principle of transformation.

Just as the position of sun or moon in a particular sign of the Zodiac indicates the strong points of the personality of a man or woman, so the position of Saturn indicates the weak points; that is, the *INFERIOR FUNCTION*.

Jupiter: Intuition. The religious impulse: the creative power that shapes myths, and thereby governs the destiny of man. The ideals of man, his highest aims, in contrast with his depths (see *ABOVE*/Below). Jupiter and Saturn together form the opposite poles, the top and bottom of the Cosmic *AXIS*, and the Vertical line (see *PATTERNS*).

Mars and Venus: Complement Sun and Moon, as male and female forces, showing additional subsidiary aspects of the character, or of the Animus and Anima. More personal facets, drawn from the store of human types. As Liz Greene points out, Astrology is the oldest surviving source of the typology of human nature, which is still basic to any real understanding of the human psyche.

Mercury: Myth and astrology are closely interrelated and, like the God (Mercury/Hermes/Thoth), this planet represents the *TRICKSTER* figure on the borders of conscious and unconscious, who provides the possibility and the means of integrating unconscious content.

The outer planets, Uranus, Neptune and Pluto: Represent supra-personal forces not unlike the topmost spheres on the tree of life in the Kabbalah where the seven other spheres – like the planets above – are also more closely related to the destiny of man.

These move against the backcloth of the circle of the Zodiac, and it is the particular position of all of them at the time and place of birth which indicates the particular personal characteristics of the individual potential; the possibilities in the future, rather than any predetermined end or result.

The One.

In the night sky the Pole Star is symbol of the *ORIGINS*, splits into the opposites. It is the *CENTRE* of the Zodiac.

The Opposites.

As with symbolism generally, the *OPPOSITES* of the Zodiac are many and varied, and cannot be equated. Apart from the opposition of the planets above, the main division between conscious and unconscious is marked by the Ascendant sign – the particular constellation rising above the horizon in the East at the moment of birth – and the Descendant, the opposite constellation sinking in the West. It is especially for this aspect of the birth-chart – which changes on the hour, as it were, by the cosmic clock measuring the day and night into twelve grand double-hours – that the precise time and place of birth is needed. The qualities of the Ascendant sign are expressed in the individual's conscious behaviour (often more so than the sun-sign) and the Descendant expresses his unconscious, to be found within himself (as Inferior *FUNCTION*); as well as in others; often a partner, chosen to complement his or her deficiencies.

The opposition of *MASCULINE* and feminine is depicted in the planets but also in the signs. The masculine features in the individual's particular birth-chart will be more accessible to men and less to women; and vice versa.

It is precisely the complexity that builds up from these basic ingredients that enables the Zodiac to do justice to the living situation, arising from its map of possibilities. 'Everything in the birth-chart has its opposite' (Greene, Liz).

The Four.

The Zodiac can be divided broadly into Earth, Air, Fire and Water, by its cardinal points (i.e. by four major signs), indicating the overall sequence of life. Judging from the general tendencies in the development of symbolism – compare, for example, the *I CHING* – this was related to the older eight-sign Zodiac with four cardinal male signs and four female consorts. *This has been further elaborated and subdivided, into three series of Earth, Air, Water, Fire:* The basic human types (Sensation opposite Intuition, Thinking opposite Feeling) are depicted, within the general overall human sequence of development, that is, made personal by the particular situation of the planets.

The elements in astrology.

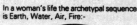

In a man's life the archetypal sequence is Earth, Air, Water, Fire:-

In a woman's life the archetypal sequence is Earth, Water, Air, Fire:-

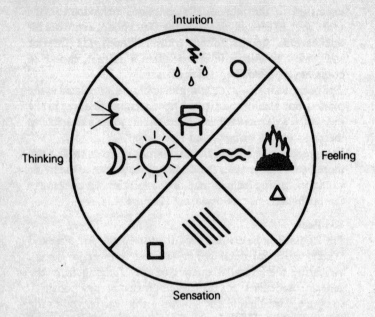

Intuition

Thinking

Feeling

Sensation

Note to Chart:-
Jung pointed out that Capricorn, (depicted as the Mesopotamian Water God, Ea, the goat with fish's tail,) Aquarius, (the Water Carrier,) and Pisces may originally have all been water signs. Which suggests an earlier bolder grouping of the *ELEMENTS*. Compare diagram p 437.

But with symbolism it is important to remember the way the Elements act in Nature, in close conjunction with each other, almost inseparable, which is what makes them all suitable as symbols of the *FUNCTIONS* in the psyche. For example, it is the *Fire of lightning* which heralds the rain that refills the springs of fresh water. In this context, Fire is the prophet, the herald, the flash of foresight, and insight which is Intuitive. Whereas the warming *Fire in the hearth* corresponds to the Emotions, and *the sunlight* which differentiates forms is an image of the Intellect. Just as the elements bind, interweave and interrelate, so do the different *FUNCTIONS* within the psyche and the different psychological Types within society. It is only the intellect which would like to dissect them for the sake of order and clarity, till there is no living interaction left.

The Four Beasts in Ezekiel, related to the four figures symbolizing the Evangelists (the Tetramorphs) were probably originally associated with the four cardinal signs of the Zodiac in the age of Taurus:

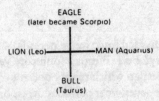

```
              EAGLE
        (later became Scorpio)


LION (Leo)━━━━━━━╋━━━━━━━MAN (Aquarius)


              BULL
            (Taurus)
```

The Four Ages of Man is Astrology:-

The Age of Taurus, from before 4000 BC to c. 2000 BC: The emergence of the river cultures between the Tigris and the Euphrates (see *MESOPOTAMIAN MYTH*) and on the Nile, which are sometimes regarded as the foundation of Western Civilization and possibly of the Indus Valley and Eastern Civilization as well. It culminates with the Pyramid Age in Egypt. At the end of it, there was considerable upheaval, with the vividly described horrors of the First Intermediate period in Egypt and the collapse of the Early Bronze Age civilization elsewhere.

The Age of Aries between c. 2000 BC and 0 BC: The Heroic Age, of evolving consciousness and will.

War, with warrior Gods – and Goddesses – presiding, and Law.

The Age of Pisces between c. 0 AD and 2000 AD – the fish swimming in opposite directions: The split between opposites. The duality of man and his Shadow, of mind and matter, of spirit and flesh, etc. An age ruled by the hostile *BROTHERS.*

The Age of Aquarius between c. 2000 and 4000 AD – i.e. the Future from now: 'Will constellate the problem of the *UNION* of the Opposites': Through becoming conscious of what have hitherto been the unconscious factors, and thereby integrating them. Synthesis leading to cohesion of the human family: the new age is conceived, but the labour pains of giving birth are still ahead.

Note:-

These Four Ages correspond to the usual symbolic *SEQUENCE,* of *ORIGINS, SPLIT, OPPOSITES, UNION* of Opposites.

The Twelve.

If life can be divided into twelve periods of seven years each – making the symbolic lifespan fourscore years and four, i.e. 84, an ideal lifespan which reality doesn't often match – and if each of these seven-year periods corresponds with a sign of the Zodiac (which is what symbolism suggests) then this leads to interesting possibilities regarding the symbolic pattern and sequence of life.

It suggests a more realistic (though more complex) method of cultivating the psychological functions, overlaying and in conjunction with the four main periods of life. The first twenty-one years of life can then be seen as the period of grappling with the three major functions, and the age of twenty-one becomes an important transition because it is the first moment of facing the *INFERIOR* Function, and integrating it in a partial, embryonic way. As Liz Greene shows there is a progressive sequence of development in each of the signs belonging to a particular element. So that ideally, by the age of twenty-eight, all four *FUNCTIONS* would have had a certain amount of attention lavished on them. And the cycle within the cycle would be ready to start again.

Symbolism depicts life rather like those Chinese carved ivory spheres within spheres which sometimes took generations of carvers to complete.

Related Symbolism:-

OLYMPUS; KABBALAH; MYTH. Also *ARCHETYPES.*

Books:-

Greene, L. *Relating* (1977), and *Saturn* (1976).

Also:

Arroyo, S. *Astrology, Psychology, and the Four Elements* (1975).

West, J. A. and Toonder, J. G. *The Case for Astrology* (1970).

The Zodiac as the earliest chart of the Psychological Types. From the overall archetypal pattern of Man's progressive development below, the particular combinations indicated by the individual birth-chart can be plotted.

The cardinal points would indicate the major transitions of life: the time for dreams of crossing with minor transitions at seven, fourteen, etc.

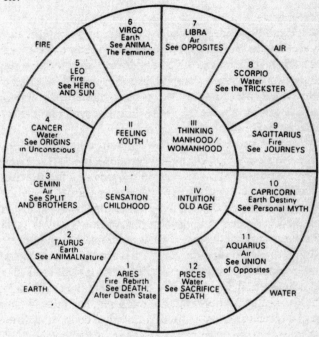

Index of Authors

All references to authors mentioned in sectional bibiliographies. For other authors See General Index.

General Index

See also Index of Authors, p. 439.

INDEX

INDEX

Dictionary for Dreamers

TOM CHETWYND

Distilled from the collective wisdom of the great interpreters of dreams – Freud, Jung, Adler, Stekel and Gutheil, among others – this comprehensive key to the baffling language of dream symbolism is a thought-provoking and invaluable guide to the uncharted country of the mind. Tom Chetwynd has isolated for the first time the rich meanings of over 500 archetypal symbols from the indiscriminate mass of dream material, and rated the likelihoods of the various possible interpretations in each case. Here are the essential clues to understanding the ingeniously disguised, life-enriching, often urgent messages to be found in dreams.

Dictionary of Sacred Myth

TOM CHETWYND

'There is only one symbolic language – and that is used by dreams, creative imagination and myths.'

Myths depict the archetypal patterns in the drama of the psyche, the universal processes of life. The language of myths and dreams is simple and direct – but we have forgotten the art of interpreting it. In this fascinating compilation, Tom Chetwynd explores this oldest and most universal method of communication, drawing on the mythologies of the ancient world, Egypt, Classical Greece and Rome, as well as the insights of psychology and the mystical traditions of the world's religions.

As sacred myth is an attempt on the part of the human psyche to reflect the dynamics of nature and the universe, so working with myths and symbols can bring renewed understanding of the ways of the soul.

The Age of Myth

TOM CHETWYND

The oldest literature – the first words of civilized man to reach us – reveal a symbolic world view, a mythological perspective. From them we get a glimpse of a time when the human psyche was still largely governed by dreams and visions. They provide valuable insights into the long formative period of the Unconscious. The Ancient Near East was the cradle of the unconscious mind, where humanity's creative imagination found full expression for the first time. It was also where the modern conscious ego, with its intellectual bias, showed the first signs of mature development. In between these two psychological events lies the Age of Myth.

Egyptian, Greek and other Semite myths throw new light on a cycle of Hebrew myth underlying a tradition that is at the root of the major living religions of the West. This cycle of myth appears to have been based firmly on the zodiac – a universal ancient cult in which the Hebrews shared, with their twelve tribes corresponding to the twelve celestial signs.

This period of history is the lost childhood of mankind, partly forgotten, partly repressed and derided by the intellect, but still surviving in the depths of the Unconscious, waiting to be retrieved like the Golden Fleece or the Grail.

Symbolic & Mythological Animals
J. C. COOPER

From the time when humans and animals faced the same world, living in close proximity and observing each other's every movement, people have ascribed certain powers and significance to the birds and beasts around them, and folktales, rituals and symbolism have sprung up to describe and interpret the creatures of the real and imaginary worlds.

What is the heraldic significance of the dragon? Why is the beaver a sacred animal to the Blackfeet Indians of North America? How far-reaching is the cult of the werewolf, and what are the roots of superstititions about black cats?

Gleaned from a wealth of cultural sources, *Symbolic and Mythological Animals* offers an enlightening account of the role animals – real and fantastical – have played in shaping the myths, religions and customs of the world, from ancient times to the present day. A complete A–Z of the insects, fish, reptiles, birds and mammals – and combinations of these – that have inspired human artistry and lore, these entries contain abundant information on the meaning and symbolism associated with different animals by distinct societies and traditions.

Bringing together the folklore and mythologies of ancient Rome, Greece, Britain, Babylon, Egypt, and North and South America, as well as of the peoples of present-day Europe, Australasia, Africa and the Americas, this illustrated sourcebook is a cornucopia of fascinating and informative detail about the abiding power and beauty of the natural world, and the place animal myth and symbolism hold in the collective history and culture of humanity.

| DICTIONARY OF DREAMERS | 1 85538 295 4 | £5.99 | ☐ |
| DICTIONARY OF FESTIVALS | 0 85030 848 8 | £7.99 | ☐ |

All these books are available from your local bookseller or can be
ordered direct from the publishers.

To order direct just tick the titles you want and fill in the form below:

Name: _____

Address: _____

_____

_____ Postcode: _____

Send to: Thorsons Mail Order, Dept 3, HarperCollins*Publishers*,
Westerhill Road, Bishopbriggs, Glasgow G64 2QT.

Please enclose a cheque or postal order or your authority to debit your
Visa/Access account –

Credit card no: _____

Expiry date: _____

Signature: _____

– up to the value of the cover price plus:
UK & BPFPO: Add £1.00 for the first book and 25p for each
additional book ordered.
Overseas orders including Eire: Please add £2.95 service charge.
Books will be sent by surface mail but quotes for airmail despatches
will be given on request.

24-HOUR TELEPHONE ORDERING SERVICE FOR
ACCESS/VISA CARDHOLDERS – TEL: 0141 772 2281.